Forms of List-Making: Epistemic, Literary, and Visual Enumeration

Roman Alexander Barton
Julia Böckling • Sarah Link
Anne Rüggemeier
Editors

Forms of List-Making: Epistemic, Literary, and Visual Enumeration

palgrave
macmillan

Editors
Roman Alexander Barton
University of Freiburg
Freiburg, Germany

Julia Böckling
University of Freiburg
Freiburg, Germany

Sarah Link
University of Freiburg
Freiburg, Germany

Anne Rüggemeier
University of Freiburg
Freiburg, Germany

ISBN 978-3-030-76972-7   ISBN 978-3-030-76970-3   (eBook)
https://doi.org/10.1007/978-3-030-76970-3

Cover illustration: WORDS AND MEANINGS/MARK SYKES / Alamy Stock PhotoCover design: eStudioCalamar

This Palgrave Macmillan imprint is published by the registered company Springer Nature Switzerland AG.
The registered company address is: Gewerbestrasse 11, 6330 Cham, Switzerland

PREFACE

The concern of this book is the versatility of the list. Considered as an epistemic, literary, or visual form, it has contributed to arts and sciences since the beginnings of civilization. This edited volume brings together scholars from various disciplines to analyze the manifold functions of enumeration, thus contributing to an emerging field dedicated to the study of lists. As such, it presents the outcome of our engagement in the project *Lists in Literature and Culture: Towards a Listology* funded by the European Research Council (ERC Starting Grant No. 715021). We want to express our heartfelt gratitude to Eva von Contzen, the principal investigator of our project, for her intellectual guidance and kind support. We are further grateful to Nathan Anderson for his laborious translations and corrections as well as Franca Leitner and Philomena Wolf for their thorough proofreading. Thanks is due also to the peer reviewers, who have provided us with many helpful suggestions, as well as the European Research Council for financing this book. Some thoughts developed in the contributions to this volume were presented at the conference "Enumeration, Epistemology, Etcetera" which took place in July 2019 at the Freiburg Institute for Advanced Studies.

Freiburg im Breisgau, Germany
December 2020

Roman Alexander Barton
Julia Böckling
Sarah Link
Anne Rüggemeier

CONTENTS

Notes on Contributors

Agnes Blümer is a member of the academic staff (akademische Rätin) at the University of Cologne. She teaches at the Center for Children's and Young-Adult Media Research (ALEKI), and has previously worked at the Department for Children's and Young Adult Literature Research (Goethe University Frankfurt). She has authored a book on the translation of children's literature during the 1950s and 1960s. Her current research project is concerned with lists in children's literature.

Alyson Brickey is assistant professor of English at the University of Winnipeg. Her work focuses on American literature and critical theory, specifically the relationship between literary aesthetics and philosophical ethics. She is working on a monograph entitled *America's Walls* that argues for a reconsideration of American literary representations of thresholds—walls, hedges, gates, and doorways—as having much to tell us about contemporary US political debates surrounding border security, incarceration, migration, and detention. Her work can be found in *Mosaic, intervalla, Walt Whitman Quarterly Review*, and is forthcoming in *Journal of Modern Literature*.

Ottmar Ette holds the chair of Romance Literature at the University of Potsdam. He is the co-founder of various DFG-Research Training Groups and the BMBF projects "Alexander von Humboldt's American Travel Diaries" and "Alexander von Humboldt's Journeys – Science on the Move" at the Berlin Academy of Sciences. Since 2010, he is ordinary member of the *Academia Europaea* and in 2012 was appointed *Chevalier dans l'Ordre des Palmes Académiques*. Ette is honorary member of the

Modern Language Association of America (MLA). His publications include *Writing-Between-Worlds* (2016) and *TransArea. A Literary History of Globalization* (2016).

Juri Joensuu is a senior researcher in Literature at the Department of Music, Art, and Culture Studies, University of Jyväskylä, Finland. Since his doctoral dissertation on Finnish procedural literature (2012), he has taught creative writing and published on literary humor, conceptual writing, literary recipes, and experimental movements of Finland in the 1960s.

Lennart Lehmhaus is an assistant professor and a lecturer (akademischer Rat) at the Eberhard Karls University of Tübingen. After projects focusing on Midrash and early medieval Jewish ethical traditions, his current projects and his habilitation explore rabbinic medical knowledge in comparison with Greco-Roman and Ancient Near Eastern traditions in late antiquity. He has edited several peer-reviewed thematic volumes and is the founding editor of the series ASK—Ancient Cultures of Sciences and Knowledge.

Stefanie Lethbridge is Professor of English Literature and Culture at the University of Freiburg, Germany. Her major research interests lie in English print culture from the Renaissance to the early twentieth century and popular culture since the nineteenth century. Her monograph *Lyrik in Gebrauch* (2014) explores British poetry anthologies in the context of British print culture since the mid-sixteenth century. Her current research projects focus on hero cultures in gothic and sensation fiction of the nineteenth century, the significance of spaces and ecocriticism.

Theresa Schön is an assistant professor at the Interdisciplinary Centre for European Enlightenment Studies (IZEA) of Martin Luther University Halle-Wittenberg. After obtaining a degree (Diplom; equivalent of MA) from Martin Luther University Halle-Wittenberg, she received a PhD scholarship from the Center of Excellence "Enlightenment – Religion – Knowledge" for her project on the early eighteenth-century character sketch in British periodical literature. She completed her PhD in early 2017. Her dissertation has been published as a book, *A Cosmography of Man: Character Sketches in "The Tatler" and "The Spectator,"* in 2020. In her postdoc project, she examines patterns of deviance in British non-canonical novels since the eighteenth century.

Anja Schürmann is working as a postdoctoral fellow at the Institute for Advanced Study in the Humanities Essen (KWI). She previously worked as an assistant professor at the Institute of Art History at the University of Düsseldorf, where she also completed her doctorate with a systematic analysis of ekphrasis as an art historical methodology. Her postdoc project deals with visual narration in the photobook. She recently published a thematic issue of the journal *Fotogeschichte* (2021, together with Steffen Siegel) which offers new perspectives on photobook research.

Martin Stöckinger is a lecturer (wissenschaftlicher Assistent) at the University of Cologne. Prior to this, he taught at the University of Heidelberg and at the Humboldt University of Berlin. He has co-edited a volume entitled *Horace and Seneca. Interactions, Intertexts, Interpretations* (2017) and authored a book entitled *Vergils Gaben. Materialität, Reziprozität und Poetik in den Eklogen und der Aeneis* (Heidelberg 2016) as well as numerous articles on Roman literature of the Republican, Augustan and early imperial ages. His current research project is concerned with the depiction of writing in Roman historiography.

Ulrike Vedder is a professor at the Institute for German Literature at the Humboldt Universität zu Berlin. Earlier, she served as a research assistant at the Zentrum für Literatur- und Kulturforschung (Center for Literary and Cultural Research), Berlin, among other places. She has concluded a doctorate on the media history of the discourse of love and a postdoctoral thesis on wills and inheritance in nineteenth-century literature. Her current research foci are literature and material culture; aesthetics of the museum; narrations at the gates of death; and genealogy, inheritance, generation. She is co-editor of *Zeitschrift für Germanistik*. Her recent book publications include *Museales Erzählen. Dinge, Räume, Narrative* (co-ed., 2020); *Handbuch Literatur & Materielle Kultur* (co-ed., 2018); *Herausforderungen des Realismus. Theodor Fontanes Gesellschaftsromane* (co-ed., 2018); *Alter und Geschlecht. Soziale Verhältnisse und kulturelle Repräsentationen* (ed., 2018); *Gegenwart schreiben. Zur deutschsprachigen Literatur 2000–2015* (co-ed., 2017); *Konversionen. Erzählungen der Umkehr und des Wandels* (co-ed., 2017).

Eva von Contzen is tenure-track Professor of English Literature including the literatures of the Middle Ages at the University of Freiburg, Germany. Since 2017, she is the principal investigator of the project "Lists in Literature and Culture: Towards a Listology (LISTLIT)," funded by the European Research Council. Apart from lists, her research interests include historical narratology, medieval saints' legends, the epic catalogue, and cognitive literary studies.

Daniela Wagner is Assistant Professor of Art History at the University of Tübingen with a specialization in medieval visual art. Research interests include plural image configurations, enumerations, sound, and the visual representation of time and temporality. As a principal investigator of the CRC 1391 "Different Aesthetics," she explores the pictorial use and functionality of personifications. At present, she is working on a book on images of enumerations in the Middle Ages.

LIST OF FIGURES

CHAPTER 1

Introduction: Epistemic and Artistic List-Making

Roman Alexander Barton, Julia Böckling, Sarah Link, and Anne Rüggemeier

The etymology of the term *list* reveals more about the nature of the thing itself than is commonly acknowledged.[1] Derived from the Old High German *lista* and the Old English *liste*, the word originally designated a small strip of cloth, a hem, a piece of braid, or border. Its first metaphorical use appears to have been due to its synonymity with *border*: until early modern times, *lists* could signify land borders.[2] More groundbreaking of course was the term's application to the field of writing and literature, an association that was perhaps to be expected given the traditional semantic proximity of *text* and *textile*, both derivatives of the Latin *texere*. The word *list*, then, more so than other related terms such as *enumeration* or

This introduction is the outcome of our joint research conducted in the project *Lists in Literature and Culture* (LISTLIT), funded by the European Research Council Starting Grant no. 715021

R. A. Barton (✉) • J. Böckling • S. Link • A. Rüggemeier
University of Freiburg, Freiburg, Germany
e-mail: roman.barton@anglistik.uni-freiburg.de; salink@uni-wuppertal.de;
anne.rueggemeier@anglistik.uni-freiburg.de

R. A. Barton et al. (eds.), *Forms of List-Making: Epistemic, Literary, and Visual Enumeration,*
https://doi.org/10.1007/978-3-030-76970-3_1

1

catalogue, carries the denotation of handiwork. It implies a made product or, more precisely, a subproduct in bigger textile or textual endeavors. When the proximity of text and textile is made explicit in literary works of the Middle Ages, authors appear to reflect on their "wordweaving," the *poiesis* of literature.[3] Accordingly, the term *list* puts stress on the *making* of enumerative texts and their contents. It invites us to reflect on how art or knowledge is produced through enumeration. With this edited volume, we have accepted that invitation and brought together scholars from various disciplines to explore list-making as a means of epistemic and artistic creation.

Perhaps the most striking similarity between a strip of cloth and a textual enumeration, and thus perchance the ground of their etymological connection, is their shared appearance or form. Though this form is easily recognizable, scholars have found it difficult to pin down and indeed are undecided whether it is a graphic or a grammatical structure. Theorizing the form of the textual list is very challenging because, as many have pointed out, versatility is its most remarkable feature.[4] In the emerging field of list studies, the list's form as well as its pivotal functions continue to be debated or renegotiated as more and more specific contexts of enumeration are taken into account. Moreover, lists are elusive: although they have classified, organized, and categorized the world since the early high civilizations,[5] they also, and sometimes simultaneously, have shown a tendency to confuse and overwhelm their readers. This tendency is perhaps best captured in the much-cited fictional taxonomy of animals by Jorge Luis Borges, supposedly of ancient Chinese origin, which is both intentionally unintelligible and evidently playful.[6] What Borges' example suggests, among other things, is that the list, however elusive, has been a mainstay in both epistemic and artistic endeavors since ancient times. In spite of this, the list has received, until recently, little or no attention in histories of knowledge, literature, or the visual arts.

The past decade or so has seen a growing interest in the role that lists play in knowledge-making, an interest that could possibly be explained by the prominence of enumerative structures in contemporary digital formats. Part I of our book seeks to contribute to the current debate by examining the epistemic functions of the list in a diachronic perspective. Most previous research on the subject is based on the assertion that, because list-making originates in administration, administrative textual practices have defined the scientific list ever since.[7] This view has prompted invaluable studies on the often underestimated *politics* of the list, the invisible power structures that define the selection and arrangement of a list's contents in governance and beyond.[8] The first section of this volume pursues a different approach in that it points out the impact of some of the other genres traditionally associated with list-making as a means of knowledge-making, namely historiography, wisdom literature, natural history, and the character sketch. By providing new case studies, it continues the work performed in Lucie Doležalová's edited volume *The Charm of a List: From the Sumerians to Computerised Data Processing* (2009) and Liam Cole Young's monograph *List Cultures: Knowledge and Poetics from Mesopotamia to BuzzFeed* (2017), two attempts to think about the allure of lists in different fields of knowledge. Though we agree with these authors that the list is and has always been an indispensable cognitive tool that helps to manage (big) data, we wish to encourage further research on the long and eventful epistemic history of the list: to what extent has scientific list-making been subject to epistemological shifts throughout history?

Like the scientific list, the literary list has lately become a "hot topic," and the second part of this book acknowledges as much. While the epic catalogue has been a subject of research in classical philology for quite some time,[9] the list as a literary form was taken seriously only after the turn of the millennium. Nor has the related concept of *enumeratio*, which originates in ancient rhetoric, received much scholarly attention until the past few years.[10] In fact, rhetorical and hence much poetological knowledge about enumeration has been handed down the centuries more or less unchanged (Schöpsdau 1994). Reflections on the enumerative in literature have gained currency only since the publication of Sabine Mainberger's pioneering monograph *Die Kunst des Aufzählens: Elemente zu einer Poetik des Enumerativen* (2003), which presents a multifaceted overview of the mutability and manifold functions of literary enumeration.[11] Subsequently, a range of more detailed and specific studies on the subject, which cover individual works or epochs, have appeared in print. Terminologically speaking, they all favor the more neutral and inclusive designation *list* over the more specifically rhetorical term *enumeration*.[12] Perhaps most notably, Robert Belknap's monograph *The List: The Uses and Pleasures of Cataloguing* (2004) discusses lists in the works of four prominent American Renaissance authors, namely Emerson, Whitman, Melville, and Thoreau, as well as across different genres.[13] Taking a broader diachronic approach, Eva von Contzen has called for a "listory," that is, "a literary history of lists" (2016, 241) as well as an investigation of the relationship of narration and enumeration. Her edited special issue for the journal *Style* brings together a group of narratologists to explore literary list-making throughout the centuries. The distinctive tension between the list and the narrative here examined is also taken up in a recent issue on "Lists and Narrative" (*Literatur in Wissenschaft und Unterricht* 1:2 2020), which highlights the multidirectional potential of the list both as a literary and a socio-cultural form. Part II of our book continues this work and, in so doing, follows Caroline Levine's *Forms: Whole, Rhythm, Hierarchy, Network* (2015) in its conviction that *form* is not only a rewarding focus for the study of literature but also for the study of culture and that an examination of formal features can produce insights into socio-cultural contexts.

Building on the supposition that the list is not only a grammatical but also (and perhaps even more so) a graphic structure, the third and final part of this edited volume explores the role of lists in the visual arts. It thus takes up an argument first presented in one of the most widely cited publications on list-making, Umberto Eco's *The Infinity of Lists* (2009). This anthology, which emerged from a series of conferences and exhibitions that Eco organized at the *Musée de Louvre*, draws attention to the challenging and multifarious richness of the list in literature and painting. Perhaps the most intriguing question that the book raises is whether or not there is such a thing as the "visual list," a term that is introduced with disarming naturalness and yet remains suspiciously under-theorized. The present volume investigates visual list-making in the domains of book illustration, painting, and photography in an attempt to stimulate further research on the topic.

In summary, *List-Making: Epistemic, Literary, and Visual Enumeration* brings together scholars from various academic fields to critically review previous list research and examine further how lists enabled the production of scientific, literary, and art work throughout the ages. The twelve single-authored chapters place the list in different well-researched historical contexts to fully grasp the epistemic, poetic, and aesthetic needs or potentialities that it can express and afford.

(List-)Making Knowledge

The versatile form of the list is central to knowledge-making in that it records, stores, and communicates various kinds of intelligence. Although the list is ever-present in scientific literature from antiquity to the present, it has rarely attracted the interest of intellectual historians. Only in more recent times, which have witnessed the advancement of digital networking and the prominence of enumerative structures in social media formats, a special urgency for research into the epistemic practice of enumeration has been recognized. As information circulates with ever-greater speed in the digital age, list-making, perhaps the most time-efficient means of processing intelligence, is recognized not as an inferior but a pivotal means of producing knowledge.[14]

Pointing out the *longue durée* of the list, many have suggested that enumeration is a universal concept or, at the very least, an anthropological constant.[15] Though it is fascinating that lists were apparently as prominent in ancient Mesopotamia as they are today, as suggested by Liam Cole Young (2017), it does not follow that enumeration is an invariable concept or form. As research on the role of paper and pen in the production of knowledge has revealed, the (early) modern period witnessed significant revolutions in paper technology that, as a result, revolutionized list-making.[16] Also, when seen from an epistemological perspective, the list appears to transform throughout the centuries. Considered as a cognitive tool that responds to epistemological shifts, the list reveals profound changes in the ways of thinking and knowing.

The aim of the first part of this book is to highlight the list's longstanding epistemic history. Chapters 2, 3, 4 and 5 work toward an understanding of the list as an epistemic tool that connects various contexts and evolves across centuries. Rather than treating the list solely as a literary or a rhetorical form, a manner of composition and arrangement in various kinds of literature, the four authors acknowledge that it is furthermore (and often at the same time) a cognitive tool which affords intellectual activity, a claim first made by Jack Goody (1977).[17] However, and this Goody paid no attention to, the list as a cognitive tool transforms, just as the epistemes themselves are subject to gradual but significant change. Traditionally, of course, the term *epistēmē* has been contrasted with that of *technē* to distinguish immutable theoretical knowledge from empirical insight that develops over time.[18] Epistemes are not mere deductions from experience but the conditions under which humans create empirical knowledge in the first place. At least since the emergence of discourse studies, however, epistemes are no longer considered as fixed, but in flux. In *The Order of Things* (1980), a work which famously commences with the discussion of a list, namely the aforementioned Chinese taxonomy of Borges, Michel Foucault has argued that epistemes are the ground of and prior to discourse.[19] They signify historically specific ways of knowing, "apparatuses" with which to distinguish what counts as valid from what counts as invalid in a certain field at a particular point in time. Notably, for Foucault, not only human knowledge itself but the conditions of knowing are prone to historical change. Both *what* we know and *how* we know differs throughout the ages. As they are thus subject to transformation, epistemes define and redefine how knowledge is made, not least in the textual list.

The list could thus perhaps be understood as an evolving "epistemic genre" much like the *question* or the *case*.[20] As recent scholarship has shown, these are modes of thinking which employ a specific recognizable pattern and, in so doing, raise discursive validity claims that are historically specific. It seems that the list with its itemizing pattern is just such a mode. The notion of "epistemic genre" as defined by Gianna Pomata and others is certainly not without its pitfalls. In the instance of the *case*, for example, it somewhat obscures the specific origin of the genre in administrative paperwork. The list, however, is much more ubiquitous; it already played an important role in so many contexts in antiquity that this consideration is not an issue. More problematically, perhaps, theorizing the list as an epistemic genre could blur differences and suggest that, for example, an exegetical list and a botanical list are more similar than they really are. To remedy this potential fallacy, our book brings together specialists from various academic fields who place the respective lists in well-researched contexts. Telling part of the epistemic history of the list, the first four chapters demonstrate how enumeration enabled intellectual work in classical historiography, ancient and medieval wisdom literature, early modern moral weeklies, and nineteenth-century botanical geography.

In Chap. 2, Martin Stöckinger shows that lists allowed Roman imperial and early medieval historians to give a complete but contingent record of dates, events, or persons of the past. Taking the list of the *Res Gestae Divi Augusti* as example, he argues that, rather than establishing causalities, imperial lists are a "monument" of an Emperor's achievements. Due to their dignity, these enumerations cannot be expanded or otherwise altered and, because of their great length, they also convey a sense of magnitude: no other list can compare. By contrast, lists in Gregory of Tour's *Historia Francorum* transform previous enumerations and are open to continuation. Thus, the cognitive tool of the list enabled pre-modern historiographers to either finalize the record of a specific past or chronicle the progress of time. In other words, both their summative and their additive intellectual work relied on the epistemic practice of list-making.

In Chap. 3, Lennart Lehmhaus puts into perspective the traditional view that scholarship in the ancient Near East was inferior to Greco-Roman schools of thought because of its tendency to produce (mere) lists. The Rabbinic lists, he argues, had important epistemological functions. In ancient Talmudic texts, they are used to appropriate, transmit, and create medical or moral knowledge. By affording recipes and regimens, the epistemic form of the list enabled the rabbis to instruct on how to lead a healthy way of life. Meanwhile, in midrashic works, the list is key to theological exegesis and is thus a powerful hermeneutic tool. As such, it impacts the cognitive act of understanding itself. Crucially, the Rabbinic lists come to be expanded, shortened, or rearranged. They are open to continuation and thus open to new hermeneutic endeavors.

Chapter 4 argues that in the periodicals of Joseph Addison and Richard Steele, the *Tatler* and the *Spectator*, lists such as the virtuoso's testament and Leonora's library catalogue enumerate the possessions of a certain character type, thus revealing the owner's moral deficiencies. Theresa Schön demonstrates that, as they lack apparent order, such enumerations give form to what appear to be chance empirical observations. They imply a survey of the reader's bookshelves or the contents of a virtuoso's house, respectively. Consequently, these lists allow the reader to make moral deductions as if from experience. Due to their overt experiential quality, the lists of Addison and Steele make new the well-known and established typology behind the character sketch, a genre which harks back to antiquity. They do so in that they signal "the (technically) infinite nature of observation" (Schön). Thus, these eighteenth-century lists reveal the impact of Empiricism on the list-making of knowledge.

Focusing on Alexander von Humboldt's *American Travel Journals*, Chap. 5 discusses how the scientific list took on new functions in the wake of a paradigm shift in the history of knowledge around 1800. Ottmar Ette shows that Humboldt's list-making shaped and was shaped by his novel trans-areal as well as trans-scalar conception of science. Rather than composing static taxonomies, his lists make reference to geographies of natural entities, showing their evolution or migration. The list, now considered as necessarily infinite, emerges as an ideal tool to showcase scientific study as a quintessentially nomadic process that is never completed or flawless, much in contrast to traditional monadic science. Often combined into tables to represent the multi-relationality of natural life, Humboldt's lists are thus strategically incomplete and inconsistent.

In summary, Part I of this book points out basic epistemic functions of enumeration, that is, the role of lists in summative, additive, didactic, and hermeneutic endeavors, yet it also points to certain shifts in the epistemic history of the list. In particular, the case studies suggest that the emergence of Empiricism and Evolutionism had a remarkable impact on enumerative knowledge-making, an issue that deserves further comment not least because it touches on two commonplaces in list research. From an epistemological perspective, both the assertion that lists are closely related to the concept of infinity and the claim that they easily combine into tables to represent multi-relationality merits greater attention.

First, the conviction that all knowledge is gained from experience seems to have produced the insight that (empirical) lists are necessarily infinite. Arguing against Jack Goody (1977), for whom the list with its classificatory tendency "establishes the necessity of a boundary, the necessity of a beginning and an end" (105), Umberto Eco famously claimed that the list in general is a "form of representation" which "suggests infinity almost *physically*, because in fact *it does not end*, nor does it conclude in form" (Eco 2009, 17). However, his assertion that lists not only convey the notion of infinity by aesthetic means but are also and have always been logically infinite is a bit of a stretch.[21] The dilemma that enumeration can neither encompass nor represent everything or, more precisely, everything in sufficient empirical detail, and therefore must progress ad infinitum, is distinctly modern. Only in the eyes of the empiricist, who came to dominate the scientific field in the eighteenth century, no finite list is ever enough.[22]

Second, it is remarkable how the making of modern life sciences has resulted in the understanding that the list, considered as the outcome of additive intellectual work to be continued ad infinitum, is necessarily interrelated with other lists. As Alexander von Humboldt's example shows and recent research on tabular tallying in nineteenth-century medicine implies,[23] scientific lists come to serve as hermeneutic tools for one another and thus become mutually productive. This is highly significant because, speaking with the logician Charles Sanders Peirce, the list is dyadic. An enumeration of the items A, B, C, and D signifies no more than that A is related to B, B is related to C, and C is related to D. In other words, any list is composed only of dyads. The *medium* between the list's items, the answer to the question what connects them (for instance, their all being trees), no list can make explicit in and of itself. In the words of Peirce, the list lacks *thirdness* because it features only relates and correlates, but no interpretant.[24] Unless the enumeration has a title (such as "Trees") or is embedded in a narrative that interprets it, the logic of the list remains in the dark. A science (only) of lists remedies this logical insufficiency in that it asserts the necessary interaction of scientific enumerations. One list supplies another with an interpretant and so the transformation of one or both of these lists is the likely result. For instance, to put it very simply, a taxonomy of plants can be a tool with which to interpret a list of trees, namely because it includes the item "tree." As a result, a normative title or narrative becomes obsolete. Thus, perhaps for the first time in Western civilization, the mere combination of lists (and flawed or incoherent lists especially) is acknowledged as a sufficient means of knowledge-making. Further research on how scientific list-making came to be characterized by multi-relationality is needed and, with this edited volume, we hope to encourage it.

LISTS VERSUS NARRATIVES

"One does not *read* but only *uses* a list" (2009, 1) writes Lucie Doležalová in her introduction to *The Charm of a List* and thus situates enumeration firmly in the realm of functionality rather than that of literature. It is, however, the list's very usability that qualifies it as a cognitive tool which invites its users to order and link its constituent items, to examine which connections can be drawn between them, and to determine how they relate to one another or the larger framework in which they are presented. (Certainly, in some cases, lists may want the user to blindly accept the connections they imply.) Nevertheless, lists and narratives are commonly regarded as contraries: while the latter are based on sequential or causal relationships and establish meaningful connections, the former are characterized by itemization or computationality. Insofar as they are a phenomenon pertaining to the descriptive or the argumentative mode of writing, lists can be conceptualized as "anti-narrative" texts. One could even argue that lists, "as inherently nonnarrative elements, constitute 'the Other' in a literary work" (von Contzen 2016, 245). However, lists have the potential to be transformed into narratives when readers interact with them. This transformative potential suggests that lists and narratives are not diametrically opposed to one another. Rather, as the contributions to Part II of this book demonstrate, there are degrees of narrativity which can be realized more or less fully in the list: enumerative texts can acquire a somewhat narrative quality.

Placing enumerative texts on a sliding scale between narrative and non-narrative corresponds with Robert Belknap's definition of lists as frameworks "that hold separate and disparate items together" (2004, 2). Lists, somewhat like narratives, allow us "to order our surrounding world, verbally or symbolically putting everything into a sequence and an arrangement we desire" (Belknap 2004, xxii). It becomes obvious that the realms of enumeration and narrative are not as clearly separable as they initially seem. However, while lists produce order primarily through their form, narratives tend to join items by causal concatenation. More so than narratives, lists draw attention to their own constructedness and thereby make transparent how order can be created. Such transparency endows lists with the potential to explode or subvert established ordering systems by laying bare and then reimagining the structures upon which they are based. Chapters 6, 7, 8, 9 and 10 examine how the connections that lists invite their readers to draw between item and item or item and formal framework create a tension between enumeration and narrative. This tension, which lists in a literary context almost inevitably create, renders them productive in a variety of ways. Lists thus address issues such as canon-formation and counter-culture.

The invisible political agenda behind lists—the so-called politics of the list—is the topic of Eva von Contzen's contribution (Chap. 6). She explores the list as a cognitive form which elicits a range of affordances that vary according to the context they are used in. Von Contzen suggests that lists should be read symptomatically and suspiciously. Drawing on lists and catalogues in works as diverse as Daniel Defoe's *Robinson Crusoe* and Leanne Shapton's *Important Artifacts and Personal Property from the Collection of Lenore Doolan and Harold Morris*, she unmasks the capitalist narratives that are intricately interwoven with these texts. Underneath the surface of the list, von Contzen argues, there is "potentially an abyss of contradiction and manipulation."

Chapter 7 explores how, without actually having to narrate, lists imply certain narratives. Stefanie Lethbridge illustrates this phenomenon by examining the table or list of contents in the context of canon formation.[25] She demonstrates how British poetry anthologies make use of the form of the list to create epistemic, cognitive, and affective frames that govern the reception of literature. Through sequence and proximity, and through intertextual connections and resonances, these frames influence whether a poem will be read as a work by a certain author or else as a typical example of a literary period, theme, or mood. Remarkably, tables of contents thus elicit a narrative response by capitalizing on the "human predilection for creating teleological connections" (Lethbridge).

That both list-making and storytelling assert and establish authority has become clear in recent debates about the role of narratives in political discourse. De Goede et al. (2016) and Stäheli (2016) have convincingly argued for the invisible power that governs the politics of the list. However, lists do not only solidify but also destabilize political power. Alyson Brickey illustrates this in her discussion of enumeration in Allen Ginsberg's "Howl." (Chap. 8) The speaker uses the form of the list to break with continuous narration and foreground the poem's a-narrative character. The feelings of alienation and "aesthetic unrest" thus created combat established (and potentially oppressive) power structures. Brickey's reading of "Howl" demonstrates how the poem not only inextricably links the form of the list to questions of ethics but itself performs ethical work. As a Beat Generation poem, "Howl" is firmly rooted in counter-culture and is generally read as a response to an increasingly conservative American cultural sphere after the Second World War.

The subversive potential of the list also features prominently in Juri Joensuu's discussion of twentieth-century Finnish recipe poems. In Chap. 9, Joensuu emphasizes how lists both unify and fragment the (textual) spaces they create. By employing the rigid and traditional form of the recipe or menu to present scandalous or deliberately alienating content, these poems demonstrate a refusal to conform to established literary and societal norms. In the processual context of recipe writing, the list form evokes connotations of order, sterility, and objectivity that clash with the recipe poems' contents which center around sensuality, (sexual) taboo topics, and disgust. The list thus creates a shock effect that constitutes a deliberate attack on established (aesthetic) norms and values.

While Brickey and Joensuu shed light on the list's propensity to be used in counter-cultural art and discourse, Ulrike Vedder's contribution explores the self-reflexive potential and embodied nature of poetological lists (Chap. 10). The lists Vedder examines draw attention to their own constructedness by highlighting the processual nature of writing. Through their loose connections and fragmentariness, lists evoke the impression of spontaneity or immediacy. Vedder demonstrates this across a variety of genres. For example, turning to a poem by Inger Christensen, she shows how the order that lists establish can constitute an act of creation.

Furthermore, in her reading of Jack Kerouac's manifesto *Belief & Technique for Modern Prose*, Vedder points out the unique temporality of lists. Finally, she theorizes the literary list in her discussion of *roland BARTHES par roland barthes* (1975), which explores fragmentation as a form of narration.

In summary, Part II of this book addresses the ability of the list to challenge both our notion of narrative and the grand narratives of our culture.[26] The four contributions show that the tension between enumeration and narrative often evokes a "desire for creative disruption" (Richardson 2016, 328): literary lists twist conceptions of order in that they take shapes which expose their constructedness. They scrutinize established ways of sense-making and thereby invite the reader to question the power structures that underpin dominant cultural narratives.

THE VISUAL LIST

The third and final part of this book is dedicated to a specific research desideratum in list studies. Despite its visual quality, that is, its typographically specific, often framed, and vertical layout, we associate the form of the list, first and foremost, with a verbal, written, or even printed form of publication.[27] Yet there are no convincing reasons why a succession of written objects should be called a list, while a series of shown—that is, drawn or photographed—objects should not. The very basic definition of the list as "a structural schema of enumeration in which particular items [...] are arranged in a series" (Fludernik 2016, 309) can be applied to both the verbal and the visual list.[28]

Eco, in his fascinating and widely cited *The Infinity of Lists*, shows the current relevance of the topic. Eco refers to both poets and writers who use lists in their literary works *and* painters who accumulate things in their paintings. As he invents a language for what he conceives as the essential nature of lists, he describes the oscillation between completeness and infinity, that is, between form and delimitation of form, as essential (Eco 2009, 7). If Eco's lists are defined at all, then this is done only with regard to their effect, but never by describing their formal characteristics. Moreover, Eco reduces the definition of the visual list to only one of its effects, its suggestion of an etcetera: "how [can] a picture [...] present things and yet suggest an 'etcetera' as if to admit that the limits of the frame oblige the picture to say nothing about an immense number of other things" (Eco 2009, Introduction).

It seems that Eco's very cover image, a detail from Sir Edward Coley Burn-Jones' *The Golden Stairs* (1880)—which is not mentioned once in the rest of the book—has the potential to develop a set of formal criteria that can be seen as responsible for its "effet de liste" (see Milcent-Lawson et al. 2013). We see a sequence of women dressed in creamy white, silvery antique robes, as they descend a staircase. The vertical arrangement of the canvas is decisive for its list effect. The eye of the observer wanders downward, literally following the long parade of somewhat identical women step by step (the feet are visible despite the long robes). In terms of hairstyle, skin color, and clothing, they resemble each other, thus creating the impression of repetition in variation,[29] a characteristic pattern, which in art history—but also in literature and media studies—has thus far primarily been designated with the term *series*. The list and the series are united by their reflexive function: they evoke an emphasis on and thus a reflection of the *how* of representation as opposed to a simple focus on the *what* of representation. While the visual series as a primarily aesthetic form demands the consistent application (or further development) of certain pictorial and design rules, the visual list as a form—perhaps precisely because the term has no tradition in visual art—is less prescriptive. In contrast to the series, where the individual objects must always be related to each other semantically, the connection between the individual elements of a list can be established solely through their belonging to a shared whole.

As a form that transcends context, the list can manifest in visual art in variable ways. The list affords a "unifying gesture" that helps to visually organize the multiplicity of singular or rather singularized (i.e., previously decontextualized, cut, or consciously selected) elements. This "unifying gesture" could be a title, or some framing effect, or simply the (material or mental) meeting place of the list: for example, a canvas, a page, a spontaneously torn off piece of paper, or, for oral lists, a concept in the mind. The list can do both: it can suggest a unity that relies on a relation between the parts (repetition and variation) and a relationship that only relies on what we have called "unifying gesture," something that creates a whole to which the diverse and entirely disconnected parts stand in relationship with. It can therefore be noted that the prominent features of visual lists are (1) the manifestation of a pattern of repetition in variation and/or (2) the highlighting of the relationship between a whole and its parts.

Given these characteristics, what is the added value of the concept of the *visual list*? The answer is twofold. In visual studies, where the term *series* has become too narrow and specific, it opens a new perspective on enumerative structures in art. Meanwhile, it counteracts the fuzziness of the notion of *series* in other disciplines (which can signify everything from the scale of nature to television instalments)[30] and draws attention to the form of the enumerative, the "made" character of the list.

It is often an artifact's title that creates and draws attention to the productive tension between the parts and the whole. This is the case when numerical values are part of the title. Albrecht Dürer's *The Martyrdom of the Ten Thousand Christians* (1508) can serve as an example. The discrepancy between the number *Ten Thousand* mentioned in the title and the number of bodies actually depicted (about sixty) is striking. Eco states that visual lists express their own "incapacity to … show them all" (2009, 39). The list conveys exemplariness: what is represented stands for a larger (social, historical, political) whole, which becomes clear precisely through the formal power of the list to represent an obviously incomplete enumeration.[31] Hence visual lists afford exemplarity in the sense of exhibiting a selection of details that vary or share a certain theme and which indicate and reference a continuation of that which is shown beyond the frames of the canvas, the paper, or the screen. Visual lists exemplarily refer to events, contexts, and ideas that go beyond what is actually shown.

Last but not least, the reception of certain images as visual lists is a consequence of contextualization in a shared cultural heritage. The *Golden Stairs*, for example, can be interpreted as making an intermedial reference to the biblical narrative of Jacob's dream of the ladder to heaven as it is described in the book of Genesis (Gen. 28:10–22).[32] The steering of a specific viewer response and reception through the evocation of certain cultural knowledge and intermedial references should not be underestimated.

To sum up, visual lists can be described by drawing on the following criteria: a vertical or horizontal sequence of similar but usually different and individual (possibly clearly separated and carved out) objects, reminiscent of an enumeration (suggested for example by steps/gradations), which create the effect of repetition in variation. Moreover, less neatly arranged accumulations of individual objects can still be perceived as visual lists if the relationship between a whole and its parts is accentuated in a prominent way. All of these characteristics can be found to a greater or lesser extent in the detailed analyses of the individual contributions to Part III of this book.

Agnes Blümer's contribution (Chap. 11) focuses on forms, functions, and processes of knowledge construction in diverse genres of children's literature including children's poetry, folklore, novels, and picturebooks. While Blümer addresses the list's educational and didactic purpose, she also draws attention to the fact that lists in children's literature can deliberately subvert the supposed didactic function: "Their tendency for excess, for puns and for comical effects seems to undermine the traditional educational value of the list form" (Blümer). In her discussion of lists in picturebooks, Blümer highlights the interactive experiences that lists in children's literature often evoke. Picturebooks famously use lists as a tool to "archive the everyday" and to convey the yet unknown to the child. Yet, as "a multi-purpose form" that affords educational, aesthetic, and interactive functions, lists in children's literature do not simply order knowledge, they also subvert it.

In Chap. 12, Daniela Wagner's contribution explores different versions of medieval representations of the *Arma Christi*, a term that refers to weapons, torture devices, or other objects related to the suffering of Jesus Christ. Since *Arma Christi* representations are only roughly defined by the context of the Passion narrative, there are various versions that differ both in terms of the selection of elements and regarding their combination and arrangement. These processes of selection and combination highlight the "list-like character" of many *Arma* representations. For the visual list, as for the verbal list, the tension between "the cohesion of the whole and the separation of the parts" (Wagner) is essential. Wagner shows that it is specifically through innovative uses of framing that the simultaneous demarcation of the individual parts and what she calls "visual merging" becomes possible. As many representations of the *Arma* give rise to an "interplay of overview and disorder" (Wagner), the viewer is prompted to draw connections between the individual parts (the various *Arma*) as well as the relationship between the parts and the whole (the body of Christ). As Wagner further shows, it is the specific interaction of content and form that renders the motif of the *Arma* particularly effective for the practice of piety.

Finally, in Chap. 13, Anja Schürmann turns to the medium of photography. As photography can "freeze time" (Schürmann), the medium is particularly well suited for isolating subjects from their surroundings and putting them into other contexts in which new meanings can be forged.

By initially anchoring the genre of the conceptual documentary photo-book in its serial and conceptual legacy, Schürmann emphasizes both the principle of distancing as well as the principle of repetition as constituting moments of visual lists. As Conceptual Documentary photography typically explores "a single, often banal idea from many different angles" (Miles 2010, 50), repetition and variation inform their visual aesthetics: "Its formal and abstract aspects are reinforced while what is depicted loses relevance" (Schürmann). As she provides an analysis of three contemporary photobooks, Schürmann applies Peter Bexte's considerations on "the etcetera" as a verbal, a visual, and a philosophical form of conceptualization to highlight the synthetic (rather than the analytic) and the open or non-hierarchical structure of the presented art works. The enumerative structure of Conceptual Documentary photobooks, she argues, effects interpretive gaps between the individual images and thus fosters a receptive autonomy which ultimately reacts to and comments on the moralizing tendencies of documentary photography.

Critical readers of Chaps. 11, 12 and 13 will agree that the assertion that there *is* such a thing as the visual list will always lead us into problems of definition. Even though plural images or "hyperimages" (Thürlemann 2013) have gained attention in art history and visual studies alike, they have not been described as *lists* but rather were treated under terms such as *series*. The media scientist Knut Hicketier, when he experienced the difficulty of demarcating a ubiquitous form (in his case the series), suggested not to assume (or construct) an essential and fixed idea of the concept but rather to follow an inductive approach and to describe it as a product of the recipient's perception.[33] A visual list would then be whatever is perceived as a visual list, that is, what is produced, communicated, received, and processed as such. If we follow this inductive approach, we can begin to focus on the meaningful re-reading of visual artifacts *as* visual lists and to pay attention to the innovative interpretive contexts and connections this perspective on and framing of the material affords. The term *visual list*—precisely because of its odd novelty—disturbs and defamilarizes the common categorization of plurality in art as serial or series. The concept of the visual list asks us to realize how arbitrary and vague the notion of series has become and re-focuses attention on the issue of form: how does the aesthetic effect (and maybe also "the message") of a piece of art change when it is read against the background of the formal aesthetics of the list?

Christiane Frey and David Martyn have suggested that lists challenge us when our attempt to assign them to a common denominator is frustrated: "It is precisely because the category, which would have allowed to subsume the individual items under a general heading and thus to be put aside and done with, is missing, that the individual items can emerge in their detail" (90).[34] It is this 'putting aside and being done with' that is provoked by titles such as *The Martyrdom of the Ten Thousand Christians*. By referring to a specified whole, and thus manipulating the reception of the artwork, it reduces the visibility of the individual elements in their respective individuality and peculiarity (see Frey and Martyn 2016, 91). One way to challenge this customary primacy of the whole is to stress a discrepancy between the title and the content of the picture (as Dürer does when he refers to *Ten Thousand* but only represents sixty). Thus, a certain mismatch is evoked that counteracts the dominance of the whole over the details. To read visual material as a visual list furthers our understanding of the ways in which these works offer resistance to the hierarchical subsumption of particularities under generalizing umbrella terms (see Frey and Martyn 2016, 96). Visual lists ask us to remain specific as they afford the representation of "the plural experience of singularity" (Frey and Martyn 2016, 90)[35] and as such oppose generalization. Somewhat paradoxically, the visual list allows us to perceive categories, yet also makes us honor the individual elements.

Together, the twelve contributions to this book highlight the list's striking versatility, its ability to produce scientific, literary, and art work across times and cultures. They provide answers to Jack Goody's (1977) famous question "What's in a list?" in that they point out various affordances of this all but simple textual or visual form. With its interdisciplinary approach, *List-Making: Epistemic, Literary, and Visual Enumeration* aims to contribute to an emerging field dedicated to the study of lists.

Notes

1. See *Deutsches Wörterbuch von Jacob und Wilhelm Grimm Online*, s.v. Liste. See also *OED Online*, s.v. list, n.3. Both accessed 9 Dec. 2020.
2. The *OED* entry (see note 1) provides a quote from G. Fletcher's 1591 *Of Russe Common Wealth* to show the longstanding association with the term *border*: "the very farthest part and list of Europe, bordering vpon Asia."
3. See, for example, the monograph of Greber (2002) and the most recent article on the subject by Hyer (2019).

4. See, for example, Spufford 1989.

5. For the significance of lists in antiquity, see Goody 1977, Wassermann 2021.

6. In *The Analytical Language of John Wilkins* (1973, 103), Borges gives expression to the playfulness of lists which, according to Goody (1977, 89), is characteristic already for ancient lists. Foucault (1980) begins his *The Order of Things* by quoting Borges' list.

7. See, for example, Goody (1977) and Hess and Mendelssohn (2010). See also Gitelman's monograph on *Paper Knowledge* (2014).

8. In a special issue for *Society and Space*, De Goede et al. (2016) discuss list-making as a practice of governance that relies on particular ways of knowledge production and world-ordering procedures. Similarly, the sociologist Urs Stäheli (2011, 2016, 2017) has repeatedly emphasized that list-making is not just an activity to create order in the sense of an overview, but that it also involves invisible power structures which define processes of pre-selection and arrangement.

9. See, for example, Kühlmann 1973, Visser 1997, Sammons 2010.

10. Schumann (1942, 1944, 1945) is an exception to the rule. His observation that literary enumeration can be both "conjunctive" and "disjunctive," that is, that it can add items so as to create a whole or, by contrast, itemize a whole into its parts, is crucial. However, his scope is limited to the works of Whitman and German expressionist poets. In French criticism, the pioneering study of Frédéric (1986) comes to a similar conclusion in that it differentiates between *énumération homologique* and *énumération chaotique*.

11. This study, though it draws on a selected corpus of mostly canonical texts, aptly discusses the rhetorical as well as the poetological aspects of enumerative writing and points to the frequent self-reflective nature of literary enumeration.

12. See Belknap 2004, Sève 2010, Milcent-Lawson et al. 2013, Turin 2017. An earlier example is Spufford (1989). His *The Chatto Book of Cabbages and Kings: Lists in Literature* provides an anthology of literary lists.

13. Though it focuses on lists in a particular epoch, Belknap's study also examines lists and catalogues across different genres: the essay, poetry, the novel, and the memoir. Other genre-specific studies of literary enumeration include: Cotten (2008) for lists in concrete poetry; Poletti (2008) for lists in personal zines; Rüggemeier (2019, 2020) for lists in life writing and graphic novels. Forthcoming is a study on lists in detective fiction by Sarah Link. A broader genre-based approach to literary list-making is still wanting.

14. See, for example, Young 2017, 12, 109–129.

15. For instance, Eco (2009) develops a vague philosophical concept of list-likeness, which supposedly is characterized by excess and infinity. For

Young (2017), who discusses ancient Sumerian inventories alongside BuzzFeed listicles, "listing activities are the infrastructure of culture" (19). Eva von Contzen (2017) has taken a more nuanced view and suggested that the versatility of the list, its remarkable sensitivity to historical contexts, is due to potentialities inherent in the form of the list. Drawing on the new formalist study of Levine (2015), she has termed the many potential functions of the list *affordances.*

16. See Te Heesen 2005, Hess and Mendelssohn 2010, Müller-Wille and Charmantier 2012.

17. Goody (1977) claims that list-making influences cognitive processes, a claim that he explores with respect to lists in ancient Mesopotamia and Egypt. He argues that writing, and list-making especially, impacts human cognition, namely as it allows for the re-arrangement and examination of words or word sequences.

18. This definition harks back to pre-Socratic traditions. For a detailed account of the term's history, see *Historisches Wörterbuch der Philosophie,* s.v. "Episteme." See also "Episteme and Techne," *Stanford Encyclopedia of Philosophy Online,* https://plato.stanford.edu/entries/episteme-techne/. Accessed 6 Jan 2021.

19. See Foucault 2002, esp. xxii–xxv. For a precise definition of the term, see Foucault 1980, 197: "If you like, I will define épistème retrospectively as the strategic apparatus which permits the separating out from among all the statements which are possible those that will be acceptable within, I won't say a scientific theory, but a field of scientificity, and which it is possible to say are true or false." For a discussion of Foucault's interpretation of the list by Borges, see Ottmar Ette's chapter in this volume.

20. For Pomata 2010, esp. 196–197, *epistemic genres* are literary structures that afford specific ways of arranging given material and, thus, allow for certain epistemic endeavors. See also Urmann 2017 (on the epistemic genre of the *question*) and Pomata 2013 (on the epistemic genres of the *case* and the *recipe*).

21. Eco differentiates between the (subjective) aesthetic effect that derives from the idea of infinity, which Kant defines as the sublime in his *Critique of Judgement,* and so-called "objective" infinity. According to Eco, the latter rather than the former finds expression in the list. See Eco 2009, 17.

22. The list as a classificatory tool with which to divide and subdivide materials, as described by Goody (1977), must be infinite in the perspective of Empiricism. This paradigm shift in the epistemic history of the list no doubt deserves more attention and research than it can receive in this introduction. It is discussed at greater length in Roman Alexander Barton's forthcoming article "Endless Lists in Sprawling Narratives: Enumeration in the Sternean Novel."

23. See Hess and Mendelsohn (2010), esp. 299: "Running the eye down any given organ column [in the anatomical table of Pierre Charles Alexandre Louis] and keeping the duration in view, one would see in an almost automatically tallying mode what proportion of cases, in each duration range, presented a given range of descriptive terms."

24. See, for example, Peirce, *Collected Papers*, VIII, 226, where Peirce discusses the lack of an interpretant or "mental element" in dyadic relations, without which there can be no semiosis or sign, properly speaking: "In A's putting away B, there is no thirdness. In C's taking B, there is no thirdness. But if you say that these two acts constitute one single operation by virtue of the identity of the B, you transcend the mere brute fact, you introduce a mental element."

25. See Mainberger (2020), who engages with the table of contents as a visual phenomenon.

26. The belief that stable constructs of meaning ("grand narratives") can exist on a large scale is explored in Jean-François Lyotard's *The Postmodern Condition: A Report on Knowledge* (2006).

27. See also Mainberger who regards the shopping list as the prototype of the *list*: "If we ask what a Liste is, everyone will most certainly give the shopping list as an example" (2020, 9).

28. For a consideration and first remarks on the differentiation between verbal and visual lists, see Rüggemeier 2018, 56.

29. See Deleuze (1994), who defined variation as the condition of repetition. Derrida also connected the notion of repetition with variation ("Signature Event Context," 1988).

30. See *Historisches Wörterbuch der Philosophie*, s.v. "Series."

31. For a consideration of the list as a reduced and reducing form that highlights the tension between the things mentioned (shown) and the things not mentioned (not shown) see Rüggemeier 2019.

32. Art critics have repeatedly emphasized the dream-like quality of Burn-Jones's picture. See Wildman and Christian 1998.

33. "Serie ist, was als Serie verstanden, d.h. als solche produziert, vermittelt, rezipiert und verarbeitet wird" (Hicketier 1991, 8).

34. Translation of the German original: "Gerade weil die Rubrik fehlt, die es erlaubt hätte, sie (die Einzeldinge) unter ein Allgemeines zu subsumieren und dadurch gleichsam *ad acta* zu legen, können sie in ihrer Einzelheit hervortreten" (Frey and Martyn 2016, 90).

35. See also Deleuze on the distinction between generalization (where something can be substituted with something else) and repetition which stands in relation to "something unique or singular which has no equal or equivalent" (1994, 1–2).

References

Belknap, Robert. 2004. *The List: The Uses and Pleasures of Cataloguing*. New Haven: Yale University Press.

Borges, Jorge L. 1973. The Analytical Language of John Wilkins. In *Other Inquisitions 1937–1952 By Jorge Luis Borges*, 101–105. Trans. R.L.C. Simms. London: Souvenir Press.

Cotten, Ann. 2008. *Nach der Welt: Die Listen der Konkreten Poesie und ihre Folgen*. Vienna: Klever.

Deleuze, Gilles. 1994. *Difference and Repetition*. Trans. Paul Patton. New York: Columbia University Press.

Derrida, Jacques. 1988. Signature Event Context. In *Limited Inc*. Trans. Samuel Weber and Jeffrey Mehlmann. Evanstone: Northwestern University Press.

Doležalová, Lucie, ed. 2009. *The Charm of a List: from the Sumerians to Computerised Data Processing*. Newcastle upon Tyne: Cambridge Scholars Publishing.

Eco, Umberto. 2009. *The Infinity of Lists*. New York: Rizzoli.

Fludernik, Monika. 2016. Descriptive Lists and List Descriptions. *Style* 50 (3): 309–326.

Foucault, Michel. 1980. *Power/Knowledge*. Ed. Colin Gordon. New York: Pantheon Books.

———. 2002. *The Order of Things*. London/New York: Palgrave.

Frédéric, Madeleine. 1986. Enumération, énumération homologique, énumération chaotique: Essai de caractérisation. In *Stylistique, rhétorique et poétique dans les langues romanes*, ed. Jean-Claude Bouvier, 103–117. Provence: Université de Provence.

Frey, Christiane, and David Martyn. 2016. Listenwissen: Zu einer Poetik des Seriellen. In *Noch einmal anders. Zu einer Poetik des Seriellen*, ed. Elisabeth Bronfen, Christiane Frey and David Martyn, 89–103. Zürich/Berlin: diaphanes.

Gitelman, Lisa. 2014. *Paper Knowledge*. Durham/London: Duke University Press.

De Goede, Marieke, et al. 2016. Introduction: The Politics of the List. *Environment and Planning D: Society and Space* 34 (1): 3–13.

Goody, Jack. 1977. *The Domestication of the Savage Mind*. Cambridge: Cambridge University Press.

Greber, Erika. 2002. *Textile Texte: Poetologische Metaphorik und Literaturtheorie – Studien zur Tradition des Wortflechtens und der Kombinatorik*. Cologne/Weimar/Vienna: Böhlau.

Te Heesen, Anke. 2005. Accounting for the Natural World: Double-Entry Bookkeeping in the Field. In *Colonial Botany. Science, Commerce, and Politics in the Early Modern World*, ed. Londa Schiebinger and Claudia Swan, 237–251. Philadelphia: University of Pennsylvania Press.

Hess, Volker, and J. Andrew Mendelssohn. 2010. Case and Series: Medical Knowledge and Paper Technology, 1600–1900. *History of Science* 48 (3/4): 287–314.

Hicketier, Knut. 1991. *Die Fernsehserie und das Serielle des Fernsehens.* Lüneburg: Kultur-Medien-Kommunikation.

Hyer, Maren Clegg. 2019. Text/Textile*:* "Wordweaving" in the Literature of Anglo-Saxon England. *Medieval Clothing and Textiles* 15: 33–51. https://doi. org/10.2307/j.ctvb4bvnq.8. Accessed 6 Jan 2021.

Kühlmann, Wilhelm. 1973. *Katalog und Erzählung: Studien zu Konstanz und Wandel einer literarischen Form in der antiken Epik.* PhD dissertation, University of Freiburg.

Levine, Caroline. 2015. *Forms: Whole, Rhythm, Hierarchy, Network.* Princeton: Princeton University Press.

Lyotard, Jean-François. 2006. *The Postmodern Condition: A Report on Knowledge.* Minneapolis: University of Minnesota Press.

Mainberger, Sabine. 2003. *Die Kunst des Aufzählens: Elemente zu einer Poetik des Enumerativen.* Berlin/Boston: de Gruyter.

———. 2020. A List Is (Not) a List: Some (Non-Conclusive) Remarks on Lists and Literature. *lwu: Literatur in Wissenschaft und Unterricht. Theme Issue: Lists and Narrative* 1 (2): 9–21.

———. 2020. Musing About a Table of Contents: Some Theoretical Questions Concerning Lists and Catalogues. In *Lists and Catalogues in Ancient Literature and Beyond,* ed. Rebecca Laemmle et al., 19–34. Berlin/Boston: de Gruyter.

Milcent-Lawson, Sophie, Michelle Lecolle, and Raymond Michel, eds. 2013. *Liste et effet liste en littérature.* Paris: Classiques Garnier.

Miles, Melissa. 2010. The Drive to Archive: Conceptual Documentary Photobook Design. *Photographies* 3 (1): 49–68. https://doi. org/10.1080/17540760903561108. Accessed 6 Jan 2021.

Müller-Wille, Staffan, and Isabelle Charmantier. 2012. Lists as Research Technologies. *Isis* 103: 743–752.

Poletti, Anna. 2008. Where the Popular Meets the Mundane: The Use of Lists in Personal Zines. *Canadian Review of American Studies* 38 (3): 333–349.

Pomata, Gianna. 2010. Sharing Cases: The Observationes in Early Modern Medicine. *Early Science and Medicine* 15 (3): 193–236.

———. 2013. The Recipe and the Case: Epistemic Genres and the Dynamics of Cognitive Practices. In *Wissenschaftsgeschichte und Geschichte des Wissens im Dialog – Connecting Science and Knowledge,* ed. Kaspar von Greyerz, Silvia Flubacher, and Philipp Senn, 131–154. Göttingen: Vanderhoeck & Ruprecht.

Richardson, Brian. 2016. Modern Fiction, the Poetics of Lists, and the Boundaries of Narrative. *Style* 50 (3): 327–341.

Rüggemeier, Anne. 2018. The List as a Means of Assessment and Standardization and Its Critical Remediation in Graphic Narratives About Illness and Care. *Closure* 5: 55–85.

———. 2019. Lists in Life Writing: The List as a Means to Visualize the Trace of the Absent. *a/b Auto/Biography Studies* 34 (2): 329–341.

———. 2020. Life Writing and the Poetics of List-Making: On the Manifestations, Effects, and Possible Uses of Lists in Life Writing. *a/b Auto/Biography Studies* 35 (3). https://doi.org/10.1080/08989575.2020.1815371. Accessed 6 Jan 2021.

Sammons, Benjamin. 2010. *The Art and Rhetoric of Homeric Catalogue*. Oxford/New York: Oxford University Press.

Schöpsdau, Klaus. 1994. Enumeratio. In *Historisches Wörterbuch der Rhetorik*, vol. 2, ed. Gert Ueding. Tübingen: Max Niemeyer Verlag. https://db.degruyter.com/view/HWRO/ enumeratio. Accessed 6 Jan 2021.

Schumann, Detlev W. 1942. Enumerative Style and Its Significance in Whitman, Rilke, Werfel. *Modern Language Quarterly*. 3 (2): 171–204.

———. 1944. Observations on Enumerative Style in Modern German Poetry. *Publications of the Modern Language Association of America* 59 (4): 1111–1155.

———. 1945. Conjunctive and Disjunctive Enumeration in Recent German Poetry. *Publications of the Modern Language Association of America* 60 (2): 517–566.

Sève, Bernard. 2010. *De haut en bas. Philosophie des listes*. Paris: Seuil.

Spufford, Francis, ed. 1989. *The Chatto Book of Cabbages and Kings: Lists in Literature*. London: Chatto and Windus.

Stäheli, Urs. 2011. Das Soziale als Liste: Zur Epistemologie der ANT. In *Die Wiederkehr der Dinge*, ed. Friedrich Balke, Maria Muhle, and Antonia von Schöning, 83–101. Berlin: Kulturverlag Kadmos Berlin.

———. 2016. Indexing – The Politics of Invisibility. *Environment and Planning D: Society and Space* 34 (1): 14–29.

———. 2017. Traveling by Lists: Navigational Knowledge and Tourism. *Zeitschrift für Literaturwissenschaft und Linguistik* 47: 361–374.

Thürlemann, Felix. 2013. *Mehr als ein Bild: Für eine Kunstgeschichte des 'hyperimage'*. Munich: Wilhelm Fink Verlag.

Turin, Gaspard. 2017. *Poétique et usages de la liste littéraire: Le Clézio, Modiano, Perec*. Genève: Droz.

Visser, Edzard. 1997. *Homers Katalog der Schiffe*. Stuttgart: Teubner.

von Contzen, Eva. 2016. The Limits of Narration: Lists and Literary History. *Style* 50 (3): 241–261.

von Contzen, Eva. 2017. Die Affordanzen der Liste. *Zeitschrift für Literaturwissenschaft und Linguistik* 3: 317–26.

Wassermann, Nathan. 2021. Lists and Chains: Enumeration in Akkadian Literary Texts (with an Appendix on This Device in Borges and Hughes). In *Lists and Catalogues in Ancient Literature and Beyond: Towards a Poetics of Enumeration*, ed. Rebecca Laemmle et al., 57–80. Berlin/Boston: de Gruyter.

Wildman, Stephen, and John Christian. 1998. *Edward Burne-Jones: Victorian Artist-Dreamer*. New York: The Metropolitan Museum of Art.
Young, Liam Cole. 2017. *List Cultures: Knowledge and Poetics from Mesopotamia to BuzzFeed*. Amsterdam: Amsterdam University Press.

PART I

(List-)Making Knowledge

CHAPTER 2

Between Narrativity, Memory, and Administration: Lists in Roman Historiography

Martin Stöckinger

Introduction: Lists as History, History as List

The relationship of lists, cultural memory, history, historiography, and narrativity has always been intimate. Let me start with an example of a text type with which most students of the humanities are familiar:

BC
753   Legendary foundation of Rome
510   Traditional date of expulsion of kings and foundation of the
           Republic
270   Callimachus, Theocritus, Aratus active
100   Birth of Julius Caesar
84   Birth of Catullus
70   Birth of Virgil, 15 October
[…]

M. Stöckinger (✉)
University of Cologne, Bonn, Germany
e-mail: mstoecki@uni-koeln.de

© The Author(s) 2022
R. A. Barton et al. (eds.), *Forms of List-Making: Epistemic, Literary, and Visual Enumeration,*
https://doi.org/10.1007/978-3-030-76970-3_2

27

43	Birth of Ovid, 20 March; death of Cicero
[…]	
25	Ovid begins *Amores*
[…]	
AD	
2	*Metamorphoses* and *Fasti* in progress
[…]	
14	Augustus dies, succeeded by Tiberius
17/18	Death of Ovid in exile (Hardie 2002, 368–369)

What we see here is a timeline from the final pages of a random academic book, in this case *The Cambridge Companion to Ovid*. The timeline spans from the foundation of Rome in 753 BCE to Ovid's death in the year 17/18 CE. I have chosen this example to underscore the contrast it builds with my initial thoughts on the relationship between history, historiography, and lists. I began with the assumption that in any form of historiography, the predominant manner of treating lists of events would be to transform "chronicles" into narratives (i.e., "stories" and "plots") which in turn would create historical meaning, a phenomenon Hayden White has famously described as "emplotment."[1] But what we find here is the opposite: these timelines at the end of modern academic books are conceived to reduce complexity after the author(s) have laid out their case in a prose narrative in the work itself. They ban and reduce the causalities between events into an assemblage of "pure facts." This is not to say that timelines of this kind do not have their own "narrativity" or "rhetoric,"[2] but they are obviously designed to serve as a more condensed, purer, less complex, and better manageable set of historical data than the narrative that precedes them in the book that they conclude.[3] Students of the respective past, confused by or unfamiliar with the mass of information offered in the book, can find orientation in these lists. Mnemotechnics offers another case in point (think of examinees who prepare for a test and need a survey of the relevant material in a digestible form): history, in one of its most basic definitions, is the act of recording things, events, and persons that are worth being remembered, and lists can help with this, both on an individual and on a collective level.

In what follows, I will examine some functions of lists in Roman historiography. I use the term *list* in the sense of Robert Belknap's definition as a "framework[…] that holds separate and disparate items together" and "a formally organized block of information that is composed of a set of members" (Belknap 2004, 2 and 15). It is, of course, not possible to treat every Roman historian from every period. The compilation of a "list of lists in Roman historiography" would bring about the same problems as any list (such as completeness, selectivity, closure, and order) and, what is more, it would not be a very appealing endeavor, neither for its compiler nor for its reader. What we can say is that in antiquity, both in Greece and Rome with its late-antique successor provinces, lists feature prominently in commemorative practices from the earliest times on—a formulation that is meant to embrace historiography, but also other genres such as the epic and non-literary texts such as inscriptions as well as other media such as ancestral portrait galleries.[4] Names of notable magistrates, rulers, priests, and persons regarded as exemplary, but also events, troops, provinces, monetary resources, and dispenses such as dedications, and so on, have often been collected and converted into lists, not seldom in their chronological sequence. By using and including lists, historiography mirrors this wider cultural commemorative practice to a certain extent.

In my analyses, I will focus on four examples, the first and the last of which (the *Annales Maximi* and Gregory of Tours) mark the margins of what we might call "Roman historiography," while the second and third, a passage from Tacitus' *Histories* and the *Res Gestae Divi Augusti* (*RGDA*), are selected from the early principate. Each of them comes with its own interpretive difficulties and a huge bulk of scholarship to which I can only refer selectively. I will start by examining the relationship between lists and historical narratives as introduced above. More specifically, I will demonstrate that this relationship can operate in two ways: whereas the traditional view (that lists lack causality) is present in Cicero's discussion of the *Annales Maximi*, Tacitus uses a list for the very purpose of explaining reasons and causes. The Tacitus example, which subtly grapples with an administrative list compiled by the emperor Augustus, will prepare the ground for the two sections to follow. Here I will argue that historical lists can be used to display political and religious power even beyond death: The *RGDA* consists of lists that, by the means of accumulation, create an effect of sublimity, thus intimating a bid for posthumous deification. Gregory closes his historical work with a list of the bishops of Tours, including himself as the then current bishop. On the one hand, this list is meant to secure his own fame as a religious leader and historian, yet on the other hand it remains open for continuation in order that Gregory's diocese might persist until the final days.

History Without Rhetoric: The *Annales Maximi*
(with Credits to Cicero)

Perhaps the oldest form of written history in Rome was a list: the so-called *Annales Maximi* (literally the "greatest annals")[5] were daily records written on a tablet by the chief priest in Rome, the Pontifex Maximus, and put on display at the priest's house.[6] According to Servius, they contained "things worthy of mention which had been done at home and abroad, by land and sea, day by day" (Serv. Aen. 1.372–3 = FRHist T3).[7] These records were collected and preserved in 80 books and were an invaluable source and point of reference for the Republican Roman historians until Livy.

But despite their dignity, the *Annales Maximi* soon became subject to severe criticism: Cicero says about them that "nothing could be more arid" (Cic. leg. 1.6 = FRHist T4)[8] and, in another context on which I will focus in my argument, he complains that those Republican authors who wrote in the vein of the *Annales Maximi* present us with "records just of dates, persons, places, and events, which lack rhetorical adornment" (Cic. de orat. 2.53 = FRHist T2).[9] Today, our direct evidence for the *Annales Maximi* is very small: in his edition of the *Fragments of the Roman Historians*, Tim Cornell collects no more than six verified fragments and another six doubtful fragments of the *Annales Maximi*; in short, we are not in the position to judge whether or not Cicero's criticism is justified (Cornell 2013, vol. 2, 10–31).

What we can do is reconstruct Cicero's argument and its premises. One can wonder why Cicero introduces the category of rhetorical adornment here and, more importantly, what exactly he means when referring to the lack thereof. Within the context of this volume, narrativity and the role it plays therein are of particular importance. As an orator, Cicero is naturally interested in negotiating the relationship between historiography and rhetoric, that is, in the Roman context public political and juridical speech. An orator—be it in court or in a political debate—constantly has to construct narratives in order to convince his audience, and we know that the ancients were aware of this fact: in the traditional rhetorical taxonomy the central part of a speech, in which the argument is developed, is called *narratio*.[10] The excerpt in question forms part of a longer passage (Cic. de orat. 2.51–64),[11] in which Cicero, through his character Antonius, meditates on this relationship between historiography and rhetoric and, more precisely, on the question of how history should be written.[12] Hence the introduction of rhetorical adornment as a category comes quite naturally and it is reasonable to suspect that narrativity does indeed play into it.

But what precisely is meant when Antonius complains about the lack of rhetorical adornment? Interestingly, not quite what we might associate with the term: Antonius contrasts Cato, Pictor, and Piso, whose writings are indebted to the list-like *Annales Maximi*, with Coelius Antipater, whom he counts under the *exornatores rerum* (Cic. de orat. 2.53–54). So we might assume that, in Cicero's and his characters' eyes, Coelius' style seems particularly beautiful—laden with rhetorical devices. Yet, in the next sentence, it emerges that both characters (Antonius and Catulus) agree on quite the opposite:

> But even that Coelius of yours did not embroider his history with any variety of colouring nor did he give a finishing polish to his work by the arrangement of words or by a placid and uniform drawn-out style. [...] and yet, as you say, he did surpass his predecessors. (Cic. de orat. 54)[13]

In short, the elaboration which was intended to distinguish Coelius from the list-like *Annales Maximi* and from his predecessors who rely on these lists "has *nothing to do with style*," as Tony Woodman puts it; rather, "Antonius is talking about elaboration of *content by means of content*" (1988, 78; Woodman's italics).

As becomes clear in the sections to follow, the crucial element in this kind of elaboration is also a crucial element of narrativity in general: when Antonius propounds his theory on how history should be written he puts particular stress on the category of motivation, that is, of creating causality between otherwise isolated events.[14] He states that "it [...] requires [...] for the events a statement not only of what was done or said but also of how, and, when the outcome is discussed, that all the causes are explained, whether the result of chance, wisdom or recklessness" (Cic. de orat. 63).[15]

If we combine this phrase with his criticism of the list-like and in his words un-rhetorical *Annales Maximi*, we find that Cicero's view is not very original: Aristotle had already criticized the genre of historiography in general for relating actual—and we could add: contingent—events; poets, by contrast, narrate "events that might occur (be they actual or invented) [...] in terms of probability and necessity" (Arist. Poet. 1451b8–9).[16] Gerrit Kloss has demonstrated that the Greek words for probability and necessity in this passage are exactly equivalent to what modern narratologists understand by "causality" or "motivation" (Kloss

2003). For the sake of clarification, it should be noted that Aristotle's criticism of historiography relies on some false assumptions and is therefore erroneous: Greek and Roman historians of all times had a special interest in the causality of and between historical events, see for example, the programmatic passages by Herodotus (pref.) or Polybius (3.6.1–7 and 3.7.4–7), who make explicit use of the catchword αἰτία ("reason"/"cause"), as well as the remarks made by many other writers.[17] But a lack of motivation in the *Annales Maximi* might be the reason why later Roman historians used these lists only as a source of historical facts (*fundamenta* "foundations" in Cicero's words, cf. Cic. de orat. 2.63) rather than a strict model for their own writing (*exaedificatio* "superstructure" in Cicero's words, cf. Cic. de orat. 2.63). This idea of quarrying historical data from a list and constructing causal relationships between them resembles and in a way anticipates Hayden White's theory of emplotment.

TACITUS, HIST. 1.4–11 BETWEEN LOGBOOK AND CAUSALITY

My second example is also my first example from the imperial era. It is closely related to the *Annales Maximi*—a point to which I will turn in the middle of this section. At the beginning of his first major historical work, the *Histories*, Tacitus declares that he wants to lay out the number of Rome's troops and provinces, the state of the capital, and the surrounding nations, and so on (1.4.1). The passage features eight chapters (Tac. Hist. 1.4–11) and records a chronological retrospective and a geographical survey before Tacitus starts the account of his actual subject, that is, the events of the years from 69 (after the death of Nero) until the year 96, when Domitian died. Chapters 4–7 treat Rome, chapters 8–11 the provinces.[18]

To start a historical work with a longer or shorter chronological retrospective is a traditional means of setting the ground for a historian's actual purpose, known from Thucydides and Sallust, and usually labeled as "archaeology." While chapters 4–7 of our passage seem not so innovative, the second half of the passage, that is, the survey of the military forces of the provinces in chapters 8–11, is more unusual. In Ronald Syme's words, "it lack[s] precedent or parallel in ancient historiography" (1958, 146, quoted in Damon 2003, 99).[19]

To be clear: to label Tacitus' passage a list in Belknap's sense as introduced above would be inaccurate. Admittedly, it amounts to slightly more than just "a framework that holds separate and disparate items together" in that it features brief story bits which prepare the main narrative. Yet these story bits are only loosely linked or even wholly unconnected, and so the label of list seems justified. To illustrate this, let us have a brief look at the beginning of the first half of the passage, which describes the state of affairs in Rome (*status urbis*) after the death of Nero:

> Still, the senators were overjoyed, and promptly permitted themselves considerable freedom of speech in their negotiations with an emperor who was new to his task and absent from the capital. The leading members of the equestrian order were hardly less delighted than the senators. Hopes were raised among respectable Roman citizens who were connected to the great households, and among the dependants and freedmen of condemned men and exiles. The low-life types who had grown accustomed to the circus and theatres, the most villainous of the slave population and the squanderers who had been the recipients of Nero's degrading charity were gloomy and hungry for the latest rumours. (5) The city garrison (Tac. Hist. 1.4–5)[20]

Tacitus provides a survey of the different social classes in Rome. It features a top-down arrangement, starting with the highest rank, the senators, and ending with the lowest class, namely the slaves and the criminals, before turning to the military class in the following chapter. This conveys the impression of completeness—an important category of what Umberto Eco calls "practical lists."[21] Of course, what we find here is only a guise of completeness: from the perspective of a modern historian, the list does contain its silences, if we think of women, children, or immigrants, all of which the city of Rome had many, to name but a few social groups which are not mentioned here.[22] In his analysis of the social and political functions of lists, Urs Stäheli has worked out various techniques of inclusion and exclusion inherent to lists (Stäheli 2011, 2016); following up on Bruno Latour, he stresses the openness of lists, that is, their potential to be continued (2011, 93–95). As demonstrated above, a modern historian can indeed continue Tacitus' list. However, for the imperial historian himself (and perhaps for his audience), the list he provides is a closed one. In his striving for exactitude, Tacitus aims to cover the entire ground that he considers relevant before beginning his main narrative.

In the second half of the passage, the geographical survey (Tac. Hist. 1.8–11), Tacitus also "provides far more than numbers of places," as Cynthia Damon has pointed out (2003, 99). Here he conveys the impression of completeness by giving a clockwise survey of the provinces around the Mediterranean, which starts in Spain, proceeds with the Gallic provinces, Germany, Upper Germany, Lower Germany, and Britain, then moves to Syria, Palestine, Egypt, and Africa, and ends by what I would call an *et cetera*-section of provinces which cannot be subsumed under the clockwise scheme.[23]

What is more, this list is related to an actual document, namely the *breviarium totius imperii*, a logbook, which Augustus as the first princeps had drafted himself and which after his death was handed down to his successors (see Tac. Ann. 1.11.3–4); Suetonius describes it as "an overview of the whole empire," the first half of which catalogues Rome's military resources.[24] Tacitus, as a historian of the empire, works not so differently from Republican historians. While the latter often conceive parts of their works in relation to the *Annales Maximi*, Tacitus alludes to the form of the *breviarium totius imperii*, written by Augustus, who is not only the military and political ruler, but from 12 BCE onward also the Pontifex Maximus. The responsibility of the records of the state remains in the hands of the ruling class of Rome or, to put it differently, the administrative power over lists is identical with the political and religious power and has a great impact on Rome's cultural memory.[25] By alluding to this actual administrative document, Tacitus shows an awareness of these entangled power relations—an aspect to which I will come back in the conclusion.

One final point about Tacitus' list: in my introduction and in the section on the *Annales Maximi* I have argued that lists of historical events lack causality. This is strikingly different in Tacitus: the narrative elements that constitute the list display a great amount of linguistic markers which insinuate, or at the very least prompt the reader to construct causality. By way of example I give a sentence we have already seen, this time in English and Latin:

> the senators were overjoyed, <u>and promptly permitted themselves considerable freedom of speech</u> (i.e., 'since they had promptly permitted themselves considerable freedom of speech') in their negotiations <u>with an emperor who</u> (i.e., 'because the emperor with whom they negotiated') was new to his task and absent from the capital.

> *sed patres laeti, <u>usurpata statim libertate</u> licentius ut erga principem nouum et absentem;* (Tac. Hist. 1.4.3)

Two points are worth mentioning here: first, the fact that the emperor Galba was new in his office and absent from Rome is obviously set in relation to the senators' behavior in the negotiations (the notoriously polysemous conjunction *ut* can be and has been read in a causal sense here).[26] The translation by Wellesley revised by Ash which I have given (Welleslay and Ash 1995/2009) somewhat obscures the exact meaning; I have therefore inserted a more explicit translation in parentheses. Second, that the senators make use of their freedom of speech is expressed by an ablative absolute with a perfect participle (*usurpata*). Again, it is well possible to paraphrase this construction with a causal clause: the senators' use of their freedom of speech is a completed action at the time that they are overjoyed (*laeti*), and it is a reason for their joy. Moreover, the word *statim* ("promptly") suggests a "temporal antithesis" (Damon 2003, 102 ad loc.) to the time under Nero, further augmenting the senators' joy. So even in this short phrase, which is, I would argue, representative for the entire section, we already find at least two instances of causality:

- Emperor's absence and inexperience *lead to* the senators' freedom of speech.
- The senators' use of freedom of speech *leads to* their joy.

What is more, Tacitus states that he introduces the entire list specifically in order "to appreciate not only the actual course of events, whose outcome is often dictated by chance, but also their underlying logic and causes" (Tac. Hist. 1.4.1).[27] In other words, Tacitus impugns the assumption that historical lists and causality exist on two separate continents. He makes use of the same terminology here as Cicero in the passage I have examined above (see n. 15 [Cic. de orat. 2.63 = FRHist T2] with n. 27: *casus, euentus, causae*). Cicero spoke of the tasks of a historian who does not confine himself to the list-like style of the *Annales Maximi*. Tacitus, however, uses these words to assert that his list is not a coincidental assemblage of contingent historical facts but a means to create causality.

The Sublime List of the *Res Gestae Divi Augusti*

Augustus must have been very fond of lists, or so the *breviarium totius imperii* suggests. Perhaps even more famous is the so-called *Monumentum Ancyranum* or *Res Gestae Divi Augusti* (*RGDA*), an account of his achievements, which he claims to have written in the final year before his death (chapter 35).[28] It was first published in the session of the senate following his death in the late summer of 14 CE. Augustus commissioned that it was carved on bronze tablets and put on display in front of his mausoleum in Rome, but later it received even wider circulation: the text came down to us on three temple inscriptions in Asia minor, the best preserved of which is found on the Temple of Augustus and Rome in Ankara, from which the *Monumentum Ancyranum* derives its name. The inscription is bilingual (Latin and Greek) and features no less than 35 chapters written in the first person plus an appendix of another four paragraphs written in the third person which summarizes the chapters. Theodor Mommsen therefore called the *RGDA* the "queen of ancient Latin inscriptions."[29]

Its structure is complex: after a section on the honors (*honores*) which Augustus received (chapters 1–14), a larger section follows (15–35), in which his achievements (*res gestae*) and expenses (*impensae*) are intertwined. The text does not follow a clear-cut narrative scheme: there are only traces of chronology and scholars have therefore searched for other patterns. To highlight just two of the more recent and persuasive approaches, it has been suggested that the underlying principle of the text is the presentation of continuous moments of increase that chime in with the etymology of the name *Augustus* (< *augeo* "to increase," which is discussed in chapter 34);[30] another interpretation lays particular stress on the interrelation of media (written text, monument, performance) which helps Augustus represent and consolidate his *auctoritas*.[31] What we can say with certainty is that Augustus does not relate his achievements in a chronological sequence but groups them thematically. Categorization, which can ultimately lead to veritable taxonomies, has been a vital strategy of list-making in all periods (Eco 2009, 216–229, Mainberger 2013, 37–118.). Hence one can easily regard the inscription in its entirety as one massive list. This marks a crucial difference to the Tacitus example above: while Tacitus' *Histories* is a narrative that contains a list, the *RGDA* can be viewed as a list that contains some smaller narratives. If we look at the text more closely, we see that this list comprises in itself not only narratives but also various other lists, for example:

- Chapters 15–18: list of donations to the people of Rome and the veterans
- Chapters 19–21: list of buildings, renovations, dedications (mostly of temples) in the city of Rome
- Chapters 22–23: list of games
- Chapters 26–33: list of conquests (subdued provinces and rulers)

The text abounds with numbers and exact figures, most notably in the chapters on the monetary donations (15–18). To give a small but vivid impression about these accounts, let us have a look at chapter 15. Here Augustus lists the following sums which he donated over the course of the years: for the plebs 300 sesterces, two times 400 sesterces each, 12 grain rations, another 400 sesterces; for the urban plebs 60 denarii each; for the colonists 1000 sesterces each; and for the commoners 60 denarii. What is more, the list is peppered with the estimated numbers of beneficiaries of the donations: "never fewer than 250,000 members of the plebs" (15.1), "320,000 members of the urban plebs" (15.2), "about 120,000 colonists" (15.3), and "200,000 commoners" (15.4). This account-holder mentality can also be found in the chapters on the games where Augustus meticulously records how often he arranged this or that game or where, for instance, he reports that in 26 hunting shows around 3500 wild African beasts were killed (22.3).[32]

Enumeration is an important formal principle in the *RGDA*; when we move to its contents, we see that exoticism is perhaps one of its most central issues. We have glimpsed that in the previous example of the hunting shows, but nowhere is this more palpable than in the section on Augustus' world conquest (26–33). Alison Cooley counts no less than "fifty-five geographical names, many of which must have sounded distinctly exotic to a Roman audience" (Cooley 2010, 36). Thus, Augustus presents himself as the conqueror of and ruler over the known world, following the footsteps of Alexander the Great. But this exoticism is conjoined with a great mass of information about Augustus' building activities in the city of Rome (19–21).[33] We do not know whether Augustus had a diffusion of the text to the borders of the empire in mind, but just as the intended readership at his tomb in Rome could marvel at the exotic names, so too could readers in Asia marvel at the passages on the impressive architecture of the empire's capital. The main rhetorical feature of these lists is that of *accumulatio*: they gather a multitude of different items, thus expressing a great richness. But these *accumulationes* are hardly random; they have a clear goal in that they transcend the huge distances between the center and the periphery of the Roman empire and serve as a means to represent Augustus' power over *urbs* and *orbis*.[34]

Much ink has been spilled quarreling over the true motive behind the *RGDA*. Simple answers cannot be found, and it is well possible that Augustus had more than one ulterior motive behind the text.[35] Perhaps the most attractive interpretation, which is shared by many scholars, is to read the *RGDA* as a bid for posthumous deification. I would phrase this slightly differently: As a young man Augustus had written an autobiography;[36] by writing the *RGDA* shortly before his death, he renounces traditional narrative forms of this kind, which by introducing causality always involve interpretive elements and which are themselves subject to interpretation. Instead, he chooses the pure format of a list, which does not display explicit causal nexus between its elements. By doing so, Augustus allows the enumeration of his deeds speak for himself, thereby making himself independent from the decision of the senate or his successor: the immense list that is the *RGDA*, along with all its shorter constituent lists, constitutes an astounding personal monument notwithstanding the question of whether or not he was to be deified.

This interpretation is germane to, but not identical with the views brought forward by Jaś Elsner and Michèle Lowrie (see Elsner 1996 and Lowrie 2009, 279–309). Elsner stresses the *RGDA*'s position on monuments and argues that the inscription conveys its imperial message particularly through its architectural, archaeological, and religious context (Elsner 1996, 49–53); Lowrie sees the iterability inherent in the medium of writing as the crucial element in fulfilling Augustus' desire for "self-perpetuation."[37] I would argue that it is neither the monuments nor the medium of writing but the format of a list which does the talking. The *RGDA*, however, is not a list which functions as a tool to provide a neatly arranged survey much like the timelines I mentioned in the introduction. It does not transform the items it contains into a more manageable set of historical data; rather, the text functions as a vast accumulation of events which illustrate Augustus' grandeur. These events are carefully selected and ordered but constitute such a mass of information that it is not possible to absorb them all, especially not if one perceives them as an inscription and not as a text in a book. As such, I would argue they create an effect of sublimity. In his discussion of the mathematical sublime, Immanuel Kant defines that "the sublime is that in comparison with which everything else is small."[38] For Kant the sublime is closely linked to the idea of infinity, which is not explicitly present in *RGDA*: its lists assemble many but not infinite honors and achievements; they cannot be continued endlessly. However—and this is the critical point—for Kant, sublimity lies not in the object per se but in the judging person's state of mind when perceiving the object: "We hence see also that true sublimity must be sought only in the mind of the [subject] judging, not in the natural Object, the judgement upon which occasions this state."[39]

The sublime might be an interpretive key to the *RGDA*. On a general level, we can remind ourselves that the desire for deification that scholars suspect in the *RGDA* has areas of overlap with the idea of the sublime. In *An Essay on the Sublime*, John Baillie counts "desire of fame and immortality" under "the affections unexceptionably sublime" (Baillie 1747/2018, section III). When we return to the more specific Kantian concept of the sublime as introduced above, we can see the sublime's economic mechanisms at work: the huge sums of money in the chapters on the donations and dedications, the sheer mass of honors attributed to Augustus, the number of games over which he presided, and his building activities, conquests, and victories as presented in the *RGDA* are barely comprehensible in their own right, especially since the reader learns nothing about the causes and underlying intentions of these events. Despite the exact numbers and figures given in the text, these honors and achievements paradoxically elude any clear calculation, and a purely mathematical estimation becomes inadequate (one of Kant's key criteria). Taken together, all the different items contribute to Augustus' symbolic capital, yet they are not so easily—if at all—convertible into each other. From a strategical standpoint, the text purports to be an arid and wholly rational approach to the life of Augustus when in fact the *RGDA* overwhelms its readers by presenting an incomparable mass of prestigious accomplishments.

Lists as Source and Sphragis in Gregory of Tour's *Historia Francorum*

Lists and catalogues remained important for historians throughout late antiquity and the early Middle Ages. This can be illustrated by Gregory of Tours' *Historia Francorum*, written in sixth-century Gaul, which has a great affinity to lists.[40] Let us start with two examples from the second book: in 2.9 Gregory quotes from consular tablets, which in their original form were mere lists of names of the Roman consuls.[41] Interestingly, Gregory seems to have found here more than a list of names, namely an elaborate narrative of at least two sentences, which contains the murder of King Theudemer and his mother Ascyla and the introduction of King Chlodio. After that, the reported speech breaks up, and we do not know from which sources Gregory has the information for the rest of his chapter. Only a few chapters later, a passage (2.18–19) remarkably interrupts the surrounding narrative of marvels and miracles and gives a rather dry and somewhat disruptive list of events of the 460s. It has therefore been suspected that in these two chapters Gregory reworks or even literally quotes annals of the city of Angers, a chronicle which also must have had a list-like format (Buchner 1990, XXXVI and 100 n. 1). These two examples illustrate that in his historical research, Gregory, who made use of a great number of texts from various genres, obviously also consulted list-like formats.[42]

The most significant list in the *Historia Francorum* is the list of the bishops of Tours in the final chapter of the tenth book, which concludes the work (10.31). It is not very likely that Gregory compiled this list completely by himself. Rather, he may have found models in the archives which he could continue or at the very least use as a source. Nevertheless, as will become evident below, the insertion at the end of the historical work, and some other aspects, give this list an individual touch. We are dealing with a record of the 19 bishops of Tours from Catianus (#1, 249–301 CE) to Gregory himself (#19, 573 CE). Its form is modeled after the *Liber Pontificalis*, a chronicle of the popes, which had first been published some decades before Gregory's *Historia Francorum* (see Duchesne 1910, vol. 2, 283).

A few things are remarkable here: first, like the list in 2.18–19 briefly mentioned above, this list interrupts the flow of the narrative, but in a different manner, as it repeats and summarizes times and events that were related before. One might be willing to regard this list as a paratext in a vein similar to the timelines in modern academic books mentioned above.

But, and this is my second point, this would be a very special paratext, since it does not cover the entire time span which is treated in the *Historia Francorum* (which does not begin with the first bishop of Tours but with the creation of the world) and also because the dates and details given in this list are at times not in accordance with the preceding narrative.[43] One can only speculate as to why this is the case. The most plausible answer is that Gregory made use of different sources which were themselves contradictory.

This leads to my third observation, namely that this list provides us with an interesting mix of narrative and list. Each section on a bishop can be regarded as a micro-narrative, or to put it more precisely, as a micro-biography, sometimes written in the style of saints' legends.[44] But frequently, these lists are nothing but accounts of achievements of the respective bishop or contain themselves various lists, which makes them comparable to the *RGDA*. For instance, we learn that Perpetuus (#6) rebuilt the church over the tomb of St. Martin and founded five other churches. Moreover, he reorganized the order of fasts and feasts, which is presented in a list of 21 items. In short, Gregory's list of bishops is not only a list but in fact a "list of lists" or a "meta-list," so to speak. In the section about his own life (#19), which closes the entire work in an auto-biographic fashion, Gregory lists the churches he has built or renovated. What distinguishes him from his predecessors are his literary achievements, which can be listed: ten books of *Histories*, seven books of *Miracles*, one on the *Lives of the Fathers, Commentaries on the Psalms*, and a book on the *Offices of the Church*. Consequently, the end of Gregory's list can be read as a *sphragis* ("seal"), a traditional technique by which classical authors hint at their identity and literary achievements at the closure of their works.

This brief glance at the section about Gregory himself leads to a fourth and final point, namely that Gregory highlights that his list of bishops is not complete in a strict sense: it is complete at the very moment in which it is written, but since history continues, the list that records this history is to be continued as well.

> Nevertheless I conjure you all, you Bishops of the Lord who will have charge of Tours cathedral after my unworthy self, I conjure you all, I say, [...], that you never permit these books to be destroyed, or to be rewritten, or to be reproduced in part only with sections omitted, for otherwise when you emerge in confusion from this Judgement Day you will be condemned with the Devil. Keep them in your possession, intact, with no amendments and just as I have left them to you. Whoever you are, you Bishop of God, even if our own Martianus Capella himself has given you instruction in the Seven Arts [...] and if, as a result, what I have written seems uncouth to you, despite all this, do not, I beg you, do violence to my Books. You may rewrite them in verse if you wish to, supposing that they find favour in your sight, but keep them intact. (Greg. Hist. 10.31)[45]

It is here that the indebtedness of Gregory's list to the *Liber Pontificalis* becomes palpable: for early historians of Christianity such as Gregory and the author(s) of the *Liber Pontificalis*, the history of the church is a history of (apostolic) succession. This principle is vital not only for Rome and the popes but also for smaller units of the Church such as the diocese of Tours. A list is the most natural format for relating this sort of succession history. It transfers the temporal sequence into a sequence that unfolds spatially on the final pages of Gregory's book. What is more, the list is a format which lends itself perfectly for continuation (see Stäheli 2011, 93–95): while it is true that Gregory's own time as bishop of Tours is the *telos* of both his *History* and its closing list, the list remains open to the future. And although Gregory shares a certain eschatological expectation with many contemporaries, even his following calculation of years, which reaches from the creation of the world down to the present day, must be regarded only as a subtotal. Gregory uses the open format of the list to secure and underscore the persistence of his diocese after his death until the Last Days.

Finally, Gregory makes some most interesting metaliterary claims here: by addressing both his successors as a group (*omnes sacerdotes Domini, qui post me …*) and his immediate successor (*o sacerdos Dei, quicumque es*), he shows an awareness that he will not be the last bishop of Tours. The bishops after him will continue to write the history of his diocese. I deliberately choose the formulation of "writing history" here because it can be understood in two ways: Gregory's successors continue to "write" the history because they are the future of the diocese of Tours and, viewed from a later point, their names and achievements will be part of the list as #20, #21, #22, and so forth. On the other hand, Gregory seems to be aware that they too might "write" history in a very literal sense inasmuch as they will be in charge of the archives of the diocese (see Breukelaar 1994, 116–118). Gregory fashions himself and his successor bishops as similar to the Roman Republican Pontifices Maximi, as the keepers of both the religious sphere and the records of their community. Earlier, I suggested reading Gregory's list as a *sphragis* to his work. Having discussed Gregory's warnings, which are addressed to his successors, and thus look into the future, a slight amendment seems to be in order: we should rather, in an oxymoronic formulation, speak of Gregory's list as an "open seal."

CONCLUSION: THE SOCIAL LIFE OF ROMAN HISTORICAL LISTS

By way of conclusion I would like to stress three overarching aspects we have encountered in one way or another in the examples I have discussed. The first issue is so obvious that we barely reflect upon it, but it nevertheless merits some contextualization: it is the medium of writing on which all of the lists I have presented rely. The *Annales Maximi* and the *RGDA* are conceived as inscriptions, Tacitus' list playfully alludes to an actual document, namely Augustus' logbook of the empire, and Gregory, in his list of bishops, explicitly refers to his work as a piece of writing which is handed down to his successors and which may not be destroyed, cut, or shortened (see section "Lists as Source and Sphragis in Gregory of Tour's *Historia Francorum*"). As I have mentioned, we may not be all too surprised by this focus on writing, but we would do well to remind ourselves that lists can exist and have always existed in oral forms as well.[46] Moreover, in recent years, scholars have stressed the oral aspects of the production, transmission, and performance of large parts of Latin literature, including historiography.[47] While this movement is to some extent justified, the aspects of orality in Roman literature have been overstated to a certain extent.[48] The texts I have presented in this contribution decidedly counteract the image of an oral Roman literature in that they put the role of writing front and center.

Closely related to the preeminence of writing is the role of bureaucracy, account keeping, and, most importantly, archives as stores of historical knowledge: of course, the *Sitz im Leben* of the production of the respective texts has changed in the transitions from the Republic to the age of Augustus, to the imperial, and finally to the early Christian medieval eras. But all authors discussed in this contribution certainly had access to, or were even responsible for, archives. The Pontifex Maximus was the keeper of the records of the state. Tacitus may not have examined the *breviarium totius imperii* with his own eyes, but as a member of the senatorial class he could ask for permission to examine the archives of the senate and read the so-called *acta senatus* and the *acta diurna* (see Schmal 2011, 108–111 and Woodman 2009, 8–10). Gregory as the bishop of Tours had access to the archive of his diocese and the scriptoria of the monasteries in the diocese. This means that on the one hand not everyone could have compiled the lists that I have discussed, but on the other hand it means that we have to rethink our notions of authorship of these lists, because each historical writer had to rely on information collected by others (predecessors in the respective office, secretaries, scribes, slaves, monks, etc.). In other words, we are dealing with forms of shared or collective authorship here.

Last but not least, we can see in all the lists that I have examined the intimate entanglement of memory and political power. From its beginnings until at least the times of Tacitus, Roman historiography was a project of the elite, which meant that members of the ruling class wrote history about themselves and for themselves (disclaimer: this does not mean that history could not be critical or polemic). We therefore label large parts of the historiographical production of this period as "senatorial historiography." Strikingly, more than 400 years later, Gregory of Tours preserved this model in the Gallic provinces. He, too, is a member of the senatorial (and now also episcopal) elite and essentially writes a history about and for his peers (see Breukelaar 1994, 116–132). Among my four examples, Tacitus is the only one to disentangle this relationship between political and administrative power on the one hand and memory on the other: by alluding to the logbook of the empire, he claims that he has the same wide and complete overview over the resources of Rome and its provinces as only the emperor and his secretaries can have, who themselves are in charge of this document (see Sailor 2007, 178–182). By composing his own list he opens the view for a different and I would say deviant perspective on a period of the imperial history of Rome and its causalities.

It is a fruitful, and for a literary critic perhaps the most natural way to examine lists in historiography vis-à-vis narratives. As demonstrated, these two formats always stand in one or another relation to each other and sometimes even overlap: lists which function as chronicles or datelines such as the *Annales Maximi* collect material for a more "elaborate" historical narrative; other lists like Tacitus' list in the *Histories* are embedded into or precede a narrative; closely related is the case of Gregory, where a list concludes and to a certain extent summarizes the historical narrative; and finally there is a fourth type, where—as in the *RGDA*—historical lists can function as narratives in their own right with their own specific effects on readers. Furthermore, I hope it has become clear that the question of causality is vital for both narratives and lists. One of the aims of this contribution, however, was to pave the way for a slightly broader perspective than a purely narratological one. We only understand historical lists when we also take other, perhaps less literary aspects into account. Their medium, peculiarities of their authorship and audience, and other conditions of their production, reception, and circulation all contribute to their complexity. Historical lists, in other words, lead a social life which demands further critical attention in current and future scholarship.[49]

Notes

1. For the terminology ("transformation from chronicle to story," "providing the meaning of a story = explanation as emplotment") see White 1973, 5–11 and *passim*.
2. On the literariness of lists see von Contzen 2016.
3. As von Contzen 2017 demonstrates, it is tempting but requires quite some modification in detail to regard lists as "simple form" in the vein of critics of literary simplicity such as Jolle, Dill, Bakhtin, and Iser.
4. For a concise survey of the more recent scholarship on the Homeric catalogue of ships see von Contzen 2016, 247–248. For lists on Greek historical inscriptions see Osbourne 2011, 103–105 and 112–118. In the Roman context—apart from the *Annales Maximi* to which I turn in section "History Without Rhetoric: The *Annales Maximi* (with Credits to Cicero)"—the consular *fasti* and the triumphal *fasti* deserve mention (see Cooley 2011, 250–251). Wiseman 2007, 70, speculates on further lists of magistrates in Rome. Finally, ancestral portrait galleries in private houses display a list-like format and commemorative practice (see Cooley 2011, 248–249). The vast galleries on the Forum of Augustus in which statues of notable men (*summi viri*) and mythical and historical ancestors of the *gens Julia*, accompanied by inscriptions, are put on display, pick up on this tradition (see Cooley 2011, 254–257 and Zanker 2009, 196–217).
5. Both text and translation, if not otherwise indicated, are taken from Cornell 2013, abbreviated as "FRHist."
6. For a comprehensive introduction to the *Annales Maximi* see Rich 2013.
7. *domi militiaeque gesta per singulos dies.*
8. *nihil potest esse ieiunius.*
9. *sine ullis ornamentis monumenta solum temporum, hominum, locorum, gesatrumque rerum.*
10. For the Greek background see Asper 2020 with further bibliography; for Rome and especially Cicero see Berger 1978.
11. The following translations from this passage are those by Marincola 2017.
12. I borrow this formulation from Woodman 1988, 78.
13. *sed iste ipse Caelius neque distinxit historiam varietate colorum neque verborum conlocatione et tractu orationis leni et aequabili perpolivit illud opus; [...] vicit tamen, ut dicis, superiores.*
14. On causality/motivation as a general criterion for narrative texts see Martínez and Scheffel 2012, 111–126.

15. *et in rebus gestis declarari non solum quid actum aut dictum sit, sed etiam quo modo, et cum de eventu dicatur, ut causae explicentur omnes vel casus vel sapientiae vel temeritatis.*

16. τὰ δυνατὰ … κατά τὸ εἰκὸς ἢ τὸ ἀναγκαῖον. (Both text and translation are those by Halliwell 1999.)

17. See the references in Marincola's thematic index s.v. "causation (causes, consequences)," Marincola 2017, 565.

18. The Tacitus translation I give is that by Welleslay/Ash 1995/2009.

19. In ann. 4.4.3–5, Tacitus has Tiberius give a speech which might serve as an interesting (but later) parallel. It is likewise positioned at the beginning of a larger section, namely the beginning of the second half of the Tiberius plot (books 1–6 of the *Annales*), and features a catalogue of troops, yet this time in an anti-clockwise scheme: it starts in upper Italy, Gaul, and Germany and moves to Spain, Africa, Egypt, and Syria, before ending in Thrace, Pannonia, Moesia, and finally Dalmatia.

20. *sed patres laeti, usurpata statim libertate licentius ut erga principem novum et absentem; primores equitum proximi gaudio patrum; pars populi integra et magnis domibus adnexa, clientes libertique damnatorum et exulum in spem erecti: plebs sordida et circo ac theatris sueta, simul deterrimi servorum, aut qui adesis bonis per dedecus Neronis alebantur, maesti et rumorum avidi.* [5] *Miles urbanus …*

21. On the differentiation of "practical" versus "poetical" lists, see Eco 2009, 112–129.

22. Contra Fuhrmann 1960, 256 ("*Sind* auf diese Weise *sämtliche* Gruppen der Einwohnerschaft genannt, […]," my italics).

23. It treats the two Mauretanias (Tingitana and Caesariensis), Raetia, Noricum, Thrace, as well as the ungarrisoned provinces and Italy itself. As Eva Noller pointed out to me, Tacitus' contemporary, the Elder Pliny, follows a similar, yet not identical scheme in the geographical books of his *Naturalis Historia* (3–6) in that he also starts in the west and moves eastward. Unlike Tacitus, he treats first the territories adjacent to the Mediterranean (Spain, Italy, Greece) and the more northern provinces (Gaul, Germania, Britain) only afterward; what is more, in his treatment of Africa and Asia, he does not proceed in the clockwise scheme, but again starts in the very east and moves westward.

24. See Suet. Aug. 101.4: "in the third of the three rolls, a summary of the condition of the whole empire; how many soldiers there were in active service in all parts of it, how much money there was in the public treasury and in the privy-purse, and what revenues were in arrears. He [i.e., Augustus] added, besides, the names of the freedmen and slaves from whom the details could be demanded." *Tribus voluminibus, […] tertio breviarium totius imperii, quantum militum sub signis ubique esset, quan-*

tum pecuniae in aerario et fiscis et vectigaliorum residuis. Adiecit et liberto-
rum servorumque nomina, a quibus ratio exigi posset.

25. The fact that the *breviarium* was deposited with the Vestals underscores the religious connotations of this piece of writing, see Sailor 2007, 180.

26. See Damon 2003, 102 ad loc., referring to OLD s.v. *ut* 21a.

27. *ut non modo casus euentusque rerum, qui plerumque fortuiti sunt, sed ratio etiam causaeque noscantur.*

28. Text and translations from Cooley 2009.

29. Mommsen 1887, 385 = 1906, 247. Quote in the original: "Wer die im Römerreich lateinisch geschriebenen Inschriften zählt, wird leicht an die hunderttausend hinankommen; wer sie wägt, dem wiegt schwerer als die zahllosen übrigen die eine, die Königin aller, das Denkmal von Ancyra."

30. Schwindt 2013, 69–76.

31. Lowrie 2009, 279–309.

32. "I gave to the people hunting shows of African wild beasts in my own name or in the name of my sons and grandsons in the circus or forum or amphitheatre twenty-six times; in these around 3,500 beasts were killed." *[ven]ation[es] best[ia]rum Africanarum meo nomine aut filio[ru]m meo-rum et nepotum in ci[r]co aut in foro aut in amphitheatris, popul[o d]edi sexiens et viciens, quibus confecta sunt bestiarum circiter tria m[ill]ia et quingentae.*

33. Lowrie 2009, 304, speaks of the *RGDA* as "a metamonument that lists all the other monuments Augustus built or restored."

34. On this aspect see Elsner 1996, 48–49 and 52.

35. See the survey in Cooley 2009, 30–41.

36. According to Suet. Aug. 85.1, this work is called *De vita sua*, is 13 books long, and has covered the years until Augustus' campaign in Spain in the year 25 BCE. See Malitz 2003.

37. Lowrie 2009: 279–309, and here especially 299–309 (quote on 304 and 308).

38. Kant 1793/2006, 113 (translation by Bernard 1914). Quotation in the original: "Erhaben ist das, mit welchem in Vergleichung alles andere klein ist."

39. Kant 1793/2006, 121 (translation by Bernard 1914). Quotation in the original: "Man sieht hieraus, daß die wahre Erhabenheit nur im Gemüte des Urteilenden, nicht in dem Naturobjekte, dessen Beurteilung die Stimmung desselben veranlaßt, müsse gesucht werden." The reason for this is that (in Kant's words) "the numerical concepts of the Understanding, by means of progression, can make any measure adequate to any given magnitude" (120). In consequence, our estimation of sublime objects is not a mathematical but an aesthetical one: Although it might be possible to comprehend something by mathematical means, the mind feels a certain

"inadequacy" (a term Kant uses several times) of both reason and imagination when faced with objects of this kind.

40. The translations I give are those by Thorpe 1974.
41. "We read in the consular lists that" *in consularibus* [*sc. tabulis*] *legimus* [...].
42. For Gregory's sources see Buchner 1990, XXV–XXX.
43. On this issue see Duchnese 1910, 283–287. See for example, the order of the bishops between Theodorus and Proculus (#10) and Leo (#13) which deviates from the order given in book 3; moreover, some time spans diverge, too.
44. For example, in the section of St. Martin (#3) where Gregory mentions that Martin restored three dead people to life and stresses that "he manifests himself still today by many miracles" (*et praesenti tempore multis se virtutibus declarat*) or in the section on Gregory's immediate predecessor Eufronius (#18).
45. *tamen coniuro omnes sacerdotes Domini, qui post me humilem ecclesiam Turonicam sunt recturi,* [...] sic *numquam confusi de ipso iudicio discedentes* cum *diabolo condempnemini, ut numquam libros hos aboleri faciatis aut rescribi, quasi quaedam eligentes et quaedam praetermittentes, sed ita omnia vobiscum integra inlibataque permaneant, sicut a nobis relicta sunt. Quod si te, o sacerdos Dei, quicumque es, Martianus noster septem disciplinis erudiit,* [...] *si in his omnibus ita fueris exercitatus, ut tibi stilus noster sit rusticus, nec* sic *quoque, deprecor, ut avellas quae scripsi. Sed si tibi in his quiddam placuerit, salvo opere nostro, te scribere versu non abnuo.*
46. For more "oral" lists, see the contribution by Lennart Lehmhaus in this volume.
47. See, for example, the study of Wiseman 2015.
48. See, for example, the review of Woodman 2015 by Feeney 2017.
49. I am grateful to Eva Noller, Cédric Scheidegger Lämmle, and Kathrin Winter, who read and commented upon earlier versions of this paper.

REFERENCES

Asper, Markus. 2020. Storytelling in Greek Law Courts. In *Thinking in Cases*, ed. Markus Asper, 49–66. Berlin/Boston: De Gruyter.

Baillie, John. 1747/2020. *An Essay on the Sublime* (published posthumously). http://sublime.nancyholt.com/Baillie/index.html. Accessed 23 Sep 2020.

Belknap, Robert E. 2004. *The List. The Uses and Pleasures of Cataloguing.* New Haven/London: Yale University Press.

Berger, Dorothea. 1978. *Cicero als Erzähler: Forensische und literarische Strategien in den Gerichtsreden.* Frankfurt/Main: Peter Lang.

Breukelaar, Adrian H.B. 1994. *Historiography and Episcopal Authority in Sixth-Century Gaul: The Histories of Gregory of Tours Interpreted in Their Historical Context*. Göttingen: Vandenhoeck & Ruprecht.

Buchner, Rudolf. 1990. *Gregor von Tours: Zehn Bücher Geschichten*, 7th ed. Trans. W. Giesebrecht. Darmstadt: Wissenschaftliche Buchgesellschaft.

Cooley, Alison E. 2010. *Res Gestae Divi Augusti: Text, Translation and Commentary*. Cambridge/New York: Cambridge University Press.

———. 2011. History and Inscriptions: Rome. In *The Oxford History of Historical Writing. Volume 1: Beginnings to AD 600*, ed. Andrew Feldherr and Grant Hardy, 244–264. Oxford: Oxford University Press.

Cornell, Tim J. 2013. *Fragments of the Roman Historians*. 3 volumes. Oxford: Oxford University Press. (Abbreviated as 'FRHist'.)

Damon, Cynthia. 2003. *Tacitus. Histories, Book I*. Cambridge: Cambridge University Press.

Duchesne, Louis. 1910. *Fastes épiscopaux de l'ancienne Gaule*. 2nd ed. 3 volumes. Paris: Fontemoing.

Eco, Umberto. 2009. *The Infinity of Lists: From Homer to Joyce*. Trans. Alastair McEwen. London: MacLehose Press.

Elsner, Jaś. 1996. Inventing Imperium: Texts and the Propaganda of Monuments in Augustan Rome. In *Art and Text in Roman Culture*, ed. Jaś Elsner, 32–53. Cambridge: Cambridge University Press.

Feeney, Denis. 2017. Review of Wiseman 2015. *Gnomon* 89: 412–418.

Fuhrmann, Manfred. 1960. Das Vierkaiserjahr bei Tacitus. *Philologus* 104: 250–278.

Halliwell, Stephen. 1999. *Aristotle XXXIII: Poetics*. 2nd ed., ed. and trans. Stephen Halliwell, 1–141. Cambridge, MA: Harvard University Press.

Hardie, Philip, ed. 2002. *The Cambridge Companion to Ovid*. Cambridge: Cambridge University Press.

Kant, Immanuel. 1793/2006. *Kritik der Urteilskraft: Beilage: Erste Einleitung in die Kritik der Urteilskraft*, 2nd ed., ed. Heiner F. Klemme. Hamburg: Felix Meiner Verlag. English edition: Kant, Immanuel. 1914. *Kant's Critique of Judgement*, 2nd ed. Trans. John H. Bernard. London: Macmillan.

Kloss, Gerrit. 2003. Möglichkeit und Wahrscheinlichkeit im 9. Kapitel der aristotelischen Poetik. *Rheinisches Museum für Philologie* 146: 160–183.

Lowrie, Michèle. 2009. *Writing, Performance, and Authority in Augustan Rome*. Oxford: Oxford University Press.

Mainberger, Sabine. 2013. *Die Kunst des Aufzählens: Elemente zu einer Poetik des Enumerativen*. Berlin/New York: De Gruyter.

Malitz, Jürgen. 2003. Autobiographie und Biographie römischer Kaiser im 1. Jhdt. n. Chr. In *Propaganda—Selbstdarstellung –Repräsentation im römischen Kaiserreich des 1. Jh.s n. Chr*, ed. Gregor Weber, 227–242. Stuttgart: Franz Steiner Verlag.

Marincola, John. 2017. On Writing History: From Herodotus to Herodian. Trans. with an Introduction and Notes by John Marincola. London: Penguin Classics.

Martínez, Matías, and Michael Scheffel. 2012. *Einführung in die Erzähltheorie*. 9th ed. Munich: C.H. Beck.

Mommsen, Theodor. 1887. Der Rechenschaftsbericht des Augustus. *Historische Zeitschrift* 57 = new series 21: 385–397. Reprinted in: 1906. Gesammelte Schriften, vol. 4. Berlin: Weidmannsche Verlagsbuchhandlung, 247–258.

Osbourne, Robin. 2011. Greek Inscriptions as Historical Writing. In *The Oxford History of Historical Writing. Volume 1: Beginnings to AD 600*, ed. Andrew Feldherr and Grant Hardy, 97–121. Oxford: Oxford University Press.

Rich, John W. 2013. Annales Maximi. In *The Fragments of the Roman Historians*, ed. Tim J. Cornell, vol. 1, 141–159. Oxford: Oxford University Press.

Sailor, Dylan. 2007. *Writing and Empire in Tacitus*. Cambridge: Cambridge University Press.

Schmal, Stefan. 2011. *Tacitus*. 3rd ed. Hildesheim/Zürich/New York: Georg Olms Verlag.

Schwindt, Jürgen Paul. 2013. Der Sound der Macht: Zur onomatopoetischen Konstruktion des Mythos im Zeitalter des Augustus. In *La costruzione del mito augusteo*, ed. Mario Labate and Gianpiero Rosati, 69–87. Heidelberg: Universitätsverlag Winter.

Stäheli, Urs. 2011. Das Soziale als Liste: Zur Epistemologie der ANT. In *Die Wiederkehr der Dinge*, ed. Friedrich Balke, Maria Muhle, and Antonia von Schöning, 83–101. Berlin: Kulturverlag Kadmos.

———. 2016. Indexing—The Politics of Invisibility. *Society and Space* 34 (1): 14–29.

Syme, Ronald. 1958. *Tacitus*. Oxford: Oxford University Press.

Thorpe, Lewis. 1974. *Gregory of Tours: The History of the Franks*. Trans. Lewis Thorpe. London: Penguin Classics.

von Contzen, Eva. 2016. The Limits of Narrativity: Lists and Literary History. *Style* 50: 241–260.

———. 2017. Grenzfälle des Erzählens: Die Liste als einfache Form. In *Komplexität und Einfachheit*, ed. Albrecht Koschorke, 221–239. Stuttgart: J.B. Metzler.

Wellesley, Kenneth, and Rhiannon Ash. 2009. *Tacitus: The Histories*. 2nd ed. Trans. Kenneth Wellesley. London: Penguin Classics.

White, Hayden. 1973. *Metahistory: The Historical Imagination in Nineteenth-Century Europe*. Baltimore: Johns Hopkins University Press.

Wiseman, Timothy Peter. 2007. The Prehistory of Roman Historiography. In *A Companion to Greek and Roman Historiography*, ed. John Marincola, 67–75. Malden: Wiley-Blackwell.

———. 2015. *The Roman Audience: Classical Literature as Social History*. Oxford: Oxford University Press.

Woodman, Anthony J. 1988. *Rhetoric in Classical Historiography: Four Studies*. London/Sydney/Portland: Taylor & Francis.

———. 2009. Introduction. In *The Cambridge Companion to Tacitus*, ed. Anthony J. Woodman, 1–14. Cambridge: Cambridge University Press.

Zanker, Paul. 2009. *Augustus und die Macht der Bilder*. 5th ed. Munich: Verlag C.H. Beck.

CHAPTER 3

Lore and Order: Enlisting Rabbinic Epistemology

Lennart Lehmhaus

Most probably, all of us like a good list.[1] Lists condense information and make us feel organized and in control. Some might describe life as a chain of incidental happenings, and lists help to structure and tame the often-times disempowering sensation of chaos which follows in its wake. Studies have pointed out that it is precisely the ubiquity of and our familiarity with enumerations or lists that make them almost disappear from our minds as an actual discursive strategy, literary form, and cultural practice.[2] Most scholarship, even on premodern lists, tends to focus almost exclusively on the pragmatic aspects. Lucie Doležalová has pointed out that the list

> is most frequently a tool – a table of contents, dictionary, phone book, etc. One does not read but only uses a list: one looks up the relevant information in it, but usually does not need to deal with it as a whole – and is happy about this fact. (Doležalová 2009a, 1)

L. Lehmhaus (✉)
Eberhard Karls University of Tübingen, Tübingen, Germany
e-mail: lennart.lehmhaus@uni-tuebingen.de

© The Author(s) 2022
R. A. Barton et al. (eds.), *Forms of List-Making: Epistemic, Literary, and Visual Enumeration,*
https://doi.org/10.1007/978-3-030-76970-3_3

While this observation might apply to the already very elaborate forms of lists mentioned in this quote, lists, throughout history, were often conceptualized or perceived as more coherent entities with complex literary and epistemic dimensions. In the case of rabbinic and other premodern lists, this includes the production of ad hoc lists as notes or lists as an addendum to a copied text. Eva von Contzen has pointed out the manifold *affordances* of the list.[3] The list's great functional potential is worth bearing in mind when analyzing how enumerations that are passed on through time are expanded, shortened, or otherwise altered. The following discussion addresses the problem that lists do not usually supply any further explanations as to their theoretical underpinnings. The singularized items which they are composed of are not contextually embedded and thus they tend to be elliptic. However, as such, they are open to (re)interpretation. They invite future reutilizations and transformations that alter or add structure, contents, and commentaries (Mainberger 2003, 20).

This chapter will explore the manifold manifestations of lists in rabbinic texts of late antiquity and the strategies of structuring, producing, and conveying knowledge through lists. Those traditions form the basis of and remain important sources for Jewish religious ideas and practices even today. The discussion is embedded within a broader perspective on (the scholarship of) lists as didactic and epistemic tools within ancient cultures of the Mediterranean and the Middle East. I argue that lists play an important role in the production of knowledge in premodern Jewish history. The following examples aim at demonstrating that in Talmudic medical discourse, legal prescriptions, exegetical or ethical midrashic texts lists function as versatile "epistemic forms." The main bi-partite section presents different interrelated figurations of lists. First, many rabbinic texts feature different kinds of simple lists or enumerations. Second, one may find more complex versions of such enumerations as compound or growing lists featuring interdependent sequences that complement and cross-reference each other.[4] I will focus on sample texts from two different realms: (a) the Talmudic discourse on illness and health that utilizes lists (recipes, preventive advice, therapeutic instruction) in ways similar to other ancient medical traditions; (b) midrashic works with exegetical, homiletical, and ethical interest.

LISTS IN THE MAKING: FROM ANCIENT PRACTICE TO MODERN THEORY?

With a rather derogatory attitude, cultures of the Ancient Near East were primarily conceived by early scholars through the paradigm of a "science of lists" (*Listenwissenschaft*). The term expresses the extent to which "Eastern" knowledge systems were regarded as inferior to Western "Science" (with a capitalized S), which built upon the theoretical discourse of Greco-Roman traditions.[5] Such assumptions about the "Oriental mind" as structurally incapable of abstract, theoretical scientific thinking have long been dismissed in favor of a more nuanced study of the historical and cultural factors in the production of knowledge.[6] Accordingly, scientific thought is a socially embedded cultural practice of generating, ordering, and transmitting knowledge about and within the (empirical) world. The lack of an explicit concept of "science" (and related issues) or a fully fledged theoretical or epistemological discourse should not be taken as a proof for the historical absence of any systematic thinking in our sources. Rather, in several ancient traditions (Egyptian, Mesopotamian, Jewish) first- and second-order procedures of knowledge production (like sequencing, hierarchization, comparison, binary and oppositional thinking, abstraction, synthesis, and generalization), which often underlay the extant discourse, but rarely were addressed openly, are embodied and can be studied in lists.[7]

Lists as artifacts—on a clay tablet, in a scroll, codex, or written on a napkin—constitute the material embodiment of epistemic conventions within a certain culture and time at a specific locality. The deployment of lists for the production of knowledge and its didactic imparting becomes a part of the represented items, since the form has an impact on the cognitive act itself.[8] The specific blending of form and content as well as language and discursive framing played a crucial role for the creation and transmission of knowledge in Jewish traditions and their dynamic exchanges with other cultures.[9] Ancient scientific usage of lists was often intertwined with scribal education and the field of exegesis and interpretation, that is, the core expertise of the rabbinic sages.[10] From ancient times onward, lists had a decidedly epistemological function: they created and (re)presented patterns or concepts that guided the cognitive processes of their authors and their audience.[11] However, due to the dearth of sources (for triangulation), the inquiry into the function(s) of lists within their contexts or the scientific concepts underlying specific lists is often a difficult, if not impossible task.

In the following, I will explore how lists display a rather stable enumerative form across different times and cultures whose flexible and hybrid nature allowed for various adaptations to specific purposes and contexts.[12] While Belknap's broad and inclusive understanding of lists as a "block of information that is composed of a set of members"[13] is certainly applicable to rabbinic texts, a typographical or medial definition of lists as an entity using columns or rows would be rather inexpedient for the material at hand. Although rabbinic lists are thus represented in modern-day scholarly editions for analytical purposes, this is not what they looked like in the manuscripts or the most common earlier prints. Be that as it may, I will use the term *list* in the sense of a flexible enumerative format.[14] Besides preliminary studies by Wünsche and Towner, Roy Shasha's first form-critical study of lists as a literary device in early rabbinic traditions (Mishnah) describes a textual unit featuring a caption with a deictic ("these are they"/*we-ʾilu hen*) and/or a numerical reference ("Three things do/are X") to items following within the list.[15] Lists can be simple or compound, combining several lists or addressing more than one topic.[16] Lists may serve to introduce a particular topic (agenda) at the beginning of a chapter. Some lists may be comparative or contrastive, while others connect heterogeneous items under one rubric.[17] Moreover, the density and brevity of lists help to create coherent units for transferring knowledge, since they function not only as a literary device but also form an effective tool for instruction and information storage (see Cancik-Kirschbaum 2010, 2012).

Introduction to Rabbinic Sources: Background, Dating, and Characteristics

Diverse forms of lists and approaches to list-making served as discursive and epistemic tools in Jewish traditions that were composed in Hebrew and Aramaic throughout late antiquity and early medieval times, roughly from the first to the tenth century. One strand of rabbinic tradition, namely *Halakha* (lit. "way of life"), developed a set of religious normative rules and related (theological) issues that strove to include almost every realm of life—from rituals, liturgy, or festivals to agriculture, business ethics, and even medical topics. This corpus includes the early Mishnah (m.)

and its companion, the Tosefta (t.), from circa third-century Palestine. Two later Talmudic traditions commented and elaborated upon those earlier texts, often adding new material from their respective cultural background: the Palestinian/Jerusalem Talmud (y.), from the sixth century; and the Babylonian Talmud (b.), a vast tradition compiled between the sixth and the eighth centuries in the region of today's Iraq. This body of texts is accompanied by other works subsumed under the label *midrash*, mainly from Palestine, which can be described as "exegetical literature" in the broadest sense of the term. These texts include exegetical and homiletical examinations of the Hebrew Bible and also feature ethical teachings.[18]

Although rabbinic traditions commonly ascribe certain teachings to named sages, this polyphonic concert of rabbinic voices appears in texts with an anonymous and collective authorship. These teachings are thought to have been transmitted orally or else as written notes over quite a long time before they were compiled in written collections. This supposed orality of earlier rabbinic traditions ties in well with theoretical considerations regarding the form of the list. While some scholars see list-making primarily as a writing practice, media scholar Liam Cole Young has compellingly emphasized that the list "challenges the common assumptions about a dichotomy between orality and literacy/writing" because it occupies "a liminal or interstitial space between orality and literacy; 'savage' and 'domestic'; 'primitive' and 'advanced'" (Young 2013a, 501–502). Since lists were inherent parts of the curriculum learned by heart, at least in Babylonia, rabbinic list-making may have emerged as a mnemonic device that builds a bridge between the oral and written traditions. Some contents or additions to compound lists were probably added at a later point, when rabbinic teachings already circulated for some time in writing.

Lists in Ancient Jewish Texts

Before discussing the sample texts, a brief historical contextualization of rabbinic list-making seems in place. Already the Hebrew Bible features genealogies, lists of kings and priests, lists on places ("itinerary of biblical stories"), or about ritual procedures or objects.[19] Prescriptive lists figure also prominently as ordering devices in biblical (Decalogue) and later Jewish law. Enumerations of converts from different ethnic backgrounds who, to varying degrees, are permitted to intermarry with Israelites exemplify the list's political or religious power of inclusion and exclusion.

Detailed lists of items within the biblical dietary laws—specific types of beasts, wild animals, fowl or fish and plants, fruits or trees—did not only have a prescriptive purpose; they were also crucial for the ongoing formation of identity. Moreover, these lists demonstrate the terseness and specificity of the form. Devoid of further explanations regarding their items, these lists pose a challenge during their history of reception/transmission. Post-biblical traditions (e.g., texts from Qumran) and especially the Talmudic refinements of biblical law struggled with many of these names, yet oftentimes found creative solutions. Talmudic authors between the West (Syria-Palestine) and the East (Babylonia) had to translate and actualize transmitted lists according to their contemporaneous and regional contexts (specific plant life, animals, etc.).

Lists were also used to convey ethical ideas and knowledge about the order of the world in Wisdom traditions like Ecclesiastes (Qohelet), Proverbs or Sirach/Ben Sira, which were appropriated by later rabbinic ethical texts (*Avot, Avot de-Rabbi Nathan, Derekh Eretz* etc.).[20] In the post-Talmudic, early Islamic period, one may observe an increased interest in and the frequent deployment of lists. Some texts, like *Pirqe de-Rabbi Eliezer* ("Chapters of R. Eliezer"/ henceforth: *PRE*) or *Seder Eliyahu Zuta* ("The Minor Order of Elijah"/*henceforth: SEZ*), feature thematic lists on key concepts such as charity (*PRE* 33/*SEZ* 1 and 5), repentance (*PRE* 43), or righteousness (*SEZ* 1 and 3). In particular, *PRE* utilizes lists and enumerations as compositional patterns for chapters and the whole work, thereby restructuring biblical chronology according to lists about the seven days of creation, ten things created at twilight, or ten descents of the divine presence.[21] Moreover, in *PRE* lists connect between biblical traditions, Jewish religious custom, and scientific knowledge of different sorts (astrology, cosmology, etc.).[22]

Of special importance are the so-called *Ma'asseh-Torah* traditions.[23] For the first time, these texts accumulated and (re)arranged lists and other material from earlier rabbinic traditions into thematic clusters of lists.[24] The increased interest in condensing information about various fields of knowledge in lists which are combined in one work appears to have been triggered by the "beginning of Hebrew scientific literature" (Langermann 2002) in post-Talmudic Jewish texts as well as by both the penchant for florilegia or compendia and a broader model of education/learning (Arabic: *adab*/أدب) in early medieval (Byzantine) Christian and Islamic cultures.[25]

RECIPES AND RULES FOR A HEALTHY LIFESTYLE IN LISTS

As mentioned before, lists served as stock formats within ancient Jewish traditions. Moreover, lists played an important role in various ancient medical traditions (Egyptian, Mesopotamian, Greco-Roman) as an aid in therapeutic instruction, advice on *dieita* ("healthy lifestyle"), diagnosis, and prognosis.[26] Enumerations take center stage in pharmaceutic works and in recipes. They work as *aide-mémoires* for the practitioner or as handy forms to distribute and transmit pertinent knowledge through prescription-formulas to non-experts or later recipients. In rabbinic medical discourse, as in other traditions, recipes and their lists were altered, expanded, or shortened, while sometimes a piece of empirical evidence was added by way of an anecdote or a statement (efficacy label).[27]

The list structure in recipes often follows a rather simple scheme: the indication (i.e., disease), a list of ingredients or *materia medica* ("healing substances"), steps for preparation and/or application, and, sometimes, alternative therapies. However, lists should not be perceived only as an accumulation of the single items contained in it; rather, lists can intersect, accumulate, and form sequences. In general, medical or recipe lists tend to appear in clusters of lists. Sometimes two or more lists are contiguous or exhibit a close textual and/or thematical proximity. Often such lists show a high degree of either coherence or contrast as in the following brief example from the Babylonian Talmud that contains advice on health regimens. The text is embedded in a longer discussion, mostly in Hebrew, deploying lists of three, five, six, or ten items. Those lists deal with positive and negative signs in dreams or with things that are beneficial or harmful for the human body and mind:

> Three things enter the body without benefiting it: *gwdgdnywt*/גוגדניות (a fruit/plant), *kphnywt*/כפניות (spadix of palms?), and *pgy tmrh*/פגי תמרה (unripe dates?).[28]

> Three things benefit the body without entering / being absorbed by it: washing, anointing, and usage [of one's bed] (*tashmish* = intercourse). (Babylonian Talmud, b. Berakhot 57b, in Hebrew)[29]

The connection between these lists is twofold: first, both are introduced by the same numerical value (three); second, using an antithetical rhetoric they refer to specific items that interact with one's body in opposing ways.

The marked action of "entering the body" is clearly derived from the process of ingestion or consumption. The items are plants or fruits which grant no particular benefit or pleasure to one's body. The second list, by contrast, focuses on bodily activities that improve the body's constitution from the outside without entering into it. The antithesis is developed along two dichotomies: internal/food for consumption versus external/treatment, care, or action in relation to one's body.

One may note that, in this case, the introductory phrases with their numerical value (*deixis*) strongly resemble the enigmatic and learned questions that are abundant in the common ancient genre of "questions/riddles in a contest of wisdom."[30] Complying with the standard feature of brevity, the two lists do not provide any explanation whatsoever—neither why these particular items were subsumed under these inverse categories, nor what their (non-)beneficial qualities are. The recipients of these lapidary enumerations must either receive this message without further questioning or be familiar with knowledge from other sources. This might point to a certain degree of acquaintance with non-rabbinic expertise in the field of dietetics and personal health, which was an especially thriving genre in Greco-Roman cultures.[31] However, background information on the issues at hand might be gleaned also from other teachings dispersed throughout various Talmudic traditions. For instance, various types and parts of dates as well as the plant(s) *gwdgdnywt/gdgdnywt* figure frequently in Talmudic recipes and dietetic advice.[32]

Similarly, beneficial behaviors or practices (nutrition, toilet habits, bathing, anointing, or massaging)[33] are discussed extensively in rabbinic texts, often deploying lists as part of the discourse. Thus, a bath house is included in b. Sanhedrin 17b in a list of the absolutely necessary "infrastructure" in a dwelling place for rabbinic scholars—apart from a doctor, bloodletter, or a public privy. Sexuality, an important subfield within physical well-being, is understood as an integral part of divine creation whose importance for the individual (intimacy, companionship) and the collective (procreation) is highlighted. The sexual impulse and various social conventions and practices with regard to sexuality were discussed in rabbinic traditions mostly in a positive way, while also creating religious and cultural boundaries.[34] The positive attitude toward sexual relations is stressed also through a list that is added to our enumerative pair: "Three things are a reflection of the world-to-come; and these are they: Sabbath, sun and usage (*tashmish*/תשמיש), i.e. sex." Accordingly, sexual activity ("usage") is likened to savoring a small bit of the eternal gratification expected for an eschatological or otherworldly state.[35]

ACCUMULATION, STRUCTURE, AND ORDERLY SEQUENCE

The following list on sexual practices and the perils of pregnancy discusses the impact of external factors on the conception and gestation of the baby in the mother's womb. Also, it is embedded in a lengthy discussion about actions (e.g., intercourse) and products that are deemed bad for breast-milk, that is, harmful for the nursed infant. In a typically associative manner the Talmudic text in b. Ketubbot 60b-61a adds in Aramaic:

1-A Woman who has intercourse in a [public] mill will have epileptic children.[36]
2-[A woman] who has intercourse on the ground will have children with dislocated legs.
3-[A woman] who treads on donkey's blood will have children with scrapings (a skin disease?).
4-[A woman] who eats mustard [seed] will have gluttonous children.
5-[A woman] who eats cress will have blear-eyed children.
6-[A woman] who eats [fish] brine will have children with sparkling eyes.
7-[A woman] who eats clay will have ugly children.
8-[A woman] who drinks 'beer' will have dark-skinned children.
9-[A woman] who eats meat and drinks wine will have healthy children.
10-[A woman] who eats eggs will have children with big eyes.
11-[A woman] who eats fish will have graceful children.
12-[A woman] who eats parsley will have bright children.
13-[A woman] who eats coriander will have fleshy children.
14-[A woman] who eats etrog will have fragrant children.

This list supplements the preceding discussion focused on breastfeeding with other factors that affect the future child's character or bodily constitution. Instead of a caption this list features recurring conditional or propositional statements (*protasis-apodosis*) with a strict if-then logic introduced by "a woman who [does X]," thus focusing on the future mother's responsibility. The 14 items—another instance of abundance or accumulation—form three distinct areas of impact: the sexual act (1 and 2), contact with specific substances (3), eating, and drinking (4–14). So, the majority of the list items is concerned with nutrition, which is also the most important branch of ancient medical tradition.

The first two strands (sexual conduct/contact) may seem odd to a modern reader and burdened with moralizing implications or, probably, ideas of ritual impurity.[37] However, the same concept is corroborated in another Talmudic tractate (b. Nedarim 20a) by a Hebrew teaching in list-form about the impact of conception on fetal development:

R. Yoḥanan b. Dahavai said: "The ministering angels told me four things:

1) People are born lame because they (their parents) 'turned their table' (i.e., practiced some other position / sort of cohabitation).
2) [People are born] mute, because they kiss 'that place' (i.e., the sexual organs).
3) [People are born] deaf, because they talk [lewdly] during sex.
4) [People are born] blind, because they look at 'that place' (i.e., the sexual organs)."

The transmitter of this teaching, an early rabbinic scholar from Palestine, refers to a superhuman, angelic source of his surplus knowledge. This list specifies the exact bodily reciprocity between supposedly improper sexual conduct of various kinds (practice, speech, vision) and the resulting congenital disabilities. Accordingly, muteness is caused, for instance, by practicing oral sex. One has to add that the majority opinion in the Talmud does not grant R. Yoḥanan's report any legal status, that is, no prohibition of said sexual practices, but they also do not reject his moralizing claims about their consequences.[38] In general, such a connection between non-normative behavior producing (anatomically or mentally) non-normative offspring is based on ancient ideas of teratology. This branch of knowledge was concerned mainly with exploring the teratogenic causes of "wondrous births" and congenital disorders. In Jewish traditions, non-normative bodies were categorized and discussed in lists.[39] Simultaneously, a discourse on the dichotomy of (ritual) un/fitness often excluded a person from many basic religious commandments and social practices (prayer, rituals, sacrifice, marriage, etc.) that defined the Jewish community.[40]

The ideas underlying the list above have many parallels in ancient concepts of gestation and pregnancy as attested in various medical and other texts. Many authors (Plato, Aristotle, Hippocratic texts, Pliny the Elder, Soranus, etc.) agree that the unborn child, "planted" into the woman's womb, depends on the mother's nutrition, while being endangered by her unhealthy actions and conditions. In addition, not only physiological factors but even certain sensations affecting the mother during conception or pregnancy will shape the physical appearance, mental faculties, and character of the fetus.[41]

Yet, when one ignores the strict mechanical causality, the general idea that the actual behavior and especially the nutrition of the mother may benefit or harm the child sounds not at all alien to modern ears. Anyone acquainted with pregnancy advice literature might also notice that these books eagerly make use of lists as a format for conveying their message. The emphasis on the mother's behavior and thus her responsibility seems rather familiar and indeed has a long history.[42]

The above enumeration is not a straightforward list of admonitions, however. Rather, the Talmudic authors included both harmful and beneficial actions—this time not in well-distinguished groups but mixed up and with a slight preponderance of positive effects. Through its conditional structure, this list does more than just itemize things under one caption. The format does not only produce topical coherence: the lists' model of causality (if the mother does X, the child will be Y) also reflects an understanding of world coherence (*sympatheia*). The list points to a complex interplay between the human body, nature, and the cosmos ("creation") at large. Similarly, rabbinic and other Jewish traditions reiterate a model of perfect correspondence between the macrocosmic dimension of God's creation and its tool or blueprint (the Torah) and the microcosmic sphere of human experience, nature, and specifically the body.[43] Furthermore, prediction or prognosis seems of particular importance here, since it harbors an interest in the temporal dimension and divinatory aspects similar to those that prevailed in Greco-Roman, Mesopotamian, or Persian traditions.

MIDRASHIC LIST-MAKING: BETWEEN VERSE, EXEGESIS, AND ETHICAL DISCOURSE

In regard to exegetical and ethical discourse in rabbinic traditions (midrash), midrashic lists and those discussed before are not mutually exclusive. Moral topics are often linked to questions of a healthy way of life and deploy bodily imagery, as shall be seen in a moment.

The sample text comes from *Seder Eliyahu Zuta* (*SEZ*), a unique tradition in Hebrew from the ninth or tenth century combining discourse on moral behavior and Jewish (religious) identity. In *SEZ* and its sibling tradition *Seder Eliyahu Rabba* (*SER*), lists are utilized as powerful discursive tools for exegetical, homiletical, and ethical purposes.[44] The following list is embedded in a chapter discussing the human origin of evil and the initial divine plan of a perfectly good and just world order.

1) Three things/words a man ought to meditate upon every day:

    (a) the hour when he makes use of a privy,
    (b) the hour when he is bled [as part of a therapy],
    (c) the hour when he stands over a dead body.

        a1) When he makes use of a privy, he is reminded, 'Behold, your ways are like the ways of the beast'.
        b1) When he is being bled, he is reminded, 'Behold, you are [only] flesh-and-blood'.
        c1) And when he stands over a dead body, he is reminded, 'Behold, where you are going'.

2) And still, he does <u>not</u> return in penitence [to right conduct].

    A) rather, he keeps saying things that are inappropriate, as it is said [in Scripture], *When a man's folly brings his way to ruin, his heart rages against the Lord (Prov. 19:3)*;
    B) and about lies [Scripture] says: *Keep far from a false charge, and do not kill the innocent and righteous, for I will not acquit the wicked (Exod. 23:7)*;
    C) and [about malevolence Scripture] says: Do *not plot evil in your hearts against one another, and love no false oath, for all these things I hate, declares the LORD (Zech. 8:17)*.

But how?[45]

   I) When a man makes himself act like a righteous man and speaks the truth, he is assigned an angel who acts towards him in the way of the righteous and speaks the truth.
  II) When a man makes himself act like a pious, being willing to suffer all, he is assigned an angel who acts towards him in the way of pious and helps the man to accept all suffering.
 III) If, on the other hand, a man makes himself act like a wicked man, deceiving and lying, he is assigned an angel who acts towards him in the way of the wicked by deceiving and lying.[46]
 IV) And if a man makes himself follow a middle way, he is assigned an angel who acts towards him in the middle way.

So, we are told by the Holy One Himself: *I the Lord search the heart, I examine the minds (lit. 'kidneys'), in order to give every person [an angel/reward] according to their ways, according to the fruit of their deeds (Jer. 17:10).* (Seder Eliyahu Zuta 3)[47]

This is a complex version of a compound list or an enumerative cluster that functions as an epistemological device for the ethical agenda of *SEZ*. Within a broader narrative and homiletical discourse, this passage deploys four deeply intertwined lists in order to stress the importance of moral mindfulness. The first double-set exemplifies how to apply techniques of consciousness or self-awareness to reach a state of humility leading to virtue.[48] It starts with a typical caption phrase that points to three occasions as opportunities to guide one's mind and behavior. Those occasions are specified briefly in the first list. This is followed by a repetition of those occasions accompanied by the actual moral advice for each setting, which is derived from previous traditions. The contemplation focuses on human corporeality or mortality and brings one to abstain from or repent immoral actions.[49]

Given the general topic of the "human origin of evil," the text integrates the case of the inconvincible who, even after such strong admonition, keeps up his unethical behavior. This taxonomy of the wicked person (2.A–C) is amplified by the biblical proof-texts focusing on the different sins listed. The listed verses clearly show not only that the said transgressions are already discredited in Scripture, but also that divine punishment awaits those who stubbornly follow an immoral path.

The final list, which has no introductory caption, characterizes four types of behavior and how angelic beings react to them: the righteous, the pious, the wicked, and the average. This list, along with its several parallels in various rabbinic texts, proves that the divine system of "reward and punishment" works, as there is a chance for every person to change one's own ways. The reference to another proof text (Jeremiah 17:10) firmly underlines *SEZ*'s key concepts: human freedom of choice, divine justice, and the chance to repent. Moreover, with this verse, in particular its expression "to give every person according to their ways," the authors refer back to the tenet preceding this list in *SEZ*, chapter 3: "Accordingly, humans are judged because of their ways. They are judged according to their ethical behavior (*derekh eretz*) in order to save them on the Day [of Judgment]."[50]

Lists in *SEZ* function on three interconnected levels of ethical knowledge production. First, as shown above, the lists form a dense cluster that weaves together instructions on ethical mindfulness with a taxonomy of the wicked person and teachings on the divine system of "reward and punishment." So, it provides a didactically efficient but still brief summary of ethical and theological key concepts to its audience, combined with practical advice (techniques of the self). Second, these lists function within the third chapter featuring other complex lists on human ethical traits and within the broader context of *SEZ* as a whole.[51] Third, *SEZ* deploys lists as tools in order to participate in a shared discourse on a much broader scale. One may compare its discourse to similar techniques of teaching morality through lists in various (Jewish, Persian, Arabic) ethical traditions in late antiquity and early medieval times.[52]

Conclusion: Making Lists Rabbinic—Format, Discourse, and Epistemic Values

Seizing on an already developed stock of list-making and enumeration, rabbinic authors cultivated and advanced these strategies in surprising ways that suited their discursive needs and their epistemic project. They took advantage of the fluidity and versatility that make lists powerful discursive forms. The manifold contexts of usage include, as in *Seder Eliyahu*, exegetical operations and narratological deployment for instruction and moral advice. Other sample texts demonstrate how rabbinic texts use lists in order to appropriate, transmit, and create medical knowledge in the form of recipes, therapeutic advice, and instructions for well-being (diet and regimen). In all cases, one notices their function as a general texturing element within a broader discourse, wherein lists work hand in hand with other literary and epistemic micro-forms (e.g., question-and-answers, exempla, dialectic speech, dialogues, parables, case-stories).

The affinity between rabbinic discourse and lists might be explained by one of their shared dimensions. As "lists function to facilitate various forms of interaction between human beings [...] while also standing as a record or an index of [...] this interaction,"[53] so do rabbinic texts, especially when concerned with normative or legal questions (*Halakha*). Lists form an integral part of that (late) ancient Jewish tradition, namely because they trigger a prescriptive momentum while also creating a record or index of historical or ideally imagined rabbinic (normative) culture. For instance, the rabbis adopted and created lists of items forbidden or permitted for ritual reasons such as items you may carry with you for healing purposes on Shabbat. Other texts list elements of a healthy diet or prescribe the right way to behave during conception or pregnancy. This corroborates the notion that lists are intriguing instruments of organizing and producing information, while serving also as "technologies of power" that are crucial for communities, institutions, and states to communicate and implement rules and structures (taxation, census, administration, etc.).[54]

Another similarity can be adduced that connects lists with the heart of ancient rabbinic discourse. Both modern scholarship and the tradition itself have highlighted that Talmudic texts originate in an oral tradition complementing revealed Scripture. Within this context of transmitting teachings, (hybrid) lists perform the function of a structuring, mnemonic device that facilitates the study and transfer of whole chunks of tradition.[55] This holds true for pairs of opposing lists, thematically bound enumerative sequences or clusters of repetitive elements (e.g., the ethical discourse in *SEZ* 3).

Furthermore, it has been emphasized that selection and decontextualization of the singular items are prerequisite for list-making, which is supplemented by their (re)contextualization within the lists and its broader context (Mainberger 2003, 19). Studies on rabbinic literature have likewise stressed that the rabbis built their discourse on the purposeful selection, segmentation, and atomization of biblical verses, words, or Talmudic teachings from which they developed their exegetical, homiletical, and legal thinking. These techniques were adumbrated through careful actualization, intertextual relations, and their embedding into new discursive coherencies.[56] Lists seem to chime in well with this preference. In simple or contrasting form, they enumerate diverse items connected only by their respective caption or a broader theme. Consequently, the rabbinic preference for atomization forms a solid base for the itemization in lists. In rare cases, the ancient and indeed the modern recipient is in the position to identify the particular sources of lists as well as their ways of transmission so as to better understand their (different) functions and purposes.

In most of the above examples, we could see that lists are not standalone elements. They are deeply embedded in discourses on moral behavior, religious law and lore, or on historical, sociological, and scientific knowledge about the world and human life in particular. These overarching themes define the various functions of rabbinic lists. Conversely, the lists themselves shape the discourse. However, lists constitute only one discursive element among others. Most lists neatly interact with other stylistic and instructional elements from rabbinic tradition such as exempla, anecdotes, parables, or dialectic reasoning. In *Seder Eliyahu Zuta*, we saw how lists use biblical verses or quotes from Jewish tradition, thereby drawing on the core-expertise of rabbinic sages—namely the knowledge and interpretation of Scripture and religious law.

Finally, the texts have shown that rabbis employed lists and enumerations within various and, at times, converging contexts—from recipes and health advice to exegesis and ethical formation—but to the same ends. For those small text forms do not only constitute a simple device or container for indexing and conveying already self-contained knowledge; rather, they serve as powerful cognitive tools or vehicles that offer additional epistemic value and advance the broader project of the production of rabbinic knowledge. The use of numerical list captions, guiding questions, or categories resemble core features of what Gianna Pomata designates as "epistemic genres," where they serve as "signposts indicating direction for further observation and enquiry" (see Pomata 2014; here: 8). While facilitating the classification of phenomena, observations, or experiences, they "challenge extant knowledge formations, but also create new ones [...] (which amount to new ways of seeing and doing)."[57]

In his seminal study from 1977, while clearly pushing back dichotomies such as Western/Oriental or Modern/Ancient, Jack Goody emphasizes that the production of lists as a cultural practice is connected to specific "modes of thought," which he subdivides into three types or functions. First, *retrospective* lists that form a kind of inventory of persons, objects, or events (e.g., lists of kings, treasures, or battles). These can store and transmit data. Second, *prescriptive* lists, which are mainly geared toward a particular action, event, or process (shopping lists, administration procedures, flowcharts, guest lists, etc.). Although the function of such lists is not primarily related to storage, their reception may shift them into lists of the first category (i.e., guest lists of a certain event). Third, *lexical* or *encyclopedic* lists combine a bundle of concepts or practices that may serve as a proto-dictionary/lexicon of a culture or a handbook for a certain field.[58] Rabbinic lists for the most part appear to combine all three of Goody's functions in astonishing, multifarious, and often inextricable ways. Lists constitute epitomes of information received in a form that represents and affords order, accessibility, and usability. As such, lists helped the rabbinic authors to structure and authorize their discourse, while creating new insights, orders, and hierarchies—be it through sociological-ethical categorization of behavioral patterns and character types, lists of symptoms, or via elaborated disease taxonomies or catalogues of therapies.[59] Accordingly, lists contributed to the rabbinic project(s), primarily as collections of law and lore that functioned simultaneously as cultural inventories, store houses of knowledge, and practical reference works.[60] They thus facilitate the transfer of knowledge of the world and the body into the world of the rabbinic study house and eventually into the quasi-canonical Talmudic corpus, an encyclopedic body of knowledge. Although we know little about how rabbinic lists were used by contemporary readers, it is worth noting that early medieval traditions (e.g., the "midrash of lists") valued Talmudic list-making as a crucial cultural practice, a means of making sense of religious lore and the order of the world.[61]

Notes

1. I am very grateful to the LISTLIT work group at Freiburg for organizing a truly inspiring, interdisciplinary conference and for their diligent editing of this volume. I am also indebted to the questions and comments on my paper during the conference and the editing process as well as to my colleagues' presentations from which I have learned much. My study of lists within the medical discourse in rabbinic texts is based on my research as a member (2013–2020) of the transdisciplinary working group A03 "The Transfer of Medical Episteme in the 'Encyclopedic' Compilations of Late Antiquity" as part of the DFG-funded Collaborative Research Center SFB 980 "Episteme in Motion" at the Freie Universität Berlin. Moreover, I have learned a lot about lists within ancient Mesopotamian culture from the members of the ERC-funded research group BabMed (Babylonian Medicine): Markham J. Geller, Ulrike Steinert, and J. Cale Johnson. I am much obliged to Markham J. Geller, who read and commented on a previous version of this article.
2. Mainberger 2018, 97. On ad hoc lists, see Doležalová 2009b.
3. See von Contzen 2017. See also Young 2013a, 498–499 on the multifariousness of the list.
4. For a detailed discussion of such compound lists, see the discussion on the midrash *Seder Eliyahu* later. The overlap and differences between rabbinic clusters of lists and complex list formats such as tables, catalogues, or indices will be further discussed in Lennart Lehmhaus, Rabbinic Lists as "Epistemic Genre": exegesis, ethics, and science, in *Lists and Synopses* (forthcoming 2021).
5. See von Soden 1936, 411–464 and 509–557. For *Listenwissenschaft* as a concept, a survey of the reception and critique of this idea, see Hilgert

2009; Cancik-Kirschbaum 2010, 13–18, and most recent Van De Mieroop 2018. Visi 2009, esp. 12–14, questions the uncritical adoption of this idea in disciplines that deal with different sources and cultural backgrounds.

6. For a sharp critique of the traditional approach (van Soden), see Veldhuis 1997, 137–139.

7. Cancik-Kirschbaum 2010, 19–33. See also Rochberg 2016.

8. On ancient Egyptian and Mesopotamian lists and their didactic purposes, see Cancik-Kirschbaum 2010, esp. 19–21; Veldhuis 1997, 137–146; Quack 2015. See Steinert 2018, and the other contributions in the same volume on *Assyrian and Babylonian Scholarly Text Catalogues* dealing with lists that form a curriculum or field of knowledge.

9. Reed 2014, 25, in her theoretical discussion states: "attention to choices of literary form and framing, as possible clues as to the different settings of 'scientific' training and transmission; not just to consider the content of the extant records of 'ancient Jewish sciences,' but to ask what their literary context might reveal about the 'context of transmission of scholarly knowledge'—'what textual formats or genres of scientific writings are attested? And what sort of authorial strategies did ancient Jewish scholars pursue?'"

10. See Neusner 1990, 317–321; here 317: "The logical basis of coherent speech and discourse derives from *Listenwissenschaft*. The paramount mode of reasoning in the Mishnah is 'analogical contrastive reasoning'. The logic may be expressed very simply. All persons, things, or actions that fall within a different species of that same genus follow a single rule. All persons, things, or actions that fall within a different species of that same genus follow precisely the opposite rule. Reasoning by analogy and contrast dominates in the formation of the Mishnah's rules, and is, therefore, its generative mode of thought."

11. See Young 2013a. On the knowledge-producing function of lists, see Pommerening 2015 (ancient Egypt); and the other contributions in Deicher and Maroko 2015.

12. Young 2013a, b, 499: "No matter which epistemological order determines the conditions of truth and knowledge of an epoch—be it conceptualized as an episteme, 'mode of thought,' monopoly of knowledge, or otherwise—the list persists." See also Schaffrick and Werber 2017.

13. Belknap 2000, 35–36.

14. While not following her terminology, I very much agree with Mainberger 2018, 92, who argues against a medial/visual definition: "Entscheidet man sich aber statt der Rede von 'Listen' für diejenige vom 'Aufzählen' und vom 'Enumerativen', hat man eine in viele verschiedene Richtungen offene und Vorentscheidungen (auch für mediale Aspekte) vermeidende Terminologie gewählt."

15. See Wünsche 1911; Nador 1962; Towner 1973; Shasha 2006. The encyclopedic character of the Mishnah is emphasized in the title of its recent German translation (see Correns 2005).
16. Shasha 2006, 36–51 (for a definition) and 52–79 (for a form-critical description).
17. For example, ethical concepts, knowledge of nature, hermeneutical, lexical, syntactical, legal, or exegetical analogy; see Towner 1973, esp. 59–212.
18. For an introduction to rabbinic literary formats, see Samely 2007.
19. See the instruction for the specific garments of the (High) priests (Ex. 28), the inventory of items stolen by Nebuchadnezzar from Jerusalem (Ezra 1:7–11), the detailed census and genealogy of the exiled in Babylonia (Ezra 2). See Scolnic 1995. On lists in post-biblical Jewish traditions, see Tzoref 2011 (Qumran); Brady 2009 (eschatological lists in Targum), Swartz 2018, esp. 135–149 (incantations and curses).
20. See the survey in Lehmhaus 2015.
21. On the 18 benedictions of the daily *Amidah*-prayer as a list-making device, see Adelman 2009, 265–268. On the trope of Abraham's ten trials in ancient Jewish tradition, see Noegel 2003. For different usages of the list in *PRE*, see Keim 2016, 209–211.
22. See Reed 2014, 31: "In *Pirqe de Rabbi Eliezer*, moreover, ethical, ritual and 'scientific' materials are all presented in terms of a *Listenwissenschaft* that raises intriguing possibilities of some connection to pedagogical practice. Through numbered lists, the cycles and principles of Jewish piety are depicted as part of the divine order that permeates, enlivens, and supports the entire created world." See also Langermann 2002, 169–176.
23. This tradition comprises different branches of texts: the "Midrash of Three and Four," the "Seven Canopies" or "Canopy of Elijah" and the "Chapters of our Holy Master" (*Pirqe Rabbenu ha-Qaddosh*). The major part of all texts contains lists with three and four items. All traditions feature a constantly growing number of items in the lists but differ with regard to the highest number in a given text. In *Ḥuppat Eliyahu* the number of list items grows up to 24 (God's gifts to the priesthood in Israel) in the last one. The *Midrash Three and Four* even adds a list concerning the 70 names of Torah. However, the text omits some lists and has after 13 items only 18, 24, and 70. The most condensed range of those three traditions has the midrash *Pirqe Rabbenu ha-Qaddosh* proceeding only from 3 to 12 items (12 important parts of the human body).
24. While all three traditions share this overall structure, the exact sequence, comprehensiveness, and content of these texts and the various lists contained vary significantly. For a discussion of the non-eclectic but creative momentum of knowledge-making and the different topics covered by those lists (i.e., biology; the human body; diet, health and illness; biblical

events, figures and places; linguistic peculiarities; rituals and customs; dream interpretation; astrology/astronomy; cosmology; eschatology; ethics; scholarly etiquette), see Lehmhaus 2015, esp. 71–83.

25. See Lehmhaus 2018 on interaction between post-Talmudic Jewish traditions (midrash etc.) and new models of writing, thought, education, and cultural behavior in early Islamic times.

26. See Nutton 2013, 43–44, 72, 152 and 174–182 (Dioscorides, Scrribonius, Pliny, the Elder).

27. On lists and recipes as a key genre in ancient Mesopotamian traditions, see Geller 2010, 89–117 (and the literature mentioned there); Goody 1977, esp. 129–145. See Telle 2003, for discussions of recipes as a (literary) genre. On rabbinic recipes, see Amit 2017; Lehmhaus 2017; and the other chapters in Lehmhaus and Martelli 2017. On efficacy labels, see Lehmhaus 2019, esp. 150–152; Steinert 2015.

28. The exact meanings of the Hebrew terms for plants or fruits used in this list are far from obvious. The standard translations refer to either "melilot ('sweet clove'?), date berries, and unripe dates" or "cherries, bad dates, and unripe dates." See the lists in b. Eiruvin 28a and b. Gittin 70a, Avot de-Rabbi Nathan (ARNa) 41, 66b. Löw 1881, 94–96 questions the medieval and early modern understanding of *gdgdnywt* as "cherries." Based on Syriac evidence he proposes the reading *grgrnywt*. Also y. Peah 8,5 (21a) and y. Eruvin (20a) mention *gdgdnywt*. Rabbinic texts (e.g., t.Shevi'it 3:21, t. Ma'asser Sheni 1:14, y. Orla 1,7, 61b) mention *kpnywt*, which the Academy of the Hebrew Language connects to Aramaic and Arabic *kwpr^ʾ* ("inflorescence of palms"). On *pgy tmrh* for "unripe dates," see Löw 1881, 390–391, and Sokoloff 1992, 424.

29. For my translations of this and other Talmudic texts, the manuscript versions and printed editions in the Sol and Evelyn Henkind Talmud Text Databank of the Saul Lieberman Institute of Talmudic Research (http://www.lieberman-institute.com) were consulted. The same list figures in Kallah Rabbati 8:1, and in the above-mentioned *Ma'asse Torah* tradition (see Eisenstein 1915, *Pirka Rabbeinu Ha-Kaddosh* ch. 1, list 58).

30. Such questions figure in the genre of riddle-tales (e.g., the *Story of Ahikar*, Samson's biblical riddle in Judges 14:14; *Midrash Mishle* (Proverbs), or the questions posed to the protagonist by King Nebuchadnezzar in the early medieval *Tales of Ben Sira*) but are also deployed in several rabbinic traditions such as the contest between rabbis or the elders and Alexander the Great or the wise men of Athens. See Yassif 1982; Lassner 1993, esp. 9–24, Hasan-Rokem 2000, esp. 39–66.

31. See Donahue 2016a & 2016b.

32. See Lehmhaus 2017.

33. See Avot de-Rabbi Nathan B, chapter 30; Leviticus Rabbah 34,3 (toilet); m.Berakhot 2:6 and y.Berakhot 2:7 (5b); t.Shabbat 12:13 amd y.Shabbat 14:3 (14c); b.Shabbat 41a (discussion of the practice and benefits of bathing); see y.Shev 8:2 (38a); y.Ma'asser Sheni 2:1 (53b); y.Shabbat 8:1 (11b); y.Shabbat 14:3–4 (14b-d); b.Berakhot 43a-b; b.Yoma 77b (anointing against different ailments).

34. See Satlow 1995. On the distinct nature of Jewish discourse on sexuality in comparison to Greco-Roman and early Christian traditions, see Boyarin 1993. On the Persian-Iranian contexts, see Kiel 2016.

35. The anonymous compilers, however, questioned the understanding of "usage" (*tashmish*) as referring to sex because of the supposedly weakening of the body through intercourse. Rather, they recommend the meaning of "usage" as referring to the body's orifices and the act of excretion. This interpretation would comply with the crucial importance of functioning digestion and purgative measures within Greco-Roman health regimens.

36. See parallels in Leviticus Rabba 16,1; Kalla Rabbati 1. See b.Pesahim 112b. and b.Gittin 70 for other sexual practices that cause epilepsy in adults and children.

37. Sex omens in ancient Mesopotamian traditions that also link the specific circumstances of the intercourse to different effects—such as various diseases, bodily, the sex of the conceived child, the prognosis for a healthy pregnancy—might compare to those Talmudic lists. See Guinan 1997 and Geller 2004, esp. 34–35.

38. For a careful and learned analysis of the coital discourse of the rabbis in their ancient contexts, see Bickart 2016.

39. Such lists include: for example, priestly blemishes in m.Bekhorot 7; those exempted from the pilgrimage festivals because of disabilities, sickness, age, gender, and so on (m. Ḥagigah 1:1). See Abrams 1998, 16–70; Wyszynski 2001.

40. See Belser/Lehmhaus 2016, esp. 436–442.

41. See Bien 1997: 79–84 (during conception) and 130–42 (during pregnancy). A Talmudic tradition in y.Ḥagigah 2:1 (77b-c) explains the later apostasy of a famous scholar via the smell of sacrificial wine and meat from gentile temples that drew his mother's attention during pregnancy.

42. See Mulder 2015.

43. See Lehmhaus 2019, 133–134, and the literature mentioned.

44. On lists in *SEZ* 1 as devices to define and convey the integrated concept of justice, righteousness and charity, see Lehmhaus 2015, 66–71.

45. This question might refer either to the system of judgment according to one's ways (the core topic of *SEZ* 3) or to the problem how one is supposed to change one's ways.

46. I argue that, since *SEZ* focuses on return and repentance, by doing so the angel mirrors the person's deeds and eventually makes them change their ways.
47. *SEZ*, ch. 3. The translation is my own, based on the edition by Friedman 1902, 176. See translation by Braude/Kapstein 1981, 375.
48. Such techniques of self-awareness and mindfulness are also applied in SEZ, ch. 13 (see ARNa 20,70) to emphasize the triad of study, righteousness, and charity as well as the crucial importance of Torah and human dependence on God. On these techniques, see Schofer 2005, 106–115 and 147–160.
49. See similar lists with ethical advice in Hebrew traditions such as Avot 3,1; *Derekh Eretz Rabbah* 3,1; *Derekh Eretz Zuta* 4,9; ARNa 19,69; y.Sota 2:2 (18a); Leviticus Rabbah 18:1; Kalla Rabbati 6: "Meditate upon three things and you will not descend into transgression: Know from where you are, where you are going, and before whom you will give account. From where do you come? From a putrid drop. Where will you go? To a place of dust, worm, and maggot. And before whom will you give account? Before the King of king, the Holy One, blessed be He." On such techniques, see Foucault 1988.
50. *SEZ*, ch. 3, 375 (Braude/Kapstein translation) and 176 (edition Friedman). Divine "surveillance" is stressed in Avot 2:1; ARNb 32,70.
51. In *SEZ*, ch. 3 follows another cluster of lists introduced by a numerical caption ("Generally a man marries for one of four reasons"), which is then specified (lust, wealth, fame, sake of heaven) and adumbrated with short narratives and biblical proof texts. On other lists in *SEZ*, see ns. 46 and 47.
52. For ethical traditions, see Schofer 2007. See Sperber 1990; Bernard 2008 (*Avot*) for lists within rabbinic manuals of ethical conduct. Those lists focus on modest or pious behavior of the learned sage but also specify the hardships to expect by choosing a "life of Torah study." Other lists contain social observations about different types of behavior, hatred, social classes, and so on. Cf. Charles 2000 on similar taxonomies (wirtues and vices) in other traditions.
53. Young 2013a, 501–502 and 505.
54. See Vismann 2008, 71–101.
55. On the orality/literacy of lists, see Young 2013a, 499–501. On their mnemonic function, see Mainberger 2003, esp. 64–75. On rabbinic orality and mnemonics, see Jaffee 1995; Hallo 2003.
56. Among others, one may mention here Samely 2007, esp. 25–77.
57. Young 2017, 26 (on Goody). See Young 2013b, and von Contzen 2016, 257: "Lists, because they encapsulate the tensions and fascinations of narration and dis-narration, are a perfect way of throwing new light on the complex interplay of the creation of meaning in and through narratives, of

involving the readers in the processes of sense-making, and, ultimately, of the inextricable connection between form and function that lies at the heart of all literature."
58. On the last point in Mesopotamian contexts, see below n. 12.
59. For the use of lists to create disease taxonomies or therapeutic catalogues, see Lehmhaus 2015, 83–93, and Lehmhaus, Rabbinic Lists as "Epistemic Genre," see n. 4.
60. See Towner 1973, 4, who sees lists "as devices for systematizing observations about nature, geography and man, and as pedagogical and mnemonic tools for conveying this information to students and posterity."
61. On lists as scaffold of the *Ma'asseh Torah* and its sibling traditions, see Lehmhaus 2015, 71–83.

References

Abrams, Judith Z. 1998. *Judaism and Disability: Portrayals in Ancient Texts from the Tanach Through the Bavli*. Washington, DC: Gallaudet University Press.

Adelman, Rachel. 2009. *The Return Return of the Repressed: Pirqe de-Rabbi Eliezer and the Pseudepigrapha*. Brill: Leiden.

Belknap, Robert. 2000. The Literary List: A Survey of Its Uses and Deployments. *Literary Imagination* 2 (1): 35–54.

Belser, Julia W., and Lennart Lehmhaus. 2016. Disability in Rabbinic Judaism. In *Disability in Antiquity*, ed. Christian Laes, 434–452. London/New York: Routledge.

Bernard, Daniel. 2008. *Listing and Enlisting: The Rhetoric and Social Meaning of Tractate Avot*. PhD dissertation, Concordia University, Montreal.

Bickart, Noah B. 2016. Overturning the 'Table': The Hidden Meaning of a Talmudic Metaphor for Coitus. *Journal of the History of Sexuality* 25 (3): 489–507.

Bien, Christian G. 1997. *Erklärungen zur Entstehung von Mißbildungen im physiologischen und medizinischen Schrifttum der Antike*. Stuttgart: Franz Steiner.

Boyarin, Daniel. 1993. *Carnal Israel: Reading Sex in Talmudic Culture*. Berkeley: University of California Press.

Brady, Christian M. 2009. The Use of Eschatological Lists Within the Targumim of the Megilloth. *Journal for the Study of Judaism* 40: 493–509.

Braude, William G., and Israel J. Kapstein, trans. 1981. *Tanna Debe Eliyyahu: The Lore of the School of Elijah*. Philadelphia: Jewish Publication Society.

Cancik-Kirschbaum, Eva. 2010. Gegenstand und Methode: Sprachliche Erkenntnistechniken in der keilschriftlichen Überlieferung Mesopotamiens. In *Writings of Early Scholars in the Ancient Near East, Egypt, Rome, and Greece: Translating Ancient Scientific Texts*, ed. Annette Imhausen and Tanja Pommerening, 13–45. Berlin: De Gruyter.

———. 2012. Writing, Language and Textuality: Conditions on the Transmission of Knowledge and the Emergence of Systematic Thought in the Ancient Near East. In *Globalization of Knowledge and Its Consequences*, ed. Jürgen Renn, 125–151. Berlin: Edition Open Access.

Charles, J. Daryl. 2000. Vice and Virtue Lists. In *Dictionary of New Testament Background: A Compendium of Contemporary Biblical Scholarship*, ed. Stanley E. Porter and Craig A. Evans, 1252–1257. Downers Grove: Inter-Varsity Press.

Correns, Dietrich. 2005. *Die Mischna: Das grundlegende enzyklopädische Regelwerk rabbinischer Tradition*. Wiesbaden: Marix.

Deicher, Susanne, and Erik Maroko, eds. 2015. *Die Liste: Ordnungen von Dingen und Menschen in Ägypten*. Berlin: Kadmos.

Doležalová, Lucie. 2009a. Introduction: The Potential and Limitations of Studying Lists. In *The Charm of a List: From the Sumerians to Computerised Data Processing*, ed. Lucie Doležalová, 1–8. Newcastle upon Tyne: Cambridge Scholars.

———. 2009b. Ad Hoc Lists of Bernard Itier (1163–1225), Librarian of St. Martial de Limoges. In *The Charm of a List: From the Sumerians to Computerised Data Processing*, ed. Lucie Doležalová, 80–99. Newcastle upon Tyne: Cambridge Scholars.

Donahue, John F. 2016a. Culinary and Medicinal Uses of Wine and Olive Oil. In *A Companion to Science, Technology, and Medicine in Ancient Greece and Rome*, ed. Georgia L. Irby, 605–617. Chichester: Wiley Blackwell.

———. 2016b. Nutrition. In *A Companion to Science, Technology, and Medicine in Ancient Greece and Rome*, ed. Georgia L. Irby, 618–632. Chichester: Wiley Blackwell.

Eisenstein, Judah D., ed. 1915. *Otzar Midrashim: A Library of Two Hundred Minor Midrashim*. New York: Grossman.

Foucault, Michel. 1988. Technologies of the Self. In *Technologies of the Self*, ed. Luther H. Martin, Huck Gutman, and Patrick H. Hutton, 16–49. Amherst, MA: University of Massachusetts Press.

Friedman (Ish-Shalom), Meir. 1902. *Seder Eliahu rabba und Seder Eliahu zuta (Tanna d'be Eliahu)*. Vienna: Israelitisch-Theologische Lehranstalt.

Geller, Markham J. 2004. *Akkadian Healing Therapies in the Babylonian Talmud*. Berlin: Max Planck Institute for the History of Science.

———. 2010. *Ancient Babylonian Medicine Theory and Practice*. Chichester: Wiley-Blackwell.

Goody, Jack. 1977. What's in a List? In *The Domestication of a Savage Mind*, ed. John R. Goody, 74–111. Cambridge: Cambridge University Press.

Guinan, Ann K. 1997. Auguries of Hegemony: The Sex Omens of Mesopotamia. *Gender and History* 9 (3): 462–479.

Hasan-Rokem, Galit. 2000. *Web of Life: Folklore and Midrash in Rabbinic Literature*. Stanford: Stanford University Press.

Hilgert, Markus. 2009. Von ‚Listenwissenschaft' und ‚epistemischen Dingen': Konzeptuelle Annäherungen an altorientalische Wissenspraktiken. *Zeitschrift für allgemeine Wissenschaftstheorie* 40 (2): 277–309.

Jaffee, Martin S. 1995. Writing and Rabbinic Oral Tradition: On Mishnaic Narrative, Lists and Mnemonics. *Journal of Jewish Thought and Philosophy* 4 (1): 123–146.

Keim, Katharina. 2016. *Pirqei deRabbi Eliezer: Structure, Coherence, Intertextuality.* Leiden: Brill.

Kiel, Yishai. 2016. *Sexuality in the Babylonian Talmud, Christian and Sasanian Contexts in Late Antiquity.* New York: Cambridge University Press.

Langermann, Tzvi. 2002. On the Beginnings of Hebrew Scientific Literature and on Studying History Through 'Maqbilot' (Parallels). *Aleph* 2: 169–190.

Lassner, Jacob. 1993. *Demonizing the Queen of Sheba: Boundaries of Gender and Culture in Postbiblical Judaism and Medieval Islam.* Chicago: Chicago University Press.

Lehmhaus, Lennart. 2015. *Listenwissenschaft* and the Encyclopedic Hermeneutics of Knowledge in Talmud and Midrash. In *In the Wake of the Compendia: Infrastructural Contexts and the Licensing of Empiricism in Ancient and Medieval Mesopotamia*, ed. J. Cale Johnson, 59–101. Berlin/Boston: de Gruyter.

———. 2017. Beyond Dreckapotheke, Between Facts and Feces: Talmudic Recipes and Therapies in Context. In *Collecting Recipes: Byzantine and Jewish Pharmacology in Dialogue*, ed. Lennart Lehmhaus and Matteo Martelli, 221–254. Berlin/Boston: de Gruyter.

———. 2018. Hidden Transcripts in Late Midrash Made Visible: Hermeneutical and Literary Processes of Borrowing in a Multi-Cultural Context. In *Exegetical Crossroads–Understanding Scripture in Judaism, Christianity and Islam in the Premodern Orient*, ed. Regina Grundmann et al., 199–242. Berlin/Boston: de Gruyter.

———. 2019. Bodies of Texts, Bodies of Tradition: Medical Expertise and Knowledge of the Body Among Rabbinic Jews in Late Antiquity. In *Finding, Inheriting or Borrowing? Construction and Transfer of Knowledge About Man and Nature in Antiquity and the Middle Ages*, ed. Jochen Althoff, Dominik Berrens, and Tanja Pommerening, 123–166. Bielefeld: transcript.

———. Forthcoming 2021. Rabbinic Lists as "Epistemic Genre": Exegesis, Ethics and Science. In *Lists and Synopses*, ed. Ronny Vollandt and Teresa Bernheimer.

Lehmhaus, Lennart, and Matteo Martelli, eds. 2017. *Collecting Recipes: Byzantine and Jewish Pharmacology in Dialogue.* Berlin/Boston: de Gruyter.

Loew, Immanuel. 1881. *Aramaeische Pflanzennamen.* Leipzig: Wilhelm Engelmann.

Mainberger, Sabine. 2003. *Die Kunst des Aufzählens: Elemente zu einer Poetik des Enumerativen.* Berlin: de Gruyter.

———. 2018. Ordnen/Aufzählen. In *Literatur und materielle Kultur*, ed. Susanne Scholz and Ulrike Vedder, 91–98. Berlin/Boston: de Gruyter.

Mulder, Tara. 2015. Ancient Medicine and Fetal Personhood. *Eidolon*, October 16. https://eidolon.pub/ancient-medicine-and-thestraw-man-of-fetal-personhood-73eed36b945a/. Accessed 20 Jan 2021.

Nador, G. 1962. Some Numerical Categories in Ancient Rabbinic Literature: The Numbers Ten, Seven and Four. *Acta Orientalia* 14: 301–315.

Neusner, Jacob. 1990. The Mishna's Generative Mode of Thought: *Listenwissenschaft* and Analogical-Contrastive Reasoning. *Journal of the American Oriental Society* 110 (2): 317–321.

Noegel, Scott B. 2003. Abraham's Ten Trials and Biblical Literary Convention. *Jewish Bible Quarterly* 21: 73–83.

Nutton, Vivian. 2013. *Ancient Medicine*. 2nd ed. Abingdon: Routledge.

Pomata, Gianna. 2014. The Medical Case Narrative: Distant Reading of an Epistemic Genre. *Literature and Medicine* 32 (1): 1–23.

Pommerening, Tanja. 2015. Bäume, Sträucher und Früchte in altägyptischen Listen – eine Betrachtung zur Kategorisierung und Ordnung. In *Die Liste: Ordnungen von Dingen und Menschen in Ägypten*, ed. Susanne Deicher and Erik Maroko, 125–166. Berlin: Kadmos.

Quack, Joachim Friedrich. 2015. Ägyptische Listen und ihre Expansion in Unterricht und Repräsentation. In *Die Liste: Ordnungen von Dingen und Menschen in Ägypten*, ed. Susanne Deicher and Erik Maroko, 51–86. Berlin: Kadmos.

Reed, Annette Y. 2014. Ancient Jewish Sciences and the Historiography of Judaism. In *Ancient Jewish Sciences and the History of Knowledge in the Second Temple Period*, ed. Jonathan Ben-Dov and Seth L. Sanders, 195–254. New York: New York University Press.

Rochberg, Francesca. 2016. *Before Nature: Cuneiform Knowledge and the History of Science*. Chicago: University of Chicago Press.

Samely, Alexander. 2007. *Forms of Rabbinic Literature and Thought: An Introduction*. Oxford: Oxford University Press.

Satlow, Michael. 1995. *Tasting the Dish: Rabbinic Rhetorics of Sexuality*. Providence, RI: Brown Judaic Studies.

Schaffrick, Matthias, and Niels Werber. 2017. Einleitung: Die Liste, paradigmatisch. *Zeitschrift für Literaturwissenschaft und Linguistik* 47 (3): 303–316.

Schofer, Jonathan W. 2005. *The Making of a Sage: A Study in Rabbinic Ethics*. Madison: University of Wisconsin Press.

———. 2007. Ethical Formation and Rabbinic Ethical Compilations. In *The Cambridge Companion to the Talmud and Rabbinic Literature*, ed. Charlotte E. Fonrobert and Martin S. Jaffee, 313–335. Cambridge: Cambridge University Press.

Scolnic, Benjamin. 1995. *Theme and Context in Biblical Lists*. Atlanta: University Press of America.

Shasha, Roy. 2006. *The Forms and Functions of Lists in the Mishnah*. PhD dissertation, University of Manchester. Retrievable at: http://www.melilahjournal. org/p/2007.html. Accessed 23 Oct 2020.

Sokoloff, Michael. 1992. *A Dictionary of Jewish Palestinian Aramaic of the Byzantine Period*. Ramat Gan: Bar Ilan University Press.

Sperber, Daniel. 1990. Manuals of Rabbinic Conduct During the Talmudic and Rabbinic Periods. In *Scholars and Scholarship: The Interaction between Judaism and Other Cultures*, ed. Leo Landmann, 9–26. New York: Yeshiva University Press.

Steinert, Ulrike. 2015. "Tested" Remedies in Mesopotamian Medical Texts: A Label for Efficacy Based on Empirical Observation? In *In the Wake of the Compendia: Infrastructural Contexts and the Licensing of Empiricism in Ancient and Medieval Mesopotamia*, ed. J. Cale Johnson, 103–145. Berlin/Boston: de Gruyter.

———. 2018. Catalogues, Texts and Specialists: Some Thoughts on the Assur Medical Catalogue, Mesopotamian Medical Texts and Healing Professions. In *Assyrian and Babylonian Scholarly Text Catalogues: Medicine, Magic and Divination*, ed. Ulrike Steinert, 158–200. Berlin: De Gruyter.

Swartz, Michael D. 2018. *The Mechanics of Providence: The Workings of Ancient Jewish Magic and Mysticism*. Tübingen: Mohr Siebeck.

Telle, Joachim. 2003. Das Rezept als literarische Form: Zum multifunktionalen Gebrauch des Rezepts in der Deutschen Literatur. *Berichte zur Wissenschaftsgeschichte* 26: 251–274.

Towner, Wayne S. 1973. *The Rabbinic "Enumeration of Scriptural Examples" – A Study of a Rabbinic Pattern of Discourse with Special Reference to Mekhilta D'R. Ishmael*. Brill: Leiden.

Tzoref, Shani. 2011. 4Q252: *Listenwissenschaft* and Covenantal Patriarchal Blessings. In *'Go Out and Study the Land' (Judges 18:2): Archaeological, Historical and Textual Studies in Honor of Hanan Eshel*, ed. Aren M. Maeir et al., 335–357. Leiden: Brill.

Van De Mieroop, Marc. 2018. Theses on Babylonian Philosophy. *Journal of Ancient Near Eastern History* 5: 15–39.

Veldhuis, Nick. 1997. *Elementary Education at Nipur: The Lists of Trees and Wooden Objects*. PhD dissertation, University of Groningen. Retrievable at: https://www.rug.nl/research/portal/files/14460166/thesis/pdf. Accessed 23 Oct 2020.

Visi, Tamas. 2009. A Science of Lists? Medieval Jewish Philosophers as List-Makers. In *The Charm of a List*, ed. Lucie Doležalová, 12–33. Newcastle upon Tyne: Cambridge Scholars.

Vismann, Cornelia. 2008. *Files: Law and Media-Technology*. Trans. Geoffrey Winthrop-Young. Stanford: Stanford University Press.

von Contzen, Eva. 2016. The Limits of Narration: Lists and Literary History. *Style* 50 (3): 241–260.

———. 2017. Die Affordanzen der Liste. *Zeitschrift für Literaturwissenschaft und Linguistik* 47 (3): 317–326.

von Soden, Werner. 1936. Leistung und Grenze sumerischer und babylonischer Wissenschaft. *Die Welt als Geschichte: Zeitschrift für universalgeschichtliche Forschung* 2: 411–464; 509–557.

Wünsche, August. 1911. Die Zahlensprüche im Talmud und Midrasch. *Zeitschrift der Deutschen Morgenländischen Gesellschaft* 65: 57–100.

Wyszynski, Diego F. 2001. Dysmorphology in the Bible and the Talmud. *Teratology* 64: 221–225.

Yassif, Eli. 1982. Pseudo Ben Sira and the 'Wisdom Questions' Traditions in the Middle Ages. *Fabula* 23 (1): 48–63.

Young, Liam. 2013a. Un-Black Boxing the List: Knowledge, Materiality, and Form. *Canadian Journal of Communication* 38: 497–516.

———. 2013b. On Lists and Networks: An Archaeology of Form. *Amodern 2.* https://amodern.net/article7on-lists-and-networks/. Accessed 18 Dec 2019.

———. 2017. *List Cultures: Knowledge and Poetics from Mesopotamia to BuzzFeed.* Amsterdam: Amsterdam University Press.

CHAPTER 4

Moral Curiosity Cabinets: Listing and the Character Sketch in Addison and Steele's Periodicals

Theresa Schön

An essentially collaborative project undertaken by Joseph Addison and Richard Steele, the *Tatler* (1709–1711) and the subsequent *Spectator* (1711–1712/1714), capture the authors' efforts to establish and communicate a set of moral norms as the basis of what they designed to be a fundamentally polite society. Observing a careful balance of entertainment and instruction, Addison and Steele implemented their wide-ranging moralistic program with the help of their personae Isaac Bickerstaff, Esq. (*Tatler*) and Mr. Spectator (*Spectator*), whom they sent out to observe and describe the manners and morals of fictionalized contemporary London society.

In addition to the very explicit moralizing of their personae, Addison and Steele's method of choice was the Theophrastan character sketch, a genre of high popularity in seventeenth-century England. Easily lending

T. Schön (✉)
Interdisciplinary Centre for European Enlightenment Studies (IZEA) of Martin Luther University Halle-Wittenberg, Halle, Germany

81

R. A. Barton et al. (eds.), *Forms of List-Making: Epistemic, Literary, and Visual Enumeration*,
https://doi.org/10.1007/978-3-030-76970-3_4

itself to satire, a character sketch represents an ethical, social, moral type of man or woman, commending (or exposing) behavioral norms to the reader and, thus, providing orientation in an increasingly complex world (Hockenjos 2006, 35–85). Traditionally plotless, the usually fairly short verse or prose sketches simply enumerate—vertically or horizontally—typical examples of the type's (linguistic) behavior, outward appearance, and sometimes short anecdotes (Smeed 1985, 276–284). Each sentence underlines the type's nature, often anaphorically adding ("He … He …") yet another detail to the picture as it develops over course of the sketch, thus creating coherence among seemingly disparate instances. Usually published in so-called *character books*, the collections present the sketches in no apparent order; they are a more or less random list of characters without a narrative frame.[1]

Addison and Steele's character sketches differ broadly from traditional Theophrastan examples. Expanding the anecdotal element found in earlier material and embracing the first-person perspective as well as the circumstantial style of their French predecessor Jean de la Bruyère,[2] they used a fundamentally empirical approach and chose to represent their moral types *in interaction*. Shown in concrete (fictionalized) situations, in public and private, in fictionalized contemporary London, individualized and endowed with personal (and usually telling) names, the types meet and converse with the personae as well as the numerous other types of men and women populating the periodicals. Yet, while the majority of their sketches are characterized by a strong narrative element, the periodicals also experiment with the genre's essential affinity to enumeration and feature a small group of texts in the form of lists.[3] In contrast to Theophrastan character sketches, however, in which each item or sentence in the text more or less straightforwardly confirms the nature of the type, the epistemological process in Addison and Steele's examples is more complex. They combine the character sketch with contemporary non-literary forms of notation (last will and testament, inventory, genealogy, library catalog).[4] In order to understand the texts (adequately), the readers need to be familiar with the methodological specificities and the socio-cultural implications of these forms. Although the texts ultimately serve a moralistic purpose in exposing moral excess, the forms Addison and Steele adapted in these cases carry different affordances that inform the readers' response and affect the epistemological dimension of these texts: the form of the text defamiliarizes the (more or less well-known) content (i.e., the moral types), which readers may have known from their reading or the theater. The list decelerates the reading process, heightens the readers' attention, and encourages them to pause; in turn, this pause prompts readers to reflect on the knowledge the list communicates as well as on the manner in which this moral knowledge relates to their experience of the world.

In the following pages, I will examine two such lists from the *Tatler* and the *Spectator* in detail: the will and testament of the Virtuoso Nicholas Gimcrack (*Tatler* no. 216) and the library catalog of the Romance Heroine Leonora (*Spectator* no. 37)—two forms intimately related to the practice of collecting. Briefly considering the traditions the texts relate to, I shall trace the mechanisms of the epistemological process for each text individually before considering them comparatively in their position in the periodicals' collection more generally. The capacity of these texts as character sketches and their place in the periodical project endow them with an additional quasi-scientifick,[5] quasi-sociological function: The texts list naturalist and bibliophile curiosities; at the same time, these lists (and the moral types captured by these lists) emerge as collectibles themselves, as curiosities gathered by Bickerstaff and Mr. Spectator to become part their moral curiosity cabinets.

The Will of a Virtuoso (*Tatler* No. 216)

Testaments represent the testators' attempt of reaching out from beyond their death to the living. They endow a voice to one who is no longer able to speak. Hence, the testament, as Ulrike Vedder has explained, is a medium of return from death to life, of transition from life to death, and of transfer of the testator's legacy to the heirs (2011, 23). In this function, the testaments (and testators) continue to interfere with their family's affairs and society more generally. In particular, the legacies may determine the heirs' future lives, being a symptom or even a cause of social, legal, and cultural conflict (Vedder 2011, 24). A functional text used by social representatives from the husbandman to the king, the testament is, as Ulrich Bach explains, characterized by a dual purpose relating to a person's earthly, material existence on the one hand—that is, the legal document regulating the bequeathal of property from the dying testator to the heirs—and to the testator's religious fate on the other—that is, the relationship to God and the salvation of the soul (Bach 1977, 39/41). This dual purpose entails a tension between the plain (and formulaic) language and ordinary content of the document, laying out the details regarding the testator's property, and its "high" purpose, its function as religious instrument and legal record (Bach 1977, 41). Endowed with an important epistemic dimension, the testament reflects on the testator as well as the relationship between testator and heirs. The epistemic quality relies on the symbolic force of the individual legacies, which assume the role of *tertium comparationis*. In its capacity as an object deemed important enough to explicitly figure as a legacy, the object sheds light on the character (and the identity) of the testator and—depending on the (un-)suitability of the match (legacy/heir)—on the character of the heir.

The example in *The Tatler* is clearly indebted to the tradition of the mock testament, which goes back to antiquity, and its comic-satiric parodies often taking the form of beast testaments, and attests to the appeal of mocking sublime forms. According to Bach (1977, 77–80), mock testaments build on the testament's function of revealing the speaker's nature, thus enabling the satirical denunciation of the speaker/author and/or the heirs. Relying on the moral weight of last words, they use the legacies' closed range of items to criticize particular social or political groups, moral flaws, and particular circumstances. Their critical impetus reveals the affinity of the testator to the fool: like the fool, the testator has the freedom of mocking others without punishment, as the testament is only opened after death (Vedder 2011, 50). A particularity of mock testaments is linked to the conventional and fairly rigid form of last wills—a three-part structure with opening formulae, legacies, and closing formulae (Vedder 2011, 50); so, the form quintessentially participates in creating meaning beyond the particular content of the testament (Bach 1977, 48). As the document represents the authority of the church, the respective jurisdiction, and so forth, the approach of the satirist at least partly touches the authorities themselves by playing with the conventional form.

The *Tatler*'s issue no. 216 reprints the will of Nicholas Gimcrack, the eponymous Virtuoso of Thomas Shadwell's Restoration comedy (1676).[6] The issue primes the reader for the will adequately by providing an inset generic character sketch of the type of the Virtuoso, that underlines the type's nonsensical obsession with trivialities, with "mean and disproportioned Objects," with "the Refuse of Nature" (Bond 1987, vol. 3, 132–133), and thus emphasizes the ideal of temperance and modesty.[7] The introductory passage explicitly refers to the type's inclination to *collecting*, "hoarding up in their Chests and Cabinets such Creatures as others industriously avoid the Sight of" (Bond 1987, 133). Tracing back to the Renaissance, collecting as an end in itself, driven by a particular propensity and performed with some manner of expertise, often at the cost of social duties, as it is suggested here, mirrors the collector's fear of the contingency of the world, a pleasure comparable to that of the hunter as well as a disposition toward order and ostentation (Stagl 1998, 41–45).[8] The collector compiles a collection, a form of materialized memory, a structured entity of previously unconnected parts which are then related in a meaningful way and, thus, represent that section of the world from which they have been taken (Stagl 1998, 41). As a means to capture such a collection in writing, the list graphically mirrors this process, allows the collectors to communicate with their peers even in their absence, and provides the grounds for the (listed) collection to be removed from its original setting (the collector's cabinet) to new and different contexts such as a satirical paper, thus enabling discursive mobility.

The testament's form follows the traditional structure (see Bach 1977, 36–37) and is immediately recognizable by its formulaic beginning (and conclusion): "I Nicholas Gimcrack being *in sound Health of Mind, but in great Weakness of Body*, do by this my last Will and Testament *bestow my Worldly Goods and Chattels* in Manners following: [...]" (Bond 1987, vol. 3, 133, emphasis added). The text's standard reference to the testator's "sound Health of Mind" satirically exposes Gimcrack. Though no clear indication of madness, the testator's beliefs and behavior as suggested by the following list strongly contrast with the concept of a "sound mind" and appear to lie beyond the confines of reason. Gimcrack's reference to his "Worldly Goods and Chattels" anticipates a significant void in his will: Gimcrack devotes his text exclusively to the management of his worldly, ephemeral affairs and ignores the other core ideas traditionally found in testaments, namely, soul, body, and sins (Bach 1977, 82).[9] Gimcrack's disregard for the fate of his soul suggests that he has lost sight of, or is indifferent to, the concept and meaning of salvation and eternal happiness.

In characteristic parallel sequencing (Bach 1977, 37), the following list allots individual items to the heirs.

> *Imprimis*, To my dear Wife,
>> One Box of Butterflies,
>> One Drawer of Shells,
>> A Female Skeleton,
>> A dried Cockatrice.
> *Item*, To my Daughter *Elizabeth*,
>> My Receipt for preserving dead Caterpillars:

As also my Preparations of Winter *May*-Dew, and Embrio Pickle.
Item, To my little Daughter *Fanny*,
Three Crocodile's Eggs.
And upon the Birth of her First Child, if she marries with her Mother's Consent,
The Nest of an Humming Bird.
(Bond 1987, vol. 3, 133–134, emphasis in original)

The text takes up the standard combination of legacy and heir. Appearing in a very condensed form, Gimcrack's will refrains from more elaborate and possibly affectionate explanations and largely presents a vertical enumeration of items (per heir).[10] The text only breaks with this pattern toward the conclusion of the testament, where Gimcrack sets down the legacies to his son Charles. Whereas the previous entries singled out individual items, this passage contains the remainder of his possessions, merely presented as unspecified (and, by implication, unordered) accumulation, that is, "all my Flowers, Plants, Minerals, Mosses, Shells, Pebbles, Fossils, Beetles, Butterflies, Caterpillars, Grashoppers, and Vermin, not above specified: As also all my Monsters, both wet and dry" (Bond 1987, vol. 3, 135). While, of course, allowing the periodical's editors to adhere to the spatial limitations of the folio half-sheet, the text thus presents the individual items in "the Apartment of a Virtuoso," in his "Chests and Cabinets" (Bond 1987, 132–133) in a visually easily accessible format. The nature of the items is, indeed, telling in several ways. Gimcrack exclusively passes on items related to the natural sciences, collectibles associated with contemporary curiosity cabinets, that apparently constitute his estate. The items on the list are of a domestic—for example, butterflies, grasshoppers, mosses, pebbles—and foreign origin—for example, the "Crocodile's Eggs" and the "Nest of an Humming Bird" cited above, or "The Mummy of an *Egyptian* King" and the "Horned *Scarabaeus*" (Bond 1987, 134), pointing to the extensive travels natural historians undertook, to the scientifick excursions to parts of the earth as yet unknown, and to the exploration of the minute and invisible. Some legacies suggest methodological knowledge developed by and necessary to contemporary naturalists (e.g., Gimcrack's "Receipt for preserving dead Caterpillars," Bond 1987, 134). Most of the items represent rarities of an exotic, if not monstrous nature and are, hence, of a high scientifick (and possibly also monetary) value. In some instances, the scientifick value clashes with contemporary notions of propriety, an aspect that the form of the testament emphasizes by linking individual testators with certain items: Considering, for instance, that corpses (e.g., for scientifick purposes such as anatomical dissections) could not be acquired legally and usually belonged to criminals, Gimcrack's legacy of a "Female Skeleton" to his wife clearly distances him from the periodical's moral standards. Indeed, the list builds toward a climax, moving from the "Female Skeleton" via "[m]y Rat's Testicles and Whale's Pizzle," Gimcrack's legacy to his fellow Virtuoso "Dr. Johannes Elscrickius" (Bond 1987, 134), to Gimcrack's deceased daughter "whom I keep by me in Spirits of Wine" and who represents but one example of his "Monsters, both wet and dry" that he gives to his second son Charles. As evidence of the owner's choices and values, the nature of the objects is clearly designed to suggest Gimcrack's monstrous morals.

This reading is confirmed and consolidated by the symbolic dimension of the items in Gimcrack's testament. For instance, the first three items that he bequeaths to his wife (see block quotation above) have a broadly positive connotation, entailing ideas of metamorphosis (butterflies), of Christ (shells), and memento mori (skeleton), the first two of which highlight the collector's habit of ordering ("Box," "Drawer"). The fourth legacy, the "Dried Cockatrice," however, is associated with superstition (cockatrice as basilisk, see *OED*) as well as pride, envy, and slander (see Butzer and Jacob 2012, 230–231). The emblematic meaning of the items largely relies on the literary-cultural tradition and, particularly, on specific knowledge of the Bible.[11] The text suggests that Gimcrack is unaware of his legacies' symbolic dimension, an aspect which is betrayed by the list and its arrangement as well as by the context of its publication: While the individual item in the collection assumes its meaning as collectible by being part of the collection, a meaning which is relevant, primarily, to other collectors, the testament, and particularly its publication in a satirical periodical, relocates the item to a different context (law, religion, society), in which the item's socio-religious connotation moves center stage. This mechanism further gains momentum by the text's coupling of the items with the respective heirs. The list thus reveals his unawareness or, even worse, his ignorance that surely results, the text implies, from his exclusive focus on "the Refuse of Nature" (Bond 1987, vol. 3, 134). At the same time, the items' symbolic meaning—in true mock testament fashion— reflects on the heirs, who are publicly exposed through Gimcrack's cultural illiteracy.

As the most important worldly purpose of a gentleman's testament is to provide economically for his surviving relatives, Gimcrack's heritage appears to confirm Bickerstaff's earlier criticism: Gimcrack's preoccupation with nature has disconnected him "from the Knowledge of the World" (Bond 1987, 132). The legacies he bestows on his wife, that is, her dower on which she was to subsist for the remainder of her life, are scientifick collectibles whose (monetary) value, if any, may well be unknown to the non-naturalist. The widow's lack of expertise might, in turn, entail the loss of the object—she may simply give it away or throw it out—and, hence, the loss of money and subsistence.[12] What is more, the testament's distribution of wealth deviates from the prevalent contemporary social and moral norms. Gimcrack, it appears, allots his legacies according to naturalist interests, not according to family or legal tradition. His wife's dower strongly contrasts with the legacies Gimcrack bequeaths to his "learned and worthy Friend Dr. *Johannes Elscrickius*" (Bond 1987, 134, emphasis in original), namely, his "Rat's Testicles, and / Whale's Pizzle" (Bond 1987, 134). Taking rarity as the crucial contemporary criterion for a curiosity to sell well, for example, at auctions (Cowan 2005, 135), Gimcrack's testament clearly favors his fellow Virtuoso over his wife: the scientifick network, whose international scope is emphasized by Elscrickius' Germanic name, undermines the traditional social network, that is, the family (Daston 2011, 102–103; Stagl 1998, 49–51).[13]

Gimcrack's testament thus unsettles the social hierarchy and the social structure. It can be seen as a symptom of existing and the cause of further social conflict. This conclusion is confirmed by the explanation Gimcrack provides for disinheriting his eldest son John, thus violating the laws of primogeniture. As Gimcrack's commentary reveals, his decision is again based on scientifick loyalty, rather than filial/family duty:

> My eldest Son John having spoken disrespectfully of his little Sister whom I keep by me in Spirits of Wine, and in many other Instances behaved himself undutifully towards me, I do disinherit and wholly cut off from any Part of this my Personal Estate, by giving him a Single Cockle Shell. (Bond 1987, vol. 3, 134–135)

In this passage, Gimcrack's implicit auto-characterization serves as confirmation of his monstrous morals. He ranges his daughter's fetus, conserved in alcohol and surely resulting from a miscarriage, before his breathing son, thereby demonstrating his preference for death over life. More than that, the list prior to this passage, which evidently represents its moral climax, indicates that his emotional relationship to the fetus results from scientifick interest rather than a close familial bond. The text achieves this effect fundamentally by means of its formal shape. The list defamiliarizes the well-known content. The fact that the Virtuoso is wholly taken up by his study of odd (natural) objects and consequently estranged from his family was a common reproach at least since Shadwell's comedy. The *Tatler* condenses this knowledge into the connection between item and heir. Although the text does provide an explanatory narrative frame that helps to situate the testament, it is the reader's task to decipher the socio-moral meaning of the item/heir relation.

A Lady's Library Catalog (*Spectator* No. 37)

Akin in kind to the inventory, the library catalog has an important administrative function, keeping track of the publications and manuscripts available and simultaneously facilitating the retrieval of single (or several) volumes (Rösch 2012, 97–100). It assigns a place to each item and thus creates a spatial as well as an ideological order. The order of the items can be chronological, alphabetical, or thematic; it can be guided by the volumes' size (folio, quarto, octavo, etc.; see Jacobs 1999) or by genre. Depending on the order that is chosen, the catalog (and library) suspends temporality by bringing different periods together, setting them next to each other, thereby suggesting (or encouraging reflection on) the kinship of the items placed on the shelves (and on paper). As library space is so (over)loaded with (visual) information as to potentially overwhelm the viewer, the catalog serves as orientation—as a map—guiding the reader from the written/printed word(s) to the medium of the book (Krajewski 2012, 82–83). The creation of a catalog requires skill and education. In addition to being literate, the author needs literary, philosophical, and scientifick knowledge, as well as taste and judgment. Like the testament, the catalog reflects on the identity of the books' owner: the choice of books to be stored in the library and listed in the catalog mirrors the owner's values, preferences, and interests. In its educational (and economic) function, the catalog becomes an essential tool for shaping and storing the cultural capital necessary for social progress and, more particularly and very much in the spirit of *The Spectator*'s historical context, for enlightenment.

The catalog of books in *Spectator* no. 37 has an anecdotal frame introducing the central character constellation that provides the occasion for Mr. Spectator's ensuing observations: one of the Spectator Club members, Sir Roger de Coverly,[14] asks Mr. Spectator to deliver an important letter to an acquaintance of his, "Leonora," as she is christened by Mr. Spectator. The observations themselves can be divided into three parts: Mr. Spectator first devotes some time to describing the "Lady's Library" (Bond 1965, vol. 1, 153) as a physical space, that is, the room and its organization, before he provides the catalog of books and finishes the issue with a description of Leonora's character (her marital and social situation, her current passion, her country seat).

Mr. Spectator's approach to Leonora's library seems to be designed to arouse the reader's interest in what follows. In accordance with what Lorraine Daston has found to be the contemporary "psychology of natural philosophical inquiry" (Daston and Park 2001, 305), Mr. Spectator expresses his wonder at being invited "to walk into [the] Lady's Library" which, in turn, sparks his "great Curiosity" (Bond 1965, vol. 1, 153) and heightens his attention. Although his description of the room does not correspond to a (clear-cut) list, his text does mirror an enumerative and what appears to be a quasi-scientifick, systematic approach: he follows—or, rather, his eyes follow—the organization of the books on the shelves, arranged "in a very beautiful Order" (Bond 1965, 153), from the *Folios* via the *Quartos* to the *Octavos*, each separated by a corresponding combination of *China*. Together with the remaining decorations adorning the room—including "one of the prettiest Grotesque Works that ever I saw, and made up of Scaramouches, Lions, Monkies, Mandarines, Trees, Shells, and a thousand other odd Figures in *China* Ware"—the interior design of the library (as physical space) prepares Mr. Spectator's reading of and judgment on Leonora's books (as captured by his catalog) and, ultimately, her character: "I [...] did not know at first whether I should fancy my self [*sic*] in a Grotto, or in a Library" (Bond 1965, 154). Leonora shares with the Virtuoso a fascination for strange, exotic objects, which, in her case, have a different origin and serve a different function.

The catalog of books is explicitly marked as a *selection*, an extract from the books on the shelves and the list Mr. Spectator notes down: "Among several that I examin'd, I very well remember these that follow. [...] I was taking a Catalogue in my Pocket-Book of these, and several other Authors, when *Leonora* entred [*sic*]" (Bond 1965, 154/157, emphasis in original). Hence, it is very much Mr. Spectator's perspective and choice—first, in situ at Leonora's library and, second, later when preparing the issue—that determines the nature, shape, and function of the list created by Mr.

Spectator so as to represent Leonora's character. It contains 33 works in vertical format and in no apparent order, for example:

> *Ogleby*'s Virgil.
> *Dryden*'s Juvenal.
> *Cassandra.*
> *Cleopatra.*
> *Astrea.*
> Sir *Isaac Newton*'s Works.
> The *Grand Cyrus*: With a Pin stuck in one of the middle Leaves. (Bond 1965, vol. 1, 154, emphasis in original)

The works include titles of literary, philosophical, moralistic, and political works of modern and ancient origin. Contrary to a (professional) library catalog, Mr. Spectator's list presupposes a well-read reader. Most of the entries feature shortened titles, for example, "*Sherlock* upon Death" (Bond 1965, 155) for William Sherlock's *A Practical Discourse Concerning Death*, also reflecting on the bestselling nature of the works; the majority of the entries drop the authors' names (particularly for the literary works, the classics sometimes including translators), and lack any reference to the place or date of publication.

Very much like Gimcrack's legacies, Leonora's collection of books metonymically mirrors her character. The titles on the list can be divided into seven (thematic) categories: romance/literature, natural philosophy/learning, morality—as the largest groups—as well as education, courtship, and politics/current affairs. Thus, at first sight, Leonora's library suggests a broad interest in various fields of socio-cultural (learned) activity. Yet, Mr. Spectator's initial proviso and his later observations qualify this reading. He introduces the catalog claiming:

> Upon my looking into the Books, I found there were some few which the Lady had bought for her own use, but that most of them had been got together, either because she had heard them praised, or because she had seen the Authors of them. (Bond 1965, vol. 1, 154)

With this qualification, Mr. Spectator insinuates Leonora's failure of actively engaging with the majority of the books on her shelves, which she possesses, one might infer, in order to appear, rather than to be learned.[15] Among the selection that Mr. Spectator represents in his paper, only five of the works bear traces of Leonora's engagement with them: Mr. Spectator finds Leonora's copy of Madeleine de Scudéry's *Artamène or the Grand Cyrus* "with a Pin stuck in one of the middle Leaves" (Bond 1965, 154), John Locke's *Essay Concerning Human Understanding* "With a Paper of Patches in it" (Bond 1965, 155), Thomas D'Urfey's *Tales Tragical and Comical* "Bound in Red Leather, gilt on the Back, and doubled down in several places", Leonora's copy of Madeleine de Scudéry's *Clelia* "Which opened of it self [*sic*] in the Place that describes two Lovers in a Bower", and "A Prayer Book: With a Bottle of *Hungary Water* by the side of it" (Bond 1965, 156). The markings and signs of wear mirror the reading process and, by implication, provide insight into the intellectual priorities of the reader. Surely, the text implies, the books that bear such traces are those most often and most earnestly read. The material evidence Mr. Spectator finds on the shelves reveals that Leonora prefers romance, a literary genre commonly related to the female reader. Hence, Mr. Spectator uses an empiricist framework—(attentive) observation and note taking (Daston 2011)—as a means to authenticate his claim on Leonora's character: she emerges as a romance heroine.

This reading is confirmed by the remainder of the issue in which Mr. Spectator unveils the relationship between Leonora's reading and her perspective on the world to the reader. In a truly inductive manner, he observes that the books she reads have an effect on her character: "As her Reading has lain very much among Romances, it has given her a very particular Turn of Thinking, and discovers it self [*sic*] even in her House, her Gardens and her Furniture" (Bond 1965, vol. 1, 158). Sir Roger's description of Leonora's country estate that "looks like a little Enchanted Palace [… with] Artificial Grottoes […], shady Walks, […] Bowers, and […] Cages of Turtles" (Bond 1965, 158) serves as final evidence. A crucial part of his observational method, Mr. Spectator uses the list as a mnemonic device, allowing him to graphically represent his perceptions and to store them for future reflections.[16]

All in all, Mr. Spectator reconstructs his visit to Leonora chronologically, moving from his observations of the spatial to the bibliographical particularities of her library, completing his findings (and hypothesis) with further evidence provided by Sir Roger. Within this structure, the catalog provides him with a means to account for and, importantly, alert the reader to the cause of Leonora's strange taste and nature. Her particular biographical situation as widowed and childless woman (see Bond 1965, 157–158)—thus being, Mr. Spectator suggests, without a purpose— allows her to devote her time to her library. It is her choice of reading, her preference for publications that are "of little more use than to divert the Imagination" as opposed to "Books as have a tendency to enlighten the Understanding" (Bond 1965, 158), that turned her into a Romance Heroine—a conclusion confirmed by her library (in its double sense). Mr. Spectator opposes Leonora's want of judgment with his own skill in choosing adequate—"enlighten[ing]"—reading for her (and other women). Faced with the multitude of impressions assembled in the library (furniture, accessories, books), he extracts those that allow him to arrive at an understanding of the owner's motivation and character. At the same time, his catalog becomes a source of social power, determining in pre-scriptive manner the proper reading material for his female readers.

CONCLUSION

In sum, the two lists share a number of characteristics. Both testament and library catalog list the possessions of a type. The possessions metonymically reveal the character of the owner, suggesting past choices and prevalent values, thus being indicative of the owner's identity. While all testaments and library catalogs certainly indicate the preferences of their owner, in this case, the symbolic dimension of the items (and lists) is emphasized by being printed in Addison and Steele's periodicals. The periodicals' self-proclaimed intention of reforming society as well as the texts' frame in the individual issues explicitly encourages the reader to read between the lines. Both lists have a vertical structure and are empirically closed, that is, ontologically limited by what is available to the senses. What is more, both propose selections from a larger group of items. The magnitude and shape of the catalog is determined by Mr. Spectator's memory (assisted by his notes); so, the catalog essentially mirrors *his* choice. By contrast, the testament, an ego-document, is governed by Gimcrack's choice: he decides which items to accentuate among his stock of belongings, thus making the testament an instance of deliberate self-fashioning. Both lists represent emphatically written forms, guiding the reader from the printed word to the material object. In the case of the catalog, the written form has a double reference: first, to Mr. Spectator's notes in his "Pocket-Book" (Bond 1965, vol. 1, 157) and, second, to the published catalog in the *Spectator* issue. While Gimcrack's testament follows the culturally established format, it lacks any of the conventional religious references—an element that is, of course, telling and relates to the mainstream moralistic criticism of contemporary naturalists allegedly neglecting their religious duties for their obsessive preoccupation with nature. The implication is that Gimcrack thus jeopardizes his afterlife.[17] Furthermore, the two lists relate in similar ways to class and gender. Both forms are associated with the propertied, endowed, at least in some manner, with enough leisure time for collecting and for reading as well as pursuing naturalist inquiries. Both texts (or types) clash with gender norms. For Gimcrack, this clash is primarily relational: he ignores his social duties as patriarch and even interrupts the established social order. The catalog adds another element. At the time, the library was still perceived as a space of "retreat and solitude" (Williams 2017, 50), as Mr. Spectator's surprise at being invited to enter the "Lady's Library" suggests (Bond 1965, vol. 1, 153). By contrast, Leonora has, as Mr. Spectator finds, turned this allegedly intimate and private space into a "place for public display" (Williams 2017, 50), ultimately defeating the library's purpose, namely self-reflection and learning or, as Mr. Spectator puts it, "enlightenment."

Although the lists are both tailored to the same purpose, that is, capturing the nature of a socio-moral type of man and woman, the way they operate reveals fundamental differences. Gimcrack implicitly characterizes himself by explicitly rating the items and relationships.[18] Furthermore, the testament is an official document extending, in some manner, into the public sphere. Gimcrack thus explicitly sets up a grid that exposes his moral disposition. At first glance, the procedure of rating the individual objects according to value appears to be similar to the weight individual books receive in Leonora's library, worn by use. However, Leonora's reading leaves involuntary traces (e.g., in the case of the book that opens by itself in one place), not necessarily meant for others to see. Her library represents a private space, voluntarily disclosed to Mr. Spectator who then makes it public in his enumerative description and catalog. Hence, the lists are additionally differentiated by agency: Gimcrack exposes himself, while it is Mr. Spectator's observational skills and interpretive glance that make Leonora's character accessible to the reader. The form of the testament, and Gimcrack's testament in particular, creates a hierarchy between individual items in his collection by singling out legacies and by allotting them to respective heirs.[19] The result is a hierarchy of scientifick (and, possibly, monetary) value. The catalog, by contrast, levels hierarchy by listing books in no apparent order; each book, the catalog implies, has the same cultural value. In order to effectively capture Leonora's character, Mr. Spectator's list undermines this equalizing function of the catalog in some measure; the signs of wear create the hierarchical structure of the type's reading. The catalog as a whole, however, contains books of different moral value (high value of philosophy/morality versus low value of romance); it is in their blend that they achieve a balance of moral (and cultural) value. Furthermore, the issues in which the lists are published differ with regard to their epistemological procedure. The *Tatler* issue proposes a deductive framework, leading from a generic, abstract definition of the type (Bond 1987, vol. 3, 132–133) to a representative example located in space and time, Gimcrack's will. The *Spectator* issue, by contrast, works inductively with Mr. Spectator as a representative observer showing the reader how to come to terms with what he sees. In this context, Mr. Spectator uses the catalog to provide evidence for his reading, that is, for his hypothesis of Leonora's character.

Ultimately, both lists mirror the activity of collecting: natural and cultural curiosities in Gimcrack's testament and books in Leonora's case. Their incorporation into the periodicals—a publication format intricately connected to the idea of listing and enumeration[20]—transforms them into items in a collection, in a process that very much resembles the creation of the catalog in *Spectator* no. 37. As a result, the lists—and the socio-moral types captured by these lists—become collectibles themselves and are, in turn, incorporated in yet another list: the index in the collected editions.[21] As much as testaments in literature always implicitly address the question of the literary archive and of cultural memory (Vedder 2011, 27), the two lists analyzed here serve to register in satirical fashion exaggerated behavioral patterns marked as typical of their time and, thus, as memorable.[22] The types emerge as moral curiosities in the *Tatler*'s and the *Spectator*'s curiosity cabinets. Hence they are evidence of the authors' "hoarding up in their Chests and Cabinets such Creatures as others industriously avoid the Sight of" (Bond 1987, vol. 3, 133), a practice very much akin to the Virtuoso's activities, yet allegedly inspired and morally justified by their dedication to the "commonweal."

Notes

1. This design, together with the contemporary practice of ever-expanding editions, hints at the (technically) infinite nature of observation and, by implication, of character writing, with new observational details and new types simply added to a constantly increasing repertoire. An exception is

Joseph Hall's early seventeenth-century character book, which arranges the types in two parts according to their predominant virtues and vices.

2. See *Caractères ou les Mœurs de ce Siècle*, which were published in eight continuously expanding editions in Paris from 1688.

3. With Eva von Contzen, I define the list as a formal unit consisting of distinct parts with a very loose, if any, link to the surrounding narrative (2017b, 222). The relationship between the components of the list is complex: As Robert Belknap argues, they "cohere to fulfil some function as a combined whole, and by discontinuity the individuality of each unit is maintained as a particular instance, [...]. Each unit in a list possesses an individual significance but also a specific meaning by virtue of its membership with the other units in the compilation [...]" (2004, 15). Depending on the way the list is contextualized, it may have a variety of affordances; crucially, it may provide or reflect identity or order, invite the reader to fill the gaps between its parts and tell a story, and have a range of different purposes—legal, religious, administrative, therapeutic, and, indeed, didactic (von Contzen 2017a, 322).

4. This methodological choice testifies to the contemporary significance of the list, a crucial instrument for naturalists in their attempts at systematically understanding and ordering nature for Bacon's *Instauratio magna*, which is reflected, for instance, in Robert Boyle's advice to naturalists to use "*General* heads of Inquiry" in their exploration and description of nature (Boyle 1665/1666, 186) or Patrick Blair's systematic description of the anatomy of an elephant including a tabular synopsis of the animal's skeleton (Blair 1710, 143). For a discussion of late seventeenth-century attempts at systematizing science, see Hunter 2007.

5. The archaic spelling of the term is meant to indicate the somewhat elaborate epithet "natural philosophical and natural historical," while emphasizing that the term "science" in its modern understanding only emerged in the mid-nineteenth century (see *OED*).

6. While Addison and Steele take up Shadwell in Gimcrack's aversion to *useful* knowledge ("I seldom bring anything to use; 'tis not my way. Knowledge is my ultimate end" Shadwell 1966, 47), as the quintessential characteristic of their Virtuoso, their catalog of Gimcrack's possessions seems to be more indebted to Mary Astell's sketch of the Virtuoso in her *Essay on the Defence of the Female Sex* (1696) which refers not only to entomological artifacts (e.g., caterpillars), but also to specimens of a marine origin (e.g., "Shells and Pebbles of all Shores") and to the type's activity of conserving: "He preserves carefully those *Creatures*, which other Men industriously destroy, [...]. He is the Embalmer of deceas'd Vermin, and dresses his Mummy with as much care, as the Ancient *Egyptians* did their

Kings" (Astell 1696, 96–99). For an analysis of Astell's sketch of the type and its history more generally, see Houghton 1942.

7. As in most other characters, Bickerstaff attacks the imbalance in the Virtuoso and the type's neglect of the affairs of life that his exclusive focus on "trivialities" entails. Gimcrack's telling name confirms his nature.

8. In the type's affinity to collecting and the collector, the Virtuoso is linked to the Pedant, the Antiquary, and the Critic, broadly popular in seventeenth-century character books. See Assmann 1998.

9. Thus, the text equally leaves the pattern of traditional mock testaments that typically made a legacy of the testator's sins (see Bach 1977, 81).

10. This conforms to the literary tradition of the mock testament, as Bach's examples illustrate (e.g., Bach 1977, 80–85), and contrasts with historical examples such as the naturalist Robert Boyle's testament (see Boyle 1772, clviii-clxxi).

11. At the same time, a familiarity with the tradition of the mock testament certainly promotes the reflection on the symbolic meaning of the legacies on the part of the reader.

12. He conceptualizes the "Nest of an Humming Bird" as a reward for his daughter Fanny's complying with her mother's wishes, thus for conduct that accords with her filial duties. The same applies to the recompense for his brother's support of his son. In this passage, he even equates installing someone into an estate ("Lands") with a "Collection of Grasshoppers" (Bond 1987, vol. 3, 134), supposedly level due to the sheer size of the collection.

13. Gimcrack emphasizes his bias toward his naturalist friends in his comment on his legacies to Elscrickius which he defines as "an eternal Monument of my Affection and Friendship for him" (Bond 1987, vol. 3, 134), the only extensive expression of emotion and, remarkably, the only reference to eternity and the afterlife in his will. The sexual connotation of the legacies hint at a homosexual relationship and, by extension, suggest a potential threat to the welfare and subsistence of society.

14. The Spectator Club allows the periodical's authors to expand their perspective on contemporary society by assembling a number of "experts." Each member represents a central social sphere: the country gentry (Sir Roger de Coverly), trade (Sir Andrew Freeport), the church/religion (the Clergyman), literary criticism (the Templar), and fashionable society (the Restoration Rake Will Honeycomb).

15. Through this detail, Leonora is associated with the type of the Book Pedant, personified in *Tatler* issue no. 158 as Tom Folio, who is more interested in the outside of the books he collects and their material quality than in their actual content (see Bond 1987, vol. 2, 384–387; and Assmann 1998, 271–272).

16. In *Spectator* 46, Mr. Spectator provides another specimen of his notes (see Bond 1965, vol. 1, 195–199).
17. This connects with his legacy of the "Female Skeleton" which indicates Gimcrack's disregard of the commands of religious piety, disrespecting the body's right of eternal rest. While, of course, criminals forfeited such rights, the use of corpses for scientifick purposes was highly contested at the time, not least for religious reasons.
18. He elevates the legacy he bestows upon Johannes Elscrickius "as an eternal Monument of my Affection and Friendship" while he degrades the legacy to his eldest son, whom he deprives of his inheritance "by giving him a Single Cockle-Shell" (Bond 1965, vol. 1, 134–135).
19. For the link of enumeration and hierarchy, see Mainberger 2003, 7–8.
20. The individual issues are published consecutively in *numerus currens* format, technically an "infinite list," ultimately collected in bound editions (in close proximity or simultaneously to original publication) with an index.
21. The first collected editions were published during the papers' initial run and reissued in differing formats and by different editors throughout the eighteenth century and beyond. Collections also included (and include) selected editions (see, e.g., Erin Mackie's fairly recent *Commerce of Everyday Life: Selections from The Tatler and The Spectator*, Bedford/St. Martin's 1998).
22. The authors express a playful, yet acute awareness of posterity/future readers, especially in *The Spectator* (see Bond 1965, vol. 1, 422–426).

REFERENCES

Assmann, Aleida. 1998. Der Sammler als Pedant. In *Sammler – Bibliophile – Exzentriker*, ed. Aleida Assmann, Monika Gomille, and Gabriele Rippl, 261–274. Tübingen: Narr.

Astell, Mary. 1696. *An Essay in Defence of the Female Sex*. London.

Bach, Ulrich. 1977. *Das Testament als literarische Form: Versuch einer Gattungsbestimmung auf der Grundlage englischer Texte*. Düsseldorf: Stern-Verlag.

Belknap, Robert E. 2004. *The List: The Uses and Pleasures of Cataloguing*. New York: Yale University Press.

Blair, Patrick. 1710. A Continuation of the Osteographia Elephantine: Or, a Description of the Bones of an Elephant, Which Died Near Dundee, April the 27th, 1706. *In Philosophical Transactions* 27 (327): 117–168. https://doi.org/10.1098/rstl.1710.0009.

Bond, Donald, ed. 1965. *The Spectator*. 5 vols. Oxford: Clarendon.

———, ed. 1987. *The Tatler*. 3 vols. Oxford: Clarendon.

Boyle, Robert. 1665/1666. General Heads for a Natural History of a Countrey, Great or Small. In *Philosophical Transactions (1665–1678)*, vol. 1 (1665–1666), 186–189.

Boyle, Robert. 1772. *The Works of the Honourable Robert Boyle*. Vol. 1. London.

Butzer, Günter, and Joachim Jacob, eds. 2012. Metzler Lexikon literarischer Symbole. Stuttgart: Metzler. https://doi.org/10.1007/978-3-476-05302-2.

Cowan, Brian. 2005. *The Social Life of Coffee: The Emergence of the British Coffeehouse*. New Haven: Yale University Press.

Daston, Lorraine. 2011. The Empire of Observation: 1600–1800. In *Histories of Scientific Observation*, ed. Lorraine Daston and Elizabeth Lunbeck, 81–113. Chicago: University of Chicago Press.

Daston, Lorraine, and Katharine Park. 2001. *Wonders and the Order of Nature: 1150–1750*. New York: Zone books.

Hockenjos, Katrin. 2006. *Frauenbilder in englischen Charakterskizzen des 17. Jahrhunderts*. Tübingen: Narr.

Houghton, Walter E. 1942. The English Virtuoso in the Seventeenth Century. *Journal of the History of Ideas* 3 (51–73): 190–219.

Hunter, Michael. 2007. Robert Boyle and the Early Royal Society: A Reciprocal Exchange in the Making of Baconian Science. *The British Journal for the History of Science* 40 (1): 1–23.

Jacobs, Edward H. 1999. Buying into Classes: The Practice of Book Selection in Eighteenth-Century Britain. *Eighteenth-Century Studies* 33: 43–64.

Krajewski, Markus. 2012. Die Bibliothek als Meta-Medium. In *Handbuch Bibliothek: Geschichte, Aufgaben, Perspektiven*, ed. Konrad Umlauf and Stefan Gradmann, 81–89. Stuttgart: Metzler. https://doi.org/10.1007/978-3-476-05185-1.

Mainberger, Sabine. 2003. *Die Kunst des Aufzählens: Elemente zu einer Poetik des Enumerativen*. Berlin: De Gruyter.

Rösch, Hermann. 2012. Die Bibliothek und ihre Dienstleistungen. In *Handbuch Bibliothek: Geschichte, Aufgaben, Perspektiven*, ed. Konrad Umlauf and Stefan Gradmann, 89–100. Stuttgart: Metzler. https://doi.org/10.1007/978-3-476-05185-1.

Shadwell, Thomas. 1966. *The Virtuoso*. Eds. Marjorie H. Nicolson and David S. Rodes. Lincoln: University of Nebraska Press.

Smeed, John William. 1985. *The Theophrastan 'Character': The History of a Literary Genre*. Oxford: Clarendon.

Stagl, Justin. 1998. Homo Collector: Zur Anthropologie und Soziologie des Sammelns. In *Sammler – Bibliophile – Exzentriker*, ed. Aleida Assmann, Monika Gomille, and Gabriele Rippl, 37–54. Tübingen: Gunther Narr Verlag.

Vedder, Ulrike. 2011. *Das Testament als literarisches Dispositiv: Kulturelle Praktiken des Erbes in der Literatur des 19. Jahrhunderts*. Munich: Fink.

von Contzen, Eva. 2017a. Die Affordanzen der Liste. *Zeitschrift für Literaturwissenschaft und Linguistik* 47: 317–326.

———. 2017b. Grenzfälle des Erzählens: Die Liste als einfache Form. In *Komplexität und Einfachheit*, ed. Albrecht Koschorke, 221–239. Stuttgart: Metzler. Springer Nature. https://doi.org/10.1007/978-3-476-04357-3_13.

Williams, Abigail. 2017. *The Social Life of Books: Reading Together in the Eighteenth-Century Home*. New Haven: Yale University Press. https://doi.org/10.12987/9780300228106.

CHAPTER 5

The Lists of Alexander von Humboldt: On the Epistemology of Scientific Practice

Ottmar Ette

THE EPISTEMOLOGIST'S LAUGHTER

Together, a list and laughter gave rise to perhaps the most well-known book on contemporary epistemology. The first paragraph of the preface in *Les mots et les choses* is filled with and famously makes reference to the imaginative power of literature:

> This book first arose out of a passage in Borges, out of the laughter that shattered, as I read the passage, all the familiar landmarks of my thought – *our* thought, the thought that bears the stamp of our age and our geography – breaking up all the ordered surfaces and all the planes with which we are accustomed to tame the wild profusion of existing things, and continuing long afterwards to disturb and threaten with collapse our age-old distinction between the Same and the Other. This passage quotes a 'certain Chinese encyclopedia' in which it is written that 'animals are divided into: (a) belonging to the Emperor, (b) embalmed, (c) tame, (d) sucking pigs, (e)

O. Ette (✉)
University of Potsdam, Potsdam, Germany
e-mail: ette@uni-potsdam.de

101

R. A. Barton et al. (eds.), *Forms of List-Making: Epistemic, Literary, and Visual Enumeration,*
https://doi.org/10.1007/978-3-030-76970-3_5

sirens, (f) fabulous, (g) stray dogs, (h) included in the present classification, (i) frenzied, (j) innumerable, (k) drawn with a very fine camelhair brush, (l) *et cetera*, (m) having just broken the water pitcher, (n) that from a long way off look like flies'. In the wonderment of this taxonomy, the thing we apprehend in one great leap, the thing that, by means of the fable, is demonstrated as the exotic charm of another system of thought, is the limitation of our own, the stark impossibility of thinking *that*. (Foucault 1970, XV)

In *Les mots* (first published in 1966 by Gallimard) Michel Foucault opts not only for a literary text as a launching point for his "archaeology of the human sciences," but also begins with the Argentinean Jorge Luis Borges, a representative of that particular brand of Latin American literature which, during the 1960s, experienced a dramatic ascension to worldwide renown. In doing so, he of course did not select a text which could be categorized as belonging to the authors of the so-called boom in Latin American literature, but rather a text from *that* Argentinean who would soon be considered one of the primary references and forerunners for what is generally regarded as "postmodernism."[1] After a several decade-long delay Borges would grow to be esteemed as its founder within the Western order of world literature. His laughter over such classifications and categorizations is certainly understandable.

The matter of situating Michel Foucault within structuralism or post-structuralism, within modernism or postmodernism, rather than opening the door for any serious reflection, serves as a reminder that such "alternatives" ought to be regarded as case-in-point evidence of a striking lexical and conceptual deficiency. Still, it is worth highlighting that Foucault meditates on the breaking up of "the thought that bears the stamp of our age" (1970, XV) and, in doing so, introduces a spatial-temporal limitation traversing millennia of occidental thought and history, which undoubtedly constitutes Foucault's intention when he writes of *our* thought, for the relationship between words and objects which he examines is evidently one which bears with it such spatial-temporal restrictions.

Accordingly, it is the epistemologist's laughter which is situated at the heart of the initial excerpt from *Les mots and les choses*—a downright Rabelaisian cackle in the face of cognitive limits, which literature may well be able trace out and perhaps even grasp by means of artifice but which now prove (categorically, at least) unfathomable for Western philosophy. And at the crux of Foucault's interest is the "impossibility of thinking *that*" (1970, XV). But what precisely is that which has been designated as *impossible to think*?

At the center of Borges' "The Analytical Language of John Wilkins" (as cited by Foucault) is a list which is subdivided into thirteen cataloged points. This list proves unintelligible, owing to "our age-old distinction between the Same and the Other" (Foucault 1970, XV). In other words, it cannot be conceived of on epistemological grounds. Following the French philosopher Vincent Descombes, it is clear that a significant part of the history of twentieth-century French philosophy can be regarded of in terms of these two concepts as a history revolving around *le même* and *l'autre* (see Descombes 1981). It is this (occidental) episteme to which Foucault refers as he begins his preface.

Suppose it were the case that this episteme precluded the possibility of our comprehending Borges' thirteen-item long list. As a corollary, of course, it would not follow that the individual entries be generally unintelligible. Rather, it would simply be the case that they cannot be conceived in terms of one and the same logic. Hence, what is required is either a different logic to understand Borges' list or a composite of disparate and diverse logics, a multilogical thought structure from which various divisions and subdivisions might be conceived of. Literature—including world literatures—circumvents such complications. It represents such a multilogical system.

Upon closer examination of the list, the chinoiserie as recounted by Borges, we find that it contains a small list embedded within it. The first point consists of a kind of *mise en abyme*, designated here by a formulaic expression for lists—"and so on"—which, as a general rule, tends toward infinity. It thus contains, as it were, the entire list in the form of pars pro toto, in which we may detect the *ars pro toto* and the Argentinean's pleasure associated with it. For the formula "etc." or "et cetera" opens up the possibility of expanding a given list and, if necessary, of permitting it to grow on into a limitless list of endless indulgence and boundless delight.

Yet the epistemologist's laughter is more likely about the *occidental* impossibility of thinking of this multilogical list. Is it laughter arising out of perplexity or rather laughter accepting a challenge? At the same time, it denotes the point at which, in the face of a list, the acknowledgment of a historical *burden* is broken, an acknowledgment which, of course, on a meta-level, releases that pleasure which is able to find expression in the form of laughter. If we allow this pleasure space, it does not, in the face of the historical burden, remain fixed in place to deny further service. Rather, it gives rise to certain lists which make it possible to contemplate the task that the list of conceivable animals poses. Delight sets the lists in motion, as it were.

The Borgesian text offers a glimpse into the epistemology of et cetera. Indeed, it would be conceivable, given the possibilities of our thought, to open the invitation received in Borges' text to a *praise of "and so on,"* to a *eulogy of* "et cetera," thereby conceiving of an *epistemology of widening and expansion* existing beyond Foucault's laughter (see Ette 2016). But our task in the following deliberations is not aimed at altering the occidental episteme, but rather at exploring the thinking of one of the main representatives of science grounded in that episteme, whose 250th birthday we celebrate this year.

The Emergence of the Humboldtian Science

Let us begin with a factual statement: There are hundreds, indeed, thousands of lists and enumerations throughout the entirety of Alexander von Humboldt's scientific works. If we hope to achieve an overview of the thinking, writing, and scientific style of the Prussian natural and cultural scientist,[2] his *Amerikanische Reisetagebücher* offer a most promising starting point, for they have come to stand for something along the lines of the birth certificate, the record of origin for the Humboldtian science. And even within them, the distinction between practical and poetic lists, as introduced by Umberto Eco, proves hardly pertinent (see Eco 2009, 113). For it was not only in his *Ansichten der Natur* that Alexander von Humboldt sought to harmonize literary aims with purely scientific ones[3]: in his printed works as well as in his manuscripts, both fields flow into one another again and again.

One would be hard-pressed to find any document or text which bears such precise traces of the lengthy and sometimes arduous process which marked the rise of the science for which the younger of the two Humboldt brothers with all his personality was responsible. They constitute the true core and, at the same time, the biography of the academic and author who recorded hypotheses, measurements, observations and insights in his *Amerikanische Reisetagebücher* not only during his voyage through the American tropics, but over a period of almost seven decades. They thus accompanied him throughout his entire life and serve as a testimony to the development of the transdisciplinary work which has come to be associated with the name Humboldt.

In order to recognize the significance of these travel manuscripts, it is important for the contemporary reader to bear in mind that, with the onset of his journey to America in 1799, Humboldt was rounding off the first of three phases of his life and entering the second, much more self-determined phase. Born in Berlin beneath the blessing of a comet in 1769, Humboldt spent the first nearly thirty years of his life as a self-proclaimed "nomad," as a "stranger" amongst the sciences.[4] He had traversed the most disparate of disciplines from chemistry and mathematics to botany and geography all the way to history and cameralistics, which he had studied on the "frosty banks of the Oder" at the Viadrina in Frankfurt an der Oder. A long list of subjects, indeed.

The youthful Humboldt had—at times in succession, at times simultaneously—busied himself with myriad and diverse disciplines, further expanding the horizons of his knowledge at the University of Göttingen in anthropology, philology, and surely in philosophy as well. Complementing this was his time at the Commercial Academy in Hamburg where he continued to refine his knowledge in cameralistics. He completed his studies in mining technology in the famous Saxon town of Freiberg in one-third of the normal period of study and proceeded to embark on a career in the Prussian mining service. There he quickly experienced a rapid rise from prospective mining assessor to government mining official. But Humboldt had his sights set on higher things.

For after the death of his mother he unceremoniously turned his back on Prussia and turned his inheritance into tinkling coins, which he would then be able to use for a planned and long-desired trip to non-European regions. After several false starts, his voyage from 1799–1804 through the Spanish colonial regions of America—a journey through today's Venezuela, Cuba, Colombia, Ecuador, Peru, Mexico, again Cuba and the United States—would ultimately transform him into an international star in the scientific community. He quickly began acquiring membership status in both national and international academies alike. Humboldt had long since given up compiling an unwieldy list of different sciences: he had stumbled into the conception of a new science.

Indeed, decisive for this new development was a new, forward-looking understanding of science: the Humboldtian science, founded through his voyages and established with his subsequent writings. Alexander von Humboldt was not only the founder of individual disciplines such as phytogeography or Native American Studies but also, sensu Michel Foucault, a founder of discourse, the inventor of a new understanding and a new scientific practice which defied the increasingly popular nineteenth-century trend of separating nature from culture. His equally comprehensive and complex concept of life understood both nature and culture as an inseparable living entity.

For his journey into the New World marked the dawn of a profound nexus of thought amongst all those disciplines in which Humboldt had previously familiarized himself and deepened his knowledge. His concept of science remained deeply nomadic and by no means monadic. His brother Wilhelm had already recognized early on that his younger sibling's great gift lay in creative combination: the ability to join by dint of thought what at first glance does not belong together.[5] It was the beginning of a transdisciplinary science whose relevance even today defies obsolescence. On the contrary: our times of ecological catastrophes call for a way of thinking that opens up our planet Earth in all its relations and interactivity and which ensures that the various influences of the world's cultures on nature are no longer culpably neglected.

The immense, albeit temporary success of Daniel Kehlmann's bestseller *Die Vermessung der Welt* has branded the Prussian as a mere world surveyor. Alexander von Humboldt was certainly a man of numbers, constantly taking measurements, running different measurement series day and night. Yet he never let his measurements lie untouched; they always led into more general observations inspired by his spirit of creative combination. For him, it was always about the big picture.

Numbers undoubtedly testify to his profound shift toward empiricism and the empirical basis implicit in the conception of his science. Thus we find in his writings a myriad of lists and enumerations with different measurements in both the natural and cultural sciences alike. But the numbers sometimes took on the same significance that Dante—whom he admired— ascribed to them in the universe of his *Divine Comedy*, that is, in his cosmos. While such numerical symbolism did not obscure the precision of his data, it always aimed at the universal. Recent research from a Toulousain research group led by Pierre Moret came to the hardly surprising conclusion that his *Tableau physique des Andes* (1807)—to which we will have to return in detail—ought not to be taken too literally and empirically, as his entries were certainly not derived solely from Chimborazo, but rather encompass the entirety of today's Ecuadorian high Andes (see Moret et al. 2019). They offered a fractal model as opposed to a precise list of the locations of certain plants at a particular volcano, for Chimborazo served more than anything as a symbolic mountain for him: he had never reached its summit. Here, rather than yielding to failure, Humboldt emphasized that science is a pursuit without telos, that there is always a way forward and beyond, as he also indicated in his *Naturgemälde*.

Alexander von Humboldt was a precise observer of people, and not least of the indigenous population in the Americas. He quickly overcame his initial prejudices whose roots derived from the relevant writings of the *philosophes* of the eighteenth century; indeed, he became increasingly absorbed in American cultures and would ultimately come to be known as the founder of Native American Studies, the study of the diverse cultures across the Americas. Here, too, he surveyed everything he came across. But his primary interest lay not in measurements and numbers, not in measuring and calculating, for he developed a profound understanding of the cultural developments that the various American peoples had lived through and sought to juxtapose them with Western antiquity and with cultures worldwide. Drawing on Clavijero's work and many other studies, he developed a historically sound picture of the indigenous American civilizations. Furthermore, as his later writings such as *Vues des Cordillères et Monumens des Peuples Indigènes de l'Amérique* indicate, he began to study complex relationships between the world's most diverse cultures,[6] integrating them into a grand overview of human cultures.

The younger of the Humboldt brothers hardly limited himself to the study of natural phenomena. To label him as a mere natural scientist is indeed as traditional as it is false. Such a view has been known to flow about in Germany and occasionally in other European countries, but never in Latin America; for there his intensive engagement with, for instance, American history and culture is well known. For Humboldt, nature and culture were intimately intertwined. This process of insight into the indissoluble relationship between culture and nature is documented in his *Amerikanische Reisetagebücher* in a very precise and yet quotidian manner. This resulted in far-reaching scientific consequences.

To be sure, it is not entirely clear how the central axiom of the nascent Humboldtian science made its way into his travel reports. Situated in the midst of a disparately formatted passage scribed in French, it almost literally glowed in German: "Alles ist Wechselwirkung" (Everything is reciprocity).[7] The axiom emerges like an epiphany. Very suddenly the all-encompassing fundamental formula was found: the basic formula of the scientific practice that Humboldt had long since developed on his journey through the American tropics—the Humboldtian science. The location and surroundings seem to indicate a spontaneous moment of enlightenment, something Humboldt had certainly long since contemplated and derived but had never expressed with such simplicity. But thereafter he saw even more clearly how intimately everything was connected via reciprocity and, above all else, inter*actions.*

It is fascinating to peek over Humboldt's shoulder amidst this cognitive process in his *Amerikanische Reisetagebücher*. Indeed, his daily field research is currently being transformed into a series of transdisciplinary investigations: beyond the network of rivers ranging from the Orinoco to the Amazon and the network of volcanoes in the high Andes of present-day Ecuador, the interconnectivity between the indigenous languages and the interrelationships among the different cultures of America are also becoming increasingly visible. Lists appear everywhere: lists of languages, lists of volcanoes, lists of rivers.

And what is more: Humboldt recognized on multiple occasions and with great clarity the extent to which humans with, for example, agriculture encroach on seemingly inexhaustible natural resources and, through deforestation for shipbuilding or access to more cultivable land, devastate the water balance. Historical sources had already alerted him to the destructive effects of human culture. He develops this into a recognition of ecosystems, yet all of this is coupled with an assessment of the respective culture of the corresponding population groups. The matter of biodiversity is not a purely bioscientific issue, but rather one that essentially involves cultural aspects.

Indeed, it is cultural backgrounds that determine people's actions, as he illustrated by singling out the destruction of the lake area in the heart of Anáhuac in present-day Mexico:

> The Spaniards treated the water as an enemy. Apparently, they want this New Spain to be as dry as the inner districts of their Old Spain. They want nature to resemble their morals, and they are not doing a bad job of it. [...] They have not managed to reconcile the two objectives: the security of Mexico City and the irrigation of the land. The lack of water makes the valley infertile, unhealthy, the salt level increases, the dryness of the air increases.[8]

Humans intervene in nature according to culturally shaped ideas and, in Humboldt's words, harbor the desire for nature to resemble the respective group's morality as well as its origin. These are insights into the interwovenness of culture and its destruction of nature which, until recently, had hardly been used in research and thus remain largely unaddressed. There exists a plethora of natural science institutions bearing the name Humboldt, yet a shortage of such institutions which represent equally both the natural sciences as well as cultural studies.

The realization that *Alles ist Wechselwirkung* brings together geology and volcanology with the mythology and the symbolism of the indigenous populations, infusing into what Humboldt perceived in the American tropics as the grand majesty of nature an awareness of scientific knowledge still to be pursued while, in turn, also alluding to the fragility of all human knowledge. For not only is everything connected with everything: everything inter*acts* (interagiert) with everything. Here it is also worth noting to what extent Humboldt increasingly resorts to the knowledge of the indigenous peoples, often relying on repeated reminders from his Indian guides for the names of animal noises amidst the darkness of the jungle and also admiring their ability to find their way around in utter darkness.

Returning from Chimborazo and searching out in pitch-darkness the proper path down, Humboldt again revealed his almost compulsive affinity for numbers, this time not without a stroke of self-directed irony:

> We moved first on foot, then on horseback. We amused ourselves by counting how many times each one of us fell whilst walking. In less than three hours, Don Vicente Aguirre, who strode behind me, counted 123 falls for me, and I counted 34 for the Indian walking ahead of me. It thus follows that the skill of an Indian compared to a white man is 34 to 123.[9]

Nothing was beyond the scope of Humboldt's interests. He recorded everything in his *Amerikanische Reisetagebücher*, annotated extensively and wondered all the meanwhile how his recordings and insights might be related—that is, *almost* everything. Indeed, Humboldt's reticence is also of significance: reticence which speaks volumes, but which can only briefly be addressed at present.

It is thus hardly imaginable that the Prussian researcher, whose scope of interest nothing eluded, would have abstained from experimentation with the indigenous hallucinogens whose presence in certain regions of the high Andes had been well known for centuries. Yet his travel reports contain no mention of such. Humboldt was well aware of the fact that his *Amerikanische Reisetagebücher* would one day be publicly accessible and, accordingly, remained silent, concealing his more intimate emotions: such was not intended for public scrutiny.

But the knowledge and insight of the Native Americans proved at once interesting, intriguing, and fascinating to Humboldt. Exemplary of his interest is a passage from Report VII, which highlights both the boundaries of his own knowledge as well as his own senses.

> When we botanized, we consulted Indians to find out the names of trees. Here one encounters trunks that tower so high that one cannot distinguish the foliage. The Indian takes the bark in his mouth, chews on it and then says with the utmost certainty that it is such or such tree. I, in turn, chewed on the bark, and could not detect any difference in taste among 15 trees. They all seemed to me to be equally tasteless.[10]

The tedious learning process reflected in his *Amerikanische Reisetagebücher* would ultimately encompass all branches of science and knowledge. Humboldt proved willing to reexamine all areas of his knowledge against reality and empiricism and to correct manifest errors. And where his mistakes proved salient, he grew more sapient. Thus, during his American journey, the Prussian travel writer evolved from a staunch Neptunist who, like Goethe or his mentor Werner, believed in the rock-forming power of aquatic sedimentation, into a budding Plutonist, who saw volcanic phenomena as holding a far greater influence on the formation of rocks. Yet throughout his life, he enjoyed a warm friendship with Goethe and Werner: even if Goethe resented him, Humboldt was a diplomatist, and a skilled one at that.

The roughly 4000 manuscript pages containing some 450 sketches and drawings (see Ette and Maier 2018) constitute a detailed image of a tropical world in which Humboldt quickly felt both happy and homely. But it was not only in various climates where he felt at home: Humboldt wrote in a great range of languages, convinced that the world's complexity could not be adequately expressed when restricted to the viewpoint of one single language. If a report began in German, he was wont to transition into French as the journey progressed, neglecting neither Latin nor Spanish and often including references to other (and especially indigenous) languages. Humboldt was truly multilingual both in tongue and thought.

Allow me here to briefly touch on the materiality of his writing: He mixed his inks himself which, beyond allowing for the very precise dating of certain passages from his *Amerikanische Reisetagebücher* (see Thiele 2016; Bispinck-Roßbachere 2016), after the cap-sizing of his pirogue also prevented their utter destruction owing to the ink's water resistant properties. Decades later, Humboldt circled in pencil the water stains still preserved in the paper, noting affectionately, "Water from the Orinoco." More importantly, however, his writing and penmanship—continually rising upward and toward to top right as characteristic of him—were preserved and thus maintain all the processes of knowledge which have been passed down to us with such impressive clarity. These manuscript pages feature a myriad of lists and tables of every sort, something which we shall return to shortly. Humboldt delighted in creating lists of things that he was investigating, that he loved, that he was measuring, or that he simply wished to remember.

Let us now attempt to gain a broader perspective. Accompanying the Humboldtian science was also the development of a Humboldtian approach to writing. In his travel manuscripts, the philosopher and natural scientist from Berlin wrote neither in diary-like fashion— that is, day after day—nor in a manner typically associated with travelogues— that is, following a given travel route; he arranged his materials neither by discipline nor thematically. In other words, there exists no consistent, continuous logic in his writing, which was without a doubt not only multilingual, but also multilogical. What, then, did his writing consist in?

Lists are first and foremost linear, albeit discontinuous discourse elements. Alexander von Humboldt did not write continuously, but rather discontinuously: He often left large free spaces between his entries and later filled in these gaps successively. In doing so, he practiced an island approach to writing or, more precisely, an approach featuring small text-islands which were not recorded in a continuous sequence, but rather linked relationally with one another. Each text-island, only occasionally titled, served as a small work in itself with its own logic and voice—yet at the same time an island world insofar as each island was situated in a multi-relational network with other islands.

This enabled a much more precise implementation of the foundational principles of his scientific concept, in which everything was necessarily interwoven with everything and, moreover, interacted reciprocally with everything. Thus, in his *Amerikanische Reisetagebücher*, Alexander von Humboldt found his characteristic style, which he later tinkered with in his printed works in various ways. He thereby succeeded in implementing discontinuity as a fruitful underlying principle in his writing. This ought to prove of great importance, especially where lists are of interest.

But Humboldt was also a deeply political mind. He spoke out vehemently against all forms of slavery and servitude. His travel manuscripts included oftentimes shocking scenes of a colonial ruler exercising violence, depictions which must have literally branded themselves into his readers' memory. His criticism of colonialism, which ultimately neutralized any hopes of accessing the British Empire on the Asian continent, became harsh and biting, particularly in the second half of his travel manuscripts—a fact supported by his remarks in Report IX about the native miners in Mexico:

> Apart from their pants, they walk completely naked, sweating terribly, are usually leaning on a small stick, barely 10 inches long, and are stretched out on stairs as if walking on all fours. Unhappy offspring of a race robbed of its property. What precedent exists of a whole entire nation losing all its property? A strong Tenatero remains burdened with 12 - 14 arrobas of stone for 6 hours and walks up and down the 32000 steps in 1 shift! What contrast, people talk daily about the energy of the white race and weakness of the Indians. The latter make 8 - 10 journeys loaded, and we, we crawl, if we are unburdened and well-fed, only once out of the shelters of Valenciana daily. I have found myself quite miserable.[11]

Alexander von Humboldt continued entering additions, deletions, amendments, and updates in his *Amerikanische Reisetagebücher* with great precision and equal affection until his final days. This chronicle of his life is a treasure which alters the perception of that Prussian cultural and natural scientist and which shows us a humane and almost present Humboldt—with all his contradictions, all his vehemence, all his science, and all his truth. Consequently, any attempt to construct a monolithic image of a Humboldt compiling his lists, constellations, and tables according to a single logic, perhaps as a mere "surveyor of the world," can only be described as misguided. Never in his long life of research spanning more than seven decades was he afraid of contradictions.

CONTRADICTIONS AND WEAVING FLAWS

Attentive reading often reveals the tensions, and sometimes contradictions, between many of Humboldt's statements. It seems obvious that Humboldt deliberately built weaving flaws (Webfehler) into many other constellations and lists. The following shall elucidate some of the characteristic contradictions in Humboldt's work by way of example. Even in the "Introduction" to his *Reise in die Äquinoktial-Gegenden des Neuen*

Kontinents (dated "Paris, February, 1812"),[12] which appeared in print for more than a decade and a half, Alexander von Humboldt had drawn a clear line of demarcation between the hemispheres, between the "Old" and the "New" World, not least by including the typical objects expected by the contemporary public in travel reports:

> I am more than aware of how a traveler in America is at a disadvantage with respect to those who describe Greece, Egypt, the banks of the Euphrates or the South Sea Islands. In the Old World it is the civilized peoples and the gradations of their civilization that lend the picture its principal character; in the new world, however, the individual vanishes, as it were, together with his problems amidst a wild and imposing nature. The human race offers here only a few relics of indigenous, culturally underdeveloped hordes or the uniformity of customs and institutions that have been planted by European colonists on these distant shores.[13]

The stark contrast between a world of culture and a world of nature opened up, as it were, a travel moment which the reading public would follow for nearly two decades until the publication of the third and final volume in April 1831—and thus until the abrupt end of the actual travel report. Not long thereafter, in 1813, and again in Paris, Humboldt drafted his "Introduction" to *Ansichten der Kordilleren* and—despite numerous contradictions—would designate Ancient Greece as the locus of the world's cultures. Particularly in his *Vues des Cordillères et Monumens des Peuples Indigènes de l'Amérique*, Humboldt hands his readers a great deal of evidence for the diversity of the "monuments of the native peoples of America," which the Prussian scholar had scrupulously examined on his voyage through the most diverse regions of the Americas as well as in the libraries and archives of both the Old and New Worlds. Indeed, as his *Amerikanische Reisetagebücher* demonstrate, he had already learned much from the complexity of American cultures and would later become one of the founders of Native American Studies. Why, then, did he retain his bias toward Western antiquity—something which both his brother Wilhelm and the entire Western educational system would undoubtedly approve of—when, at the same time, he had developed a much broader, panoramic view of world cultures in his writings?

The contradictions in his œuvre would remain and even intensify. What might have prompted Humboldt to take two essentially disparate views on two distinct introductions to volumes written within a year of one another, each depicting important parts of his American travel work? Whereas in his travel report he resorted to the bromide of the American continent as the "realm of Nature"[14] which, apart from Europeans and Creoles, was populated by only "a few relics of indigenous, culturally underdeveloped hordes," in his *Ansichten der Kordilleren* he vehemently denounced the widely held prejudice that America was a continent bereft of culture and history prior to its "discovery":

> A people whose festivals were arranged according to the stars and whose calendar was engraved in a public monument probably had a higher level of civilization than it is granted by those sharp historians who have taken aim at America. These authors regarded as barbaric any such human condition far removed from a type of culture formed in accordance with certain systemic ideas they held. These rigid distinctions between barbarism and civilization are unacceptable.[15]

The alleged contrast between civilization and barbarism is in fact a constant source of controversy for Humboldt, something which we shall consider at a later point. Nevertheless, the contradictions between the two passages are striking, almost certainly owing to the fact that in the introduction of his travel report Alexander von Humboldt employed a popular cliché only to paint a much subtler portrait of the continent and its cultures at a later point in his *Relation historique*. Playing around with clichés and with the banal was by no means an uncommon Humboldtian practice: he loved to play with the expectations of his readers only to *disappoint* them in unexpected ways. Thus, the rigid dichotomy observed in the travel report between the two worlds in Humboldt's thought remains open to impugnment, especially since a "weaving flaw"—often a hallmark of his systematizing enumerations—managed to creep into the aforementioned account.

The supposedly clear division in the listings of world regions was ever so subtly fragmented by the addition of the hardly old-world South Sea Islands, which had been made famous by the travel reports of some Louis-Antoine de Bougainville, Georg Forster, or James Cook. It was with the aid of the small, apparently illogical deviations—the supposedly minor weaving flaws—that Humboldt succeeded in stripping his ideas of the dogmatic schematism which he decried as the "systematic ideas"[16] of Raynal, de Pauw, or Robertson. No, he did not seek systematic ideas.

Rather, he sought an empirical, material, and experimental basis for his vision without, of course, neglecting a theoretical view of the whole.

Both in the *Vues des Cordillères* as well as in the *Relation historique*, Humboldt proves himself fully capable of presenting the Old and New World as no longer fixed in opposition, but rather as complementary and mutually interactive. In the place of the absolute alterity that had prevailed in the so-called Berlin Debate on the New World, (see Bernaschina et al. 2015) he placed a kind of mutual interdependence which could underlie his basic formula *Alles ist Wechselwirkung*. Incidentally and unlike any of his contemporaries, he was practiced in citing cultural evidence for just such cases which, beyond the ephemeral traces of hunting populations and other nomadic tribes, rather impressively proved the presence of thriving indigenous cultures. For him, the division between civilization and barbarism constructed by dint of European pride was a chimera, both a foreign- and self-delusion.

Comparable contradictions in Humboldt's writing are also seen at other levels. What Humboldt in the first volume of his travel report denounced as "uniformity" and later in the third volume—in light of the sweeping dissemination of Spanish—heralded as an enduring "monument to national glory,"[17] was depicted in other writings as an important element in facilitating communication across national borders, which would soon benefit the future development of the Spanish-speaking world. He had already noted in his *Amerikanische Reisetagebücher* that of all the European languages, Spanish was "spoken by the largest number of people outside Europe."[18] Not even Arabic or Chinese had "spread over such a vast area from Nueva Galicia and California to Cape Horn, the Philippines and the Maluku Islands," and if one were to add Portuguese, which was closer to Castilian than Catalan or Valencian, then one could "include the whole of eastern India, Persia and the Asian archipelagoes, where Portuguese served as the language of commerce and business."[19] Although from a modern linguistic perspective the inclusion of lusophones amongst hispanophones is hardly permissible, Humboldt's reflections on Spanish as a world language are more pertinent today than ever.

The prevalence of Spanish was rivaled only by English, which in turn had spread over "the majority of North America and the West Indies, Bengal and Orissa, the coast of Madras."[20] But with altered political conditions, it was Spanish whose potential for development held the greatest promise:

> If the Spanish nation one day obtains political freedom and intellectual education, this dissemination of the nation's language will afford a great advantage primarily to Europeans. This will be particularly manifest in South America. That which is printed in Mexico can be read in Caracas, Lima, Buenos Aires and Manila. Such ease in the spread of ideas and sensibilities![21]

In this journal entry—penciled on his way to Bogotá on the Río Magdalena—Alexander von Humboldt conjured up the worldwide dissemination of those European languages on the New Continent, this "mapping" of a language atlas amplifying the contrast between North and South America—and thus between the "two Americas"—while at the same time transcending these hemispheric borders considerably. It was characteristic of Humboldt's manner of thinking and writing that even his listings of South American regions or capitals contained many inconsistencies, running contrary to any unifying logic. On the one hand, Mexico by no means belongs to the South American subcontinent—not even according to Humboldtian classification—and on the other hand, Manila—similar to the South Sea Islands in the list of places in the "Old World" discussed earlier—points beyond both South America and the entire American continent. Simple authorial lapses? Unlikely. So here, too, we come across more weaving flaws in a typical Humboldtian list of places and regions.

The frequent inconsistencies in Humboldt's lists and sequences may at first glance appear as mere slips. The frequency of his "oversights" should certainly make us sensitive to the fact that Humboldt, transcending fixed systematic ideas, was clearly concerned with the ever-changing perspectives of what prima facie appeared like simple demarcation lines. The lists of pictorial representations in his *Vues des Cordillères* also contain similar weaving flaws, the illusion of coherency a sleight of hand. Such weaving flaws always give rise to gaps in a list's consistency, and through such gaps different arrangement patterns and logics become tangible. And indeed, the individual parts of the *Vues des Cordillères* elude any consistent logic and arrangement.

We are thus initially astonished to discover that Humboldt's only systematic practices consist in traversing and undermining boundaries and divisions: fresh relationships and connections constantly pop up, terminology and perspectives appear in constant flux, and the inclusion of other phenomena always gives rise to new contexts which had previously been buried. And so arose a multi-perspectivity along with the flexible, modular divisions it affords which, owing to constant shifts and overlap between different spaces, bring into focus not the borders and the territories connected with them, but rather the relationships between individual areas and the possibilities for communication and exchange associated with them. Humboldt always offers his readers different ways of approaching the logic of a given phenomenon.

In this way, the internal relationality at the hemispheric level can be worked out in its complexity while still applying to the American hemisphere an external relationality which transcends the American frontiers, as Humboldt demonstrated with the example of languages as a means of communication *par excellence*.[22] Let us note, then, that Humboldt incorporated weaving flaws into many of his lists in order to undermine categorical classifications and to highlight transareal relationships. Behind the apparent order of a list lurks a force which pushes such order to its limits, giving way to other forms of logic.

THE *TABLEAU PHYSIQUE DES ANDES*

It is not possible in this limited context to exhaustively work through the hundreds, even thousands of lists riddled throughout Alexander von Humboldt's œuvre. The lists are too diverse to be presented critically in a single, brief overview. As such, beyond what has already been said, we can only attempt to present our considerations in a representative manner. Exemplary of this is the outstanding visualization of the Humboldtian science which, in a unique fashion, presents this concept of science in all its complexity while also capturing its integrative approach in a total view ("Totaleindruck").

So let us turn our attention to his spectacular *Tableau physique des Andes et Pays voisins*, well established as one of the most famous scientific representations of the entire nineteenth century. It goes back to a Humboldtian draft from 1802 in Guayaquil, Ecuador, which appeared in 1807 in a separate volume from his *Géographie des Plantes*, his first scientific book publication following his travels and also the foundation of phytogeography. Although it represents the state of his science around 1807 and was associated with that half-century of scientific activity, it is of fundamental importance for the entire *Opus Americanum*.

Relying both on ideas from pasigraphy as a formula language to immediately grasp complex relationships and on reflections concerning the total view or "Totaleindruck" from his brother Wilhelm von Humboldt,[23] Alexander von Humboldt's *Tableau physique* asserts a unity of nature and art. This is suggested not least by its German title, *Naturgemälde der Tropen*, which characterizes the work as the "painting" of nature. In this unique combination of science and aesthetics (aesthetics is here not to be understood as "ornamental" or "decorative," but rather as the true, artistically constructed nexus of knowledge between all areas of knowledge and science) the Prussian natural and cultural scientist was able to work out those elements of his voyage which best represented his manner of thinking, writing, and science. An emblem of the Humboldtian concept of science, the *Tableau physique* remains without a doubt unsurpassed by any of his other imaginings.

To begin, it ought to be emphasized that in that island-like stretch through the Andean volcanoes of Chimborazo and Cotopaxi, literally everything is in motion. Firstly, the continental shelf is moving: Humboldt had already noticed earlier how the contours of South America neatly fit into those of Africa, a fact which suggested a westward movement of the South American continent. Secondly, the entire geography, as represented in the tableau, is moving: the smoking maw of the volcano indicates that the rock which composes the volcanic cones is in constant "plutonic" motion. Thirdly, and most importantly, it is the plants that are on the move; and indeed, the phytogeography founded by Humboldt is not a mapping or static inventory of plant locations, but rather an investigation of the migration of plants on the surface of (and of the cryptogams below) the earth. Lastly, the various parameters such as the snow line and the various altitude levels are also in flux, the borders of both flattening out near the poles, as the *Tableau physique* notes.

It is not only nature and art that stand in such close relation in this particular *Naturgemälde* but also, and perhaps most importantly, text and image. This applies equally to both the painting itself as well as to the tables listed scientifically on either side of it, where Humboldt recorded his remarks and all measuring data imaginable. On the left hand side there appear heights listed in meters, followed by a list of height measurements of various great mountains across the globe, which at that time were known and verifiably measurable, from the peak of Chimborazo—in 1807 still considered to be the highest mountain in the world—all the way to Kinekulle in Sweden; then comes a list of electrical or weather phenomena at high altitudes followed by soil cultures as a function of altitude.

Within the previous list there is a bracketed addition from Humboldt reading: "Esclaves Africains introduits par les peuples civilisés de l'Europe." Here he clearly makes reference to the barbarism of civilization as well as to the civilization of barbarism exhibited in slavery and the slave trade, for which Europeans were responsible. The mention of African slaves also supports the presentation of a movement encompassing the entire range of nature and culture, for it was the devastating biopolitics of Europe with its enslavement and deportations that changed the population structure of the American colonial territories so fundamentally.

This addition anchors the *Naturgemälde der Tropen-Länder* without question within an ethical-political space of decisive importance for the Prussian researcher. At this point we are, of course, able to recognize one of Alexander von Humboldt's many weaving flaws and, at the same time, one of the lists which enabled him to evade pure schematics and which, naturally, incorporated the political into his scientific investigations. Indeed, this entry was doubtlessly a ruse which allowed him to allude to the burden of a colonial and colonialist past which, at that time, still persisted in the form of slavery.

Here is a cursory glance at the remaining tables or lists on the left-hand side: on the weakening of gravitation, on the blueness of the sky as determined with the aid of a cyanometer, on the decrease of humidity, and on air pressure measurements. Enough for now on the first ten listings on the left-hand side, which one could certainly examine in more detail.

The framing of the *Naturgemälde* featuring height scales in both toise and meters is carried onto the right-hand side and includes air temperature readings at various altitudes, measurements on the chemical composition of air, on the lower limit of perennial snow, information on animals located at various altitudes as well as on others such as crocodiles which do *not* inhabit that region. At this point, Humboldt sowed tiny seeds of potential narratives which he here only hints at, but which never develop into a full narrative. This is followed by information on the boiling point of water at different altitudes and on the respective geological conditions primarily of the Andes and the surrounding regions, but also with a view to relationships across the globe; here Humboldt also expressed some theories on the nature of the lowlands, plateaus, and peaks. And finally, there appears information on light intensity as a function of altitude as well as another scale with altitudes in toise.

These diverse listings possess something at once fascinating and disconcerting. On the one hand, they condense all those measurements which he had carried out during his journey through the American tropics in impressive fashion; on the other hand, they single out objects and phenomena which leave one wondering what sort of logic guided him and why he selected precisely these details instead of others. Indeed, he could have opted for completely different objects in his measurements; furthermore, it is easy to imagine a range of topics which Humboldt disregarded in his *Tableau physique*—lists on the highest established human settlements, on the location of important cities and capitals in relation to their altitude, or on the infrastructure of the Andean areas, to name but a few examples. There is no doubt that the lists obey a scientific logic within Humboldt's science but, at the same time, they possess a nature reminiscent of Jorge Luis Borges' list, which occasioned the epistemologist Foucault's laughter and prompted him to write *Les mots and les choses*. Yet it remains unclear which logic was at play as the Prussian selected his lists and equally unclear why some lists bear traits of narrative expressed to varying degrees.

The tables and listings which Alexander von Humboldt shows in his *Naturgemälde* correspond not only to the state of scientific knowledge he had arrived at in 1807. For more than fifty years—more than half a century still—he would continue to work on these observations, especially with regard to the American continent, and to expand his ideas considerably with respect to his illustration of phytogeography. From this point of view, it seems almost essential that Humboldt would have employed here an epistemology of expansion and enlargement—that his lists could have been printed as they were, but also in an utterly disparate manner while still retaining those weaving flaws which render them so readable and insightful for us today. Transdisciplinary to the core, his lists lead us down paths which traverse the Humboldtian science from all directions.

Researchers have tended to overlook the detailed title of his entire *Naturgemälde der Tropenländer*. The full title of the original French version reads: *Géographie des plantes équinoxiales. Tableau physique des Andes et Pays voisins. Dressé d'après des Observations & des Mesures prises sur les Lieux depuis le 10° de latitude boréale jusqu'au 10° de latitude australe en 1799, 1800, 1801, 1802 et 1803. Par Alexandre de Humboldt et Aimé Bonpland. Esquissé et rédigé par M. de Humboldt, dessiné par Schönberger et Turpin à Paris en 1805, gravé par Bouquet, la lettre par Beaublé, imprimé par Langlois.*

Its designation as *Tableau physique*[24] (like the German *Naturgemälde*) clearly demonstrates the mutual interrelation and influence of nature and culture (or art). Moreover, the title hints at the intimate collaboration between scientists and artists in the configuration of this particular cut through the Andes. The detailed title configures a group of authors of this *Tableau physique*. At the same time, the title gives sufficient indication of the breadth of collected measurements, which refer not only to Chimborazo, but to a large spatial-temporal expanse spanning his entire journey and, as such, represent a model which must be understood as a fractal of the entire South American subcontinent. The notes provided by the aforementioned French research team, which indicated that the data on plant height could not be verified on Chimborazo, appears to have already been anticipated in its title. To doubt the precision of the data and measurements in the *Tableau physique* would border on gross negligence, bearing in mind the exemplary character of Humboldt's visualization.

The textual entries in the *Naturgemälde der Tropenländer* themselves appear in three different forms. First, there are details about the journey itself such as the furthest point reached by Aimé Bonpland, Carlos Montúfar, and Humboldt on Chimborazo—yet another indication from the Prussian that they did not reach the summit. Second, the *Tableau* contains information on the altitudes which other expeditions in the Andes (such as those of Bouguet and La Condamine) or the Alps (such as those of Saussure) had reached, while also recording the world record for the highest altitude achieved during the ascent of a French hot air balloon shortly thereafter. Lastly, information is provided which is not merely comparative, but also relational in nature. This includes not only references to mountains that Humboldt climbed in other areas (such as Popocatépetl), but also elevations on a global scale, as his reference to Vesuvius demonstrates. Rather than drawing comparisons, these entries engender relations and thereby express Humboldt's fundamental and *transareal* understanding of the globe.

The lists of Alexander von Humboldt are thus truly wonders unto themselves. They serve the Prussian researcher's discontinuous writing style and, in many respects, can be described not only as multilingual, as are his writings, but also multilogical. They contain narrative cores, some of which Humboldt developed elsewhere, or introduce fundamentally different themes such as slavery and the barbarism of "civilized" Europeans, thereby introducing a fundamental ethical dimension to the aesthetics of the *Tableau physique*. They represent forms of writing that Humboldt employed in his travel manuscripts, but also in his printed scientific treatises as a means of naming factors involved in the fundamental process of mutual interactivity.

Last but not least, the lists and enumerations throughout Humboldt's œuvre evince their own imaginative nature, evidence that their author created them to convert the burdens of the past or present into a delight that could shape and enrich both knowledge and science. They are lists of an epistemology of constant expansion and thus allow us to occasionally make out the gentle laughter of the list-making author.

NOTES

1. For more on this topic and on the complex, asymmetrical relations to Latin American literature, see Ette (1994).
2. For a scientific overview of the various aspects of Humboldt's work, see Ette (2018).
3. See the "Preface to the second and third edition" (dated March, 1849) of his *Ansichten der Natur, mit wissenschaftlichen Erläuterungen*, 9.
4. See Humboldt, Alexander von, *Die Jugendbriefe 1787–1799*, 74.
5. See Humboldt, Wilhelm von, *Briefe an Karl Gustav von Brinkmann*, 60.
6. See the German edition from Humboldt, Alexander von: *Ansichten der Kordilleren und Monumente der eingeborenen Völker Amerikas*, (2004).
7. Humboldt, Alexander von, *Reise auf dem Río Magdalena, durch die Anden und Mexico*, vol. I: Texte, 358.
8. All quotations from Humboldt are original translations by Nathan Anderson, who rendered this article into English. In this instance, see Humboldt, Alexander von: *Reise auf dem Magdalena, durch die Anden und Mexiko*, vol. 2, 254.
9. See Humboldt, Alexander von, *Das Buch der Begegnungen*, 236.
10. See Humboldt, Alexander von, *Das Buch der Begegnungen*, 270.
11. See Humboldt, Alexander von, *Das Buch der Begegnungen*, 315.
12. See Humboldt, Alexander von, *Reise in die Äquinoktial-Gegenden des Neuen Kontinents* vol. I, 40.
13. See Humboldt, Alexander von, *Reise in die Äquinoktial-Gegenden des Neuen Kontinents*, vol. I, 35–36.
14. See Humboldt, Alexander von, *Reise in die Äquinoktial-Gegenden des Neuen Kontinents*, vol. I, 35–36.
15. See Humboldt, Alexander von, *Vues des Cordillères*, 194.
16. See Humboldt, Alexander von, *Vues des Cordillères*, 194.
17. See Bernaschina, Kraft and Kraume (2015), vol. II, 1462.
18. See Humboldt, Alexander von, *Reise auf dem Río Magdalena, durch die Anden und Mexico*, vol. I, 75.

19. See Humboldt, Alexander von, *Reise auf dem Río Magdalena, durch die Anden und Mexico,* vol. I, 75.
20. See Humboldt, Alexander von, *Reise auf dem Río Magdalena, durch die Anden und Mexico,* vol. I, 75.
21. See Humboldt, Alexander von, *Reise auf dem Río Magdalena, durch die Anden und Mexico,* vol. I, 75.
22. Regarding the spatial-geographical, temporal, social, literary, genre-specific, intermedial, and cultural dimensions of this new American discourse, see Ette (2004).
23. See Trabant (1986); Hard (1970); Schneider (2016).
24. See the important work on this aspect of Humboldt's science by Kraft (2014); it is this work which provided me with the note on African slavery in *Tableau physique.*

References

Bernaschina, Vicente, Tobias Kraft, and Anne Kraume, eds. 2015. *Globalisierung in Zeiten der Aufklärung: Texte und Kontexte zur „Berliner Debatte" um die Neue Welt (17./18. Jh.).* 2 vols. Frankfurt/Main: Peter Lang Edition.

Bispinck-Roßbachere, Julia. 2016. Ein Blick in die Tiefe – Kodikologische und materialtechnologische Untersuchungen an den Manuskripten Alexander von Humboldts. In *Horizonte der Humboldt-Forschung: Natur, Kultur, Schreiben,* ed. Ottmar Ette and Julian Drews, 193–205. Hildesheim/Zürich/New York: Georg Olms Verlag.

Descombes, Vincent. 1981. *Das Selbe und das Andere: Fünfundvierzig Jahre Philosophie in Frankreich 1933. 1978.* Trans. Ulrich Raulff. Frankfurt/Main: Suhrkamp.

Eco, Umberto. 2009. *Die unendliche Liste.* Trans. Barbara Kleiner. Munich: Carl Hanser Verlag.

Ette, Ottmar. 1994. Asymmetrie der Beziehungen: Zehn Thesen zum Dialog der Literaturen Lateinamerikas und Europas. In *Lateinamerika denken: Kulturtheoretische Grenzgänge zwischen Moderne und Postmoderne,* ed. Birgit Scharlau, 297–326. Tübingen: Gunter Narr Verlag.

———. 2004. Die Ordnung der Weltkulturen: Alexander von Humboldts Ansichten der Kultur. *HiN – Alexander von Humboldt im Netz. Internationale Zeitschrift für Humboldt-Studien* 5 (9): 8–29. https://www.hin-online.de/index.php/hin/article/view/50. Accessed 7 Jan 2021.

———. 2016. Weiter denken: Viellogisches denken/viellogisches Denken und die Wege zu einer Epistemologie der Erweiterung. *Romanistische Zeitschrift für Literaturgeschichte/Cahiers d'Histoire des Littératures Romanes (Heidelberg)* XL (1–4): 331–355.

———, ed. 2018. *Alexander von Humboldt Handbuch. Leben – Werk – Wirkung.* Mit 52 Abbildungen. Stuttgart: J.B. Metzler Verlag – Springer Nature.

Ette, Ottmar, and Julia Maier. 2018. *Alexander von Humboldt: Bilder-Welten. Die Zeichnungen aus den Amerikanischen Reisetagebüchern.* Munich/London/New York, Prestel.

Foucault, Michel. 1970. *The Order of Things: An Archaeology of the Human Sciences.* New York: Vintage.

Hard, Gerhard. 1970. „Der Totaleindruck der Landschaft": Re-Interpretation einer Textstelle bei Alexander von Humboldt. In *Alexander von Humboldt: Eigene und neue Wertungen der Reisen. Arbeit und Gedankenwelt,* ed. Herbert Wilhelmy, Gerhard Engelmann, and Gerhard Hard, 49–73. Wiesbaden: Steiner.

Kehlmann, Daniel. 2005. *Die Vermessung der Welt.* Reinbek: Rowohlt.

Kraft, Tobias. 2014. *Figuren des Wissens bei Alexander von Humboldt: Essai, Tableau und Atlas im amerikanischen Reisewerk.* Berlin/Boston: de Gruyter.

Moret, Pierre, et al. 2019. Humboldt's Tableau Physique Revisited. *PNAS* 116 (26): 12889–12894. https://doi.org/10.1073/pnas.1904585116.

Schneider, Birgit. 2016. Der „Totaleindruck einer Gegend": Alexander von Humboldts synoptische Visualisierung des Klimas. In *Horizonte der Humboldt-Forschung,* ed. Ottmar Ette and Julian Drews, 53–78. Hildesheim/Zürich/New York: Georg Olms Verlag.

Thiele, Matthias. 2016. „Im Angesicht der Dinge": Ambulatorische Aufzeichnungspraktiken und Schreibtechniken des Notierens bei Alexander von Humboldt mit Seitenblicken auf Georg Forster, Thomas Jefferson und Adelbert von Chamisso. In *Horizonte der Humboldt-Forschung: Natur, Kultur, Schreiben,* ed. Ottmar Ette and Julian Drews, 319–348. Hildesheim/Zürich/New York: Georg Olms Verlag.

Trabant, Jürgen. 1986. Der Totaleindruck: Stil der Texte und Charakter der Sprachen. In *Stil. Geschichte und Funktionen eines kulturwissenschaftlichen Diskurselements,* ed. Hans Ulrich Gumbrecht and Karl Ludwig Pfeiffer, 169–188. Frankfurt/Main: Suhrkamp.

von Humboldt, Alexander. 1939. *Briefe an Karl Gustav von Brinkmann.* Ed. Albert Leitzmann. Leipzig.

———. 1973. *Die Jugendbriefe 1787–1799.* Ed. Ilse Jahn and Fritz G. Lange. Berlin: Akademie-Verlag.

———. 1986a. *Ansichten der Natur, mit wissenschaftlichen Erläuterungen.* Nördlingen: Greno.

———. 1986b. *Reise auf dem Río Magdalena, durch die Anden und Mexico.* Teil I: Texte. Aus seinen Reisetagebüchern zusammengestellt und erläutert durch Margot Faak. Mit einer einleitenden Studie von Kurt-R. Biermann. Berlin: Akademie-Verlag.

———. 1991. *Reise in die Äquinoktial-Gegenden des Neuen Kontinents. Mit Anmerkungen zum Text, einem Nachwort und zahlreichen zeitgenössischen*

Abbildungen sowie einem farbigen Bildteil. 2 vols. Ed. Ottmar Ette. Frankfurt/Main: Insel Verlag.

———. 2004. *Ansichten der Kordilleren und Monumente der eingeborenen Völker Amerikas.* Trans. Claudia Kalscheuer and Ed. Oliver Lubrich and Ottmar Ette. Frankfurt/Main: Eichborn Verlag.

———. 2018. *Das Buch der Begegnungen: Menschen – Kulturen – Geschichten aus den Amerikanischen Reisetagebüchern.* Ed. and Trans. Ottmar Ette. Mit Originalzeichnungen Humboldts sowie historischen Landkarten und Zeittafeln. Munich: Manesse Verlag.

Lists Versus Narratives

Don't Trust the List: The Politics of Enumeration and Capitalist Discourse in the Novel

Eva von Contzen

In Chapter XIV of Laurence Sterne's first volume of *The Life and Opinions of Tristram Shandy, Gentleman*, published in 1759, Tristram muses about the pitfalls of writing historiography. If history writing were as straightforward as a direct journey between two places—a direct route from Rome to Loretto—it could be accomplished in a very short period of time. But, alas, as Tristram points out, this is "morally impossible":

> For, if he [the historiographer] is a man of the least spirit, he will have fifty deviations from a straight line to make with this or that party as he goes

This article was written as part of the research conducted in the project *Lists in Literature and Culture* (LISTLIT), funded by the European Research Council Starting Grant no. 715021.

E. von Contzen (✉)
University of Freiburg, Freiburg, Germany
e-mail: eva.voncontzen@anglistik.uni-freiburg.de

R. A. Barton et al. (eds.), *Forms of List-Making: Epistemic, Literary, and Visual Enumeration*,
https://doi.org/10.1007/978-3-030-76970-3_6

along, which he can no ways avoid. He will have views and prospects to himself perpetually soliciting his eye, which he can no more help standing still to look at than he can fly; he will moreover have various

Accounts to reconcile:
Anecdotes to pick up:
Inscriptions to make out:
Stories to weave in:
Traditions to sift:
Personages to call upon:
Panegyricks to paste up at this door;

Pasquinades at that:——All which both the man and his mule are quite exempt from. To sum up all; there are archives at every stage to be look'd into, and rolls, records, documents, and endless genealogies, which justice ever and anon calls him back to stay the reading of:——In short there is no end of it. (34–35)

The point Tristram makes here about historiography in general and his autobiography in particular is that it is arduous because it involves including many diverse sources and following sheer endless new paths. Typographically, the many possibilities for being led astray are presented in list form. The items of this list in turn point to further distinctions and ramifications and thus imply further lists. At the same time, the entries are linked to writing practices and literary artifacts: "archives [...] and rolls, records, documents, and endless genealogies." Formally as well as epistemologically, we are concerned with practices of listing.

Tristram foresees that his task will keep him busy for a lifetime: "I shall continue to do as long as I live" (35). It is not a coincidence that Sterne makes this point about Tristram's literary endeavor by using a list and that he refers to material that involves further lists. Not only are lists a key form of historical records, the argument also works the other way around: our lives can be abstracted in the form of lists; who we are, where we come from, to which groups we belong, which alliances we enter, which choices of place, faith, or possession we make, there will be traces of them in the form of lists—from our CVs and various kinds of statistics of which we form a part to genealogies, databases, social network sites, and so on. On yet another level, the passage also highlights the close interdependence of lists as containers of abstract, reductive knowledge on the one hand, and their inherent potential to offer material for constructing, or reconstructing, larger contexts, even narratives out of the individual items on the other.

The passage from Sterne's novel can be read as a concise overview of the versatility of lists: it reaches from practical contexts of ordering and archiving the world to providing the cues for narrating one's own life. Readers of the present volume will also have encountered a wide range of lists that span several centuries: from lists in the context of *Res Gestae Divi Augusti* and the *Arma Christi* tradition to the character sketch, Humboldt's tableau physique, experimental poetry, and children's literature. The range of media under discussion likewise reflects the versatility of the list form: lists can be written on bronze tablets, parchment, paper; they come in and as manuscript illuminations, images and photos, but also occur in periodicals, notebooks, and as hybrids between text and image. Their functions are manifold: to teach, to delight, to satirize, to create unrest, to gather or produce knowledge, to provide order, to commemorate, and so on.

One aspect that is implicit also in all of the essays assembled in this volume is that of the politics of the list—that is, the structures of power that underlie the list-making process in the first place (De Goede et al. 2016).[1] To various degrees, all essays grapple with the question of power relations and the list's capacity to undermine knowledge—sometimes even the very same knowledge a list establishes. Humboldt's "weaving flaws," that is, the deliberate incorporation of mistakes within the list, are a prime example of this strategy.[2] When Augustus and Gregory of Tours inscribe themselves into their lists,[3] they draw attention to the list-maker and offer insight into the power structures that made both the list and that which is listed possible. In poetry, lists are often indicative of the poet's life and times, verging into the testimonial, as the recipe poems and "Howl" illustrate.[4] A self-reflexive dimension is particularly striking also in many poetological lists, as the examples by Barthes and Calvino demonstrate.[5] In pragmatic contexts, by contrast, this meta-level tends to be absent. The lists in medieval rabbinic literature, the *Arma Christi* images, or table of contents do not invite a critical reflection on the how and why (or who) of their assembly.[6] Yet investigating the agenda behind these lists becomes all the more critical because we, as readers and potential users of the lists, may too quickly take for granted the principles and categories they offer. Against this backdrop, I am going to approach the list as a form that begs a suspicious reading. I first outline the premises and consequences of such a suspicious reading before I turn to selected examples of lists in the context of capitalism to illustrate my argument.

THE LIST AS FORM: AFFORDANCE AND SUSPICION

In a number of the essays in this volume, as well as in the introduction, the authors draw on Robert Belknap's definition of lists:

> At their most simple, lists are frameworks that hold separate and disparate items together. Lists are plastic, flexible structures in which an array of constituent units coheres through specific relations generated by specific forces of attraction. (2004, 2)

This definition is useful in several respects. Belknap directs our attention to the fact that every list has two dimensions: the immediately recognizable form of the list as a whole, and the individual items that make up the list. The one could not exist without the other. As a fixed form (or framework, as Belknap calls it), the list is static; a container of its items. These items, however, are not random; there is coherence between them. This coherence can be very loose, hence Belknap's careful phrasing "specific forces of attraction" that hold the items together. What a list is "about" can thus be approached from two different perspectives, one from within, the other from the outside. The frame "shopping list" already defines the items of said list; the individual items cohere because they fall under this heading. On the other hand, it is also possible to find a list that reads "eggs, cheese, 2 bottles of wine, tissues, 1 cucumber" and deduce from that list that it must be a shopping list. In the latter case, the items themselves create coherence by their shared context of what a supermarket has on offer. Importantly, lists do not create coherence in and of themselves— they require a reader, an interpreter, a user to connect the individual items and make sense of them. List-making and dealing with lists are fundamentally cognitive acts. In literary texts, authors can actively factor in their readership's practical knowledge of lists in the real world and invite them to reflect on the practice of list-making itself, in other words, the experience of making lists (von Contzen 2018).

While Belknap's definition is certainly helpful in highlighting the double nature of lists, it does not take into account the processual and dynamic thrust of the list as form. Caroline Levine goes one step further: she argues that form itself is dynamic, contradictory, and hybrid. Crucially, Levine also points to the inherent political entanglements of form in order to make sense of the complexity therein. Form is not an end in itself, but it conveys additional meaning, it has (overt or latent) purposes and functions. These purposes and functions may not be obvious, they may not even be necessary to be disclosed in order to make sense of a particular form. They can be understood as affordances: those aspects a particular form implies, may engender, may be "*capable* of doing" (2015, 6; emphasis in the original). Different forms, Levine argues, lay claim to different affordances. These affordances are dependent on the context; they are not isolated but set in dialogue with other organizing principles:

> [A] form does its work only in contexts where other political and aesthetic forms also are operating. A variety of forms are in motion around us, constraining materials in a range of ways and imposing their order in situated contexts where they constantly overlap other forms. Form emerges from this perspective as transhistorical, portable, and abstract, on the one hand, and material, situated, and political, on the other. (Levine 2015, 11)

Levine discusses wholes, rhythms, hierarchies, and networks as examples of forms. I would like to add the list to this list. The list is highly versatile: it is a simple form that can be used—exploited—to various purposes and thus attains transhistorical status. It is portable, crossing centuries, contexts, genres, and functions. It is also abstract—irrespective of how a list is used, it remains a list.[7] Levine's approach becomes particularly useful if one considers list-making as a cultural technique in its interdependence on changes in media, such as the changes from manuscript culture to book culture; from print culture to the internet age; from computer-based media to portable devices. These changes are not teleological; rather, the different media lead to new contexts in which lists can be used. The form of the list itself has remained stable throughout technological advancements, perhaps because it is so "simple," formally, and can be adapted easily (hence the list as "transhistorical").[8]

For Levine, the affordance-based approach to form necessarily entails a political dimension, in her words "*a generalizable understanding of political power*" (2015, 7; emphasis in the original). From a sociological perspective, Urs Stäheli tackles lists in very similar terms. He does not use the term "affordance," but what he describes is essentially a plea for including the affordances of lists in our theoretical discussions about this form and its political dimension:

> My argument is that the politics of lists has to account for the specific epistemic practices which go along with list-making – and it is only possible to

understand these practices if we account for the particular operations which the format of the list enables. From such a perspective, list-making is not only a problem of selection, but it is necessarily a transformative and performative practice: it produces the items which the list will comprise. It is the epistemic power of these practices which I call the invisible politics of lists. (Stäheli 2016, 14)

Stäheli analyzes how data, that is, individual items of information, are turned into lists; he is interested in the "transformative work" that *precedes* the making of lists (2016, 15). His approach is indebted to practice theory. Practice theory underlines the embeddedness of cultural productions and actions not only in a network of people acting and interacting with things and other people, but also in implicit knowledge systems and scripts of procedures.[9] What all kinds of lists share, no matter where or when they are used, is that they represent and reflect a certain order. Lists are tools for structuring and ordering the world. As such, they also imply power relations. Lists convey hierarchies: even in a list that seems random, there is no doubt that the first item takes precedence, simply because we read it first. In addition, the mere fact that something is included in a list means that other items are excluded. Lists are the result of selection and choice. Who or what has "made it" onto a list is itself already a matter of power (Stäheli 2016, 26).

On the surface, the list form signals objectivity and transparency. Lists invite a reading that focuses on their surface structure. It is tempting, then, to approach lists from the perspective of what has been termed "surface reading" by Stephen Best and Sharon Marcus. Best and Marcus's approach attunes to the surface of texts, that is, to "what is evident, perceptible, apprehensible in texts; what is neither hidden nor hiding; what, in the geometrical sense, has length and breadth but no thickness, and therefore covers no depth" (2009, 9). Surface reading is essentially descriptive reading; a way of approaching texts that reads, in Heather Love's phrase, closely but not deeply (2010). Lists are surface forms par excellence: they are immediately recognizable as lists, and often a superficial glance will (seemingly) reveal what they are about. Lists don't tell, they show; they require looking, not reading (Mainberger 2003, 267).[10]

Yet, when it comes to lists, surface reading (which the form very much invites), can be dangerous. The list form, in fact, calls for a symptomatic and suspicious reading. In their introduction to the special issue in *Environment and Planning D: Society and Space* on "The Politics of the

List," Marieke de Goede et al. draw attention to the politics of "the assumed prosaic nature of lists" (2016, 5) in contexts of law, regulation, and governance. The essays in their issue focus on "lists that *disguise themselves* as practical and coherent" (2016, 5; emphasis in the original). The special political force of lists, they argue, lies "(partly) in producing contingent referentialities that come to appear as obvious, and in drawing together disparate items that come to appear as commensurate" (ibid). One cannot stress enough that any list could also have been drawn up in a different way. Any system of order (or disorder) that appears in list form is preceded by the positing of this system, by the decision to set up the list in this way and not another. Analyzing lists, whether in everyday practical usage or in literary, aesthetic contexts, thus calls for a general distrust of the list as form. Only by reading symptomatically, by questioning the reasons for the list, by asking for the author(s) and authority behind it (its *cui bono?*), by deconstructing the systematization it offers, by discussing the effects in light of the performative function of the list can one do justice to this seemingly straightforward form. Despite their ostensible simplicity, lists are structures of power.

In what follows, I provide a case study of the close interdependence of everyday practices of list-making and power relations in literary texts that thematize, in the broadest sense, capitalism and its effects on the individual and on personal relationships. One could even argue that the list is the ultimate tool of exerting capitalist power: lists help us to manage the things we own, to count and measure them, to express our desire for possession and consumption, to tempt our desires in the first place.

Lists and Capitalist Discourse in the Novel

The New Economic Criticism has emphasized the multifarious links and overlaps between economic conditions and systems and literary texts.[11] We can add a further dimension to the existing approaches by focusing on the interrelationships between the specific formal arrangements of the list and how it is used in capitalist discourses. In doing so, I consider list-making as a practice that transgresses any implicit or assumed boundaries between the realms of aesthetic works on the one hand and "the real world" and its economic conditions on the other. I stress this point because one frequently comes across a distinction between "poetic" and "pragmatic" lists, originally made by Umberto Eco in *The Infinity of Lists*, which is both misleading and problematic. According to Eco, pragmatic lists, such as the shopping list, a guest list, or a library catalogue, "have a purely referential function, in other words they refer to objects in the outside world and have the purely practical purpose of naming and listing them" (2009, 113). Poetic lists, by contrast, he argues, comply with "any artistic end for which the list was proposed" (ibid.). Pragmatic lists, for Eco, are finite because they serve a practical purpose that limits these lists; the prime purpose of poetic ones, however, is to transcend finiteness and reach toward infinity, explore the margins, the ever-more, the whole world. Lists that occur in literary texts (which thus qualify as "poetic" lists) and that negotiate capitalist values, though, complicate Eco's distinction. Here the list form, in its poetic, aesthetic usage, deliberately aligns itself with the pragmatic implications of the kind of lists we make in everyday life for practical purposes. Such poetic lists that negotiate economic concerns do not make sense without the pragmatic backdrop of lists in everyday life.

The Life and Strange Adventures of Robinson Crusoe, of York, Mariner by Daniel Defoe is a case in point. The book, often hailed as the first English novel, was published in 1719. Even though—or rather, because—Robinson Crusoe, stranded on the island, is outside of any social structures and contact with other human beings, he takes careful measures to record everything he does. The form of the list is ubiquitous in this enterprise. Robinson keeps a journal in which he notes his observations and actions from right after his shipwreck until he has run out of ink (see 2012, 66–68); he provides a list of the changing seasons on the island (103); there are accounts of which items of food and clothing he stores, of the things he retrieves from the shipwreck (51–53); and a list of positive and negative ("good" and "evil") aspects of his present situation (63). Robinson frames this list of the pros and cons of the shipwreck in financial-administrative terms:

> I now began to consider seriously my condition, and the circumstance I was reduc'd to [...] I began to comfort my self as well as I could, and to set the good against the evil, that I might have something to distinguish my case from worse, and I stated it very impartially, like debtor and creditor, the comforts I enjoy'd, against the miseries I suffer'd. (Defoe 2012, 63)

Paradoxically, Robinson is a proto-capitalist in a society of one. He cannot help but construe his situation in terms that are oriented toward a system which is based on the exchange of goods and in which commodities define the self. For instance, we are given the following list of items he recovers from the shipwreck:

> I brought away several things very useful to me; as first, in the carpenter's stores I found two or three bags full of nails and spikes, a great skrew-jack, a dozen or two of hatchets, and above all, that most useful thing call'd a grind-stone; all these I secur'd together, with several things belonging to the gunner, particularly two or three iron crows, and two barrels of musquet-bullets, seven musquets, and another fowling-piece, with some small quantity of powder more; a large bag full of small shot, and a great roll of sheet lead. But this last was so heavy, I could not hoist it up to get it over the ship's side. (Defoe 2012, 51)

Robinson survives because he upholds capitalist ideas and ideals, even though his whole situation could not be further removed from them: there is no market, no production, no demand, no consumption that could influence a potential market. Critics have of course noted the novel's richness of material details and their proto-capitalist contexts, in particular its indebtedness to early eighteenth-century social and political discourses.[12] I want to put emphasis on the link between this preoccupation with economic discourses and the form of the list. On the one hand, the list is the form most evidently linked to administration and management; it reduces complexity, it provides order, and it signals clarity and stability. These functions hold true for household management just as much as they do for contexts of trading and globalization. At the same time, the list also fulfills the function of keeping Robinson sane. Dorothee Birke has situated the lists in the novel within the context of the protagonist's mental processes. She argues that the lists are indicative of Robinson's struggles with despair and isolation and function as "exercises in rational self-control" (2016, 304). Robinson masters the island by transforming his experiences into lists, in the form of a calendar, a journal, and inventories of goods. In *Robinson Crusoe*, then, the list brings together struggles of identity and proto-capitalist thinking. The two go hand in hand: Robinson's identity is defined by and ultimately stabilized by his activity as a member of a (absent but imagined) market society. His list-making is thus driven by the desire for a return to a society whose rules and values he has internalized. The list is the prime medium of translating these desires and possessions into words and thus into the narrative: Ultimately, the message is that even in complete isolation, human beings are *homines economici.*

My second example is taken from Charles Dickens's novel *Little Dorrit* (1855–1857). In the following extract, Daniel Doyce and Arthur Clennam visit the Meagles, who are friends of Clennam's. In the Meagles's house, they encounter Mr. Meagles's curious collection of souvenirs:

> Of articles collected on his various expeditions, there was such a vast miscellany that it was like the dwelling of an amiable Corsair. There were antiquities from Central Italy, made by the best modern houses in that department of industry; bits of mummy from Egypt (and perhaps Birmingham); model gondolas from Venice; model villages from Switzerland; morsels of tesselated pavement from Herculaneum and Pompeii, like petrified minced veal; ashes out of tombs, and lava out of Vesuvius; Spanish fans, Spezzian straw hats, Moorish slippers, Tuscan hairpins, Carrara sculpture, Trastaverini scarves, Genoese velvets and filigree, Neapolitan coral, Roman cameos, Geneva jewellery, Arab lanterns, rosaries blest all round by the Pope himself, and an infinite variety of lumber. There were views, like and unlike, of a multitude of places; and there was one little picture-room devoted to a few of the regular sticky old Saints, with sinews like whipcord, hair like Neptune's, wrinkles like tattooing, and such coats of varnish that every holy personage served for a fly-trap, and became what is now called in the vulgar tongue a Catch-em-alive O. Of these pictorial acquisitions Mr Meagles spoke in the usual manner. He was no judge, he said, except of what pleased himself; he had picked them up, dirt-cheap, and people *had* considered them rather fine. (Dickens 2008, 192–193)

The primary function of this (descriptive) list is clearly to poke fun at Mr. Meagles.[13] Given how eclectic and fraudulent the collection is, Mr. Meagles, who is a former banker, comes across as someone who wants to make the impression of being well-traveled and a connoisseur of art when in truth he is neither. His relationship to these possessions is complex: he claims they were "dirt-cheap" but that other people, too, considered them "rather fine." The items bear witness to an itinerary that ranges from various places in Italy, Switzerland, and Spain all the way to Egypt. His desire to collect is also an attempt to control the world, to bring it into his home. Mr. Meagles's "market" is a global one (even though most of the places turn out to be relatively close by) and linked to travel. We can situate this type of souvenir or kitsch list in the wider context of Victorian commodities and the Great Exhibition of 1851 in London.[14] As in *Robinson Crusoe,* and also similar to the character sketch,[15] goods here are a means of characterization—Mr. Meagles aims at being perceived in a certain way (a man of the world) while at the same time he is disclosed as being something else (artsy, ignorant). The form of the list encapsulates Mr. Meagles's self-understanding as a man of possession; he is what he owns, or rather, he wishes to be judged by that which he owns. The list thus functions as a means of indirect communication between the narrator and reader that allows us to share a certain opinion about Mr. Meagles's character behind his back.

In both Crusoe and Dickens, the form of the list—lists of objects and material belongings in particular—is used to impart information about a character's relationship to society and to consumption. We have seen that there is a strong element of self-definition, as in Robinson Crusoe's case, who upholds capitalist ideals even in isolation. Mr. Meagles, too, defines himself by what he has acquired, though the result is not quite what he may have envisaged. In his case, the fraudulent nature of the souvenirs renders any genuine effort to be a respected traveler vain to the point of absurdity.

In contemporary literature, literary texts continue to capitalize on lists in order to express their protagonists' sense of self, their material desires, and often also their personal relationships in the form of wish lists, gift lists, and shopping lists. These lists often establish a direct connection to the real world—online retailers, for instance, take advantage of the power of lists and provide the opportunity to create one's own wish list and saving items for later purchases. Against the backdrop of an ever-growing marketing machine that exploits the form of the list in order to speak to our material desires, it is small wonder that literary texts, too, complicate the relationship between possessing, purchasing, and desiring. The metaphor of love as a commodity, and the overlaps, gray areas, and conscious slips between love-making and prostitution are by no means new discoveries. What is new is that authors set love explicitly in these materialist contexts by using the form of the list.[16]

A good example of the use of lists and their economic, capitalist affordance is Nick Hornby's 1995 novel *High Fidelity*. The protagonist, Rob, seems to be a lost cause when it comes to finding—and keeping—a lover. Rob is a passionate lover of music; he works in a record store and occasionally DJs, too. He orders his world according to the music he likes and associates with events and people. In doing so, he relies on the form of the hit list. Hit lists, like wish lists, are expressions of material desire. Whereas wish lists are prospective (they contain wishes that have not yet been ful-filled), hit lists are retrospective (they are based on the information of how many albums or singles were sold). Rob's lists are retrospective and highly subjective. In fact, the whole plot of *High Fidelity* is based on such a hit list: Rob's five worst split-ups. The very beginning of the novel is as follows:

> My desert-island, all-time, top five most memorable split-ups, in chrono-logical order:
>
> 1. Alison Ashworth
> 2. Penny Hardwick
> 3. Jackie Allen
> 4. Charlie Nicholson
> 5. Sarah Kendrew (Hornby 2014, 1)

Rob, who is in a confused emotional state after his separation from his girlfriend Laura (with whom he is still in love), decides to visit the five former girlfriends from his list in order to find out why they broke up with him in each case. Rob's behavior toward women is highly questionable—in the words of Barry Faulk, the novel "proffers the voyeuristic charm of getting to know male psychology at its most asocial" (2007, 154), yet it does so "by disarming a romantically dysfunctional, but well-intentioned and maturing white male" (154). One symptom of Rob's "dysfunctional" handling of his personal relationship is his obsessive list-making that also informs his attitude toward women. Rob turns his former girlfriends into objects which can be ordered and ranked just like his favorite songs. Since the narrative is told from Rob's perspective, we only gradually learn why Laura left—he cheated on her while she was pregnant. In the course of the novel, Rob comes to recognize that much of the blame lies with him. By the time he gets back together with Laura (though she does not accept his marriage proposal), his process of learning has reached its peak. It may not be a coincidence that the density of lists decreases toward the end of the novel. The fact that Rob does not need the list as a form of managing his life as much as he did at the beginning of the novel may suggest that his attitude toward women, and his understanding of love and relationships, too, has changed for the better. Instead of objectifying his personal rela-tions, and thereby distancing himself from any actual confrontation with reasons and causes, he has learned to pay attention to others' feelings.

Behind each item of his "hit list" of the worst breakups, there is, after all, a whole story not just about Rob's hurt feelings, but the women's feelings, too.

Another protagonist who in a similar vein struggles to manage her life is Bridget Jones in Helen Fielding's 1996 novel *Bridget Jones's Diary*. As a diary, the entries already form a list of items, ordered chronologically. The novel begins with a list of New Year's Resolutions, and within the entries of the diary, there are lists of food and drinks consumed, but also other types of lists, such as guest lists, schedules, and shopping lists.[17] The main function of the lists in *Bridget Jones's Diary* is to characterize the eponymous heroine as someone who fails in getting her life together. Her inspiration for using lists is taken from self-help books, which recommend excessive self-monitoring. Both Rob's and Bridget Jones's lists can be read in the trajectory of what Eva Illouz has termed "emotional capitalism." According to Illouz, "emotional capitalism" describes

> a culture in which emotional and economical discourses and practices mutually shape each other, thus producing [...] a broad, sweeping movement in which affect is made an essential aspect of economic behaviour and in which emotional life – especially that of the middle classes – follows the logic of economic relations and exchange. (2007, 5)

High Fidelity is a good example of these processes. Rob, as a passionate lover of rock music, has internalized the principles of hit lists and charts to the extent that the economic logic of the music market has come to shape his perspective on his personal life, in particular his ex-girlfriends. What classic rock is to Bob is what self-help literature is to Bridget Jones. According to Illouz, the trend of a rationalization and intellectualization of personality that emerged in the 1980s was closely associated with advice literature for women, especially on the theme of intimacy (2007, 30–32). By writing down emotions—and this was explicitly advised—one could detach one's emotions from the self and thus control them. Bridget's excessive list-making thus becomes a symptom of capitalist society in which Bridget attempts to write not her own autobiography but oughta-biography, the way she wants to appear based on societal norms and expectations.[18] Not only are Bridget's love life and identity intertwined in the form of the list, they are also converted into capital that she tries to manage and invest wisely. The effect—Bridget's constant failure to live up

to her expectations—is of course comic and ultimately lays bare how problematic the perspective on relationships as economic capital is.

While Bridget Jones uses the list as an exercise in self-control and performing adulthood, the heroine of Julian Barnes's 1998 novel *England,
England* (Martha Cochrane) uses the list as a way of coping with her love
life and distancing herself from her own experiences. Here the management of her capital "love" is reified in the form of the list. At one point,
Martha reflects upon her love life so far. The list is entitled "A brief history
of sexuality in the case of Martha Cochrane" and begins with the stages of
Martha's sexual experiences, from "1. Innocent Discovery" to "7. The
Pursuit of Separateness" and "8. The Current Situation" (Barnes 1999,
82–88). Number 6 of that list ("Pursuit of the Ideal") contains yet another
enumeration: that of four men with whom Martha has been together
(numbered a to d—Thomas, Matthew, Ted, Russell), none of whom really
seemed to have loved her or could truly satisfy her.

> (a) Thomas, who took her to Venice where she found his eyes glowed before
> a Giorgione more than they did when she stood before him in her specially-
> bought night-blue bra and knickers while the back canal went slap-slap out-
> side their window; (b) Matthew, who really liked to shop, who could tell
> what clothes would suit her when they were still on the rail, who brought
> his risotto to a perfect pitch of sticky dampness but couldn't do the same for
> her; (c) Ted, who showed her the advantages of money and the softening
> hypocrisies it encouraged, who said he loved her and wanted to marry her
> and have kids with her, but never told her that between leaving her flat every
> morning and reaching his office he always spent an intimate hour with his
> psychiatrist; (d) Russell, with whom she ran away light-headedly in order to
> fuck and love halfway up a Welsh mountain with hand-pumped cold water
> and udder-warm goat's milk, who was idealistic, organized, community-
> minded and self-sacrificing. (87)

The whole list appears to be almost scientific (hence the title "a brief history"): an objective classification of Martha's failed relationships. The list,
then, is an attempt at distancing herself from what is ultimately a rather
depressing overview. In itemizing her former love interests, Martha turns
her love life into objects that can be ordered, classified, and dissected from
an analytical stance. The list is a strategy of identity management, an
expression of her coping mechanism. Ultimately, of course, Martha's list is
highly ironic: the itemization of her love experience as a way of managing
her emotional capital demonstrates that her identity work has been

successful; she is able to distance herself from these experiences by turning them into a pseudo-objective history.

The management of emotional capital is also at the center of my final example, Leanne Shapton's work *Important Artifacts and Personal Property from the Collection of Lenore Doolan and Harold Morris, Including Books, Street Fashion, and Jewelry* (2009). The subtitle is: *Strachan & Quinn Auctioneers, February 14, 2009. 10 a.m. and 2 p.m. EST.* The book presents itself as an auction catalogue; indeed, perhaps one could mistake it for one if one would not pay attention to the literary epigraphs that precede the catalogue, and only superficially glance at the images. Here the list form occurs on two levels: one is the auction catalogue itself, which is essentially a list of entries: each entry is one "item," marked by a photograph (or the absence of one). The second level occurs within these items, in the explanatory notes that accompany each "item." There are further enumerations, for instance actual lists that are included in or attached to individual items (a shopping list, a dedication, a list in a letter, etc.), or an enumeration of the things presented in an image, such as the list of the things contained in Lenore and Harold's cosmetic cases (LOT 1079 and 1080; 30–31).

Two of the essays in the present volume also discuss "visual" lists (the documentary photobook and the *Arma Christi* tradition in the Middle Ages).[19] Whether "visual" lists exist, is debatable. The term is Eco's, who has a broad understanding of lists and forms of enumerations in the first place. In their introduction, the editors of this volume make a compelling case for the existence of "visual lists" and argue that the concept of the list can provide a more nuanced understanding of different kinds of series in contexts of visual art. They single out patterns of repetition and variation as well as part-whole relationships as prominent features of visual lists. Admitting that these features are by no means hard criteria for identifying potential visual lists, they suggest following an inductive approach: "A visual list would then be whatever is perceived as a visual list".[20] The appeal of such an "inductive" (perhaps also, or rather, "intuitive") approach is that it empowers the viewer to think critically about the arrangement patterns of a work of art. At the same time, this approach begs a cognitive perspective: if one perceives of the list as a cognitive form—as a tool of and for thinking—then it can also be applied to visual representations. Shapton's book is clearly based on principles of order and itemization that reverberate with list structures and may therefore be described, in terms of its affordances, similar to a list—a visual list.

The very form of the auction catalogue already anticipates the outcome of the love story: it ended badly; Lenore and Harold have separated. The catalogue represents the sell-out of their relationship. Although a note by Harold Morris that precedes the catalogue may hint at the possibility of a happy ending, the catalogue clearly suggests otherwise. A love story is reduced to, broken down into, the items that the two former lovers owned.[21]

In the metaphor of the auction catalogue, love itself is on display. Inherent in the items, especially when they are "read" from beginning to end, is a narrative. The items tell the love story of Lenore and Harold through the objects they owned, got, and gave each other. A relationship leaves material traces, and the choice of the auction catalogue problematizes that we are what we own. What remains of this, or indeed, any love story, are things, material objects. These remains, "ruins" almost, are the afterthought of love. With the desire for the other gone, all that remains are things, the things that tell the story of their past love. Importantly, however, the story does not stop here: these things, being things, could potentially be turned into money again. The metaphor is obvious: just as the objects are on the market again, so are the former lovers. Love can be found anew, (metaphorically) "sold" anew, and thus begins new circle of goods being purchased by a potential new couple.[22]

Ultimately, Shapton's auction catalogue suggests the objectification of desire. The emotionally cool, removed, reasonable thing to do—rather than throwing the former lover's possessions out of the window—is to sell them. In a way, this decision makes obvious what the things have always been, implicitly: the material capital of a love relationship, that capital on which, at least partly, the emotional capital hinges. If the capital of love has gone, the objects that remain lose their affective power, they can be seen as purely material again. The list form both conceals this logic and draws attention to it: only if we interpret the auction catalogue in terms of Lenore and Harold's (failed) love story, we can unearth the various layers and complications of selling out one's former relationship.

CONCLUSION

I have suggested that the form of the list and capitalism are closely, inextricably intertwined when it comes to the depiction of love as material desire. Lists are commonly used to depict sales figures and profits in capitalist societies, and in our examples, the list form becomes the medium that transmits the message of a society in which love, personal relationships, and identity are bound up in capitalist discourses. The list seemingly itemizes and orders that which in truth defies order and neatly separated units, and yet the idea of one's self (self-worth even) and personal relationships as capital can be traced from Defoe to Shapton.

Clearly the form of the list has the affordance of being a capitalist instrument. It allows the depiction of identity, love, and lovers as material objects, itemizing the self and others. Apart from *Robinson Crusoe* perhaps, the lists in the examples discussed above have comic effects: we are invited to laugh about Mr. Meagle's pretence, to see through Rob's attempt to present himself as the good guy, to feel pity for both the hyperbolic failures of Bridget Jones and Martha's love history, and to recognize the ironies in Shapton's faux auction catalogue. In each case, the form of the list appears harmless; on the surface, it is a funny rhetorical move that shuns digging deeper. If we approach these lists suspiciously, however, we see their deeply political implications. If anything, we can take from the essays in the present volume a very similar message: lists are never simply containers or transmitters of knowledge and order. Under their surface of clarity and objectivity, there is potentially an abyss of contradiction and manipulation. Readers, don't trust the list.

Notes

1. See also the discussion of this issue in the "Introduction" to this volume, 9–10.
2. See the chapter by Ottmar Ette in this volume.
3. See the chapter by Martin Stöckinger in this volume.
4. See the chapters by Juri Joensuu and Alyson Brickey in this volume.
5. See the chapter by Ulrike Vedder in this volume.
6. On rabbinic literature, see Lennart Lehmhaus's chapter in this volume; on the *Arma Christi*, Daniela Wagner; on table of contents, Stefanie Lethbridge.
7. See in more detail von Contzen (2017a).
8. On the list as "simple form," see von Contzen (2017b).
9. See in more detail Reckwitz (2003).
10. Surface reading thus seems to be the natural way of reading lists because they defy the depth and concealment that has been the dominant form of critique in the hermeneutics of suspicion school. The philosopher Paul Ricoeur coined the phrase "hermeneutics of suspicion." He evoked the image of the critic as someone who, in Rita Felski's words, has to "reverse

the falsifications of everyday thought, to 'unconceal' what has been concealed, to bring into daylight what has languished in deep shadow" (2015, 31). This practice of "symptomatic reading" gained currency from the 1970s onward. Influenced by psychoanalytic and Marxist approaches to literature, it posits that the actual meaning of a literary text is suppressed, hidden, latent, not immediately visible and accessible, and thus requires the literary critic to search for this hidden meaning by "digging deep," that is, by "reading suspiciously." In recent years, the tide has appeared to be turning against symptomatic reading, as the calls for "surface" or "descriptive" reading (see Marcus et al. 2016 for the latter) demonstrate.

11. For an introduction, see Woodmansee and Osteen (1999).
12. See Schmidgen (2001) on mercantilism; Rogers (1974) on Robinson's home-building; and McMillen (2013) on the importance of food and Robinson as a global citizen. See also Watt (1957) on Robinson as *homo economicus*.
13. See also Fludernik (2016, 319–320) for an analysis of this passage.
14. See in more detail Richards (1990).
15. See Theresa Schön's chapter in this volume.
16. I can only briefly mention at this point the wider discourses of the reification of the laborer and labor in capitalist societies as Georg Lukacs (1971) has argued. Said succinctly summarizes Lukacs's arguments, drawing attention to the form of the list: "If capitalism is the embodiment in economic terms of reification, then everything, including human beings, ought to be quantified and given a market value. This of course is what Lukacs means when he speaks of articulation under capitalism, *which he sometimes characterizes as if it were a gigantic itemized list*" (1983, 232, my emphasis). Modern working conditions, in their poetic form, become a list.
17. See von Contzen (2018) on Bridget Jones's diary and the experiential dimension of lists in literary texts.
18. The term was coined by Chon Noriega and has found its way into the theory of autobiography; see Smith and Watson (2010, 258).
19. See the chapters by Anja Schürmann and Daniela Wagner in this volume.
20. See Barton et al., "Introduction", in this volume, 16.
21. See the chapter by Agnes Blümer in this volume.
22. Vedder (2012a, b) analyzes the narrative dimensions of Shapton's work (its elliptical, fragmentary nature) and its links to memory work. See also Jakubowski (2013).

REFERENCES

Barnes, Julian. 1998. *England, England*. London: Picador, 1999.
Belknap, Robert E. 2004. *The List: The Uses and Pleasures of Cataloguing*. New Haven/London: Yale University Press.

Best, Stephen, and Sharon Marcus. 2009. Surface Reading: An Introduction. *Representations* 108 (1): 1–21.

Birke, Dorothee. 2016. The World Is Not Enough: Lists as Encounters with the 'Real' in the Eighteenth-Century Novel. *Style* 50 (3): 296–308.

De Goede, Marieke, Anna Leander, and Gavin Sullivan. 2016. Introduction: The Politics of the List. *Environment and Planning D: Society and Space* 34 (1): 3–13.

Defoe, Daniel. 2012. *Robinson Crusoe*, ed. John Richetti. London: Penguin Classics.

Dickens, Charles. 2008. *Little Dorrit*. London: Vintage.

Faulk, Barry. 2007. Love, Lists, and Class in Nick Hornby's *High Fidelity. Cultural Critique* 66: 153–176.

Felski, Rita. 2015. *The Limits of Critique*. Chicago: University of Chicago Press.

Fludernik, Monika. 2016. Descriptive Lists and List Descriptions. *Style* 50 (3): 309–326.

Hornby, Nick. 2014 [1995]. *High Fidelity*. London: Penguin.

Illouz, Eva. 2007. *Cold Intimacies: The Making of Emotional Capitalism*. Cambridge: Polity Press.

Jakubowski, Zuzanna. 2013. Exhibiting Lost Love: The Relational Realism of Things in Orhan Pamuk's *The Museum of Innocence* and Shapton's *Important Artifacts*. In *Realisms in Contemporary Culture: Theories, Politics, and Medial Configurations*, ed. Dorothee Birke and Stella Butter, 124–145. Berlin: de Gruyter.

Levine, Caroline. 2015. *Forms: Whole, Rhythm, Hierarchy, Network*. Princeton/Oxford: Princeton University Press.

Love, Heather. 2010. Close but not Deep: Literary Ethics and the Descriptive Turn. *New Literary History* 41 (2): 371–391.

Lukacs, Georg. 1971. *History and Class Consciousness: Studies in Marxist Dialectics*. Trans. Rodney Livingstone. London: Merlin.

Mainberger, Sabine. 2003. *Die Kunst des Aufzählens: Elemente zu einer Poetik des Enumerativen*. Berlin: de Gruyter.

Marcus, Sharon, Heather Love, and Stephen Best. 2016. Building a Better Description. *Representations* 135: 1–21.

McMillen, Krystal. 2013. Eating Turtle, Eating the World: Comestible Things in the Eighteenth Century. In *Eighteenth-Century Thing Theory in a Global Context: From Consumerism to Celebrity Culture*, ed. Ileana Baird and Christina Ionescu, 191–207. Farnham & Burlington: Ashgate.

Reckwitz, Andreas. 2003. Grundelemente einer Theorie sozialer Praktiken: Eine sozialtheoretische Perspektive. *Zeitschrift für Soziologie* 32 (4): 282–301.

Richards, Thomas. 1990. *The Commodity Culture of Victorian England: Advertising and Spectacle, 1851–1914*. Stanford: Stanford University Press.

Rogers, Pat. 1974. Crusoe's Home. *Essays in Criticism* 24 (4): 375–390.

Said, Edward. 1983. *The World, the Text, and the Critic*. Cambridge, MA: Harvard University Press.

Schmidgen, Wolfram. 2001. *Robinson Crusoe*, Enumeration, and the Mercantile Fetish. *Eighteenth-Century Studies* 35 (1): 19–39.

Shapton, Leanne. 2009. *Important Artifacts and Personal Property from the Collection of Lenore Doolan and Harold Morris, Including Books, Street Fashion, and Jewelry*. London: Bloomsbury.

Smith, Sidonie, and Julia Watson. 2010. *Reading Autobiography: A Guide for Interpreting Life Narratives*. 2nd ed. Minneapolis: University of Minnesota Press.

Stäheli, Urs. 2016. Indexing – The Politics of Invisibility. *Environment and Planning D: Society and Space* 34 (1): 14–29.

Sterne, Laurence. 1984. *The Life and Opinions of Tristram Shandy, Gentleman*. The Florida Edition, ed. Melvyn New, Richard A. Davies, and W.G. Day. Oxford: Oxford University Press.

Vedder, Ulrike. 2012a. Weitergeben, verlorengeben: Dinge als Gedächtnismedien. In *Gendered Objects: Wissens- und Geschlechterordnungen der Dinge*, ed. Gabriele Jähnert, 17–28. Berlin: Zentrum für transdisziplinäre Geschlechterstudien der Humboldt-Universität zu Berlin.

———. 2012b. Auktionskatalog, Fotoroman, Liebesinventar: Vom Wert der Dinge in Leanne Shaptons *Bedeutende Objekte und persönliche Besitzstücke aus der Sammlung von Lenore Doolan und Harold Morris, darunter Bücher, Mode und Schmuck*. In *'High' und 'Low': Zur Interferenz von Hoch- und Populärkultur in der Gegenwartsliteratur*, ed. Thomas Wegmann and Norbert Christian Wolf, 199–216. Berlin: de Gruyter.

von Contzen, Eva. 2017a. Die Affordanzen der Liste. *Zeitschrift für Literaturwissenschaft und Linguistik* 3: 317–326.

———. 2017b. Grenzfälle des Erzählens: Die Liste als einfache Form. In *Komplexität und Einfachheit*, ed. Albrecht Koschorke, 221–239. Stuttgart: Metzler.

Watt, Ian. 1957. *The Rise of the Novel. Studies in Defoe, Richardson and Fielding*. Berkeley: University of California Press.

———. 2018. Experience, Affect, and Literary Lists. *Partial Answers* 16 (2): 315–327.

Woodmansee, Martha, and Mark Osteen, eds. 1999. *The New Economic Criticism: Studies at the Intersection of Literature and Economics*. London/New York: Routledge.

CHAPTER 7

More Than a Canon: Lists of Contents in British Poetry Anthologies

Stefanie Lethbridge

Allow me to start with a short text on the deleterious effects of modern car culture:

> Autobahnmotorwayautoroute
> Autobiography
> Autowreck
> Aye, but to die, and go we know not where

While this might not be readily recognized as a canonical poem, I would argue that it displays definite aesthetic qualities in the anaphorical "auto" at the beginning of the first three lines, that, in its ambiguous merge between a reference to the "self" and the automobile, stages life as a trip down a motorway and death as a car accident. As it happens, these are four consecutive entries in the list of contents to *The Rattle Bag* (1982), an anthology edited by Seamus Heaney and Ted Hughes. What is listed here are three poems by Adrian Mitchell, Louis MacNeice, and Karl Shapiro

S. Lethbridge (✉)
English Department, University of Freiburg, Freiburg, Germany
e-mail: stefanie.lethbridge@anglistik.uni-freiburg.de

R. A. Barton et al. (eds.), *Forms of List-Making: Epistemic, Literary, and Visual Enumeration*,
https://doi.org/10.1007/978-3-030-76970-3_7

respectively, and the first line of an excerpt from Shakespeare's *Hamlet*, as found in the list of contents to the collection.

Criticism frequently questions the literary and/or narrative qualities of lists, or at any rate describes the list as only "quasi-narrative" or "potential narrative" (Richardson 20, 328–329). Akin to description, lists interrupt the flow of a narrative and thus, according to Eva von Contzen, disrupt our sequential reading habits (von Contzen 2016, 246). At the same time, lists are considered to have a primarily pragmatic purpose and, in consequence, to be aesthetically lacking (Belknap 2000, 38); they are described as reproducing the mundane and every-day, and as an essentially "non-narrative practice" (von Contzen 2018, 325). And while the possibility of an aesthetically formed list is acknowledged—in the hands of a Homer, Milton, or Joyce (e.g., Richardson 2016, passim), this is treated as an exception, something that only temporarily dislodges the essentially utilitarian quality of the list. This insistence on the usefulness of the list is particularly noticeable for lists (or tables) of contents, which are typically identified as a type of "finding aid" or reference tool (Blair 2010, 4, 18), "in theory no more than a device for reminding us of the titular apparatus – or for announcing it" (Genette 1997, 317).[1] Among lists, a table of contents is described as uniquely restrained, "built through an externally imposed systemization, […] dictated by the sequence of the parts of the book" (Belknap 2000, 40), thus further reducing the creative potential of this type of list.

Against positions that argue the narrative and aesthetic limitations of the list of contents, this chapter will draw on suggestions that concede the at least "loosely narrative" quality of any list (von Contzen 2018, 315). Within its narrative potential, the list of contents co-determines cognitive and affective frames of reception. I will explore the narrative, even literary, potential of the lists of contents for British poetry anthologies since the Renaissance. Contextualized in a print product that claims to offer culturally and socially relevant poetic heritage, these lists of contents create narratives out of previously disconnected items, pandering to, in some cases even enforcing, the human predilection for creating teleological connections. In this sense, rather than hinder our habit of sequential reading, lists of contents might actually be said to encourage it.

ANTHOLOGIES: JOINING THE PARTS

The anthology, derived from the Greek *anthos* (= "flower") and *legeín* (= "to gather"), hence also the Latin *florilegium*, is designed to bind together separate items into a complete and coherent whole: the individual flowers are joined into a bouquet (Korte 2000, 2). At the very basic level, we have a list when at least three separate items are linked. In close parallel to this, we have an anthology when the poems of at least three different authors are presented in one collection (Benedict 1996, 3; Ferry 2001, 31).[2] Similar to the list, the anthology as publication format combines disparate units (individual poems by different authors) into some form of unity. On the material level this unity is achieved by printing and binding the poems between the two covers of a book and providing it with a title that governs the whole collection. On a figurative level, anthologies tend to provide various frameworks which justify the selection of these (rather than other) texts, and which locate the individual poem within this larger framework, thus creating a connection between individual items. For instance, poems might be arranged in terms of historical period, identifying a Chaucer poem as an early example of English poetry and placing a poem by Carol Ann Duffy as a late example, at the same time classifying both as important poets for the development of English poetry. In print culture, to some extent also in manuscript culture, anthologies communicate cohesion and coherence through paratexts: the title, address to the reader, editor's introduction, and, centrally, the list of contents which usually makes explicit the ordering system the collection uses. While the title gives a general idea of the principles governing the selection (for instance Vicesimus Knox's comprehensive program in *Elegant Extracts: Or Useful and Entertaining Pieces of Poetry, Selected for the Improvement of Youth, in Reading Thinking, Composing; and in the Conduct of Life*, 1785), the list of contents provides the details (which poem serves which purpose?). By providing both framework and structure, paratexts provide the ribbon that holds the bouquet of (poetic) flowers together.

Anthologies of English poetry made their first appearance in British print culture in the mid-sixteenth century. The first complete anthology to survive is Richard Tottel's *Songes and Sonettes*, 1557, which collects poetry by Thomas Wyatt, Henry Howard, Earl of Surrey, Nicholas Grimald, and several anonymous writers, in an effort to demonstrate "that our tong is able in that kynde to do as praiseworthily as ye rest," as Tottel states in his address to the reader—"the rest" being Latin and Italian poets (Rollins

1965, 2). Tottel attempted an overview of national poetic achievement and his example was followed by many hundreds of national survey anthologies. Famous examples include Francis Turner Palgrave's *Golden Treasury of the Best Songs and Lyrical Poems in the English Language* in 1861, Arthur Quiller-Couch's *Oxford Book of English Verse* of 1900, rejuvenated by Christopher Rick's *Oxford Book of English Verse* in 1999, and of course the many teaching anthologies that are used in schools and universities, such as *The Norton Anthology*. These collections create a poetic canon based on specific historical and/or aesthetic preferences, where certain items are included, others are excluded—indeed the power politics of their restrictive choices is part of the criticism that is frequently leveled at anthologies. The list of contents presents the story of this canon in its diachronic setting. But it does more than that. Compared across time, these lists of contents also reflect changing concepts of which criteria should be foregrounded in the link created between nation and poetic heritage: should it be the author? the theme? the poetic form? Lists of contents shape the cognitive and often also the affective frame for the reception of the poems presented in the anthology. And finally, as a *potential* literary form, a list of contents can itself create poetry.

Pointing the Way: Lists of Content and Reading Strategies

The list of contents started to appear in the twelfth century as a tool for intellectual reading, helping those, as Sabine Mainberger points out, that wished to gain an overview of the matter to come, before they started reading (2003, 134). The list of contents provided a finding tool which facilitated the non-sequential reading of the main text. It represented, according to Mary and Richard Rouse "efforts to search written authority afresh, to get at, to locate, to retrieve information" (Rouse and Rouse 1991, 221). On the other hand, prefatory tables were also frequently used for polemical purposes, "seeking to control how readers read rather than simply guiding them to material they desired" by adding explicit judgments (Da Costa 2018, 308). This tension between offering material for free access and at the same time limiting and controlling the choices that are made (Da Costa 2018, 312) is particularly noticeable in anthologies. We rarely *read* anthologies; we read *in* anthologies.[3] They are by design the type of book that offers reading in non-sequential order. This kind of dipping and skipping is possible because the individual units that make up the anthology usually stand on their own. While the publication format "anthology" thus enables highly self-directed reading strategies, the list of contents provides a convenient (and sequential) overview of the order in which the editor wished to place the items of his or her selection. As much as a preview, the list of contents also serves as an aid to recall, when the reader tries to locate or re-locate a familiar poem, or when it actually recalls the forgotten familiar. The list of contents, in other words, furnishes a map which readers can use in order to go to a place of their own choosing, selecting from the various places on offer—some of which might be familiar, others enticingly new. Thus, while the list of contents improves accessibility, it also points in very specific directions and in this sense, as Siân Echard has argued for the different *tabulae* prefixed to Gower's *Confessio Amantis*, pre-structures the reading experience by focusing on certain aspects and not on others (Echard 1997, 272).

By the 1520s lists of contents seemed to have been expected of books produced in England and publishers felt the need to apologize when they were absent, which suggests that readers had become used to the convenient summaries of a book's content provided by the *tabula* (Da Costa 2018, 305). The list of contents not only changes the reading experience, it also encourages the production of texts (by the author, the editor, or publisher and printer) which use identifiable markers to structure the main text: it makes subtitles or at the very least signature and page numbering systems mandatory (Genette 1997, 316; Da Costa 2018, 298–301). In collections like anthologies, this has the consequence that originally untitled poems are given titles, adding yet another paratext that directs interpretation. Thus, for instance, Tottel titled Thomas Wyatt's poem that starts "They flee from me, that somtime did me seke" as "The louer sheweth how he is forsaken of such as he somtime enioyed." While the first edition of the *Songes and Sonettes* did not have a list of contents, this title entered the lists of contents in later editions of the collection. Arthur Quiller-Couch, in *The Oxford Book of Verse*, retitles the poem as "Vixi Puellis Nuper Idoneus," emphatically foregrounding an intertextual link to Horace. John Press, in his revisions of Palgrave's *Golden Treasury* gives the title "Consolation" to the (originally untitled) Shakespeare sonnet "When in disgrace... ." When incipits are used as titles, the poem is likely to inscribe itself in cultural memory as incipit rather than as complete poem: "In the table of contents and then in the designative use that derives from it, this first line, as incipit, breaks away and takes on an unduly emblematic value, as if it were always, …, god-given. Hence the large number of poems of which we know only the first lines" (Genette 1997, 312; 317–18): "Shall I compare thee to a summer's day?", "There is a garden in her face," "He that loves a rosy cheek," "When lovely woman stoops to folly," "I am monarch of all I survey," "She walks in beauty, like the night," "Loveliest of trees the cherry now," "Let us go then you and I."

The early print culture anthologies, however, did not always consider the list of contents a necessary addition. Tottel's *Songes and Sonettes*, for instance, though it provided some reader guidance in the initial address to the reader (largely claiming the excellence of the collection), does not offer a list of contents. It is only in the later edition of 1574 that a table is added, though this is closer to an index than a list of contents, listing the entries alphabetically according to topic.[4] Other Renaissance anthologies did include lists of content. *The Phoenix Nest* for instance (1973) did, and at the same time emphatically directed reader judgment by pointing out that these are "most special and woorthie workes" followed by "excellent and rare Ditties".

The list of contents became common for verse collections from the late seventeenth century onward, though it was not necessarily provided at the front. The fifth volume of the influential Dryden-Tonson *Poetical Miscellanies* (1704), edited by the bookseller Jacob Tonson who used Dryden's poems and name to boost the standing of the collection, gave a list of contents at the back as "A Table on the foregoing Poems." The sixth (and last) volume of the *Miscellanies* (1709) moved the list of contents to the front.

Assuming a standard reading direction in an Anglophone environment from the front of the book, the list of contents at the back provides an overview as an afterthought, or once again, an index more than a list of contents: a tool to use in order to locate a specific item, rather than providing a general overview before the reading starts.[5] A list of contents, especially in large collections, will of course frequently be used as an index wherever it is placed in the book, given that anthologies do not require linear reading. Throughout the eighteenth century, the list of contents at the front of the book became increasingly standard for British anthologies, and, by the nineteenth century, absolutely required. Thus Palgrave's extremely skimpy and unenlightening list of contents that merely indicated "Book 1, Book 2, Book 3, Book 4," according to Anne Ferry represents "a silent revolt against the conventional plan of nineteenth-century anthologies, which dictated that they list their entries in advance" (Ferry

2001, 50). With his reduced list of contents, Palgrave evades editorial positionings at the beginning of the book, leaving readers to find their own way through the collection—unless they take a deliberately scholarly approach and consult the notes and the index of first lines in the back before they start reading. In Palgrave's case this was more than likely a deliberate choice, since Palgrave wanted to create, as much as possible, an unmediated encounter with the poems in his collection as he aimed to give treasures "more golden than gold" as he put it, allowing poetry to speak "for herself" (Palgrave 1861, 8). The *Golden Treasury*'s uniquely uninformative list of contents creates a tension, a form of not-knowing what is to come, that the American edition of the *Golden Treasury* was apparently unable to sustain: Louis Untermeyer, who published the *Golden Treasury* for the American Modern Library in 1944, supplied a list of contents. It is worth noting in this context that Quiller-Couch's *Oxford Book of English Verse*, which was Palgrave's successor in terms of cultural fame and impact, provided a list only of authors at the beginning of the regular hardback edition, but no list of contents of any form for the India paper edition: the thin version, designed to be carried around in one's pocket—and indeed it was used in this manner as letters to the press indicate—was obviously thought an appropriate vessel for an immediate reading experience, dipping and skipping at random, while the more portly standard version, also enabled a more guided and intellectual approach by offering an overview of authors in the front.[6] Other anthologies, especially at the cheaper end of production, occasionally have an incomplete list of contents. This is very likely simple negligence by the compositor. It is also possible, however, that incomplete lists of contents deliberately disguised the fact that copyrighted material was (illegally) used. John Bullar's 1822 *Selections from the British Poets*, for instance, hid as many as ten Wordsworth poems in a section of the anthology that was only vaguely given as "Miscellaneous" in the list of contents.[7]

CANON NARRATIVES IN THE LIST OF CONTENTS

The noteworthy absence of a list of contents in an anthology points to the functions such lists have when they are supplied. Sabine Mainberger groups the list of contents amongst transitive texts, texts that point toward what follows (Mainberger 2003, 21). The category of the transitive text hints at a slightly less passive role of the list of contents than Belknap's "dictated by the sequence of the parts of the book" (2000, 40). As an enumerative paratext, lists of contents organize and direct reading or reception (Mainberger 2003, 119), just as the titles do that are added in order to facilitate the list of contents. In fact, in the case of anthologies (or any type of collection of secondary texts), there are two—in the end identical—lists involved in the production of the final product: editors will proceed their labors as anthologists by producing a list of poems they want to include in the anthology. The poems on this list will then be assembled in the collection. And finally the list of contents will reflect these poems as arranged in the actual anthology.[8] In this sense, the list of contents orders and frames the list of poems selected for the anthology in a meta-list. Presenting itself as a merely neutral reflection of the material that follows, the list of contents in anthologies hides the agent(s) who decided what to include in the selection while it directs reception processes and essentially creates the content of the anthology: the influence of text on lists of contents and vice versa is two-directional. It is the choices that are expressed in the list of contents and the categorizations that it offers, which provide various narratives of their own.

There is, first of all, the canon narrative: the list of contents of a national survey anthology, in particular the "disciplinary anthology" that is used in schools and universities, carries with it the claim that these poems and not others represent a nation's poetic heritage (Mandell 2007).[9] They have (supposedly) been chosen by expert judges for their excellence and uniqueness. This canon narrative is only effective if this or similar lists are repeated elsewhere. A poem that is included *once* in *one* anthology, even if this anthology enjoys a fairly high distribution, is not a canonical poem. Contrary to popular belief, anthologies have high fluctuations in the poems that are included.[10] There is, however, a core number of poems that are repeated frequently over long periods of time. These poems are read, taught, memorized, recalled, recited at weddings, quoted in love letters, and evoked on tombstones: they become canonical as articulations of personal as well as national values and impact the ways specific cultural groups—English or British in this case—articulate their life experiences (at least in times when people still read poetry) and remember their past on a national as well as on a personal level. Thus Quiller-Couch reminisces:

> Few of my contemporaries can erase—or would wish to erase—the dye their minds took from the late Mr. Palgrave's *Golden Treasury*: and he who has returned to it again and again with an affection born of companionship on many journeys must remember not only what the *Golden Treasury* includes,

but the moment when this or that poem appealed to him, and even how it lies on the page. (Quiller-Couch 1923, ix–x)

A list of contents that evokes such canonical texts has a high level of inter-textual resonance, not only with the poems printed in the actual book that this particular list of contents refers to, but a myriad of other printings, recitations, and quotations of this poem as well. Someone who knows English poetry is likely to recall at least fragments or an emotional tone of the entire poem when reading that poem's title in a list of contents. This, I would argue, is unique to the national poetry anthology: unlike the list of contents in an academic book or even in a collection of narrative prose pieces, reading the list of contents in a standard poetry collection the well-versed poetry reader already knows what is coming, at least partly. The list of contents serves as trigger (or "echoes … met in encrypted turbulence" as Mandell describes this, quoting Marjorie Welish's poem "Cities of the Table," 2007, 4) in the head of the poetry lover. These echoes evoke the text as a whole, not word-perfect, but in terms of theme and at least some of the words and phrases of the actual poem. Depending on the degree of familiarity a reader has with canonical poetry, the list given above of well-known incipits might well be moved to here as a list that provides a site for the recall, possibly the (albeit fragmentary) re-performance of these canonical poems. It is the anticipation of the already known, as well as the knowledge that other people share this knowledge, that represents part of the attraction of any particular collection. National poetry anthologies create and affirm shared experiences among the members of a generation or a cultural group:

An anthology may form the taste of one generation, or more, but may also give shape, and voice, to those readers who have not formulated for themselves what they conceive to be their taste, but who yet yearn to be part of some supposed communal expression. … Individuals do not have a treasury but share one. (Silkin 1999, 192)

Thus, in a circular process of affirmation and reconfirmation, a collection like *The Nation's Favourite Poems* (2004)—created by popular vote on the BBC—solidifies already shared memory and at the same time creates new memories. The canon is reinscribed as already there.

The Place of the Individual Poem

Even though engagement with the canon is central to the impact of the list of contents in poetry anthologies, I indicated at the beginning of this essay that its significance goes beyond the affirmation of canonical material. In most cases, lists of contents provide categories that not only recall specific poems, but group them and thus foreground specific aspects of this poem or subsume it under specific knowledge systems. It is of course possible to have a list of contents without explicit systematization. Oliver Goldsmith's list of contents to *The Beauties of English Poesy* (1767) starts with "The Rape of the Locke" and continues with "The Hermit," "L'Allegro," and "Il Penseroso." It is thus neither chronological, nor does it mention authors; it certainly presents no explicit systematization, though one might consider the simple order of the arrangement, starting with the poem by the widely acclaimed Alexander Pope, as suggesting some form of value judgment, given that the opening poem tends to assume prime place. Historically, the preferences for ordering categories change, which indicates a change in the conceptualization of literary history more broadly. Four categories occur most frequently: (1) chronology by era, (2) chronology by authors' birth dates, (3) thematic foci, and finally, (4) categories of literary form. This last one is the least long-lived. It occurs mostly in anthologies that have an avowed didactic aim, like the *Parent's Poetical Anthology* of 1849 edited by Elizabeth Mant, which explicitly groups the poems into form categories for school recitations such as "Descriptive," "Elegiac," or "Dramatic" poems. Vicesimus Knox's *Elegant Extracts*, which was widely used in schools well into the nineteenth century, offers similar categories, adding the slightly frivolous category "Ludicrous" toward the end of the book. This form of categorization according to genres was extremely popular in the late eighteenth and early nineteenth centuries; to my knowledge it is rare after that.

It is replaced, from the beginning of the nineteenth century onward, with an interest in historical chronology. This was a change encouraged no doubt by the romantic interest in historical roots (see Mandell 2007, 19), but it was also made possible by a change in copyright legislation in 1774, which finally abolished the perpetual copyright claimed by booksellers and very suddenly made large numbers of English poets available for cheap reprints.[11] The conditions of the print market clearly helped to create a cultural interest and helped to perpetuate a focus on historical overview. As Mandell argues, "Romantic writers were the first to see literary history as printed performance within book history" (2007, 19). The nineteenth century exploded in poetry collections that created narratives of poetic development, usually starting with Chaucer. The chronological list of contents is one of the most long-lived formats: a label for the historical period heads a list of author's names which are in turn followed by the individual poems of this particular author included in the anthology.[12] Such neat division into separate periods featuring a progression of individual authors of course creates an erroneous impression of a somehow neatly separable and sequential development. Some anthologies try to correct this impression and instead reflect the rather messier situation of real-life poetry production. Paul Keegan, in the *New Penguin Book of English Verse* (2000) orders his entries in chronological order according to composition date, which recreates the simultaneity of actual writing: thus, for instance, Philip Sidney's 1598 song "When to my deadly pleasure" appears next to his sister Mary's paraphrase of the 58th Psalm and Christopher Marlowe's *Hero and Leander*, and Rochester's "Disabled Debauchee" is followed by Andrew Marvell's "Horation Ode upon Cromwell's Return from Ireland," forcing the debauchee and the puritan into uneasy proximity (Keegan 2000, ix, xvi–xvii). Generally, the chronological list of contents reflects the line of development that is created by this particular ordering of the poems, but even more so, it focuses readers' attention on the aspect of chronology and encourages a view of literature in terms of development, of what comes before and after. The ordering principle reflected in the list of contents in this sense pre-shapes the assumptions we make about poetic history and, according to Laura Mandell, when categorized into literary periods, these lists create our disciplinary objects, as "tables of contents map time onto space" (Mandell 2007, 23).

While earlier anthologies tend to be interested in poems and only rarely or intermittently in poets, the author became the second ordering principle that was increasingly privileged throughout the nineteenth century. The typical list of contents in Renaissance anthologies, like *The Phoenix Nest* (see Fig. 7.1), makes no mention of authors at all. This convention remains common until the late eighteenth century, as the example of Goldsmith's *Beauties* illustrates. The Dryden-Tonson *Miscellanies* signal an interest in authors in connection with social groupings: the list of contents gives poems addressed to aristocrats, such as "Inscribed to the Right Honourable to the Lady Viscountess Weymouth." The repeated use of the expression "by the same hand" in place of an author's name, referring back to previous entries that gave the name, also enforces a more or less

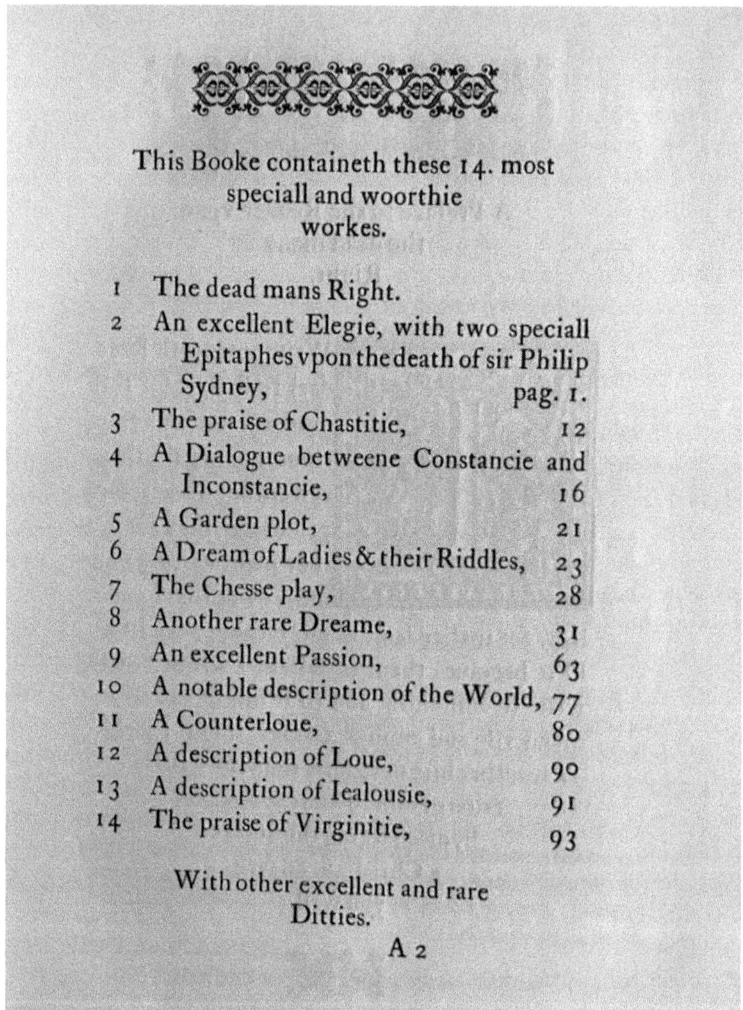

This Booke containeth these 14. most
speciall and woorthie
workes.

1   The dead mans Right.
2   An excellent Elegie, with two speciall
    Epitaphes vpon the death of sir Philip
    Sydney,   pag. 1.
3   The praise of Chastitie,   12
4   A Dialogue betweene Constancie and
    Inconstancie,   16
5   A Garden plot,   21
6   A Dream of Ladies & their Riddles,   23
7   The Chesse play,   28
8   Another rare Dreame,   31
9   An excellent Passion,   63
10 A notable description of the World,   77
11 A Counterloue,   80
12 A description of Loue,   90
13 A description of Iealousie,   91
14 The praise of Virginitie,   93

With other excellent and rare
Ditties.

A 2

Fig. 7.1   *This Booke containeth these 14. most speciall and woorthie workes* [table of contents], in *The Phoenix Nest* (London, 1593) [facsimile], private photograph

continuous reading of the list of contents, otherwise one loses track of who the author is. In some cases, this practice spreads over several pages, making it necessary to read substantial sections of the table of contents, if one wants to gather all relevant information. The list of contents, as well as the texts as printed in the collection, enforce a view of poetry that occurs in clusters connected to social groupings.

With the genius cult of the late eighteenth century, authors became essential for lists of contents: "A generation of late-eighteenth-century anthologies established [...] the rules by which future literature would be transmitted, notably the expectation that every anthology-piece bear a signature and that its signatory be dead" (Price 2000, 67). In the wake of this development, throughout the nineteenth century it was increasingly authors, not poems, that dominated the lists of contents, and anthologies encouraged readers to read poets, not poems. Accordingly, Quiller-Couch offered a list of authors at the beginning of *The Oxford Book of English Verse* (1900), and A.T. Ward's collection of 1880 was called *The English Poets*. Ward, who produced his anthology for the emerging academic market with the new university courses in English literature, was also keen to signal the academic quality of his choice. With the author of the poems, the list of contents also indicated the academic who made the selection and commented on it. In this case, acknowledged critics like Matthew Arnold or A.C. Bradley gave credit to a selection of poets within an increasingly academic system of evaluation. The desire to appropriate a poet alongside the poetry for one's own national heritage could lead to eruptions of political tensions; when, for instance, Blake Morrison and Andrew Motion chose to present Seamus Heaney in prime position as the first entry of the *Penguin Book of Contemporary British Poetry* (1982), the Irishman Heaney objected to this appropriation of his person publicly and vociferously (Stevenson 2005, 175–179).

In a variation of such forms of legitimization through famous names, some collections enlist the cultural capital of established poets who write a foreword, and this added sheen of glory is duly mentioned in the list of contents. The republications of *The Golden Treasury* furnish a striking example: Palgrave himself was advised in his choice of poems by the poet laureate of the time, Alfred Lord Tennyson, and Palgrave made this clear both in the dedication and in the introduction to his anthology. In line with this, the support of the respective poet laureate was enlisted in later editions of the *Treasury*: the 2000 facsimile edition was introduced by Andrew Motion, the 2018 collector's edition that marked 175 years of

Macmillan received its blessing from Carol Ann Duffy. In both cases the credit of the current poet laureate served to give additional sanction to the collection and the list of contents makes this explicit. Especially in the context of Palgrave's extremely reduced list of contents, the support of the poet laureate furnishes the only entry with a name and inevitably draws attention.

Rather than drawing on cognitive principles of ordering or established cultural status, the other long-standing ordering principle for poetry anthologies groups according to affect. This form of categorization originated most likely in the commonplace tradition: the habit of collecting quotes from acknowledged authors for use in one's own oral or written composition, grouped according to topic or occasion.[13] Offering poetry for personal use has been a continuous tradition since the Renaissance, one that is very much alive to this day, though often neglected by the canon debates. Thus, the Penguin *Poems for Life* (Barber 2007) offers poetry for all manner of life situation, covering Shakespeare's "seven ages of man." George Courtauld's *England's Best Loved Poems* (also 2007) arranges the poetic "enchantment of England" (the collection's subtitle) around topics such as fellowship, defiance, loss, or home. Affective groupings can functionalize individual poems in markedly differing frameworks. Thus Edward Thomas's "Adlestrop," which features in the *Norton* under World War I poetry, appears in Courtauld's collection under "Fellowship" and in Andrew Motion's *Here to Eternity* (2002) under "Travel"; William Blake's "Jerusalem" features under "Defiance" in Courtauld, but under "Music, Mystery and Magic" in A.P. Wavell's *Other Men's Flowers* (1944), while it merits no entry in the recent *Norton* as representative of romantic poetry (possibly because it is too heavily charged with nationalism).

List into Poetry

It is those editors that try most emphatically to break with established epistemic systems in their collections that are also most likely to create something poetic in the list of contents itself. Seamus Heaney and Ted Hughes's poetry anthology *The Rattle Bag* orders its entries alphabetically. This ordering framework, which is perceived as extraneous to poetry, subdues the utilitarian function of the list of contents and favors random connections—without guidance the imagination starts to roam, as the editors hoped it would: "We hope that our decision to impose an arbitrary order allows the contents to discover themselves as we ourselves gradually discovered them – each poem full of its singular appeal, transmitting its own signals, taking its chances in a big, voluble world" (Heaney and Hughes 1982, 19). In a completely fortuitous excess of meaning creation, the contiguity of list items creates the "unexpected dynamics" Belknap mentions (37) and the list of titles and first lines starts to form, cento-like or as a version of flarf poetry, poetic connections of its own, like the gloomy view of car culture cited at the beginning of this article, or what I would call "Warning to visitors not to tease zoo animals":

A crocodile
Crossing the Alps
Crossing the Water
Crystals Like Blood

These titles to poems by Thomas Lovell Beddoes ("A Crocodile"), William Wordsworth ("Crossing the Alps," an excerpt from the Prelude), Sylvia Plath ("Crossing the Water"), and Hugh MacDiarmid ("Crystals Like Blood") evoke a potential narrative: the exotic animal ("a crocodile") comes to the zoo from far away ("crossing the alps"). Teased beyond endurance, it swims across the water of its enclosure in the zoo and tears the noisome visitors into bloody shreds ("crystals like blood").[14] Obviously, such flights of the imagination do not create profundity; they revel in the chance meanings created by serendipity.

Beyond the "mere" functionality that is often ascribed to the list of contents, in poetry anthologies these lists create not only canon narratives, they offer epistemic or affective frameworks in which to place and use the texts to come—frameworks that are repeated in the collections themselves as titles, subtitles, or running headers, thus structuring the reading experience. And in some cases, the spatial proximity that a list of contents creates between "normally" separate units can itself generate playful poetic connections. The list, far from being a mere tool, develops a life of its own in all these cases, catering, as I initially claimed, to the human predilection for making teleological connections, even in cases where established systems of meaning creation (such as chronology) are subverted.

NOTES

1. Given his interest in the impact which paratexts and peritexts have on the "meaning" of a text, Genette treats the table of contents in a surprisingly cursory fashion.
2. There are fierce contentions whether such a basic definition of an anthology is valid. In particular, critics argue for a fundamental difference between collections that represent largely contemporary poetry, typical especially for the early modern period and often categorized as "miscellanies," and for collections that present an historical survey, the anthology "properly defined" according to Laura Mandell (2007, 10). While there are obvious differences between the two formats, the distinction has to be on a relative scale rather than an absolute one (see Lethbridge 2014, 20).
3. See similarly Lucie Doležalová about the usage of lists generally: "One does not *read* but only *uses* [sic] a list: one looks up the relevant information in it, but usually does not need to deal with it as a whole—and is happy about this fact" (2009, 1).
4. This is different in the twentieth-century scholarly edition by Hyder E. Rollins which, by way of table of contents, lists all of Tottel's added titles and—also different to Tottel who only mentioned the authors of the poems at the end of each section—clearly identifies authors at the beginning of the relevant listings.
5. Genette points out that the French custom is to have the list of contents at the back of the book. This is also the case for many German poetry collections, though it is rare for modern anthologies published in an Anglo-American context.
6. For the highly personal and personalized engagement of readers with Q's anthology as expressed in letters to Oxford University Press see Lethbridge 2014, 401–407.
7. Despite such efforts to make his use of the poems less noticeable, Bullar was threatened by Longmans, Wordsworth's publisher, who tried to force him to withdraw these poems from later editions, a threat which seems to have had no effect, as the *Selections* reappeared in 1830, this time with the poems of contention explicitly listed under "Modern Writers" (see Lethbridge 2014, 254–255).
8. For Palgrave's assembly and coordination of the list of poems he wanted to include in the *Treasury* with Tennyson and Thomas Woolner, see Tillotson 1988.
9. The term "disciplinary anthology" is Mandell's.
10. For an attempt to support this claim with statistical evidence see Lethbridge 2014, 33–37.
11. For the effect of this sea-change in literary production see StClair 2004.

12. The first survey anthology to introduce this format, according to Mandell, was the Chambers's *Readings in English Poetry* (1865), which was designed for a very broad readership, especially schools. The Chambers did not actually label the periods, they provided dates (Mandell 2007, 12).
13. On the connection between anthologies and the commonplace tradition see Price 2000, chapter 2, and Lethbridge 2014, 62–72.
14. The procedure is actually used in found poetry: Finnish poet Janne Nummela, for instance, created a found text from the list of contents of *Onnen Aika* by Pentti Saarikoski (Nummela 2008, 14). I thank Juri Joensuu for drawing my attention
15. to this lovely example.

REFERENCES

Barber, Laura, ed. 2007. *The Penguin Poems for Life*. London: Penguin Books.

Belknap, Robert. 2000. The Literary List: A Survey of its Uses and Deployments. *Literary Imagination* 2 (1): 35–54.

Benedict, Barbara. 1996. *Making the Modern Reader: Cultural Mediation in Early Modern Literary Anthologies*. Princeton: Princeton University Press.

Blair, Ann M. 2010. *Too Much to Know: Managing Scholarly Information Before the Modern Age*. New Haven: Yale University Press.

Chambers, William, and Robert Chambers, eds. 1865. *Chambers's Readings in English Poetry*. London/Edinburgh: William and Robert Chambers.

Courtauld, George, ed. 2007. *England's Best Loved Poems: The Enchantment of England*. London: Ebury Press.

Da Costa, Alex. 2018. 'That ye mowe redely fynde…what ye desyre': Printed Tables of Contents and Indices, 1476–1550. *Huntington Library Quarterly: Studies in English and American History and Literature* 81 (3): 291–313.

Doležalová, Lucie. 2009. Introduction: The Potential and Limitations of Studying Lists. In *The Charm of a List: From the Sumerians to Computerised Data Processing*, ed. Lucie Doležalová, 1–8. Cambridge: Cambridge Scholars Publishing.

Dryden, John, ed. 1684–1709. *Poetical Miscellanies. 6 vols*. London: Tonson.

Echard, Siân. 1997. Pre-Texts: Table of Contents and the Reading of John Gower's *Confessio Amantis*. *Medium Ævum* 66 (2): 270–287.

Ferry, Anne. 2001. *Tradition and the Individual Poem: An Inquiry into Anthologies*. Stanford: Stanford University Press.

Genette, Gérard. 1997. *Paratexts: Thresholds of Interpretation*. Trans. Jane E. Lewin. Cambridge: Cambridge University Press.

Goldsmith, Oliver, ed. 1767. *The Beauties of English Poesy*. 2 vols. London: W. Griffin.

Heaney, Seamus, and Ted Hughes. 1982. *The Rattle Bag*. London: Faber.

Keegan, Paul, ed. 2000. *The New Penguin Book of English Verse*. London et al.: Penguin.

Knox, Vicesimus, ed. 1785. *Elegant Extracts: Or Useful and Entertaining Pieces of Poetry, Selected for the Improvement of Youth, in Speaking, Reading, Thinking, Composing; and in the Conduct of Life*. London: Charles Dilly.

Korte, Barbara. 2000. Flowers for the Picking: Anthologies of Poetry in (British) Literary and Cultural Studies. In *Anthologies of British Poetry: Critical Perspectives from Literary and Cultural Studies*, ed. Barbara Korte, Ralf Schneider, and Stefanie Lethbridge, 1–32. Amsterdam: Rodopi.

Lethbridge, Stefanie. 2014. *Lyrik in Gebrauch: Gedichtanthologien in der englischen Druckkultur 1557–2007*. Heidelberg: Universitätsverlag Winter.

Mainberger, Sabine. 2003. *Die Kunst des Aufzählens: Elemente zu einer Poetik des Enumerativen*. Berlin: de Gruyter.

Mandell, Laura. 2007. Putting Contents on the Table: The Disciplinary Anthology and the Field of Literary History. *Poetess Archive Journal* 1 (1): 1–28. https://journals.tdl.org/paj/index.php/paj/article/view/29/31. Accessed 9 Jan 2021.

Mant, Elizabeth Woods. 1849. *The Parent's Poetical Anthology: Being a Selection of English Poems Primarily Designed to Assist in Forming the Taste and the Sentiments of Young Readers*. 5th ed. London: Longman, Brown, Green, and Longmans.

Morrison, Blake, and Andrew Motion, eds. 1982. *The Penguin Book of Contemporary British Poetry*. Harmondsworth: Penguin Books.

Motion, Andrew, ed. 2002. *Here to Eternity: An Anthology of English Poetry*. London: Faber.

Nummela, Janne. 2008. *Frigiditalvi*. Helsinki: ntamo.

Price, Leah. 2000. *The Anthology and the Rise of the Novel*. Cambridge: Cambridge University Press.

Palgrave, Francis Turner, ed. 1861. *The Golden Treasury of the Best Songs and Lyrical Poems in the English Language*. London: Macmillan.

Quiller-Couch, Arthur. 1923 [1900]. *The Oxford Book of English Verse 1250–1900*. Oxford: Clarendon Press.

Richardson, Brian. 2016. Modern Fiction, the Poetics of Lists and the Boundaries of Narrative. *Style* 50 (3): 327–341.

Ricks, Christopher, ed. 1999. *The Oxford Book of English Verse*. Oxford: Oxford University Press.

Rollins, Hyder E., ed. 1965 [1557]. *Tottel's Miscellany* [Songs and Sonnets]. 2 vols. Cambridge, MA: Harvard University Press.

———., ed. 1973. *The Phoenix Nest 1593. Facs. Repr.* London: Scholar Press.

Rouse, Mary A., and Richard H. Rouse. 1991. *Authentic Witnesses: Approaches to Medieval Texts and Manuscripts*. Notre Dame: University of Notre Dame Press.

Silkin, Jon. 1999. Taste-Shaping. *Victorian Poetry* 37 (2): 192.

StClair, William. 2004. *The Reading Nation in the Romantic Period*. Cambridge: Cambridge University Press.

Stevenson, Randall. 2005. *The Last of England?* Oxford: Oxford University Press.

The Nation's Favourite Poems. 1996. London: BBC Books.

Tillotson, Kathleen. 1988. Palgrave's *Golden Treasury* and Tennyson: Another Source. *Tennyson Research Bulletin* 5 (2): 49–54.

von Contzen, Eva. 2016. The Limits of Narration: Lists and Literary History. *Style* 50 (3): 241–260.

———. 2018. Experience, Affect, and Literary Lists. *Partial Answers* 16 (2): 315–327.

Ward, Thomas Humphry, ed. 1880. *The English Poets: Selections with Critical Introductions by Various Writers and a General Introduction by Matthew Arnold.* 4 vols. London: Macmillan.

Wavell, Archibald P., ed. 1944. *Other Men's Flowers*. London: Jonathan Cape.

CHAPTER 8

Aesthetic Unrest: "Howl" and the Literary List

Alyson Brickey

> At the still point of the turning world. Neither flesh nor fleshless;
> Neither from nor towards; at the still point, there the dance is,
> But neither arrest nor movement. And do not call it fixity.
> —T.S. Eliot, "Burnt Norton"

Lists are everywhere these days: not just in the familiar capitalist forms of "best seller" lists or "best albums of the year" lists, but most ubiquitously on the internet, in the form of the increasingly popular "listicle." As Wikipedia defines it, "[t]he word is a portmanteau derived from *list* and *article*. It has also been suggested that the word evokes 'popsicle,' emphasizing the fun but 'not too nutritious' nature of the listicle."[1] The listicle is an easily digestible, tasty treat. It allows us to take in a large concept in a small delicious form—an innocuous distillation of a more complex process of knowledge production. The less serious partner in the pair is, of course, the list, not the article. Lists are direct and to-the-point. They are

A. Brickey (✉)
Department of English, University of Winnipeg, Winnipeg, MB, Canada
e-mail: a.brickey@uwinnipeg.ca

R. A. Barton et al. (eds.), *Forms of List-Making: Epistemic, Literary, and Visual Enumeration,*
https://doi.org/10.1007/978-3-030-76970-3_8

brief, ordered, and clear, and they do not pretend to do the lofty intellectual work of a longer article or more involved piece of writing.

Recent scholarship on the form and function of the list, however, would suggest that lists are not, after all, to be trusted. In their introduction to the February 2016 special issue of *Society and Space*, "The Politics of the List," Marieke de Goede, Anna Leander, and Gavin Sullivan argue that lists are in fact quite nefarious. The cultural proliferation of lists, they suggest, which

> is taking place across such diverse domains [...] as finance, the environment, security, humanitarianism and health, [...] should be treated as more than a curiosity. Instead, we argue that it is important to take seriously the form and technique of the list itself and engage the knowledge practices, governance effects and ways of ordering the world that the list format enables. (2016, 3–4)

Citing examples such as watch lists, kill lists, blacklists, and no-fly lists, contributors to this special issue each elaborate what they believe to be the list's culturally oppressive characteristics: its ability to "procedure categories by making a 'cut' in the continuous flow of the world," its power to include through exclusion, and its suitability to processes which discursively restructure the world in order to benefit those in power (De Goede et al. 2016, 6).

This is something Michel Foucault intuits in much of his work, most notably in *The Order of Things*, where he outlines the epistemic processes that occasioned science's penchant, for example, for constituting the very knowledge systems that would make its "discoveries" possible. But the list, it is worth remembering, manifests in many different cultural forms, not just in science and law and finance. We also see it in aesthetic practices and artistic representations, where its ability to "cut" in the way these writers identify is complicated, and even encumbered. Umberto Eco's 2009 monograph *The Infinity of Lists* as well as the 2016 special issue of *Style* devoted to the range of literary lists throughout genres and history are a testament to this fact.

Eco distinguishes between what he calls "pragmatic" and "poetic" lists. Pragmatic lists are the kind of lists which are mundane and familiar, like telephone directories or restaurant menus. Eco argues that these kinds of lists "confer unity," and are therefore also finite (2009, 113). Poetic lists, on the other hand, are insatiable in their scope. These lists gesture outward into an abyss of referentiality and can expand infinitely. It is this second kind of list—the poetic list—with which this chapter concerns itself. While the writers in *Society and Space* argue that Eco's categories obscure the powerful ideological work that the list as a cultural technology does, suggesting that he makes a problematic distinction between high and low art, I argue that the literary list can in fact offer us a way of combating those same power structures with which these contributors are so concerned. Lists initiate a kind of restlessness within the literary text: what I term, in what follows, an "aesthetic unrest."

To elucidate this idea, I take up Allen Ginsberg's 1956 poem "Howl", a deviously restless text. This poem is constantly experimenting with movement and motion, its subjects caught up in continuous verbs, performing illicit acts and living in ways that defy state-sanctioned norms of behavior. To contextualize this kinesis, I turn to literary theory's interest in the aesthetic history of *ekphrasis*, or the linguistic representation of a visual representation. The literary list, I suggest, involves recourse to what Leo Spitzer calls the "ekphrastic impulse," which is a kind of representational reach for mimesis which always falls short and is therefore always also on the move (1962, 266).

In his discussion of literary ekphrasis, Sigurd Burckhardt positions literary works as materially unmoored, constantly searching for some reconnection to the physical world through linguistic attachment. The process of ekphrasis thus becomes a larger organizing principle, where all literary art in some sense desires to be a plastic art, and where poems can be said to have an "impulse" that tends toward the materially solid medium of sculpture. What is most relevant for my current discussion is the formulation of this impulse as an interplay between stillness and movement. To describe this phenomenon, Murray Krieger uses the term "still" not just as an adjective, but also as an

> adverb, and verb; as still movement, still moving, and more forcefully, the stilling of movement: so "still" movement as quiet, unmoving movement; "still" moving as a forever-now movement, always in process, unending; and the union of these meanings at once twin and opposed in the "stilling" of movement, an action that is at once the quieting of movement and the perpetuation of it, the making of it; […] a movement that is still and that is still with us, that is—in [Eliot's] words, "forever still." (Krieger 2019, 268)

This is Eliot's "still point of the turning world" from his 1936 poem "Burnt Norton": neither stasis nor momentum; not aesthetic arrest, but a kind of aesthetic *unrest* (Eliot 2008, 64). This paradoxical, ekphrastic quality of literature is precisely the movement that the aesthetic category of the literary list can lay bare. Lists like Ginsberg's poetically enact strange scenes that are "still moving" in their stillness. They can open a space amongst a flurry of activity: a productive space where the book exposes us, in these moments of unrest, to some kind of otherness—something strange.

This type of internal vibration—this textual restlessness that we see in Ginsberg's ecstatic chants of "holy! holy! holy!"—is indicative of an ekphrastic kinesis: a literary marker of the difficulty inherent within the process of representation itself (2008a, 1). In many ways, lists stall us, leaving us stuck between things; moored in the interstitial spaces between two or more solid, definable concepts. This is not stasis, however; and we do not experience a Joycean aesthetic arrest. It is a dynamic energy that lies at the very center of the work, and it is born out in catalogue form. In our encounters with texts like "Howl," we are thus witness to an aesthetic *unrest*: an inner oscillation that might trouble us or strike us as strange, or off-kilter. The a-narrative character of the list lends itself to this version of estrangement, but so do its ties to textual over-population, paratactic prose, and excessive descriptive passages that we might even find boring, or frustratingly unfocused.

The encounter with the list is also importantly a process of alienation and, as I show, is structurally aligned with the dynamics inherent in contemporary theoretical conceptions of ethical responsibility. Since at least Emmanuel Levinas's work in the 1950s, the philosophical conception of an ethical encounter has involved the idea of an encounter with otherness—something or someone who is strange and unfamiliar. Restless lists like the ones we find in "Howl" are, I suggest, one way that literature can expose us to otherness: that which is strange and outside of our familiar field of vision. The literary listing we find in "Howl" is strange—queer, even—not just for its evocation of sexual non-conformance, but also, importantly, for its ability to tolerate a kind of constant unease: an ontological restlessness born out in its catalogue aesthetic.

When Joyce's protagonist Stephen Dedalus lays out his aesthetic philosophy to his friend Lynch at boarding school in *A Portrait of the Artist as a Young Man*, he identifies an "esthetic emotion" that he says is "static— a face looking two ways [...] the mind is arrested and raised above desire and loathing" (Joyce 2003, 222). This passage marks the first time in literature we encounter the now-familiar idea of "aesthetic arrest," a concept that seems to name that which we have understood for so long in our philosophical discussions about art: a description of stillness in the face of beauty—an automatic response to being in the presence of artwork that moves.

The temporal and grammatical aspects of "Howl" accrue an intensity and velocity as the text progresses. Ginsberg, as many scholars have noted, was very interested in rhythm and music while writing this piece, and was particularly fond of listening to jazz great Charlie Parker while he composed his lines (see Géfin 2002, 275). Parker is perhaps most famous for his piece "Now's The Time," which aligns both thematically and formally with Ginsberg's repeated use of the continuous present tense in "Howl," as well as its simultaneity. Though he begins in the past tense, with the elegiac "I saw the best minds of my generation destroyed by madness," Ginsberg immediately shifts to the continuous present with "starving / hysterical, naked, / dragging themselves through negro streets at dawn looking for an angry / fix / [...] burning for the ancient heavenly connection" (2008b, 1–2). And while the tense shifts effortlessly throughout the poem—between different variations of the past, present, and future—it is always in the service of presenting us with extremely dynamic and perpetually moving scenes, not unlike the dynamism for which jazz music is known.

Each of these scenes is anchored by a strong verb that is very often connected to a description of an emotional force or corporeal movement. Ginsberg's rebellious young men over-populate the page with their insistent activity, which more often than not stages a socially taboo scenario. These are actors who shun heteronormativity and reject capitalist conformity. They press and impress upon us with an often violent and desperate demand for recognition and space. This is not the plural America that a loafing Walt Whitman described as his toes curled lazily in the grass; this is an America filled with young urban men on fire. These are men who chain themselves to subways, fuck each other in the ass, "walk all night with their shoes full of blood," burn cigarette holes in their arms, and "cut their wrists three times successively unsuccessfully" in a kind of living that might actually lie just adjacent to a kind of dying (Ginsberg 2008b, 44, 55).

In essence, Ginsberg presents us with a great list of unapologetically frenetic moments. When placed successively one after another, these moments accumulate to form a complex and perpetually moving scene. Ginsberg's aesthetic in fact operates in much the same manner here. Each line sets another action in motion, and these individual movements accumulate and gain momentum as the piece progresses. This process has something to do with the affective momentum of the poem as well, and by the end of the piece, when we read the supplementary "Footnote to Howl" where Ginsberg ecstatically declares that everything and everyone is "holy," we feel the weight of all that has come before it and are left with little choice but to join in, echoing his chant.

The rhythms he was encountering in Black Jazz culture, Ginsberg attempted to make each line the length of one long breath, a technique that infuses the poem with a steady pace that at once feels natural, but also always new (Géfin 2002, 275). In the first section, many lines start with the anaphoric "who," followed by some physical action performed by that subject, and then ending with an elaboration on that action. Here is a typical example: "who scribbled all night rocking and rolling over lofty incantations which in the yellow morning were stanzas of gibberish" (Ginsberg 2008b, 51). If we temporarily remove each elaboration, it becomes even more clear that the poem is asking us to recognize not just these subjects who society wants to marginalize and denigrate, but also to accept, without condition, their often brazen and illicit actions. Ginsberg wants to lift these scenes out of the shamefulness of dark corners and display them, glorified, upon a stark white page. Like Whitman's great catalogues in "Song of Myself" that expand to accommodate both the prostitute and the President, Ginsberg wants to invite those

> who blew /[...] who balled /[...] who hiccupped /[...] who lost /[...] who copulated /[...] who sweetened /[...] who faded /[...] who walked / [...] who ate /[...] who wept /[...] who scribbled /[...] who cooked /[...] who plunged /[...] who threw /[...] who cut /[...] who sang /[...] who drove /[...] who journeyed /[...] who crashed /[...] who demanded (2008b, 36–64)

and so on. These men and many more initiate moments of activity that defy prescriptive gender norms, balk at heteronormative coupling, spit at mandatory capitalist labor, howl back against the violence of war, and think anew what it might mean to live life otherwise.

"Howl" was written against the backdrop of a dominant American culture that was increasingly conservative, valuing conformity and control amidst the traumatic reverberations of World War II. Having just come out of a university experience studying English literature at Columbia, Ginsberg was frustrated by what he saw as the stale formalism of American poetry and disillusioned by higher education's ideological and financial involvement with the perverse creation of the atomic bomb. Written on the cusp of the repressive social policies of the Cold War, "Howl" represents a political, but not a utopian gesture. It reaches not toward some future time when differences would be tolerated and all would be harmonious, but rather enacts a powerful legitimization of a present moment that was being over-written by a rising white, patriarchal, upper middle-class, heterosexist culture. This is a type of resistance through the rebellion of contemporaneity: *now* was going to be the time when disaffected and disenfranchised populations were going to be taken seriously, just as Martin Luther King Jr. would articulate a short eight years later on the steps of the Washington Monument.[2]

While Ginsberg is not explicitly aligning himself with any particular political movement per se, there is nonetheless a politics here that has to do with a validation of subjects or ways of being that have been culturally suppressed or ideologically vilified. While the *Society and Space* editors are right to connect the list to politics, Ginsberg here demonstrates that the form can also be instrumentalized to fight against the very oppressive mechanisms they identify in their critique.

This last point becomes especially clear in Part III of the poem, which is addressed directly to Carl Solomon. Solomon was at the time incarcerated in a state-run psychiatric institution, and Ginsberg had in fact met him at a similar hospital in 1949 (see Hunsberger 2002, 160). This third section of the poem starts by continuing the radical dynamism I have been tracing, where lists of verbs and actors in constant and varied motion pile up, one on top of the other, multiplying and rapidly proliferating like errant cells under a microscope. These lines are filled with subjects who are nearly moving too fast for us to see; people who

> talked continuously seventy hours from park to pad to bar to Bellevue
> to museum to the Brooklyn Bridge,
> a lost battalion of platonic conversationalists jumping down the stoops off
> fire escapes off windowsills off Empire State out of the moon,
> yacketayakking screaming vomiting whispering facts and memories and
> anecdotes and
> eyeball kicks and shocks of hospitals and jails and wars, [...]
> who lit cigarettes in boxcars boxcars boxcars racketing through snow
> toward lonesome farms in grandfather night,
> who studied Plotinus Poe St. John of the Cross telepathy and bop
> kaballah because the cosmos instinctively vibrated at their feet in
> Kansas. (Ginsberg 2008b, 16–24)

Ginsberg's dual focus on simultaneity and movement comes strongly to the fore in this excerpt, as catalogues of verbs spill forth in clusters like "screaming vomiting whispering," and we are overwhelmed by having to imagine how one body could be doing all of this at once. It is as if he places multiple spinning tops on a vast floor, and one by one sets each in motion until the entire room is abuzz with kinetic activity. This sense of a cyclical rather than a propulsive movement is linguistically enacted through repetitive lines such as "who lit cigarettes in boxcars boxcars boxcars racketing through snow," which at once conjures the sound and rhythm of a forward-moving train, but also stalls the semantic progression of the sentence through repetition, and asks us to stay, moving, in the present moment (Ginsberg 2008b, 23).

While section one is filled with rebellious and subversive activity, and section two (the "Moloch" section) realizes an Inferno-like representational diagnosis of contemporary America's most insidious socio-cultural problems, section three is, by contrast, very calm and gentle in its tone. Here, Ginsberg stages a scene between just two characters, and in doing so he also stages a scene between freedom and confinement—power and powerlessness.

The section starts empathetically, where the "with" signals a kind of emotional alignment or understanding—an attempt to let the other know that he is not, in the end, alone. "I'm with you in Rockland," the speaker says over and over again,

> where you must feel very strange
> I'm with you in Rockland
> where you imitate the shade of my mother
> I'm with you in Rockland
> where you've murdered your twelve secretaries
> I'm with you in Rockland
> where you laugh at this invisible humor
> I'm with you in Rockland
> where we are great writers on the same dreadful typewriter
> I'm with you in Rockland
> where your condition has become serious and is reported on the radio.
> (Ginsberg 2008b, 96–106)

While the initial deictic location of the sentence is tied to the speaker—the "I" who is claiming to be "with" Solomon—the second line always shifts to the second person "you," emphasizing the importance of trying to understand the strangeness of being institutionalized: the perspective from which Solomon must be experiencing the world while detained in this place. Rightly or wrongly, this "I" attempts to reside in Solomon's head, taking seriously his delusions and participating in what others might think are mad, impossible scenes. Ginsberg imagines what it would be like if Solomon were not tucked quietly away and isolated, but rather treated as if his crisis were global in scale, as serious as an earthquake or another natural disaster that might be "reported on the radio."

The most powerful line of this section enacts another kind of ontological validation, but here this is accomplished through rhetorical recourse to a kind of ethical imperative. Solomon "bang[s] on the catatonic piano," spelling out a song that no one but the speaker seems able to translate, and stuck in a rhythmic yet torturous holding pattern (Ginsberg 2008b, 116). Catatonia is a kind of "inert state" characterized by the inability to move in recognizably normative physical and behavioral patterns.[3] In keeping with his theme, however, Ginsberg aestheticizes this inertness and turns it into inertia; he transforms Solomon's mental state into music, so that catatonia might now sound like a song where one note is repeated again and again, not unlike the poem's anaphoras. What results is an urgent moral statement: a run-on sentence that tells a tragic narrative and signals a need for change and recognition. "The soul," Ginsberg concludes, "is innocent and immortal it should never die ungodly in an armed madhouse" (Ginsberg 2008b, 116). This is a restlessness and unease that results in sympathetic care; the familial tone with which this stanza begins—the sibling-like adjacency that Ginsberg creates—now shifts to a guarding, parental one. This paves the way for the next few lines that seem to momentarily break from the willingness to inhabit Solomon's delusions to a more direct indictment of the realities of state-run psychiatric care. Again the speaker is "with" Solomon in Rockland, but now we are made to face directly the effects of institutionalized violence, when "fifty more shocks will never return your soul to its body again" (Ginsberg 2008b, 117).

Lest he create a hopeless scene, however, Ginsberg ends this section with a dream for a different reality, one where those imprisoned in Rockland break free from its oppressive walls and emerge triumphant to the soundtrack of a different kind of national anthem. The walls turn "imaginary" and collapse, and airplanes "roar over the roof" and drop "angelic bombs" (Ginsberg 2008b, 127). And as if the familiar orchestral swell of the Star-Spangled Banner has slowly crept into the frame, we read "O skinny legions run outside / O starry-spangled shock of mercy the eternal war is here / O victory forget your underwear we're free" (Ginsberg 2008b, 129). Ginsberg does not end with an unproblematic image of emancipation. Instead, he stages a quiet, private meeting, where he and Solomon can greet one another on equal footing, if only in an imagined space. "In my dreams," the speaker says, "you walk dripping from a sea-journey on the highway across America in tears to the door of my cottage in the Western night" (Ginsberg 2008b, 130).

The supplementary "Footnote to Howl" functions as a vital addition to the rest of the text. Ginsberg does not just make everything democratically equal, however, and he does not reach for the mechanical political metaphors he uses in other poems, like "Wichita Vortex Sutra"—words like ("legislate [...] execute [...] publish," or "approve")[4] (2007, 402). Instead, he declares that everything is sacred; holy:

> Holy! Holy! Holy! Holy! Holy! Holy! Holy! Holy! Holy! Holy! Holy! Holy! Holy! Holy! Holy! Holy!
> The world is holy! The soul is holy! The skin is holy! The nose is holy! The tongue and cock and hand and asshole holy!
> Everything is holy! everybody's holy! Everything is holy! everybody's holy! everywhere is holy! everyday is in eternity! Everyman's an angel!
> The bum's as holy as the seraphim! the madman is holy as you are my soul are holy!
> The typewriter is holy the poem is holy the voice is holy the hearers are holy the ecstasy is holy! (Ginsberg 2008a, 3–5)

This is a forceful and rebellious prayer: a sacrilegious, liturgical celebration. Here Ginsberg's parataxis works to linguistically and rhythmically equalize the poem's inhabitants—the nose and bum are praised alongside seraphims and angels—and capitalized letters fall away in favor of non-hierarchical lower-case ones. Through a whirling sea of individual actions and queer voices and incomprehensibly mad gestures, Ginsberg has made everything and everyone holy, and he has opened up a space where Carl Solomon can emerge from the sea and walk tearfully up to his cabin door in the middle of the quiet night. Ginsberg imagines a space that is hospitable even for those who have been cast away or cast out. His America is one where "when you are not safe I am not safe," and "Howl" thus remains a truly radical poetic offering.

Timothy Morton connects the notion of hospitality and what he calls "queer ecology." "To us," he argues, life-forms are strangers whose strangeness is irreducible: *arrivants*, whose arrival cannot be predicted or accounted for ("Hostipitality"). Instead of reducing everything to sameness, ecological interdependence multiplies differences everywhere [...] Strange strangers are uncanny, familiar and strange simultaneously. [...] They cannot be thought as part of a series (such as species or genus) without violence. [...] Queer ecology may espouse something very different from individualism. (Morton 2012, 277)

Here is a model of sociality that is paradoxically based on strangeness, not familiarity or understanding. Lists, in many ways, are indeed very queer. They too "multiply differences" and render the world mysterious and miraculous. They can make even the most familiar collection of things seem weird in its heterogeneity, and they can make the most bizarre things appear familiar through a cultural attachment to modes of description and definition. Ginsberg's list aesthetic, in other words, is one way representations can register that version of the uncanny that Morton identifies. Lists invite us to reconsider those familiar processes by which we are accustomed to recognizing and responding to that which is strange, other, queer, and unfamiliar.

And while the list does not necessarily entail an ethics in every circumstance, lists like Ginsberg's suggest that the aesthetic deployment of the catalogue form is not in itself harmful. It can, in fact, be quite revolutionary. This challenges the arguments made in *Society and Space*, and yet the contributors are correct in exposing the list's complicity in some extremely harmful social practices. While it is true that the catalogue form may serve oppressive aims by enabling the production of "contingent referentialities that come to appear as obvious," "absorb[ing] uncertainty," and "undermining the possibilities for political challenge," it is also true that the list can open up the possibility of radically shifting the ground upon which those kinds of aims are able to proliferate—where categories like "citizen" and "non-citizen," become very difficult to delineate and maintain (De Goede et al. 2016, 3, 6, 7).

It is in this sense that Ginsberg's lists strike us. They repeatedly disrupt any kind of linearity and can disturb conceptual associations. They overwhelm us and flood us with too much information and make navigating a textual world a disorienting and unfamiliar process. The contemporary philosophical formulation of otherness as strange carries with it an implicit demand that we must never try to domesticate or familiarize it. Giorgio Agamben writes, for example, that "if we try to grasp a concept as such, it is fatally transformed into an object, and the price we pay is no longer being able to distinguish it from the conceived thing" (2003, 80–81). The question becomes how best, then, to avoid collapsing the distance between the thing and the mimetic representation of the thing—between alterity and our ability to name it. Ginsburg's lists may offer us one way to think about that strange process of an encounter with alterity that is also, at the same time, a non-encounter: a failed meeting.

Derek Attridge argues that reading literature can be conceptualized as precisely this kind of encounter with strangeness, one which can elicit an opening up to alterity. In *The Singularity of Literature*, he writes that "it is the case, I believe, that some sense of strangeness, mystery or unfathomability is involved in every encounter with the literary" (Attridge 2004, 77). This strangeness results from an encounter with "otherness," or what Attridge defines as that which a particular culture at a particular moment must elide in order to maintain its

> normative modes. Here, alterity is figured as that which is [...] outside the horizon provided by the culture for thinking, understanding, imagining, feeling, perceiving [...] produced in an active or event-like relation [...] that which the existing cultural order has to occlude in order to maintain its capacities and configurations, its value-systems and hierarchies of importance; that which it cannot afford to acknowledge if it is to continue without change. (Attridge 2004, 29, 30, 124)

While Attridge might certainly be correct in suggesting that particular works will be experienced as more or less strange given how hospitably they are received within a given socio-cultural context, it might very well also be the case that the ekphrastic impulse embedded within the process of literary production itself means that some literary works always, to some degree, remain epistemologically alien and are never fully culturally assimilated. My sense is that lists such as those we find in "Howl" encourage this process of estrangement and render the texts in which they are found more likely to be culturally received with this attunement to alterity. Certainly, while "Howl" is by this point firmly canonical and very often anthologized, it is also its queer content and explicit language that results in its marginalization both within and outside of the English literary studies classroom—as well as the larger cultural imaginary.

This is a poem that is not easily domesticated, a fact that is intimately bound up with the aesthetic form of the list itself. The list is what allows

Ginsberg to poetically instantiate something as strange as "the game of the actual pingpong of the abyss" (Ginsberg 2008b, 114). We meet overly enumerative texts like Ginsberg's with a certain amount of trepidation; they are not easily absorbed, and they prove difficult for the task of the interpreter. These texts are restless and fidgety—somehow on edge. In the end, it is the list's ability to strangely point far beyond itself, to mark a kind of endlessness to the complexity of the representational gesture, that is perhaps most theoretically significant. These catalogues and enumerations, this paratactic and excessive prose, are ultimately able to open us to otherness: something strange—something else. The space of the list can thus become a space in which an egalitarian ethics might reside: a space where Ginsberg's "when you are not safe, I am not safe" becomes not just a utopian dream, but an ontological possibility.

Notes

1. "Listicle," Wikipedia. https://en.wikipedia.org/wiki/Listicle. Accessed 15 May 2016.
2. I am indebted to the Art Gallery of Ontario's 2015 Jean-Michel Basquiat exhibit "Now's the Time" for this rhetorical connection between King and Parker.
3. "Catatonia." *Oxford English Dictionary*, 2. https://www-oed-com.uwinnipeg.idm.oclc.org/view/Entry/28804?redirectedFrom=catatonia#eid. Accessed 20 July 2015.
4. Ginsberg, "Wichita Vortex Sutra" in *Collected Poems: 1947–1997* (2007), 92, 93, 96, 98.

References

Agamben, Giorgio. 2003. *The Coming Community*. Trans. Michael Hardt. Minneapolis: The University of Minnesota Press.
Attridge, Derek. 2004. *The Singularity of Literature*. London: Routledge.
"Catatonia." *Oxford English Dictionary* 2. https://www.oed.com.uwinnipeg.idm.oclc.org/view/Entry/28804?redirectedFrom=catatonia#eid.   Accessed 15 Jan 2020.
De Goede, Marieke, Anne Leander, and Gavin Sullivan. 2016. Introduction: The Politics of the List. *Society and Space* 34 (1): 3–13.
Eco, Umberto. 2009. *The Infinity of Lists: An Illustrated Essay*. New York: Rizzoli.

Eliot, T.S. 2008. Burnt Norton. In *The Norton Anthology of American Literature Volume 2: 1865–Present*, shorter 7th ed., ed. Nina Baym, 885–889. New York: W. W. Norton & Company.

Géfin, Laszlo. 2002. Ellipsis: The Ideograms of Ginsberg. In *On the Poetry of Allen Ginsberg*, ed. Lewis Hyde, 272–287. Ann Arbor: The University of Michigan Press.

Ginsberg, Allen. 2008a. Footnote to Howl. In *The Norton Anthology of American Literature Volume 2: 1865–Present*, shorter 7th ed., ed. Nina Baym, 1424. New York: W. W. Norton & Company.

———. 2008b. Howl. In *The Norton Anthology of American Literature Volume 2: 1865–Present*, shorter 7th ed., ed. Nina Baym, 1416–1424. New York: W. W. Norton & Company.

———. 2007. Wichita Vortex Sutra. In *Collected Poems: 1947–1997*, 402–419. New York: Harper Collins.

Hunsberger, Bruce. 2002. Kit Smart's Howl. In *On the Poetry of Allen Ginsberg*, ed. Lewis Hyde, 158–170. Ann Arbor: The University of Michigan Press.

Joyce, James. 2003. *A Portrait of the Artist as a Young Man.* New York: Penguin Books.

Krieger, Murray. 2019. Ekphrasis and the Still Movement of Poetry; or Laokoon Revisited. In *Ekphrasis: The Illusion of the Natural Sign*, 263–288. Baltimore: The Johns Hopkins University Press.

"Listicle." Wikipedia. https://en.wikipedia.org/wiki/listicle. Accessed 15 May 2016.

Morton, Timothy. 2012. An Object-Oriented Defense of Poetry. *New Literary History* 43 (2): 205–224.

Spitzer, Leo. 1962. The Ode on a Grecian Urn, or Content *vs* Metagrammar. In *Essays on English and American Literature*, 67–97. Princeton: Princeton University Press.

CHAPTER 9

Culinary List Form in the Experimental Poetry of 1960s Finland: Literary Menus and Recipes

Juri Joensuu

A reader interested in different approaches or eras of avant-garde and experimental literature—whether he or she reads concrete poetry, Samuel Beckett's or Georges Perec's prose, works of American postmodernism, or conceptual writing of the new millennium—is likely to stumble across enumeration, the list form. Reasons for the list's almost symbiotic compatibility with experimental approaches and techniques are numerous, as the literary list can serve a variety of functions. One can hypothesize that experimental writers easily, even instinctively, adopt the list because the list form can produce two situations on a smaller scale that experimental writing seeks to explore on a wider scale. First, it can bring about a break from the conventional poetic or narrative norms and expectations, and second, at the same time, it can highlight *writing* as a material and technical practice for recording, manipulating, and producing verbal information. And, in a more thematic sense, the list form is apt for dealing with order, hierarchy, or power, be it social, ideological, political, or systemic—themes

J. Joensuu (✉)
University of Jyväskylä, Jyväskylä, Finland
e-mail: juri.m.joensuu@jyu.fi

R. A. Barton et al. (eds.), *Forms of List-Making: Epistemic, Literary, and Visual Enumeration,*
https://doi.org/10.1007/978-3-030-76970-3_9

and subject matters dear to many experimental writers. This chapter tries to explore the symbiosis of enumeration and experimental literature by introducing and analyzing a peculiar subgenre of literary lists: texts that utilize culinary list forms such as the *menu* and the *recipe*.

By the term "experimental" I refer to a variety of formal, material, technical, or conceptual approaches consciously chosen by writers to explore the processes of creation, composition, or reception, as well as literary forms, norms, and values. The root word "experiment" refers to a science-like model of testing, the ambition "to extend the boundaries of [...] artistic practice," which also "implies rejection of hide-bound traditions, values and forms" (Bray et al. 2012, 2). To do these things, experimental literature is, nonetheless, quite sensitive to its own tradition: it recycles and reworks established techniques, methods, and formal approaches of writing. Typical experimental literary devices include collage, experiments with typography and spatial design, non-linear and multimodal narration as well as the application of rules and *constraints* (à la OuLiPo[1])—and, intersecting with some of these, the list form.

One specific example of experimental writing can be found in menu-poems. A menu can mean, first, a designed set of dishes and drinks to be consumed in a specific order. As such, the menu—the order of appetizers, main dishes, desserts, and appropriate drinks—represents a developed cultural order, which represents certain professional rules and tastes. A menu in this regard represents a meal as controlled, sociable eating and drinking. Second, menu can mean an optional list of dishes (*à la carte*) in a restaurant or canteen. Compared to the menu, which, according to Henry Notaker (2017, 104–105), first appeared at private dinner parties in France during the nineteenth century, the recipe has a longer and more complex genealogy. In practice, the recipe can be described as a textual formula for the purposes of preparing specific portions of food or beverages. The recipe is not necessarily textual nor culinary, but the textual form enables its two central functions: recording and consulting.[2] Besides food and drink, recipes also connect to the history of medicine, drugs, naturopathy, and esoteric areas of knowledge. As textual genres, both the menu and the recipe are recognizable, practical, non-literary text types. Both of them are also lists, listing a series of dishes, ingredients, steps, and stages of production. They present (sequential) actions that are oriented toward possible future action.

Food listings have a long tradition in the history of literature. A subgenre of the literary list, food listing can be an inventory of foodstuffs, or part of the description of a meal, its preparation, composition, presentation, or consumption.[3] Food listing can also be (a part of) a fictitious, imaginative recipes or menus, in fiction either embedded in the narration or presented as a separate list when the agent of narration is more unclear.[4] In poetry, recipes or menus can be used as a recognizable epistemic form "filled" with unexpected (poetic) content. As such, enumeration is usually one of the determining factors that provokes the reader to recognize the familiar form of the recipe or the menu. The graphical and typographical principles—the ways lists accentuate texts as images—are important, also in culinary forms. Even if "literary recipes" or "literary menus" present fictitious, sometimes impossible dishes—food and drinks that could not exist in reality—still, what seems to be decisive is the way in which they transport the reality of cooking and the cultural memory of food traditions and thus also speak to the personal culinary memories of the reader.

In the literary context of the 1960s Finnish experimentalists, the use of recipe and menu forms can be considered a part of "a series of efforts to articulate new relationships between art and the rapidly changing everyday, between 'high' and 'low' and between the different discourses in society" (Veivo 2016, 773). Eating and drinking are inevitable and mundane—everyday—activities in the very sense of the word. "When we eat," food sociologists inform us, "we are not merely consuming nutrients, we are also consuming gustatory (i.e., taste-related) experiences and, in a very real sense, we are also 'consuming' meanings and symbols. Every aliment in any given human diet carries a symbolic charge along with its bundle of nutrients" (Beardsworth and Keil 1997, 51). The examples explored in this chapter expand on this notion and represent polysemic approaches to taste, status, and cultural order. Their impact rests on the clash between the mundane and the exceptional, the everyday and the fantastic. Menus and recipes offer ways to examine these relationships in symbolically coded forms.

Besides these social implications, two viewpoints from experimental poetics can be considered. First, as both recipes and menus are usually non-literary, practical forms, their inclusion and imitation in literature is strongly connected to the tendency seen in experimental writings to draw from other sources such as recovered texts, literary *objet trouvés*, appropriations, and re-contextualizations. These practices are found in early avant-garde techniques (e.g., Duchamp, Breton), modernist writing (e.g., Eliot, Williams), post-war American experimental poetry (e.g., Ashbery,

Berrigan), as well as in the conceptual writing of the new millennium (see Epstein 2012). Second, one can ask in what ways the list form relates to constrained writing and procedural literature in the Oulipian sense (see endnote 1), meaning rules, methods, or other formal principles willfully chosen and imposed by the writer. The list as such is too broad a form to be accepted as a constraint in the Oulipian sense.[5] Yet, it can either be joined with a variety of Oulipian constraints or function as an essential background structure in certain instances of constrained writing.[6]

From the viewpoint of European or global literary studies, my material comes from uncharted territory, 1960s Finland. I hope that the alleged obscurity and marginality of my material will add insight on the versatility, universality, applicability, and incisiveness of literary lists and their areas of usage. My focus will be on the *poetic usage* of the list form: the tension between, on the one hand, the unity and the order inherent in the list form and, on the other hand, the free imaginative variation in the content. In my examples the list form ironizes order. Connected to this theme, the readings of the selected recipes and menus will reveal symbolic and ideological meanings that exceed their supposedly culinary content.

Lists in the Experimental Literature of 1960s Finland

Before I proceed with my primary material, I will give a couple of examples of the list form in 1960s Finnish experimental literature. The aim is to offer some literary-historical context and also to consider thematic and formal similarities between these starters and the main course: four texts (two menus and two recipes) that prove exceptional in the ways they combine distinctive content with inventive use of form. The four texts chosen show a representative selection from 1960s Finnish "culinary literature." The form of the list distinguishes them from conventional and non-experimental literature which is typically less cognizant of form.

Internationally, the 1960s was an active decade for experimental endeavors in art and literature. Different "neo-avant-garde" activities were born around the world, the term Conceptual art was introduced in 1961, the Fluxus Manifesto was conceived by George Maciunas in 1963, and Sol LeWitt's seminal text "Paragraphs on Conceptual Art" appeared in 1967. The 1960s also marked the beginning of postmodernism in literature (McHale 2008). Concrete poetry was vibrant in Europe, but also in Latin

America. OuLiPo was established in 1960 and consolidated its position during the decade.

Meanwhile, also the remote, in many ways still post-war and barely urban Finland "saw the rise of a new interest in the avant-garde […] especially in poetry" (Veivo 2016, 772). In many respects this was something new. The period of Finnish-language modernism only really took off in the 1950s. Before World War II, attempts to translate the innovative approaches of the European Avant-gardes (Futurism, Dadaism, and Surrealism) into the Finnish context were extremely rare. Only German Expressionism had some positive reception in Finland as figures such as "the first modernist" Edith Södergran (1892–1923) and Uuno Kailas (1901–1933) show. There are many reasons for Finland's cultural hostility toward experimental literature. The legacy of the brutal civil war (1918) politicized Finnish culture for decades. Avant-gardistic arts were regarded as suspicious imported goods in the eyes of both right-wing and left-wing political groups. Together with a lack of literary tradition, a lack of urban culture, and the linguistic "outsider" status of the Fenno-Ugric language, this created a hostile climate for avant-garde, artistic innovation, and experimentation.[7]

But in the 1960s something changed in Finnish literature along the lines of innovation and international influences in other arts (e.g., visual arts, performance, electronic music, see Hottinen 2016). Especially the short, three-year period of the mid-decade saw a burst of some 30 works of versatile experimental literature (Joensuu 2016, 28). Besides such techniques as text collage, visual text, enhanced typography, minimalism, and different intermedial applications, the list was clearly the most recurring form in the experimental endeavors of the decade. According to Harri Veivo (2016, 773), the "attempts to get to grips with changes in everyday life and to navigate in the new discursive world are visible in the use or imitation of lists and catalogues." While this is probable, other kinds of motivation and functions for the use of lists can also be assumed. According to Jan Alber (2016), postmodernist literary lists (1) foreground the linguistic medium, and thus, are self-reflexive; (2) highlight (and make fun of) our need to impose order on chaos; and (3) celebrate variety and plurality. All these claims hold true also for many of the lists found in the works of 1960s Finnish experimentalists, although labeling them postmodernists would be daring.[8] Still, the following examples of 1960s Finnish list poetry demonstrate the flexibility and variability of the list form's subject matters, approaches, and effects.

I will start with a rather abstract, almost conceptual poem which uses very non-lyrical word-lists.[9] "Informaatiota" ("Information," 1966) by Brita Polttila (1920–2008) lists different acronyms of political players of the decade. For instance, "EFTA" designates the European Free Trade Association, "YK" and "NL" are the Finnish abbreviations for United Nations and Soviet Union, respectively. The ironic end phrase translates as "Come on, get real / let's go to movies!"

INFORMAATIOTA

EFTA
NATO
EEC
ANF
MLF
OAS
YAT
YK
TN
SEATO
USA
NL
FAO
MLF MLF MLF MLF YK YK TN

– Kuule älä viitsi intoilla
mennään leffaan! (Polttila 1966, 9)

One can compare Polttila's poem to an even more abstract, untitled poem by J. O. Mallander (b. 1944), which consists of mechanical repetitions of the Swedish words "nedräkning" (countdown) and "uppräkning" (listing), combined with the word "vidräkning" (reckoning, confrontation), which appears only once (see Mallander 1969, 64). In the book, the listing of two words fills the whole page lengthways: it extends from the text area to the upper and lower edges of the page, deliberately violating the typographical margin rules. In doing so, it suggests the *infiniteness* of this list: the list goes beyond the material book. Like the poem above by Brita Polttila, Mallander's poem, too, highlights the materiality of language. Stripped of its communicative and aesthetic function and turned into a sign that signifies nothing beyond its own endless perpetuation, Mallander's objectified language almost resembles concrete poetry. It seems as if these were compiled or produced by a machine.[10] The recipe and menu poems also play with this kind of non-literary, non-lyrical, and procedural approach to writing.

As in recipes, the following poem by Kalevi Seilonen (1937–2011) seems to have a rather authoritative diction. The poem presents five rather contradictious and sometimes nonsensical statements as facts. The title is the organizing and grouping principle, binding together these five numbered main clauses.

Scientific Facts

1. Goethe had a weak understanding.
2. 97 % of Finns are German.
3. Saarikoski has 12 drainpipes.
4. Finnish Broadcasting Company offends the Constitution.
5. Champignons are no champions. (Seilonen 1965, 22, original: "Tieteellisiä tosiasioita")

All the lines are concisely phrased declarative sentences that evoke the impression of being objective facts, even though they strongly claim something rather unexpected. Far from facts or scientific findings, these claims resemble, respectively, historical and logical impossibilities, inside jokes, conspiracy theories, or tongue-in-cheek opinions. The first claim on Goethe's cognitive capabilities could indicate a rebellion against Western literary values and tastes, doubled in the non-traditional form of the poem. Pentti Saarikoski (1937–1983) was a celebrity poet of the time, renowned for his bohemian lifestyle, so "12 drainpipes" might be considered as a sarcastic allusion to his industrious drinking. Furthermore, the leftist politicization of the Yleisradio (Finnish Broadcasting Company) was a widely discussed topic in the 1960s. The last sentence is a pun, which is difficult to translate. It centers on the notion of taste: the Finnish term for champignon is "delicacy mushroom" and the speaker claims that "delicacy mushrooms are no delicacy." A pun is a very different form of knowledge than a scientific fact. While the first one is simply given, the second should be the subject of investigation. The ascending numerical presentation in the lines of the poem and the use of numericals in the text (97%, 12) ironically make use of mathematical conventions that stand in for objective knowledge, order, and hierarchy, which the very content of the "facts" makes redundant. It would be impossible to achieve the same structural irony (the delightful conflict between the serious form and the oddball content) without the numbered listing. It is this idea of (linear) order and logical sequence which is also typical for the formal arrangement of recipes.

The poems by Polttila and Seilonen discussed above make use of the non-literary list's documentary, "applicatory" function and transfer it to a context outside the realm of objective facts—a feature they share with the culinary lists discussed in the following section. Just as a list easily captures topical, current discourse, the same form can ironize and criticize the ideological dimensions of the content by laying bare contradictions that obviate the need for explanation. Irony is "potentially an effective strategy of oppositionality," even a passionate "mode of combat" (Hutcheon 1994, 29). This oppositionality can also be noticed in the following examples.

The first menu poem by Aronpuro in the following section uses the list as a realistic (probably facsimile) part of a collage, with both documentary and ideological tendencies. It also relies on the visual layout which the list form typically produces. The second menu poem by Lappalainen presents a bizzare menu, which documents mainly the workings of the poet's imagination. In the recipes by Hollo and Numminen the generic user-guidance of the recipes is ironized by oppositional, countercultural, spiritual, and psychedelic elements. These are reinforced by the procedural list formula of the recipe.

MENUS AND RECIPES: FOUR SERVINGS

Peltiset enkelit ("Tin Angels," 1964), the first collection of prolific experimentalist Kari Aronpuro (b. 1940), includes a five-page collage poem "Zodiac (aivofilmi)" ("Zodiac (Brain Film)"). Rich in typographical variety, the poem employs different types, signs, and symbols, while mirroring a stroll in an urban landscape, framed by all kinds of oncoming verbal stuff. In the mix there is also a menu (see Figs. 9.1 and 9.2). It resembles a genuine, discovered text representing a selection of foods in a workers' canteen ("Open from 9 to 23"). Instead of higher culinary cultures, this à la carte from a working-class dining environment is as street-credible as the poem's references to, for instance, public transport, cigarette commercials, or an etiquette text from a cheap booze brand ("Pöytä / viinaa / Bords / brännvin"). Most dishes on the menu are affordable, mundane grub, like oat porridge, fried herrings, or pea soup. Bread, butter, and milk—cornerstones of the 1960s Nordic cuisine—are sold separately (see

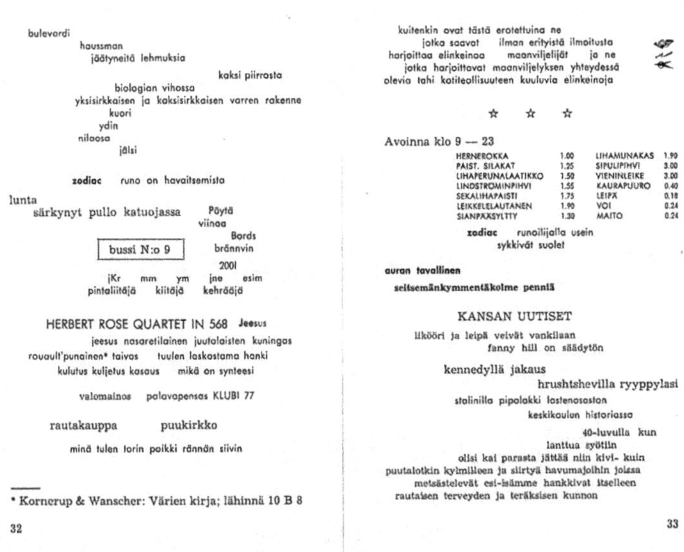

Fig. 9.1   Kari Aronpuro, "Zodiac (aivofilmi)" [a double-page spread], in *Peltiset enkelit* (Helsinki 1964), 32–33

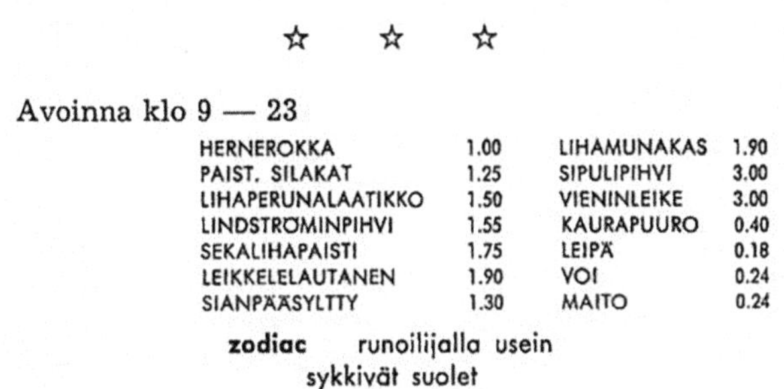

Fig. 9.2   Kari Aronpuro, "Zodiac (aivofilmi)" [excerpt], in *Peltiset enkelit* (Helsinki 1964), 33

the end of the list). Maybe the most expensive dishes, Wiener schnitzel or steak and onions (3.00 marks), spark the poem's speaker to add a less-than eloquent line underneath the menu: "a poet often has / pulsating bowels" ("runoilijalla usein / sykkivät suolet"). Instead of a romantic poet's pulsating heart, a modern poet seems to be driven by different, more material realities.

This is not the poem's only reference to poverty and hunger. Lower on the same page, there is another reference to memories of (wartime) poverty: "in the 40's when / we used to eat swede" ("40-luvulla kun / lanttua syötiin"). This cheerless root vegetable symbolizes everyday survival. Maybe this "history of hunger" is something that springs to the speaker's consciousness while seeing the range of all the unattainable dishes listed on the menu. Thus, a simple re-embedding of a list of foods to this text collage conveys an ideological significance.

This most probably authentic (a typographical facsimile) menu reflects the ethnographic impulse that collages also have: recording the everyday, unglamorous material, a canteen menu being one of the many mundane lists of the 1960s. This menu is not (originally) fictive or poetic, but it reproduces a pragmatic list and a certain, particular menu, discovered and graphically preserved. Here the list introduces a brief moment of (ironic) *order* in the midst of the wildly free multitude of graphical material that the collage presents.

The second menu is a poem by Kalevi Lappalainen (1940–1988), who had a rather peculiar, surrealistic style of writing. He lived in the USA between 1960–1964 and again from 1971 until his untimely death in a fire in 1988. His menu poem is a leap far from Aronpuro's realistic food list to more surreal servings. The effect of the form is different from Aronpuro's poem, where the list is embedded in the collage among all the other texts. In Lappalainen's text the list *is* the poem. It shows that the culinary list cannot only serve documentary purposes, but also convey culinary fantasy and imagination. Besides the title, which uses the word "menu," the reader also recognizes the form—the numbered listing, under which the servings are presented. Syntactically, the poem is a simple listing of dishes, but the contents of the menu are unusual, presenting an array of impossible foods and culinary phantasmagoria.

I WILL REVEAL MY FAVOURITE MENU

> I   serving: Embalmed Nefernefernefer.
>   Some Jimi Hendrix rubbed in oil. One fried onion.
> II serving: Fish grilled in lightning.
>   Hand soaked in water. Miss Almond tortured in fire.
> III serving: Boiled astronaut.
>   Little birds and radishes. Waist with cucumber. (Lappalainen 1968, 53,
>   original: "Paljastan teille himoruokalistani.")

The poem plainly presents a catalogue of objects, some of them referring to actual food (onion, fish, radishes, cucumber) while others refer to human beings. They are either fictitious (Nefernefernefer, a character in *The Egyptian*, a novel by Mika Waltari), real persons (Jimi Hendrix), cryptic allusions (Miss Almond), or just human body parts. Thus, in a gastronomical context of food and eating, the poem could be associated with anthropophagy—that is, cannibalism. However, further reading allows for a different interpretation which helps us to connect these bizarre combinations that seem enigmatic, disturbing, and confusing.

It is tempting to read the anthropophagic references and unconventional fusions as encoded erotic and sexual meanings. Eating and swallowing have a close relationship to physical love and eroticism, not just due to the oral dimension, but also because they symbolize procedures of internalizing, merging, and possessing. Framing normally inedible objects as edible, the poem relies on symbolic transference, where erotic impulses are converted into unexpected but powerful images. While some images exploit conventional romantic or erotic symbols (hand, little birds, waist, oil, perhaps a phallic cucumber), or otherwise clear references (Nefernefernefer, a deceitful woman who used her sexuality as a tool), some are more complicated. Both astronauts and Jimi Hendrix (at the peak of his career in 1968 renowned for his suggestive performances) were admired and adored by the masses, unlike the mysterious Miss Almond, who, instead of inner burning, is tortured in fire. Images of desire unite with weird, unappetizing images. Desire and disgust are close to each other, even "dialectically conjoined" (Ngai 2005, 332–333). Then again, Julia Kristeva's view on *abjection*—a strong, horrible disgust which shakes the foundations and boundaries of individual experience—is based on food and eating: food loathing is "perhaps the most elementary and most archaic form of abjection" (Kristeva 1982, 2). The list form is apt for highlighting and mixing the cognitive categories: the poem becomes abject because it is situated at the border (see Kristeva 1982, 75) between eroticism, food consumption, and death or decay. It is the mixture which the poem suggests that troubles us. It suggests that we are attracted by what ultimately is also repulsive. The list as a formed order or the tradition of the menu stands in stark contrast to these surreal evocations of disgust that point toward the hidden and unconscious and not to the neatly formed and known.

Once again, the form of the list as the poem's structural idea reasserts itself in the title. The title also implies the erotic and libidinal contents of the poem, something that is in strong opposition to eating as "practical," mundane nutrition. Instead of "My Favourite Menu," for instance, the title uses specifically the word *reveal*, as if referring to something previously hidden. Additionally, the word *himo* used in the original title is closer to lust, desire, or addiction, than the milder term "favourite." This "lust menu" is thus the area for the poetic imagination, where charged images and associations surpass the culinary menu and result in strange, even repulsing, surrealist servings. This private and sexual usage clearly clashes with the social and culinary user function of a menu, connected with taste, hierarchy, and order—while maintaining the form. Disturbing images are listed in the menu form and thus set in conflict with the food references this form usually is used for. The orderly listing as such highlights the discrepancy between the poem's messages. For the reader, the numerical form and the cognitive setting of "menu" ties everything into an (almost) meaningful culinary frame of reference.

The next example is by Anselm Hollo (1934–2013), certainly the most renowned Finnish poet abroad, who lived in the USA from 1967 until his death. "Good Stuff Cookies" (circa 1968) is immediately recognized as relying on the form of a recipe: it utilizes the tripartite structure with the heading, the list of ingredients, and instructions. As is so often the case in lists, here, too, the reader immediately, even before reading anything, distinguishes and recognizes the numerical list as a visual unit, and thus sets it off from the rest of the poems in the collection. This recognition and the procedural nature inherent in the recipe form are quickly short-circuited in the reading, and the reader's attention on the list form turns poetic. Hollo's way of using spaces in the middle of the lines is also conspicuous. As is the case in the previous example, here, too, the familiar culinary format is exploited by filling it with something other than real foodstuffs.

good stuff cookies

2 gods
2/3 cup hidden psychic reality
2 teasp. real world
3/4 cup sleep
2 cups sifted all-purpose iridescence
2 teasp. good stuff
1/2 teasp. pomp & pleasure

beat gods hidden psychic reality
real world and sleep together
sift together iridescence good stuff
pomp & pleasure
add to real world mixture
drop by teaspoon
2 inches apart on cookie sheet
press cookies flat
with bottom of glass dipped in sleep
bake at 400 F 8 to 10 minutes

2 dozen cookies good stuff. (Hollo 1970, 98)

All ingredients are immaterial, spiritual substances. Unlike in Lappalainen's menu, there are no edible items in the mix. Beating two gods, hidden psychic reality, real world, and sleep together seem to be like a mixture for a philosophy of life. This is enhanced by the term "iridescence," meaning rainbow-like appearance of all the colors at once. While the form of the baking recipe strongly hints at a context of middle-class communality that values sugar-coated outward appearances, Hollo's recipe seems to aim at creating individualized truth and spiritual growth that transcend the need for material proof of the recipe's successful completion. A combination of religious, psychic, and sensuous dimensions makes one ask: what is this unspecified "good stuff" that seems to be both the aim, an ingredient, and an evaluation of the result? It is hard not to acknowledge the perspective of the late 1960s alternative or countercultural context and the advent of general societal liberation, which included also psychedelic drugs. This interpretation can be supported by the repetition of slang-like wording "stuff" (drugs, booze), as well as the well-known treats of hippie cuisine, cannabis cookies. Still, the interpretation should not solely stick to the countercultural dimension. The "good stuff" can be construed as the hidden motivator of all activity: the secret ingredient in any successful recipe that remains unwritten. The recipe form thus also means an activation of the reader, a reminder of a countercultural "do-it-yourself" ethics, an impulse to seek her own good stuff. The reader must decide whether this is a serious ideological theme, or just irony.

The final example is an exceptional drink recipe by M. A. Numminen (b. 1940), a versatile artist, singer, composer, and writer. It is a set of instructions for tea in six enumerated parts using a repetitive and cumulative structure. Every unit repeats the earlier unit, but also adds a new ingredient. Some of them are rarely used in kitchens.

THE TRUE TASTE OF TEA

I   A genuine ceramic or porcelain pot is chosen. One spoonful of tealeaves is measured to the pot for each cup of tea. After this, boiling hot water is poured to the pot, and tea is left to brew from 3 to 5 minutes. Now tea is ready to be served.

II   Tea is prepared as instructed in section I. Milk is boiled lightly in a separate pot, which can be made from any material, for instance from enamel, or stainless steel. Hot milk is poured into the cup first, only then the tea.

III Tea and milk are prepared as instructed in the sections I and II. Cloves are heated in hot, not boiling water. Some of this strong "clove extract" is poured to a heated cup. Also milk, and then tea is added.

IV   Tea, milk, and "clove extract" are prepared as indicated in the sections I, II, and III. Room temperature vodka is heated by holding the bottle in hot water. First vodka, then "clove extract", milk, and tea respectively are poured into the cup.

V   Tea, milk, "clove extract", and vodka are treated according to the instructions given in the sections I, II, III, and IV. Spoonful of dried horse manure is wrapped in tin foil, which is then heated. This "hashish" thus pulverizes into thin powder. The powder is sprinkled on the bottom of a warm cup, after which vodka, "extract", milk, and tea is added.

VI   Tea, milk, "clove extract", vodka, and hashish are prepared as indicated in the sections I, II, III, IV, and V. By rubbing the penis manually, semen is drained to a warm cup. After this, the cup is further heated, to warm up the liquid. By stirring with a stick, the "hashis", vodka, "extract", milk, and tea is added. The beverage is now ready to drink. (Numminen 1971, 30–31, original: "Teen todellinen maku.")

The recipe resembles historical recipes of the naturopathy, folk medicine, aphrodisiacs, or alchemy, where certain bodily elements like semen, sweat, or hair were thought to have great power when ingested. All the ingredients have strong symbolic value: tea is an ancient ceremonial substance, milk is indispensable for calves and babies, cloves have a reputation for increasing sexual potency, vodka intoxicates, sperm impregnates. The final addition of semen, in its solemnity, is a comical double-gesture: the most "precious" ingredient is added last, accompanied with helpful instructions on how to use it.

In terms of style the text uses the laconic and passive mood known from culinary recipes (the original uses deliberately outdated, "pedagogic" diction) and quite rigid, typographically recognizable listing with chapters and roman numerals. Here they seem to stand in radical contradiction to the contents, where the sociocultural and sexual norms are ironized cunningly by using a variety of means. First of all, the structure of repetition, accentuated by the numbered procedural catalogue, is crucial. It represents the accumulation of power and possible effect that increases with each new ingredient. Even though the recipe presents a description of one sequential process, there is also some overlap: the previous phases are repeated every time, like in six *different* recipes. This illuminates Belknap's definition of the list as "simultaneously the sum of its parts and the individual parts themselves" (Belknap 2004, 15). Furthermore, there are strange assimilations and discrepancies on the textual level. Part V introduces dried horse manure, calling it "hashis" with quotation marks, which later disappear. Clove extract is later called "extract" with quotation marks thus indicating that the substances go through a magical transformation or that the language itself might be coded, directed only to a select group. Eventually, even the title references esoteric knowledge: the *true* taste of a substance, in this case tea, is hidden knowledge: only a certain, rather complex and lengthy procedure can bring it to the fore.

Conclusion

When forms inspire writers, they duplicate and evolve in the poetic imagination. Across historical eras, forms not only carry continuity but also take on ever-shifting new meanings that can reflect back on the way those forms are used. The writer's horizon of imagination can reach beyond the limits posed by their own times: the list form always refers to and carries the history of non-literary writing, the form's universality in various areas of life—one of them culinary.

An obvious reason for the attraction of lists in experimental poetry is their affordance to perform the challenging play between order and chaos: the alleged unity (brought about by the form) and the countereffect, the free movement of verbal occurrences, and the "delight in unforeseen and unexpected combinations" (Belknap 2004, 5) it brings. The 1960s experimental scene was also a countercultural youth movement, so it is reasonable to see the lists in this context as devices to challenge and ironize social hierarchy and systems of symbolic order. When "food items and food consumption events are imbued with meanings of great significance" (Beardsworth and Keil 1997, 52), the culinary forms represent developed cultural rules, order, and taste, while they simultaneously stand for deeply human, physically inevitable activities of eating and drinking. Consequently, the form addresses three levels of experience: the personal, the culture specific, and the universal.[11]

All four culinary texts refer in different ways to sociocultural realities and norms of the 1960s. All of them state something, albeit in polysemic ways, about the relationship between the individual and society. All of them comment on the mundane, either embracing it (Aronpuro) or transcending it with fierce eroticism (Lappalainen) or clandestine intoxication (Hollo, Numminen). Aronpuro's poem embeds a menu in the semiotic world of text collage, lets it "speak for itself," and claims that lists are one of the everyday text formats that constitute our lives. The typographically sensitive collage poem also implies that lists are valuable, or interesting, because they highlight linguistic form as such. Lappalainen, Hollo, and Numminen take menu or recipe formulae to fill them with (personal) mythologies, sexuality, and "hidden psychic realities." The effect of all the individual poems is highly dependent on the list form and its procedural nature, which brings a structural irony to the provocative themes and contents. The texts imply that the use of the list form, for a writer, is a method to select information "from the mind-deep pool of possibility" (Belknap 2004, 19). The list is a formal resource or pattern that precedes the writing and channels it. The writer can embrace and enhance the possibly constraining aspects.

Enumeration can yield poetic effect and intensively meaningful efficacy; it can be used to create seductive, entertaining texts—*or* highly abstract, almost illegible textual objects. All my examples take a kind of non-serious, cerebral, and comical grasp to their subject matters, and even if a list can be said to be serious, the form seems to be most suitable for humorous purposes. Jan Alber's (2016) functions of lists in postmodernist fiction—linguistic self-reflexity, mocking the human need to bring order to chaos, and celebrating plurality—can, for the most part, be agreed upon with regard to the material discussed in this article. Alber's arguments also support the impression that literary lists have a kind of deeper, even penetrating, relationship to comicality.

My examples share a number of common features. In all of them (except in Aronpuro, where the list is embedded in a collage) the *title* is an important organizational principle as it guides the reader's perception of the text. Most examples (all but Numminen's text, which is a sequential compilation of instructive sentences, thus less list-like than the others) use vertical listings so that the typical list layout is immediately visible. Leafing through experimental poetry makes us realize the importance of the appearance of the list form in general. Lists can be ways to celebrate and embrace the visual dimension and the image-like attributes of texts. Also, in all the examples, the use of numerals is conspicuous. They play important roles in all four culinary texts as well as in "Scientific Facts" by Seilonen. Numbers and numerals seem to enhance the "listness" of the list by adding a deceptive sense of order or factuality—that is, by defamiliarizing poetry or literature through the introduction of elements commonly considered to be diametrically opposed to the realms of arts and aesthetics. In experimental poetry, the use of the list form often suggests *omission* or *displacement* of conventional literary means and characteristics: lists do not need a speaker, list-language usually does not create poetic imagery. In this way, in the context of (other) experimental techniques, the list form is a continuation of literature by other means.

Notes

1. *Ouvroir de Littérature Potentielle* (Workshop for Potential Literature, OuLiPo or Oulipo), a group concentrating on formal and mathematical resources for poetic activity, was established in 1960 by Raymond Queneau, François Le Lionnais, and others, and is still active with 20 living members. Instead of the Surrealists' interests on subconsciousness and total freedom, their take on creativity was considered a kind of "anti-Surrealism," fueled by strictly defined rules and repeatable procedures that were based on (or parodies of) mathematics, set theory, artificial languages, or other system-

atic principles. The most important Oulipian concept is *constraint*, the rule that regulates and invigorates the creative process and shifts focus onto the act of writing. According to Harry Mathews, constraint "generates every work that can be properly called Oulipian" (Mathews and Brotchie 2005, 131). For information on OuLiPo, see Motte 2007, or Mathews and Brotchie 2005. For detailed readings on constrained writing, see the *Poetics Today* double issue (Baetens and Poucel 2009–2010). About the list form in the works of a pivotal Oulipian, Georges Perec, see Andrews 1996. For readings of four Oulipian literary recipes, see Joensuu 2021.

2. Besides food and drink, recipes also connect to the history of medicine, drugs, naturopathy, and esoteric areas of knowledge. Although Jack Goody (1995, 17) considers "the use of tables, lists, formulae and recipes" to be instances of "non-speech uses of language," recipes can also be drawn, acted out, filmed, or memorized.

3. One can think of culinary equivalents to all the basic types of listings as presented by R. E. Belknap (2004, 3–4): the list, the catalogue, the inventory, the itinerary and the lexicon. A recipe is a kind of itinerary, as it describes actions in temporal order. All these types can be exploited in fiction or poetry. Culinary inventories can be found in various literary works, from the novels of François Rabelais to *Robinson Crusoe*, from *Ulysses* to *Gravity's Rainbow* and *Bridget Jones's Diary*.

4. *The Flounder* by Günter Grass (1977) includes descriptions of meals, lists of their foodstuffs, and narrated recipes, often in blended fashion. In *House of Day, House of Night* by Olga Tokarczuk (1998), embedded recipes interrupt the narration. In *Hortense Is Abducted* by Jacques Roubaud (1987), a recipe is embedded in the narration in the old lyric format of *sestina*, recited by one of the characters.

5. *Oulipo Compendium* (Mathews and Brotchie 2005) is an encyclopedia of Oulipian methods, but includes no headwords for "list," "catalogue," nor "enumeration." Still, the list form is manifested in many of the examples involved therein.

6. Lipogram, like Georges Perec's novel *La Disparation* (1969), means omission of a certain letter. Thus, the writing process of *La Disparation* was regulated by the avoidance of all the French words that contained the letter "e." These forbidden words constitute a strictly defined, although invisible, lexicon—a word list that "haunts" the novel by its absence, so to say. In addition, one might claim that Robert E. Belknap's (2004, 15) definition of the list—a "formally organized block of information that is composed of a set of members"—sounds almost like a definition of any Oulipian text. Besides Oulipo, one can consider connections between the list form and other schools or approaches of experimental writing. A typology by J. M. Conte (1991, 214–237) divides postmodern poetry into *serial* and *procedural* poetry. The latter is divided into *predetermined form* and

generative devices. It is legitimate to say that the list form can add both generative and predetermined aspects to writing. Still, in many cases of experimental writing, it implements a certain predetermined form.

7. For socio-cultural and historical context, see Eskelinen 2016, 247–269; Haapala 2007, 277–278.
8. While their historical emergence seems, at first glance, to fit well with McHale's (2008) dating of the genesis of postmodernism in 1966, the term's pertinence to the Finnish context is not evident. Even if the new literary generation of the 1960s diverged from certain aesthetic traits of the 1950s modernists (Veivo 2016, 773), both the preceding modernism and the aftermath were brief.
9. All translations in the article are by the writer, except "Good Stuff Cookies" by Anselm Hollo which was originally published in English.
10. Regarding lists, Mallander's poem also poses a question about the conceptual relationship between repetition and enumeration. Does a mere repetition of, say, a single word, constitute a list? Belknap's view on this is affirmative, although, according to him (2004, 34), a "repeated single item makes for a very boring list." This is not necessarily the case with concrete poetry or experimental literature.
11. In their own way, my examples also reaffirm affects and experientiality as a "crucial category for adequately describing and making sense of the processes that come into play when we encounter lists in literary texts" (von Contzen 2018, 316), although the content of these lists is not "practical."

References

Primary Sources

Aronpuro, Kari. 1964. *Peltiset Enkelit* (Tin Angels). Helsinki: Kirjayhtymä.
Hollo, Anselm. 1970. *Maya: Works 1959–1969*. London: Cape Goliard Press.
Lappalainen, Kalevi. 1968. *Puolihevosen Hermorata* (Half Horse's Nerve Path). Hämeenlinna: Karisto.
Mallander, Jan Olof. 1969. *Out*. Helsinki: Söderström & Co.
Numminen, M. A. 1971. *Lastuja* (Chips). Helsinki: Kirjayhtymä.
Polttila, Brita. 1966. *Tapahtumista* (On Occurrences). Helsinki: Tammi.
Seilonen, Kalevi. 1965. *Tosiasioita minusta* (Facts About Myself). Helsinki: Tammi.

Secondary Sources

Alber, Jan. 2016. Absurd Catalogues: The Functions of Lists in Postmodernist Fiction. *Style* 50 (3): 342–358.

Andrews, Chris. 1996. Puzzles and Lists: Georges Perec's *Un Homme qui dort*. *MLN* 111 (4): 775–796.

Baetens, Jan, and Jean-Jacques Poucel, eds. 2009–2010. *Poetics Today* 30: 4–31: 1: Constrained Writing I–II, Special Double Issue.

Beardsworth, Alan, and Teresa Keil. 1997. *Sociology on the Menu: An Invitation to the Study of Food and Society*. London/New York: Routledge.

Belknap, Robert E. 2004. *The List: The Uses and Pleasures of Cataloguing*. New Haven: Yale University Press.

Bray, Joe, Alison Gibbons, and Brian McHale. 2012. Introduction. In *The Routledge Companion to Experimental Literature*, ed. Joe Bray, Alison Gibbons, and Brian McHale, 1–18. London/New York: Routledge.

Conte, Joseph M. 1991. *Unending Design: The Forms of Postmodern Poetry*. Ithaca/London: Cornell University Press.

Epstein, Andrew. 2012. Found Poetry, "Uncreative Writing," and the Art of Appropriation. In *The Routledge Companion to Experimental Literature*, ed. Joe Bray, Alison Gibbons, and Brian McHale, 310–322. London/New York: Routledge.

Eskelinen, Markku. 2016. *Raukoilla rajoilla: Suomenkielisen proosakirjallisuuden historiaa*. Helsinki: Siltala.

Goody, Jack. 1995 [1977]. *The Domestication of the Savage Mind*. Cambridge: Cambridge University Press.

Haapala, Vesa. 2007. Kokeellinen kirjallisuus ja kirjallinen vastarinta Suomessa – kiintopisteenä 1960-luku. In *Kirjallisuuden avantgarde ja kokeellisuus*, ed. Sakari Katajamäki and Harri Veivo, 277–304. Helsinki: Gaudeamus – Helsinki University Press.

Hottinen, Merja. 2016. Experiment, Scam, and Children's Games – The Finnish Media on Ken Dewey's Happenings in Finland, 1963–1964. In *A Cultural History of the Avant-garde in the Nordic Countries 1950–1975*, ed. Tania Ørum and Jesper Olsson, 516–527. Leiden/Boston: Brill, Rodopi.

Hutcheon, Linda. 1994. *Irony's Edge: The Theory and Politics of Irony*. London/New York: Routledge.

Joensuu, Juri. 2016. *Vuoden 1965 mania? Suomalaisen kirjallisuuden hullu vuosi*. Helsinki: Poesia.

Kristeva, Julia. 1982. *Powers of Horror: An Essay on Abjection*. Trans. Leon S. Roudiez. New York: Columbia University Press.

Mathews, Harry, and Alastair Brotchie, eds. 2005. *Oulipo Compendium: Revised & Updated*. London/Los Angeles: Make Now Press, Atlas Press.

McHale, Brian. 2008. 1966 Nervous Breakdown, or, When Did Postmodernism Begin? *Modern Language Quarterly* 69 (3): 391–413.

Motte, Warren. 2007. *OULIPO: A Primer of Potential Literature*. Trans. and ed. Warren Motte. Champaign/London: Dalkey Archive Press.

Ngai, Sianne. 2005. *Ugly Feelings*. Cambridge/London: Harvard University Press.

Notaker, Henry. 2017. *A History of Cookbooks: From Kitchen to Page over Seven Centuries*. Oakland: University of California Press.

Veivo, Harri. 2016. Everyday High and Low – Finnish Avant-Garde Poetry of the 1960s in a Rapidly Changing Society. In *A Cultural History of the Avant-garde in the Nordic Countries 1950–1975*, ed. Tania Ørum and Jesper Olsson, 772–781. Leiden/Boston: Brill, Rodopi.

von Contzen, Eva. 2018. Experience, Affect, and Literary Lists. *Partial Answers* 16 (2): 315–327.

CHAPTER 10

Poetological Lists: Writing-Scenes in Contemporary Literature

Ulrike Vedder

The textual and media form of the list is as simple as it is complex. Lists are simple in that they adhere to certain patterns, are easy to identify typographically, abbreviate, and subsume. At the same time, they are complex, ranging across the most disparate fields of tension, in which they express their rhetorical and literary efficacy. Such efficacy includes matters of tellability and untellablity; cohesion and disintegration; homogenization and heterogenization; paratext and subordination; the wielding of and criticism of power, memory, and oblivion; and reification and subjectification.

The extent to which lists can generate cohesion or disintegration, the wielding of power or anarchy, depends not only on the listing agent and his or her categorizations and subsumptions but also on the listed items themselves—be they images, icons, or linguistic signs, or be they headlines, which abbreviate facts, circumstances, or cue words, which initiate a chain of associations. They belong to a range of categories and functional contexts: when a list gathers people (e.g., such as the women seduced by

U. Vedder (✉)
Humboldt Universität zu Berlin, Berlin, Germany
e-mail: ulrike.vedder@hu-berlin.de

R. A. Barton et al. (eds.), *Forms of List-Making: Epistemic, Literary, and Visual Enumeration,*
https://doi.org/10.1007/978-3-030-76970-3_10

Don Giovanni and registered by his servant Leporello in Mozart's opera *Don Giovanni*; see Vedder 2001) or enumerates things (such as possessions recorded in inventories; see Vedder 2008) or records actions or events. Particularly revealing are those literary lists whose items thematize the process of writing, that is, those which evoke a "writing-scene" (see Campe 1991):

> The term 'writing scene' is to be understood as the framed ensemble of instrumentality, gesture and language, provided that these factors do not become the object or source of possible or actual resistance. Where, on the other hand, this ensemble, in its reluctant heterogeneity and instability, resides and problematizes itself, we can speak of a 'writing-scene.' (Giurato 2012, 306)

While a "writing scene" (*Schreibszene*) is ultimately inherent in every written text insofar as it refers as a written text to the pertinent media, materiality, and writing agents, a "writing-scene" (*Schreib-Szene*) is characterized by its thematization of the resistance to writing, that is, by its heterogenization. A fundamental assumption in the following readings is that the list—in its conspicuous (and suspicious) form and with its structural tension—is a particularly suitable genre for this purpose: if its issue is writing, that is, in the context of a poetic list, it is to be understood as a writing-scene.[1]

The following will focus on those "poetological lists" that, in the second half of the twentieth century, consolidate the self-reflexive potential of literary texts, gather seeds of narration in list form, stage the conditions for a non-linear narrative in the list, or even thematize the "genea-logic" of narrative and writing insomuch as "data, impressions and objects" which are strung together in lists are brought into a new "form liberated from their origin" (Pordzik 2017, 208). To this end, let us consider four lists from the most disparate of genres—lyric poetry, the manifesto, the novel, and the autobiography—each of which is poetically effective in its own way as a writing-scene. What is meant here are neither textual precursors (see Mainberger 2003) such as those known in the form of excerpt collections, word indices, or chapter listings for the writing processes of Jean Paul (register), Novalis (Brouillon), or Emile Zola (dossiers) nor paratextual elements such as indices.[2] Instead, the poetological lists considered below consist of a long poem (Inger Christensen), a manifesto (Jack Kerouac), a passage from a novel (Italo Calvino), and a section of an autobiographical text (Roland Barthes). Each of these lists reflects not only writing and poetics but also their respective genres.

Lyric Poetry

The naming and enumeration of that which exists is the simplest form for representing things and events. The act of registering something, meanwhile, is also a means of appropriation, which proceeds under the guidance of an order arising from the enumerator's directive—indeed, it is also an act of creation: of order, of the world. In Inger Christensen's equally simple and intricate long poem *alfabet* (1981), beginning with "a," the world, speaking and enumerating, is inventoried and simultaneously recreated. This creation follows two orders: the linguistic sequence of the Latin alphabet and the mathematical one based on the Fibonacci sequence, in which each number represents the sum of its two predecessors (1, 2, 3, 5, 8, 13, 21, 34, …). The section for the letter "a" thus contains one verse, "b" two verses, "c" three, "d" five, "e" eight, and so on. It not only lists what exists in the sense of an inventory of the world—"apricot trees exist, apricot trees exist"—but through repetition and creative combination the world is simultaneously reconstructed and conjured forth:

1
abrikostræerne findes, abrikostræerne findes

2
bregnerne findes; og brombær, brombær
og brom findes; og brinten, brinten

3
cikaderne findes; cikorie, chrom
og citrontræer findes; cikaderne findes;
cikaderne, ceder, cypres, cerebellum

4
duerne findes; drømmerne, dukkerne
dræberne findes; duerne, duerne;
dis, dioxin og dagene; dagene
findes; dagene døden; og digtene
findes; digtene, dagene, døden

5
efteråret findes; eftersmagen og eftertanken
findes; og enrummet findes, englene,
enkerne og elsdyret findes; enkelthederne
findes, erindringen, erindringens lys;
og efterlyset findes, egetræet og elmetræet

> findes, og enebærbusken, ensheden, ensomheden
> findes, og edderfuglen og edderkoppen findes,
> og eddiken findes, og eftertidern, eftertiden[3]

This list poem spans between subjective openness and systematic sequence, conjuring up things in the world[4] and, at the same time, taking aim neither at the sovereignty of the lyrical "I" nor at the wholeness of world (or of the alphabet, for the poem ends at "n" and thus shows for Christensen's part what constitutes lists: reference to that which lies beyond the limits of their textual boundaries). Instead, the intersection of alphabetical and mathematical series reveals the varying degrees of order and dispersion in Inger Christensen's strophic and list-like enumerations, which are generated by the coordinate axes:

> There they sat, those words, on large pieces of white paper, words starting with *a*, with *b*, with *c*, and so on, and if I'd kept at it much longer it would have looked like an odd, unorganized dictionary, a wilderness of disjointed phenomena. And then came mathematics. For, since phenomena themselves never occur just because they are given names, it was my good fortune that, in my search for words (in a dictionary under *f*), I happened upon numbers, specifically, the Fibonacci numbers. (Christensen 1999, 23–24)

Herein lies the crossover between Christensen's *alfabet* and the principle of the list and enumeration, as Sabine Mainberger summarizes it:

> Enumerations exhibit various degrees of connection and cohesion or disintegration and dispersion, i.e. the elements are more or less bound or independent. In enumerative passages of a text, one of two sides can come to force: either the structuring and grouping which creates order according to some principle can predominate – i.e. the organizing enumeration – or the 'mere' enumeration with its effects of fragmentation and diffusion and its propensity for formlessness is emphasized. (Mainberger 2018, 94–95)

But Inger Christensen's *alfabet* is not about escaping the "wilderness of disjointed phenomena" with the help of alphabetical-mathematical ordering patterns but about sounding out epistemological decisions, as indicated by the list form.[5] Moreover, the poem seeks to oppose in vigorous and persistent fashion the utter destruction represented by the cipher "atombomben finds"/"the atom bomb exists" (Christensen 2001), which is placed in the poem between "j" and "k" with slight variations. The constructive list, equally rational and magical in its capacity to create both worlds and continuance, thus simultaneously calls attention at its own composition and to its threatened nature, capable as such an elliptical writing-scene of evoking the world in its fragility. At the same time, *alfabet* insists on the sensuousness and reality of the world and hence also opposes—*qua* list form—"the stringent charge of aesthetic futility [...] that a postmodern age hurls against poetic endeavors."[6] In this sense as well, Christensen's list poem represents a poetological commentary on the present.

The Manifesto

The list as an *organon* in which poetological considerations are formulated is also found in literary manifestos. Both in their potential for abbreviation as well as in their unique temporality, lists generally represent a suitable form for manifestos, which are characterized by their ability to fix in a pointedly programmatic, that is, non-narrative way, what "could or, more importantly, should occur in the future" (Rieger 2014, 135). For, on the one hand, it is the abbreviation as facilitated by lists—owing, for example, to their columnal form, the syntactic incompleteness of their items or their repetitive structure—which also characterizes manifestos with their catchy, beckoning formulations:

> Nor does the manifesto develop any narrative flow. Rather, its syntax derives from an intrinsically tiered agenda, whose step-by-step processing gives the manifestos the form of a catalog of measures, whose individual items are occasionally just numbered. The texture is interrupted, thetically, structured by paragraphs, and sentences are often concluded with an exclamation mark. (Rieger 2014, 136)

On the other hand, the manifesto and the list, more precisely the "prospective list,"[7] are linked by a specific temporality. It is certainly true that lists, because they do not develop narratives, "do not possess any index of time."[8] Yet, they exhibit—not only as genealogical lists with their chronologies and memorial component—a certain temporality, be it in the aforementioned prospective sense of a future or an ordering of time generated through the rhythmization of form. Both are exemplified in a manifesto written in list form by Beat author Jack Kerouac.

Under the title *Belief & Technique for Modern Prose* (1959), Jack Kerouac assembles a numbered list of 30 items. In these "Essentials," as he refers to them, he captures his writing style—that of the "Beat Generation"—which focuses on everyday life and spontaneity, on his own body and his own life with its rhythm. Poetology is formulated in list form, which at the same time becomes performative within that same form: not only in its correspondence to the genre of the manifesto, which "is [generally] performative in its structure – as a speech act, as showing and as proclaiming something that becomes mani-fest" (Brandstetter 2017, 18), but also in the peculiarity of the Beat agenda.

In this manner, improvisation and spontaneity become apparent, which are thematized in the following items and which also appear in list form:

> 1. Scribbled secret notebooks, and wild typewritten pages, for yr own joy
> 2. Submissive to everything, open, listening
> 13. Remove literary, grammatical and syntactical inhibition
> 28. Composing wild, undisciplined, pure, coming in from under, crazier the better (Kerouac 1992, 58–59)

Indeed, Kerouac's "Essentials" do not form a well-formulated manifesto but rather give the impression of a spontaneously and hastily recorded list (in which "your" is abbreviated throughout as "yr" as if to write faster). Although the textual calculations can hardly be mistaken—this including the list format as an index of spontaneity—here the causality operates in the opposite direction: the choice of the list format is deliberately planned precisely because it opens up space for improvisation. Furthermore, the list requires a certain type of procedure—of rhythm and breathing—thus reflecting the Beat Generation's nod to contemporary jazz and its practice of improvisation, rhythmization, and controlled breathing. Indeed, with the perpetually novel positioning of the numbered items, it is the role of breathing, along with a certain driving dynamic, which comes into focus, as Stefanie Heine claims: "Precisely where nothing is written or thought, in the space reserved for breathing, the idea for that which follows is generated. […] Kerouac consciously creates this space through the list form, which demands the repeated usage of a number void of meaning" (Heine 2014, 256). What's more: with such breathing, life itself seems to animate the list as the Beat manifesto itself demands:

10. No time for poetry but exactly what is
20. Believe in the holy contour of life
25. Write for the world to read and see yr exact pictures of it

Numerous subsequent pop-writers from Rolf Dieter Brinkmann (e.g., in *Nichts*, 1965, or *In der Seitenstraße*, 1966) to Rainald Goetz (e.g., in *Abfall für alle*, 1999) follow this poetological maxim with their list literature. Brinkmann's poetological essay *Der Film in Worten* (1969) also explicitly refers to a list entry from Kerouac's manifesto (see Meyer-Sickendiek 2018, 30–31):

26. Bookmovie is the movie in words, the visual American form

The mundane ("exactly what is") demanded and practiced in the manifesto therefore also includes the contemporary media reality and with it a distinct visuality:

16. The jewel center of interest is the eye within the eye

In this sense, the list also functions, as it were, as a visual phenomenon which thematizes "seeing" in a performative manner. This becomes even more pronounced when lists are inserted into prose texts.

The Novel

Another poetological list can be found in a novel that is not just about novels—and how to become immersed in them—but which also consists exclusively of the beginnings of novels: Italo Calvino's *If on a Winter's Night a Traveler* (1993 [1979]). In addition to writing, Calvino's self-referential novel construction focuses primarily on reading, from the intimate act of reading in bed to reading guided by theses and theory:

> Lotaria wants to know the author's position with regard to Trends of Contemporary Thought and Problems That Demand a Solution. To make your task easier she furnishes you with a list of names of Great Masters among whom you should situate him. (Calvino 1993, 44)

This list "of Founders of Schools of Thought"[9] does not receive further elaboration but joins those lists in the novel that prevent pleasure reading.

This includes word lists based on digital text analyses of novels according to word frequency. A novelist (who makes reference to Calvino) is confronted with these lists by the literary scholar Lotaria, who does not read his novels herself but has them evaluated by a "computer system," as she explains:

> What is the reading of a text, in fact, except the recording of certain thematic recurrences, certain insistences of forms and meanings? An electronic reading supplies me with a list of the frequencies, which I have only to glance at to form an idea of the problems the book suggests to my critical study. (Calvino 1993, 186)

Calvino's novel cites several of these alphabetically ordered lists and ironizes the scholarly conclusions drawn by Lotaria, which, for example, derive literary depth from the frequency of "under":

> underarm, underbrush, undercover, underdog, underfed, underfoot, undergo, undergraduate, underground, undergrowth, underhand, under-privileged, undershirt, underwear, underweight...
> No, the book isn't completely superficial, as it seemed. There must be something hidden; I can direct my research along these lines. (Calvino 1993, 187)[10]

While these word counts, despite Lotaria's thesis, are certainly not poetological lists, one such list can be found right at the beginning of Calvino's multifarious novel. The first chapter describes the difficulties of even finding and buying the book in a bookstore in the first place, which will then begin with the second chapter. To that end, the novel exploits the poetological as well as visual potential of lists:

> With a rapid maneuver you bypass them [other books] and move into the phalanxes of the Books You Mean To Read But There Are Others You Must Read First, the Book Too Expensive Now And You'll Wait Till They're Remaindered, the Books ditto When They Come Out In Paperback, Books You Can Borrow From Somebody, Books That Everybody's Read So It's As If You Had Read Them, Too. Eluding these assaults, you come up beneath the towers of the fortress, where other troops are holding out:
> the Books You've Been Planning To Read For Ages,
> the Books You've Been Hunting For Years Without
> Success,

the Books Dealing With Something You're Working On
At The Moment,
the Books You Want To Own So They'll Be Handy Just
 In Case,
the Books You Could Put Aside Maybe To Read This
Summer,
the Books You Need To Go With Other Books On Your
 Shelves,
the Books That Fill You With Sudden, Inexplicable
 Curiosity, Not easily Justified. (Calvino 1993, 5)

Yet, what is described here as a dynamic attack which is said to have a certain speed in its forward movement—a stormy conquest of the bookstore as well as a tumultuous plunge into its reading—yields retarding effects. Such effects are due to the resistance of the books, which might prevent the acquisition of Calvino's novel and whose victory is not yet assured at this moment in the narrative. And, on the other hand, the retardation results from the list that unmistakably obstructs the narrative, even in a visual sense: while the first part of the enumeration, owing to the unusual use of capitalization, evokes a horizontal frontage—a kind of palisade that must be breached—the vertically arranged obstacles in the second part reveal, typographically speaking, as it were, the obstructive piles of books as "towers of the fortress."[11]

In terms of economizing narrative, the list here represents a retarding, non-narrative moment, the poetological self-reflection consisting in the fact that it is also about the retarding moments of reading which might prevent the reader from reading the book. Readers do read these interruptions but do so in a different register of signification:

As lists are usually not plot-bearing but rather break up the plot, pause and digressively or additively prolong it, they work against the narrative context in which they are embedded by introducing a structure of simplicity that places the responsibility of making sense in the hands of the reader. (von Contzen 2017, 222)

Yet, just as Italo Calvino's *If on a Winter's Night a Traveler* consists not only of lists but offers a wealth of narratives and narrative formats, which, despite their perpetual discontinuation, always captivate the novel's internal "you"-reader (as well as Calvino readers) anew, the novel is not a postmodern swan song to narrative. On the contrary:

> The narrative that does not end because it cannot be finished stands in con-
> trast to the narrative that does not end because the storytelling will never
> cease. (Moses 1990, 121)

Nevertheless, the highly reflective writing (and reading) scene of this novel from 1979 clearly emphasizes its theoretical-aesthetic contemporaneity, especially in the act of non-narrative list; this contemporaneity exists, for example, in Roland Barthes' writings both on narrative and reading (*Le plaisir du texte*, 1973; *Poétique du récit*, 1977) and on non-narrative text orders (*roland BARTHES par roland barthes*, 1975; *Fragments d'un discours amoureux*, 1977).

The Autobiography

Roland Barthes' autobiography *roland BARTHES par roland barthes* (1975) does justice to his fragmentary, scattered concept of the subject through the form of alphabetically sorted fragments that yield neither an exemplary *confession* nor a narrative identity or continuity. Accordingly, the section titled "The order I no longer remember"/"L'ordre dont je ne me souviens plus," reads: "The alphabetical order erases everything, banishes every origin."[12] Admittedly, there exists the danger of generating meaning from the alphabet by mere chance ("This order, however, can be mischievous: it sometimes produces effects of meaning").[13] In contrast, however, Barthes puts forth the idea of an "antistructural criticism," which would "not look for the work's order but its disorder,"[14] namely by viewing each text as an encyclopedic list of disparate objects which represent "the work's antistructure, its [...] polygraphy."[15] This proves all the more true for an autobiography à la Barthes', which stages and reflects its own author/subject position as an effect of such polygraphic text operations.

Hence, among the fragments is the entry, "J'aime, je n'aime pas": a typical demonstration of ego-determination through the enumeration of what the "I" likes and dislikes, at least in the first part of the entry. This constitutes a bundled but expandable ("etc.") list of heterogeneous elements, which represents a biographical-subjective accumulation as emphasized in the ever-recurrent first-person singular:

> *I like:* salad, cinnamon, cheese, pimento, marzipan, the smell of new-cut hay
> (why doesn't someone with a "nose" make such a perfume), roses, peonies,
> lavender, champagne, loosely held political convictions, Glenn Gould, too-

cold beer, flat pillows, toast, Havana cigars, Handel, slow walks, pears, […] etc.

I don't like: […] telephoning, children's choruses, Chopin's concertos, Burgundian branles and Renaissance dances, the organ, Marc-Antoine Charpentier, his trumpets and kettledrums, the politico-sexual, scenes, initiatives, fidelity, spontaneity, evenings with people I don't know, etc.[16]

What unifies the arbitrary items is hence, on the one hand, the list mode and, on the other, the subjective perspectivation. Here something along the lines of subjectivity arises out of "a list of heterogeneous objects" (Barthes 1977, 148), for this list is "a subjective evaluation system which arbitrarily assigns the same value to things, conditions, circumstances, actions and ownership of highly variable value and which cannot be meaningfully generalized" (Tauber 2018, 139). The intricacy of this becomes a systematic point in the second part of the entry:

> *I like, I don't like:* this is of no importance to anyone; this, apparently, has no meaning. And yet all this means: *my body* is *not the same as yours.* Hence, in this anarchic foam of tastes and distastes, a kind of listless blur, gradually appears the figure of a bodily enigma, requiring complicity or irritation.[17]

Barthes thus subjectivizes himself even as he calls that very act into question. Yet, he is able to declare in the form of enumeration: this is contingent, this is just who I am… His "J'aime, je n'aime pas" list hence appears first as a simple exercise, as a child's game, in order to then form the starting point for a complex analysis of the self as a writer: an analysis that in turn proceeds through the simple, certainly not high literary writing of lists, which thereby demonstrates the arbitrary fashion in which an author is made an author. The fragments do not aim at instances such as "History, Ideology, the Unconscious."[18] "Instead, Barthes profiles the movement of continuous writing" (Erhart 2015, 273), when he states: "the latter [part of the text] is nothing but *a further* text, the last of the series, not the ultimate in meaning: *text upon text,* which never illuminates anything."[19] It is therefore a matter of writing on (*das Weiterschreiben*), *text upon text,* which drives the list, which in this case is not only polygraphic but also poetological. For as little as writing has a telos and as little as autobiography stabilizes an avowed ego, the list format seems appropriate here; and indeed, the "paradigmatic structure of equivalence of the list does not allow for any metaposition" (Schaffrick and Werber 2017, 312).

CONCLUSION

With regard to the poetological lists considered here from 1957 (Kerouac), 1975 (Barthes), 1979 (Calvino), and 1981 (Christensen), a concluding remark is in order concerning their literary-theoretical contemporaneity with Beat culture and postmodernism. Insofar as lists draw attention to their writing-scenes, they represent a simple and sophisticated tool for poetological reflection and for the performative staging of writing and authorship together with the areas of contention surrounding them. In its constitutive incompleteness, the list is not only a critical instrument against cessations of meaning and narrative but also alludes with its non-narrative and arbitrary elements to reality (saturated with the extra-literary) as well as to (intertextually resonating) text materials. *Sans* metaposition, no strong authorship is restituted here; instead, the list form generates and represents both a kind of writing from the "poetic strain [...], in which various pitches – high and low, trivial and cerebral – lie close to one another, both spatially and in meaning" (Pordzik 2017, 229), as well as a polygraphic procedure of *text upon text*, that is, non-linear but continuous writing. That this is by no means monotonous or artless can be attributed to, on the one hand, the "mechanisms of friction and alienation – these disrupting or heteroclitically supplementing the regular repetition of syntactic structures, certain word types, word groups or individual words –" (Rakusa 2016, 319) and, on the other hand, to the pleasure of lists, *le plaisir des listes*, for their repetitive schemata, tonal rhythms, semantic hollowing, "for yr own joy."

NOTES

1. Particularly as lists "per se" belong to the medium of writing and—if litanies are excluded—hardly play a role in oral communication.
2. A paratextual list, however, which lists the range of allusions and knowledge in the appendix of a volume of poetry, for example, can itself regain a lyrical character—because lists resemble so closely poems in typographical terms and because the semantics of the explanations listed are aimed at an excess of meaning—such that in modern poetry, text, and paratext cannot always be clearly distinguished (see e.g., the "annotations" in Poschmann's poetry volume *Geliehene Landschaften. Lehrgedichte und Elegien;* see also van Hoorn 2018).
3. Christensen, Inger. 2001. *alfabet / alphabet.* https://sites.northwestern. edu/jac808/ 2014/02/28/alphabet-inger-christensen/. Translated by

Susanna Nied: "1 apricot trees exist, apricot trees exist // 2 bracken exists; and blackberries, blackberries; / bromine exists; and hydrogen, hydrogen // 3 cicadas exist; chicory, chromium, / citrus trees; cicadas exist; / cicadas, cedars, cypresses, the cerebellum // 4 doves exist, dreamers, and dolls; / killers exist, and doves, and doves; / haze, dioxin, and days; days / exist, days and death; and poems / exist; poems, days, death // 5 early fall exists; aftertaste, afterthought / seclusion and angels exist; / widows and elk exist; every / detail exists; memory, memory's light; / afterglow exists; oaks, elms, / junipers, sameness, loneliness exist; / eider ducks, spiders, and vinegar / exist, and the future, the future."

4. See Cotten 2008 on Christensen's *alfabet*: "In a certain way, it shares the function of the list as a symbolic substitute for a certain set of objects [...] with certain types of litanies, where it is imagined [that] by mentioning the name of a spirit or deity, when done correctly, that deity is not only asked but forced to appear" (trans. by Anderson).

5. Interestingly, the alphabet is not only a popular ordering pattern for lists but can also be traced back to the format of the list, at least according to Jack Goody's thesis (within the framework of his theory of writing), as inferred from pre-alphabetic lists of characters (e.g., in Mesopotamia): "Lists of this kind played an important role in earlier pre-alphabetic writing systems. In fact, even the mere fact that something such as the list was made may have already contributed to the development of the alphabet in Phoenicia and Palestine" (see Goody 2012, 353).

6. See in connection with list poems of contemporary poetry (without reference to Christensen) Pordzik 2017, 209–210: "the acts of taking an inventory and cataloging in the context of poetry belie the stringent charge of aesthetic futility [...] that a postmodern age hurls against poetic endeavors."

7. In addition to "lexical lists" (sensu dictionaries or encyclopedias), Jack Goody speaks of "retrospective lists" ("recording of events, functions, situations, people") and "prospective lists," "which, like shopping lists, serve as a kind of guide, a plan for future actions" (Goody 2012, 347).

8. Schaffrick and Werber 2017, 314: "The past becomes flat. While the time dimension is indispensable for the constitution of meaning in society and is usually handled with narrative, lists dissolve orders of time" (trans. by Anderson).

9. Here and in other parts of the novel, discourse quotations are highlighted by the use of capital letters.

10. Interestingly, this refers to an actual investigation, as a footnote suggests: "The [...] word lists originate from *Spogli elettronici dell'italiano letterario contemporaneo* [...], edited by Mario Alinei, Il Mulino, Bologna 1973" (Calvino 1993, 188).

11. See Mainberger 2003, 5: "'List' calls to mind a certain manner of writing, a visualization possible only in the medium of writing" (trans. by Anderson).
12. Barthes 1977, 148. Original text: "L'ordre alphabétique efface tout, refoule toute origine" (Barthes 1975, 151).
13. Barthes 1977, 148. Original text: "Cet ordre, cependant, peut être malicieux: il produit parfois des effets de sens" (Barthes 1975, 151).
14. Barthes 1977, 148. Original text: "une critique antistrucurale; elle ne rechercherait pas l'ordre, mais le désordre de l'œuvre" (Barthes 1975, 151).
15. Barthes 1977, 148. Original text: "une liste d'objets hétéroclites, et cette liste est l'antistructure de l'œuvre, son [...] polygraphie" (Barthes 1975, 151).
16. Barthes 1977, 116–117. Original text: "*J'aime*: la salade, la cannelle, le fromage, les piments, la pâte d'amandes, l'odeur du foin coupé (j'aimerais qu'un 'nez' fabriquât un tel parfum), les roses, les pivoines, la lavande, le champagne, des positions légères en politique, Glenn Gould, la bière excessivement glacée, les oreillers plats, le pain grillé, les cigares de Havane, Haendel, les promenades mesurées, les poires [...], etc. *Je n'aime pas*: [...] téléphoner, les chœurs d'enfants, les concertos de Chopin, les bransles de Bourgogne, les danceries de la Renaissance, l'orgue, M.-A. Charpentier, ses trompettes et ses timbales, le politico-sexuel, les scènes, les initiatives, la fidélité, la spontanéité, les soirées avec des gens que je ne connais pas, etc." (Barthes 1975, 120).
17. Barthes 1977, 117. Original text: "*J'aime, je n'aime pas*: cela n'a aucune importance pour personne; cela, apparemment, n'a pas de sens. Et pourtant tout cela veut dire: *mon corps n'est pas le même que le vôtre.* Ainsi, dans cette écume anarchique des goûts et des dégoûts, sorte de hachurage distrait, se dessine peu à peu la figure d'une énigme corporelle, appelant complicité ou irritation" (Barthes 1975, 121).
18. Barthes 1977, 120. Original text: "Ces instances sont l'Histoire, l'Idéologie, l'Inconscient" (Barthes 1975, 124).
19. Barthes 1977, 120. Original text: "celui-ci n'est rien d'autre qu'un texte *en* plus, le dernier de la série, non l'ultime du sens: *texte sur texte*, cela n'éclaircit jamais rien" (Barthes 1975, 124).

References

Barthes, Roland. 1975. *roland Barthes par roland barthes*. Paris: Seuil.
———. 1977. *Roland Barthes by Roland Barthes*. Trans. Richard Howard. London: Macmillan.
Brandstetter, Gabriele. 2017. Yes! Das Manifest als künstlerische Praxis. In *"Clear the Air" Künstlermanifeste seit den 1960er Jahren: Interdisziplinäre Positionen*, ed. Burcu Dogramaci and Katja Schneider, 17–36. Bielefeld: Transcript.

Calvino, Italo. 1993 [1979]. *If on a Winter's Night a Traveler*. Trans. William Weaver. London: Vintage Books.

Campe, Rüdiger. 1991. Die Schreibszene, Schreiben. In *Paradoxien, Dissonanzen, Zusammenbrüche: Situationen offener Epistemologie*, ed. Hans Ulrich Gumbrecht and Karl Ludwig Pfeiffer, 759–772. Frankfurt/Main: Suhrkamp.

Christensen, Inger. 1999. Der naive Leser. In *Der Geheimniszustand und Gedicht vom Tod: Essays*, 19–25. Munich/Vienna: Hanser.

———. 2001. *alfabet / alphabet*. Trans. Susanna Nied. https://sites.northwestern.edu/jac808/2014/02/28/alphabet-inger-christensen/. Accessed 24 Nov 2020.

Cotten, Ann. 2008. *Nach der Welt: Die Listen der Konkreten Poesie und ihre Folgen*. Vienna: Klever.

Erhart, Walter. 2015. Warum ich mich anders schreibe: Grenzen des Sich-Selbst-Vergleichens im 20. Jahrhundert. In *Sich selbst vergleichen: Zur Relationalität autobiographischen Schreibens vom 12. Jahrhundert bis zur Gegenwart*, ed. Franz-Josef Arlinghaus, Walter Erhart, Lena Gumpert, and Simon Siemianowski, 259–290. Bielefeld: Transcript.

Giurato, Davide. 2012. Maschinen-Schreiben. In *Schreiben als Kulturtechnik: Grundlagentexte*, ed. Sandro Zanetti, 305–317. Frankfurt/Main: Suhrkamp.

Goody, Jack. 2012 [1977]. Woraus besteht eine Liste? In *Schreiben als Kulturtechnik: Grundlagentexte*, ed. Sandro Zanetti. 338–396. Frankfurt/Main: Suhrkamp.

Heine, Stefanie. 2014. "First Thought, Best Thought": Jack Kerouac und Allen Ginsberg. In *Improvisation und Invention: Momente, Modelle, Medien*, ed. Sandro Zanetti, 245–261. Zürich/Berlin: Diaphanes.

Kerouac, Jack. 1992 [1959]. Belief & Technique for Modern Prose. In *The Portable Beat Reader*, ed. Ann Charters, 58–59. New York: Penguin.

Mainberger, Sabine. 2003. Von der Liste zum Text – vom Text zur Liste: Zu Werk und Genese in moderner Literatur. Mit einem Blick in Perecs *Cahier des charges* zu *La Vie mode d'emploi*. In *Entwerfen und Entwurf: Praxis und Theorie des künstlerischen Schaffensprozesses*, ed. Gundel Mattenklott and Friedrich Weltzien, 265–284. Berlin: Reimer.

———. 2018. Ordnen/Aufzählen. In *Susanne Scholz and Ulrike Vedder*, ed. Handbuch Literatur and Materielle Kultur, 94–95. Berlin/Boston: De Gruyter.

Meyer-Sickendiek, Burkhard. 2018. Lyrik, "nach Jazz-Arrangements strukturiert": Rolf-Dieter Brinkmann und die Beatgeneration. In *Stile der Popliteratur: Versuch einer intermedialen Differenzierung*, ed. Carsten Gansel and Burkhard Meyer-Sickendiek, 19–45. Munich: Text + Kritik.

Moses, Stéphane. 1990. Italo Calvino: Die Kunst nicht zu enden. In *Die Kunst zu enden*, ed. Jürgen Söring, 111–123. Frankfurt/Main: Peter Lang.

Pordzik, Ralph. 2017. Poesie der Liste: Sammelleidenschaft und Sprachkritik in der modernen deutschen Lyrik. In *Sammeln: Eine (un-)zeitgemäße Passion*, ed. Martina Wernli, 207–230. Würzburg: Königshausen & Neumann.

Rakusa, Ilma. 2016. *Listen, Litaneien, Loops – zwischen poetischer Anrufung und Inventur*. Munich: Stiftung Lyrik Kabinett.

Rieger, Stefan. 2014. Manifest: Zur Logik einer Erzählform. In *Nach Feierabend 2014: Erzählen*, ed. David Gugerli et al., 133–152. Zürich/Berlin: Diaphanes.

Schaffrick, Matthias, and Niels Werber. 2017. Die Liste, paradigmatisch. *Zeitschrift für Literaturwissenschaft und Linguistik* 47: 303–316.

Tauber, Christine. 2018. Autobiographie als Trauerarbeit. *roland BARTHES par roland barthes*. In *Das eigene Leben als ästhetische Fiktion: Autobiographie und Professionsgeschichte*, ed. Dietrich Erben and Tobias Zervosen, 117–151. Bielefeld: Transcript.

van Hoorn, Tanja. 2018. Zwischen Anmerkungslust und Reflexionszwang: Poetologische Paratexte in aktuellen Lyrikbänden. *Zeitschrift für Germanistik* 28 (2): 261–274.

Vedder, Ulrike. 2001. Leporellos Register. Sammeln und Ausstellen in Mozarts "Don Giovanni". In *Sammeln – Ausstellen – Wegwerfen*, ed. Gisela Ecker, Martina Stange and Ulrike Vedder, 124–140. Königstein, Taunus: Ulrike Helmer Verlag.

———. 2008. Inventare, Akten, Literatur: Zur Kulturtechnik des Erbens bei Stifter und Raabe. In *Logiken und Praktiken der Kulturforschung*, ed. Uwe Wirth, 179–204. Berlin: Kadmos.

von Contzen, Eva. 2017. Grenzfälle des Erzählens: Die Liste als einfache Form. In *Komplexität und Einfachheit: DFG-Symposion 2015*, ed. Albrecht Koschorke, 221–239. Stuttgart: Metzler.

PART III

The Visual List

CHAPTER 11

Between Order and Chaos: Lists in Children's Literature

Agnes Blümer

Cornflakes
Milk
Crisps
Pasta
Canned Tomatoes
Knitting needles
Yarn (Steinkellner 2015, 133)[1]

Lists are a very common but not yet widely researched phenomenon in children's literature.[2] This chapter will investigate their verbal and visual forms, their function, and processes of knowledge construction and aims to contribute toward a poetics of the list in children's literature. The typical features of lists seem to parallel some of the characteristics of children's literature itself, and this might be the reason why they are a recurrent technique in texts addressed to children and young adults.[3] Similar to the

A. Blümer (✉)
University of Cologne, Center for Children's and Young-Adult Media Research (ALEKI), Köln, Germany
e-mail: agnes.bluemer@uni-koeln.de

© The Author(s) 2022

227

R. A. Barton et al. (eds.), *Forms of List-Making: Epistemic, Literary, and Visual Enumeration*,
https://doi.org/10.1007/978-3-030-76970-3_11

perception of children's literature as a whole, lists in children's literature may be perceived as solely or mostly pedagogical in their function. This chapter intends to show that this didactic function is very important even as it acknowledges that many lists for younger readers are also intended to serve as a source of enjoyment through their reliance on rhymes, sounds, and their typical creative play with language. The didactic function is also subverted in many lists (especially in texts for older children): many lists do not transfer knowledge or moral standards but play with concepts of narration.

Lists can be found in different genres of children's literature: in children's poetry and children's folklore, in picture books and in novels for children as well as in novels for young adults.[4] At a first glance, lists seem to work quite differently in the various genres. Yet, some unifying patterns may be identified. To be able to look at the various genres and forms of lists in the vast field of children's literature, a narrow definition of the list would not be useful. Thus, I will rely on the fact that we know a list when we see one. We can also turn to children's folklore and to nursery rhymes to find pointers for the nature of the list:

> One's none,
> Two' some,
> Three's many,
> Four's a penny,
> Five's a little hundred. (Opie and Opie 1963, 164)

Apart from specific—and inevitably random—numbers of items, this example provides us with many other characteristics to be considered when defining a list: stylistic features like the parallelisms in the list above may play a role, the vertical layout seems to be important (although not mandatory), and other typographic features (like the line breaks, the commas, and the colon above) contribute to the list-like quality. Also, materiality and modality, the oral traditions, mnemotechnic, and rhetoric play a role when defining lists, and one would also have to talk about seriality and episodic structure, as well as the differentiation of lists and enumerations. Robert Belknap's (2004, 2) definition might be the most useful here: "At their most simple, lists are frameworks that hold separate and disparate items together. Lists are plastic, flexible structures in which an array of constituent units coheres through specific relations generated by specific forces of attraction."

Starting from this broad definition, the initial focus of this contribution will be on the content of lists in children's literature: which items are listed? If we look across the various genres of children's literature, the lists often contain children's treasures and belongings like toys or sweets or curious finds, elements of their everyday world, or names of characters and animals who play an important role in the child's imagination—perhaps, for example, in the form of fantastical world building. Lists in children's literature may of course be of a more paratextual nature and consist of names or places that play a key role in the text. Especially striking in their number are lists that are sets of defined and distinct objects or concepts such as the days of the week, the months of the year, the letters of the alphabet, or the parts of the human body. Obviously, the content of these lists is meant as a kind of curriculum that children are supposed to learn.

Lists Are for Learning

Head, shoulders, knees and toes,
Knees and toes.
Head, shoulders, knees and toes,
Knees and toes.
And eyes and ears and mouth and nose.
Head, shoulders, knees and toes,
Knees and toes. (https://allnurseryrhymes.com/head-shoulders-knees-and-toes/)

This nursery rhyme may serve as an example for the kind of "curricular lists" mentioned above; when performed with the accompanying gestures (pointing to the body parts in question in a kind of dance) it is meant to help toddlers or small children remember the names of parts of the body. This seems to be the first function of lists: lists in children's literature have educational purpose, they are didactic.

In its repetitions ("knees and toes"), rhymes ("toes"/ "nose"), catchy quality, and structure, this list is also a perfect example for the simplicity of a list. Lists work on an enumerative principle; therefore, they are a relatively "simple" form.[5] Their apparent simplicity of course lends itself well to pedagogical use. In her article on lists in British children's poetry, Debbie Pullinger connects lists' apparent simplicity with the typical young audience, seemingly performing a well-established move in children's literature research (if it is simple, it is for children): "If the list can be seen as a relatively simple poetic form, then we might conjecture that children's poets feel instinctively that it offers easy listening for unsophisticated ears" (Pullinger 2015, 208; Pullinger will modify this view very plausibly later in her article). This is a first parallel between the list and children's literature: their apparent simplicity. As simple forms, not only do they offer a highly accessible means of auditory engagement but also lend themselves aptly to the well-arranged and memory-friendly presentation of reality. Knowledge is broken down into items in an enumeration, no complex explanations are needed, and all the items are or seem equally accessible. With their enumerative structure, lists organize and allow to transfer knowledge without further explanation.

Maybe these simple nursery rhymes show the lists' origins in oral traditions the most clearly. Lists can be seen, as Pullinger writes, as an "out-working of oral culture's additive dynamic" (Pullinger 2015, 209). In nursery rhymes and children's poetry, memorable patterns like rhythm and rhymes but also actions which are performed with the words facilitate the learning of various things; list items that rhyme will (probably) be remembered more easily. Many poems structured according to defined and often finite sets of items seem to rely on this principle.

Lists as Aesthetic Experiences

Lists are certainly suited for educational use in their simplicity and matter-of-factness, but their affinity toward repetitions, their rhythm, their sound, and their rhymes also offer early exposure to certain literary qualities and, indeed, to literature itself—perhaps a first inkling of what Umberto Eco calls the "dizzying sound of the list" (2009, 118). This is the second intent of lists in children's literature: in their simple form, they offer children access to literature at a very young age.[6] The function of offering early literacy experiences may go hand in hand with the didactic function (as in "Heads, Shoulders, Knees and Toes"), but it may in some instances even subvert the first, the didactic function. Lists in poetry can often verge on nonsense and end up in intoxicating absurdity, as many list poems for children show. One example would be "Too many Daves" by Dr. Seuss, taken from *The Sneetches and Other Stories* (1961), a catalogue of 23 nonsensical and funny names:

Too many Daves
Did I ever tell you that Mrs. McCave
Had twenty-three sons and she named them all Dave? [...]

And often she wishes that, when they were born,
She had named one of them Bodkin Van Horn.
And one of them Hoos-Foos. And one of them Snimm.
And one of them Hot-Shot. And one Sunny Jim.
And one of them Shadrack. And one of them Blinkey.
And one of them Stuffy. And one of them Stinkey.
Another one Putt-Putt. Another one Moon Face.
Another one Marvin O'Gravel Balloon Face.
And one of them Ziggy. And one Soggy Muff.
One Buffalo Bill. And one Biffalo Buff.
And one of them Sneepy. And one Weepy Weed.
And one Paris Garters. And one Harris Tweed.
And one of them Sir Michael Carmichael Zutt
And one of them Oliver Boliver Butt
And one of them Zanzibar Buck-Buck McFate.
But she didn't do it. And now it's too late.

If a list can be this crazy, can it also be educational? Apart from the fact that children can use this list to count to 23, there seems to be little educational value in this list in that it does not transfer any factual knowledge. But as a list of (male) names with reference to the characters' decents and the inclusion of "fate," this certainly reads as a parody of epic catalogues (an intertextual reference addressed to the experienced reader). To young readers it may convey a sense of the possibilities of literature as it uses some of its more striking features: telling names (all of the names can be interpreted as displaying some rather funny features of the character in question), play with sounds (most of the names seem to be built on comical sound effects), word play (e.g., Biffalo Buff), intertextual references (Shadrack/Shadrach as biblical figure), and other rather obscure references (Paris Garters). The anapaestic tetrameter and rhyming couplets seem to accelerate the text when read aloud, contributing to the sense of escalation one feels when reading or hearing this poem.[7] The last verse ("But she didn't do it. And now it's too late") seems to provide a closure to this list, to contain it—but paradoxically, it does not succeed: Mrs. McCave may not have named her sons differently, but this list just did. Such tendency for excess, for puns, and for comical effects seems to undermine the traditional educational value of the list form, although it may absolutely function as an experience of early literacy, an encounter with elements typically associated with literary style—albeit a little distorted for fun.

The effect of reading the poem aloud points to another peculiarity of lists for children: they are often meant to be read in shared, communal, or communicative reading settings when an adult reads to one or more children or adult and child share reading "duties." Most texts for children cater to a dual or double addressee (see Barbara Wall 1991 for this distinction) and include elements addressed to young readers, others probably only to be understood by older (or more experienced) readers. Here the comical sound effects seem to benefit the young, while the intertextual and fashion references (Paris Garters, Harris Tweed) may rather be detected by the adult reader.

Lists as Interactive Experiences

Another function of lists becomes obvious here, apart from their educational value and their potential for first literary experiences. Their additive form suggests abundance, multitude, sometimes even infinity. Although the list of Daves is finite—there are only 23 of them—lists in children's literature often play with the infinite. This function of lists (referencing high numbers or big amounts of items or even alluding to infinity) is not reserved to children's literature, but here it may sometimes be used in a peculiar way: lists can be an invitation for interaction, especially when read aloud. When looking at the list by Dr. Seuss, almost any child can add or swap a crazy name to the list of Daves. Adults reading rhyming lists to children aloud will often leave gaps or stop before the end of the verse to let children fill in the next item which will complete the rhyme.

This invitation for interaction is explicit in a prompt for creative writing in Brian P. Cleary's *Underneath My Bed. List Poems*, when he first explains the structure of list poems and then suggests to young readers: "Now, don't make a list of excuses – get busy writing!" (Cleary 2017, 5) Here, the interaction is not restricted to oral situations but continues into the written form as children are encouraged to write their own lists. That this seems reasonably plausible might not only have to do with rhyming patterns of lists in poetry but also with the organization of lists. Due to their additive structure lists seem easily accessible and also easily writable. In this way, lists can be a tool for blurring the boundaries between reader and creator.

To conclude this overview of lists in poetry for children, it is also important to note that poetry in general seems to lend itself well to lists because the verse form resembles a vertical list with several items written underneath each other. The axes of paradigmatic relations are strong both in lists as well as in poetry. Relating to British children's poems, Pullinger estimates that "approximately ten per cent of the poems could be identified as employing list form – whether as a simple series of items, an elaborated series, or enclosed within a larger structure" (2015, 208). Contemporary German language children's anthologies are also full of list poems (approximately 20 percent of the poems in recent anthologies may be categorized as lists), often nonsensical ones. Current children's poets like Arne Rautenberg, Uwe Michael-Gutzschahn, Elisabeth Steinkellner, and Susan Kreller seem to appreciate the list's ability to combine the everyday, the poetical, and the comical in rather accessible texts for children.

Not only lists in children's poetry but whole genres in children's literature and folklore use an interactive principle. Cumulative tales and songs like "This is the House that Jack built" or "There was an Old Lady That Swallowed a Fly" can be read as lists. They are certainly made for shared reading experiences and in their predictability give the child an opportunity to chime in and to fill in words or verses.

Lists as Archives of Voracity

This invitation or even provocation to interact makes the list a playful form. Sabine Mainberger sees lists as "enumerative games" (my translation of Mainberger 2003, 7). This is another shared characteristic of the list form and children's literature: the importance of play and the possibilities for interaction. The child's desire for continuation may play a role here. Umberto Eco writes on the "insatiable" list: "But in traditional rhetoric there is no interesting definition of what strikes us as the dizzying voraciousness of the list" (2009, 137).

This "voracity" may find a counterpart in the child's desire for more when the joy of copiousness is expressed in the literary list. One expression of such desire can be found in wish lists in children's literature, where two kinds of voracity are brought together: one on the material and one on the auditory level. Wish lists can be spotted in any genre and sometimes in their exaggerated form make up an entire poem like Barbara Vance's poem "Dear Santa." In this proleptic catalogue, a little child lists their wishes in a very long stanza addressing Santa:

> So I've made up a list to assist you
> With the hope that it's perfectly clear:

One princess ballerina doll (the one with curly hair),
A pair of skates, a pogo stick, one fuzzy teddy bear;
A pink snow cap with matching gloves, a puppy in a box,
A stocking with my favorite sweets, a brand new set of blocks;
I want another china doll (I dropped the one I had;
I tried to make her better, but the injury was bad).
A set of drums, a big doll house, a new bell for my bike,
The sweater that my best friend has (so we can look alike);
A great big pack of bubble gum (I chew it every day),
A radio, a telescope, a massive wad of clay.
[…] (2020)

Obviously, here, the literary list mimics the child's writing, but it also becomes a fictional archive of the child's everyday life, hopes, and dreams. Wish lists may be an interesting genre to look at historically: how do the toys listed change and how is the child's world reflected in the list? The list here becomes an archive in the sense in which Moritz Baßler (2002) describes pop literature and its archival merit ("Archivierungsleistung," Baßler 2002, 21). Mundane items which normally would not be included in "serious" literature are included in the archive of the text and thus in our cultural memory.[8]

Also, Joosen and Pauwels (2018) find that "wish lists gear the young for consumerism and even greed, as they instill in children a desire for ever more commodities" (56). A kind of greediness is certainly apparent when the wish list poem, like the nonsensical list poem, seems to escalate quickly as more and more wishes are added (the text above is just an excerpt from a much longer poem). Some wish lists even seem to lack any reality in the sheer number of wishes listed. Children's literature certainly seems to abound with wish lists detailing children's longings and dreams. Not each specific object of desire seems important, but desire itself is often the topic of these escalating lists. Desire in children's literature has been seen as a necessary step toward autonomy (and toward adolescence and adulthood). Karen Coats in her psychoanalytic reading sees children's books as parameters of desire: "the child (unconsciously) uses his books […] to fill his unconscious with representations and images, shape his reality, and define the parameters of his possibilities. […] [T]his process depends on repetition—both the repetition of the same book, and the repetition of structures, images, and values across books. Hence, as her books have a definable structure, so structure becomes a psychic necessity for the child.

As her books depict a whole world, the child seeks nothing less than a whole world" (Coats 2004, 6–7). As she shows here, structure, repetition, and fullness (arguably all features of the list) play an important role in shaping the child's identity, and lists seem to play an important part in offering an almost fantastical glimpse into that desirable adult world.

The playfulness of lists, their tendency to veer toward the fantastical, nonsensical, or absurd, and their function as archives of voracity seem to be important factors when we consider their attractiveness for the intended audience. Although simplicity and accessibility are certainly some of the reasons why lists are used in children's literature, and while they are often used with educational purposes in mind, they are more than didactic tools.[9] There is another feature of children's lists that might make them attractive for their intended audience: they often combine two codes, the verbal and the visual so that advanced reading skills are not absolutely necessary to access the list.

Visual Lists in Picturebooks

Whereas wish list poems can be read as catalogues of desire, the picturebook famously uses the list as catalogue of the whole world. Picturebook lists may rely on solely visual elements or they may combine two codes: word and image. They differ in this from lists in a narrower sense, and according to Umberto Eco, we might classify them as "visual lists" (Eco 2009, 36–38). *Orbis sensualium pictus* by Amos Comenius (1653), the publication that is widely regarded as one of the first picturebooks, is essentially a list of Latin words describing the whole world. It presents, among many other topics, for example "olera," garden vegetables (picture taken from a later quadrilingual edition, 1760) (Fig. 11.1):

Under the picture of a vegetable garden, which can be read as a visual list of the vegetables in question, we find a vertical verbal list in three columns giving the names of the vegetables in Latin and German, as well as grammatical information. Both the picture as well as the words are numbered so the reader can find the correct names for the elements in the picture in the written legend (e.g., I is lactuca, Salat—lettuce). Although the verbal and the visual list here seem quite separate, they are intertwined in their equivalences and through these numbers. Clearly, the educational function is to teach the names of vegetables in different languages, and the visual cues supplement the verbal ones.

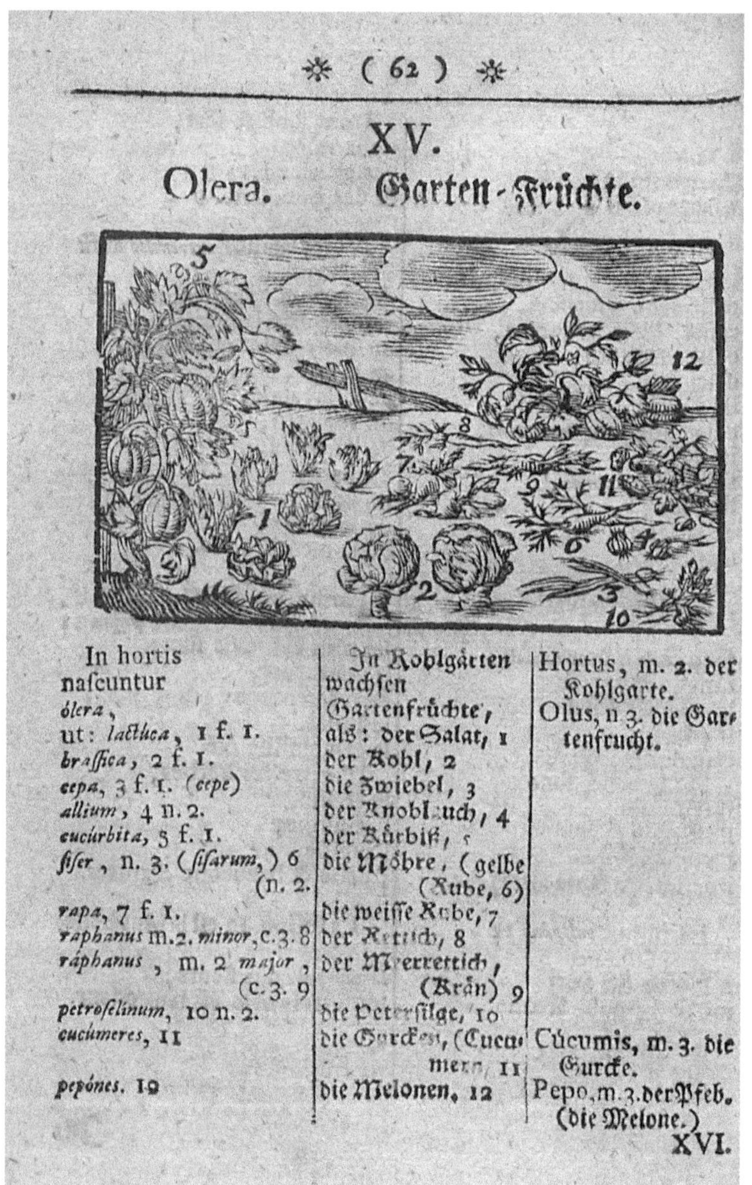

Fig. 11.1   *Olera. Garten-Früchte*, in John Amos Comenius, *Orbis sensualium pictus* (Nuremberg 1760), 62

Fig. 11.2 *At the Supermarket*, in Richard Scarry, *Best Word Book Ever* (1991), n.p.

To this day, early literacy picture books and word board books are structured in a similar fashion as lists and present knowledge to be acquired and words to be learned. Again, the use of lists here stems from an educational impulse. Like in the precursor *Orbis pictus* these lists may combine the two codes: verbal and visual. These lists, too, seem to suggest copiousness, like for example Richard Scarry's "At the Supermarket," taken from his famous *Best Word Book Ever*, first published in 1963 and again in 1980 with new illustrations (picture taken from the 1991 edition, no page numbers) (Fig. 11.2):

In the supermarket spread, especially on the right side of the double page, we can still see a pretty close connection to the vegetable list in *Orbis pictus* three centuries before. The layout in Scarry's book is different; there is no vertical list and the visual and the verbal lists are not separate like in *Orbis Pictus* but rather intertwined: the verbal list is written into the picture as little tags underneath the items in question. Still, both Scarry's and Comenius' verbal/visual list may be read as attempts to archive the everyday and also to convey the yet unknown to the child. Both examples invite the reader to interact with the list in its two codes: to learn the words, to point to the items, and to name them.

Both lists also hint at narration. Comenius prefaces the vertical list with an opening sentence ("In hortis nascuntur olera," "Vegetables are growing in the garden") like a narration, and Scarry hides snippets of narration in his tags, for example, "a piglet who wants to work in the supermarket when she grows up" to "label" the little pig girl in the shopping trolley. Scarry's introductory sentence, like Comenius', also provides a narrative context ("The Pigs are buying groceries for their family"), and the next two sentences amplify the invitation for interaction. They provide the (probably) adult reader with questions to ask the (probably) child addressee: "What would you like to buy the next time you go to the supermarket?" Like some wish lists, this question seems tied to the intent to educate the child to become a "good" client or consumer or to maybe spark a conversation about food choices.

For children's literature, it is important to note that both verbal and visual lists may be pedagogical when they serve as instruction or memory aids for learning, but both kinds can also be playful and focus on conveying sensations or offering early literary experiences. Obviously, in modern word books, lists are used to present aspects of reality in a structured way to little children, as when the supermarket items, for example, are sorted into the categories "meats," "fruits," and "vegetables." Verbal and visual lists act as catalogues of knowledge or possessions, but they are aesthetical fabrications, too, in that their pictures serve as an experience of art, color symbolism, and picture composition.

Visual lists can be found in many narrative picture books as well, as for example in Eric Carle's *The Very Hungry Caterpillar* where, again, we find lists focused on food—in this case, the caterpillar eating its way through a true inventory of (human) food. Its eating journey is narrated in double-page spreads (and the famous smaller part-pages with holes) that correspond to the days of the week (e.g., "On Monday he ate through one apple. But he was still hungry") and culminate in Saturday's menu: "On Saturday he ate through one piece of chocolate cake, one ice-cream cone, one pickle, one slice of swiss cheese, one slice of salami, one lollipop, one piece of cherry pie, one sausage, one cupcake, and one slice of watermelon. That night he had a stomachache!" (Carle 1994, no page numbers). Of course, the story may serve as learning material for the days of the week (a finite set so appropriate for a finite list) and the numbers, but the most memorable experience is probably a visual and tactile one: of touching the thick pages with their holes, of taking in Carle's collages with various textures and colors, and of reveling in the indulgent food choices.

Again, we see the list as a multipurpose form here: it seems to be educational, aesthetical, and interactive.

A huge number of narrative picture books for very young children are essentially lists. Simple sentences or structures are listed, repeated, and modified, as in Molly Bang's *Ten, Nine, Eight* (first published in 1983) or Margaret Wise Brown's *Goodnight Moon* (first published in 1947), where everything in the room is listed and bid goodnight: "Goodnight room – Goodnight moon – Goodnight cow jumping over the moon" (Brown 2017, no page numbers). Every element of the list is present both in verbal as well as in pictorial form. Stating and repeating the items is a routine process likely to offer reassurance to the child by summarizing and archiving the world that surrounds them. Again, this list prompts interaction: caregivers and children are likely to list the elements in their own room and tell them goodnight after reading this book. The parallelisms and repetitions of this process lead to a certain monotony which helps to calm the child and perhaps even lull it to sleep. Apart from these verbal-visual lists, there are also wordless picture books which can be read as lists. Those for very early literacy present one item per page to be named in reading situations with a caregiver ("duck," "ball," …). They, of course, are a prime example of the educational nature lists may have in children's literature when, again, in an interactive reading setting, children may learn the words to match the items shown.

Lists as Reading Promotion

Lists in novels for young readers may have pedagogical function, too. While these texts mostly move away from presenting items to be learned, lists seem to be used here with a different aim in mind: to promote literacy and to encourage independent reading. Lists can structure longer texts and make them more easily accessible and a quicker read. As Joosen and Pauwels (2018) put it: "From a developing reader's perspective, lists reduce the time spent on reading, without reducing the overall achievement of finishing a book." This is certainly the case for Kristin Mahoney's *Annie's Life in Lists* (2018). The novel consists only of lists but still unfolds the plot of Annie who loves making lists to help her keep track of things that seem a little out of control such as when her family moves from Brooklyn to a small town, Clover Gap. A review from the *School Library Journal* reveals what I suspect to be one aim of lists in novels for younger readers. Liz Anderson (2018) writes: "Even with its imperfections, the format, featuring illustrations throughout, will make it a great choice for reluctant readers." Lists can make longer texts more bite-sized for beginning or reluctant readers; the lists break up the continuous text and offer little breaks in between. The novel is also a very good example of how fictional child characters use lists as "coping mechanisms" (Joosen and Pauwels 2018, 53). The blurb on the front dust cover of this list novel reads: "Welcome to a year in the life of a kid just trying to keep everything in order" (Mahoney 2018). Annie is trying to make sense of her new surroundings and clings to the familiarity and order of lists when she chronicles her life after the move.

LISTS AND CONFUSION

So far, in mentioning poems, picture books, and *Annie's Life in Lists*, this chapter has dealt mostly with texts that consist of one list or several lists, that is: texts that *are* lists. But of course, one can also find lists that constitute parts of novels, where continuous text is interspersed with lists. Lists might also, by providing the title and the chapter headings as list items, structure a novel or a narrative that is mainly continuous text.[10] In *Why We Broke Up* (Handler and Kalman 2011) the list structure stems from objects and images in a box that the female protagonist Min dumps at Ed's front door after they have broken up. "This is the box, Ed. Inside is everything." In the blurb, this announcement is followed by a list of some of these objects:

> Two bottle caps,
> a movie ticket from Greta in the Wild,
> a note from you,
> a box of matches,
> your protractor,
> Joan's book,
> the stolen sugar,
> a toy truck,
> those ugly earrings,
> a comb from the motel.
> and the rest of it.
> This is it, Ed.
> The whole story of why we broke up. (Handler and Kalman 2011, back cover)

In the book, every chapter is dedicated to one of the items and each chapter is headed by an illustration by Maira Kalman. As Min says or rather writes in a long letter, the items make up a catalogue or archive of artefacts of their past relationship that lasted only a few weeks: "Every last souvenir of the love we had, the prizes and the debris of this relationship, like the glitter in the gutter when the parade has passed, all the everything and whatnot kicked to the curb. I'm dumping the whole box back into your life, Ed, every item of you and me" (Handler and Kalman 2011, 3). Here, the whole book becomes an inventory which is even more tangible because of the illustrations dividing the text into chapters and showing every single item. But this list is not an objective one: it is clearly Min's view of why they broke up, and the seemingly material objectivity of the list is undermined by several literary techniques, for example by elaborate pop culture references that lead absolutely nowhere. As Monica Edinger noted in *The New York Times' Sunday Book Review*: "Handler has made them all up, but so superbly you feel certain they must really exist" (Dec 16, 2011). As we can see here, lists in children's literature do not only provide structure and order; they can also be misleading like this list of verbal and visual references to movies, bands, songs, and books that the reader feels they must know. But if the reader, maybe confused or ashamed of their ignorance, tries to research some of the art that is described and shown in great and intricate detail, it is revealed that none of it exists.

Lists in literature for young adults often represents confusion and disorientation; they can break up the former coherence of the narration. Eva von Contzen (2017, 226, trans. by Nathan Anderson) has shown this already when talking about literary texts for adults: "When narratives employ enumeration, they initially break up the narrative coherence: that which binds them together as narratives grows feeble and inert."[11] This is what happens here as well, and of course it is significant that we do not find this so much in texts for small children but rather in young adult fiction or adolescence novels. Here, the pedagogical impulse may take a back seat, and also the fragility and changes represented by list structures are the very themes of the adolescence novel.

In Elisabeth Steinkellner's novel *Rabensommer* (published in 2015, not translated into English, the title would translate as *Summer of Ravens*) we get an impression of the protagonist's insecurity through her lists. It is the summer after Juli's matura, the Austrian capstone examination before graduation. When her life threatens to spiral out of control in the second part of the book, the cohesive text dissolves into lists, dreams, text messages, and short episodes. This is when her friend August writes a meta-list to and about Juli on a postcard:

> what I like about Juli:
> that she starts to write lists in times of crisis
> that it makes her happy to drink vanilla tea from flowered grandmother's cups
> that [...]
> that she will be gnawing at her lip when she reads this. (Steinkellner 2015, 192)[12]

Like in *Why We Broke Up*, lists are explicitly linked to crisis here, and the crisis is triggered by Niels, who breaks up with Juli, but it is also fueled by the sense of betrayal Juli feels toward her two other friends, August and Ronja, for having sex together. Both events are narrated at the end of the first part of the novel which consists of conventional continuous text. However, the opening pages of the second part show how much Juli feels thrown offtrack by these events, the first page simply reading:

> Bread
> Butter
> Milk
> Coffee (Steinkellner 2015, 97)[13]

Narration does not seem possible anymore; we get only fragments of a shopping list that seems to function as a kind of foothold, or again, a coping mechanism, for Juli. The following pages hold more pragmatic lists, many of them shopping lists.

These lists are symbols of the teenage protagonist's desperate search for stability and orientation; they are symptoms of her disorientation and helplessness. It seems that this loss of sense and orientation is represented in the fragmentation of the text, in the groping for stability—and although this is certainly true to a certain extent, it is also deceptive: lists cannot be equated with chaos here. They do not (necessarily) stop the narrative flow. When we read, for example, the shopping lists carefully, we realize they are actually foreshadowing plot elements that are narrated later. Readers can guess developments before they are narrated—or even without them being narrated in continuous text at all. For example, shopping lists hint at menus (a lentil dhal with a side of bread and butter?) and new relationships (where toothpaste and condoms seem in order):

Bread
Butter
Avocado
Cucumber
Lemon
Coconut milk
Lentils
Wine
Toothpaste
Condoms (Steinkellner 2015, 171)[14]

These lists rely on the participation of the reader, because in reading (as Eva von Contzen wrote, my translation) "the reader makes these building blocks into a narration, when before they have only been the scaffolding for a potential narration."[15] The reader builds a menu from the grocery items and notes that these groceries, unlike before, actually seem to add up to a nice meal, one for which Juli might have company over. "Toothpaste" is another sign that the young man she has fallen in love with might be the dinner companion, and the last item, "condoms," seems to confirm this. Lists as symbols of fragmentation and helplessness redirect into storylines with the readers' help. Again, lists seem to invite the reader to interact, to take part in them, to make sense of them.

Conclusion

Lists in children's literature offer structure: lists can be scaffoldings for narratives or for world building, they can represent and teach reality, they can offer reassurance, and they can make longer texts more accessible. The perceived simplicity of lists allows us to try to grasp the ineffable or infinity. Lists are clearly used for didactic purposes, and this is probably an explanation for the abundance of lists in children's literature. The list seems to offer up the characteristics of children's literature as if placed under a magnifying glass: didactic, playful, interactive, visual, and aesthetic elements become especially apparent.

Debbie Pullinger once more highlights the list's affordance to textually archive a lost world when she suggests that "since all children's literature is concerned with the eventual 'death' of the child in order to become an adult, both the elegy and the list are at the heart of children's literature" (Pullinger 2015, 214). But the list is not only an orderly archive for the child's fleeting life; the disintegration of a text into lists can also imitate the feeling of chaos. Lists can escalate quickly; they can be nonsensical or absurd to an extreme.

Lists seem to vacillate between the extremes, between simplicity and complexity, between order and chaos, between the didactic and the purely aesthetic. Evelien Neven (2018, 123) points out that "contrasts are inherently connected to the list form itself" and that lists can lean toward one or the other pole on a continuum. If we want to bring the two opposites together, I think we may view it like this: lists may convey the presence or the absence of order, depending on how we see it. Is a list a "failure," something that is not continuous text, or is it an achievement, the result of organizing various items?

At any rate, the list is an invitation: to learn, to play, to search, to name, to write, or to narrate. Depending on the genre, the reader's age and on each specific text, lists in children's literature can be more educational or more literary, but mostly they include both extremes in some form: they are orderly and chaotic, they are nonsensical and meaningful, they bring narrations to a halt, and they make them start again.

Notes

1. This is my translation. Steinkellner's book *Rabensommer* has not been translated into English yet. The original German text:

   Cornflakes
   Milch
   Chips
   Nudeln
   Dosentomaten
   Stricknadeln
   Wolle (Steinkellner 2015, 133)

2. This has begun to change recently: the most important current articles on lists in children's literature are by Debbie Pullinger (2015) and Vanessa Joosen, and Frauke Pauwels (2018 but published in 2020). I did not know of the latter article at the time of writing this paper but was kindly made aware of it by the editors of this volume for my revision. Many points we are making are very similar, so I will point to Joosen and Pauwels where appropriate.

3. Joosen and Pauwels (2018, 49) also see a parallel between children's literature and lists in the fact that they can both "make the strange familiar, and make the familiar strange." I believe this is similar to my understanding that lists can both convey order as well as chaos.

4. This article will orient itself along some of the genres of children's literature and move from poetry to folklore, picture books, novels for children, and lastly to young adults.

5. Eva von Contzen sees lists as an ambivalent form between complexity and simplicity: "ambivalente Form zwischen Komplexität und Einfachheit" (von Contzen 2017, 222).

6. Joosen and Pauwels (2018, 49) also see lists in the context of "becoming a reader."

7. Eco (2009, 118) describes similar effects when it comes to Catholic Litanies: "What matters is being seized by the dizzying sound of the list, just as in the Litanies of the Saints what matters is not so much which of them [the saints] is present or absent, as the rhythmic enunciation of the names for a sufficiently long period of time."

8. See Baßler's reading of Max Goldt's texts: "Wir kennen fast alles, was in Goldts Kolumnen zur Sprache kommt [...], aber gelesen hatten wir darüber noch nicht, es war bislang nicht Gegenstand jener künstlerischen Anstrengung gewesen, über die Dinge ins kulturelle Archiv gelangen. [...] Die Verfahren, die in der Pop-Literatur von Goldt und anderen am Werk sind, lassen sich genau als solche Mechanismen verstehen, die 'das Verhältnis zwischen dem valorisierten, hierarchisch aufgebauten kulturellen Gedächtnis einerseits und dem wertlosen profanen Raum andererseits regeln'. Das kulturelle Archiv, das dabei bestückt wird, ist das der Literatur" (Baßler 2002, 21). To be clear, Baßler is not necessarily talking about lists here, as his definition of lists is a typographical one, in which he sees line breaks as indispensable ("als Liste, also wie in Versdichtung mit Zeilenbrüchen untereinander notiert [...] statt als Fließtext," Baßler 2020, 184).

9. As Pullinger puts it: "the didactic impulse does not seem a wholly adequate explanation for the prevalence of the list" (2015, 2018) in children's literature.

10. Some examples for this technique published in the last ten years are: *Thirteen Reasons Why* (Jay Asher 2007; TV series as TH1RTEEN R3ASONS WHY, 2017), *12 Things to Do Before You Crash and Burn* (James Proimos 2011), *Why We Broke Up* (Daniel Handler and Maira Kalman 2011) *10 Things I Can See from Here* (Carrie Mac 2017), *The Bad Decisions Playlist* (Michael Rubens 2016), or *36 Questions That Changed My Mind About You* (Vicky Grant 2017).

11. Original text: "Wenn Erzählungen sich des Enumerativen bedienen, brechen sie zunächst narrative Kohärenz auf: Das, was sie als Erzählungen zusammenhält, wird brüchig, außer Kraft gesetzt" (von Contzen 2017, 226).

12. Original text:

was ich an Juli mag:
dass sie in Krisenzeiten beginnt, Listen zu schreiben
dass es sie glücklich macht, aus geblümten Omatassen Vanilletee zu trinken
dass [...]
dass sie an ihrer Unterlippe kauen wird, wenn sie diese Karte liest (Steinkellner 2015, 192).

13. Original text:

Brot
Butter
Milch
Kaffee (Steinkellner 2015, 97)

14. Original text:

Brot
Butter
Avocado
Gurke
Zitrone
Kokosmilch
Linsen
Wein
Zahnpasta
Kondome (Steinkellner 2015, 171)

15. Original text: "narrativiert der Leser die Bausteine dessen, was zunächst Gerüst einer potenziellen Erzählung ist" (von Contzen 2017, 234).

REFERENCES

PRIMARY SOURCES

Bang, Molly. 1996 [1983]. *Ten, Nine, Eight*. New York: HarperCollins.

Brown, Margaret Wise. 1947. *Goodnight, Moon*. Pictures by Clement Hurd. New York: HarperCollins.

Carle, Eric. 1994 [1969]. *The Very Hungry Caterpillar*. London: Puffin.

Cleary, Brian P. 2017. *Poetry Adventures. Underneath My Bed. List Poems*. Illustrations by Richard Watson. Minneapolis: Millbrook Press.

Comenius, Johann Amos. 1760. *Joh. Amos Comenii Orbis Sensualium Pictus Quadrilinguis Emendatus, Hoc est: Omnium fundamentalium in mundo Rerum, & vita Actionum*, Pictura & Nomenclatura, [...]. Noribergæ: Endter.

Dr. Seuss. 1961, 1989. *The Sneetches and Other Stories*. London: HarperCollins.

Handler, Daniel. 2011. *Why We Broke Up*. Illustrations by Maira Kalman. New York: Hachette.

Heads, Shoulders, Knees, and Toes. *Nursery Rhymes*. https://allnurseryrhymes.com/head-shoulders-knees-and-toes/. Accessed 26 Mar 2020.

Mahoney, Kristin. 2018. *Annie's Life in Lists*. New York: Knopf.

Opie, Iona, and Peter Opie. 1963. *The Puffin Book of Nursery Rhymes*. London: Penguin.

Scarry, Richard. 1963, 1991, 2013. *Best Word Book Ever*. London: HarperCollins.

Steinkellner, Elisabeth. 2015. *Rabensommer*. Weinheim/Basel: Beltz und Gelberg.

Vance, Barbara. 2020. *Dear Santa*. http://www.suziebitner.com/portfolio/dear-santa/. Accessed 8 Apr 2020.

SECONDARY SOURCES

Anderson, Liz. 2018. Annie's Life in Lists: Review. *School Library Journal*. https://www.schoollibraryjournal.com/?reviewDetail=annies-life-in-lists. Accessed 8 Apr 2020.

Baßler, Moritz. 2002. *Der deutsche Pop-Roman: Die neuen Archivisten*. München: C.H. Beck.

———. 2020. Katalog- und Montageverfahren: Sammeln und Generieren. In *Handbuch Literatur & Pop*, ed. Moritz Baßler and Eckhard Schumacher, 184–198. Berlin/Boston: De Gruyter.

Belknap, Robert E. 2004. *The List: The Uses and Pleasures of Cataloguing*. New Haven/London: Yale University Press.

Coats, Karen. 2004. *Looking Glasses and Neverlands: Lacan, Desire, and Subjectivity in Children's Literature*. Iowa City: University of Iowa Press.

Eco, Umberto. 2009. *The Infinity of Lists: From Homer to Joyce*. Trans. Alastair McEwen. London: MacLehose Press.

Edinger, Monica. 2011. Daniel Handler's Teenagers Out of Love. *The New York Times*, December 16. https://www.nytimes.com/2011/12/18/books/review/why-we-broke-up-by-daniel-handler-illustrated-by-maira-kalman-book-review.html. Accessed 8 Apr 2020.

Joosen, Vanessa, and Frauke Pauwels. 2018. The Pleasures of Plenitude: Becoming a Reader Through Literary Lists. In *lwu: Literatur in Wissenschaft und Unterricht. Theme Issue: Lists and Narrative*, ed. Evelien Neven, Bart Vervaeck, and Luc Herman, 49–62.

Mainberger, Sabine. 2003. *Die Kunst des Aufzählens: Elemente zu einer Poetik des Enumerativen*. Berlin/New York: de Gruyter.

Neven, Evelien. 2018. "Kraai, Krähe, crow, corneille, corvus": On Reading Lists in Peeters' Great European Novel. In *lwu: Literatur in Wissenschaft und Unterricht. Theme Issue: Lists and Narrative*, ed. Evelien Neven, Bart Vervaeck, and Luc Herman, 123–137.

Pullinger, Debbie. 2015. Infinity and Beyond: The Poetic List in Children's Poetry. *Children's Literature in Education* 46 (3): 207–225.

von Contzen, Eva. 2017. Grenzfälle des Erzählens: Die Liste als einfache Form. In *Komplexität und Einfachheit*, ed. Albrecht Koschorke, 221–239. Stuttgart: Metzler.

Wall, Barbara. 1991. *The Narrator's Voice: The Dilemma of Children's Fiction*. Basingstoke: Macmillan.

CHAPTER 12

Aesthetics of Enumeration: The *Arma Christi* in Medieval Visual Art

Daniela Wagner

On fol. 331r of the Prayer Book of Bonne of Luxembourg,[1] we find a representation that almost forces us to reflect upon the practice of enumeration as it illustrates a sophisticated conceptual understanding of the list in visual art (Fig. 12.1): thirteen objects known as the *Arma Christi* are gathered in the central space of the small page of only 12.6 × 9 cm. All of them are of importance in the narrative of the Passion. The collection is dominated by the centrally placed side wound, which measures the full height of the picture space.[2] To its left, we see the hammer, the rod with the sponge, the cross with the crown of thorns, the lance, and the empty sarcophagus. To the right are three nails, two scourges, the bucket, the flagellation column with the rope wrapped around it, and the pincers. In comparison with the other objects, the size of the side wound indicates already that the aim here was not to achieve authentic proportions. The

Funded by the Deutsche Forschungsgemeinschaft (DFG, German Research Foundation)—Project-ID 405662736—SFB 1391.

D. Wagner (✉)
University of Tübingen, Tübingen, Germany
e-mail: daniela.wagner@uni-tuebingen.de

R. A. Barton et al. (eds.), *Forms of List-Making: Epistemic, Literary, and Visual Enumeration,*
https://doi.org/10.1007/978-3-030-76970-3_12

Fig. 12.1   Prayer Book of Bonne of Luxemburg, Paris, before 1349, Metropolitan Museum, New York, The Cloisters Collection, accession number 69.86, fol. 331r

highlighting of the side wound is based on the hierarchy of meanings. As the wound that makes the body of Christ accessible to the faithful, it is the most significant of all the items gathered here.[3] Below the picture, a French text initiates a dialogue between Christ and the reader-viewer by referring to the violence performed with the *Arma,* the instruments of the Passion: "Show us, sweet Lord, your greatest goodness. How great was the suffering you bore for our sakes?"[4]

The text, the picture space, and the *bas de page* with grotesques holding the coat of arms of Bonne of Luxembourg are surrounded by a strip frame, which is left open at the top. Thorn-leaf tendrils with various birds[5] sitting on them are sprouting from this frame and spread along the margins. Of interest for the *Arma Christi* and the practice of enumeration, however, is the ladder that is laboriously handled by a hybrid creature of man and mythical beast, which is balancing at the outside edge of the frame's strip on the top left. His neck pushed through the rungs and a hand on each rail, he allows one foot of the ladder to rest casually on the frame of the *Arma* image.

On the page and in the context of the preceding pictorial program, the ladder turns out to be a figure of reflection open to interpretation. It has been seen as an ironic reference to the ascent of the soul, which is symbolized by a ladder, and also was understood as a reference to the six stages of divine love depicted on fol. 315r of the prayer book (Tammen 2006, 98). Along with fol. 315r and the miniature of a couple looking up at Christ's cross on fol. 329r, the ladder has also been interpreted as a part of the visualization of a spiritual pilgrimage (Lermack 2008). In addition to these allegorical readings, however, the connection between the ladder and the *Arma Christi* would have been most obvious to late medieval beholders, as the ladder is known from the deposition of Christ and often can be found among the *Arma Christi* in texts and images. On fol. 331r, it remains separate from the objects arranged in the picture space, but the hybrid creature apparently endeavors to move the ladder into this space to complement the *Arma* already assembled there.

This playful device, which interweaves the levels of composition and content,[6] invites viewers to complete the action in their minds and involves them in the process of enumeration. The artist, possibly Jean le Noir, to whom the book is ascribed, reflects first of all on the character of the *Arma Christi* as an enumeration, but also the openness of the motif and the term. "Arma Christi" does not mean all the objects involved in the Passion, nor does it refer to a fixed group of instruments of the Passion. "Arma

Christi" is a collective term allowing no conclusions to be drawn about which objects are actually included in the list. The possibilities of what a set of the *Arma Christi* could contain are defined roughly by the context of the Passion narrative, but without providing further specifications.

The objects gathered on fol. 331r of the Prayer Book of Bonne thus are a representation of the *Arma Christi* either way, with and without the ladder. A fixed unit is established only on an individual basis for each spoken, textual, or visual combination. But when the ladder is brought in to complete the set of instruments within the frame, the pictorial list obtains a liminal state—it is as complete as it is incomplete—and thus is captured in the process of change. With the figure holding the ladder, the painter reflects on the productive aspect of creating a list, as an enumeration of the *Arma Christi* in text or image is the outcome of a two-stage process: the selection of the elements to be included is followed in a second step by their specific arrangement.

Robert Belknap has described literary lists as "adaptable containers that hold information from the mind-deep pool of possibility" (2000, 39), and this can also be applied to the highly variable visual representations of the *Arma Christi*.[7] The diversity and flexibility of pictorial enumerations of the *Arma* apply to two levels, to that of content and that of form, reflected in the aforementioned aspects of selection and arrangement. Although the production process is rarely visualized as explicitly as it is in the Prayer Book of Bonne of Luxembourg, pictorial representations of the *Arma Christi* consistently reveal an explicit consideration of aesthetic questions, especially regarding the structuring of enumeration. Just as no fixed set of objects has been established as "the" *Arma Christi*, no binding representational system was ever consolidated on the formal level, either. Thus, in addition to depictions such as the one in the Prayer Book of Bonne of Luxembourg, which operates with size hierarchies and presents an "orderly," easily comprehensible arrangement, other depictions of the *Arma* take the forms of irregular scatterings, accumulations, grid structures, or linear and circular sequences.[8] The fact that one representation rarely resembles another indicates that for each work a new list was created and configured individually in visual terms. Over and over again, artists and/or clients considered the selection of objects and their arrangement anew and were thoughtfully merging the content of the list and its appearance.[9]

It is precisely due to this heterogeneity of combinations and their structures that the *Arma Christi* are a motif capable of shedding light on the constitution and functionality of pictorial enumerations when studied under the premise of its list-like character. As will be shown, in pictorial enumerations of the *Arma Christi* aesthetic and functional aspects are inseparably intertwined and relate to each other repeatedly in a productive way regarding the creation of meaning and the involvement of the beholder. The particular importance ascribed to aesthetics becomes apparent in the various visual reflections on the list and its characteristics in medieval art. Moments of reflection like the one in the Bonne prayer book allow us to discern an artistic awareness of the *enumeratio* as a figure of visual rhetoric.[10] Therefore, the following explorations should also present an approach to a more theoretical understanding of enumeration in visual art.

So far, enumeration and lists have been discussed primarily in literary studies.[11] Recent literary research in particular has provided a theoretical understanding of the list, which is now considered as such primarily because of its organizational structure and not due to a specific visual appearance.[12] The term "list," therefore, is applicable when three or more distinct units (words or groups of words) are arranged in a row as well as when they are placed one below the other in columns. This definition can also be used in visual art, in which ordering structures are more diverse. An identification of enumerations and lists with a specific type of appearance, therefore, seems to make very little sense in this case. Often, there is no difference made between the terms "enumeration" and "list." A distinction, however, seems to be useful in general, but especially for the approach suggested in this chapter, in which the practice of enumeration and its product are treated as separate aspects. In the following, "list" refers to the result of the process of selection and arrangement, while "enumeration" is used to address the practice and the process of list-making through selection and arrangement.

Meanings

In early medieval visual art, the *Arma Christi* function as signs of triumph and majesty, especially when they appear alongside Christ enthroned or the Lamb of God. Based on the surviving artworks, it is impossible to say whether the *Arma* could already be found as an independent motif in those times; however, there exist various, well-known early Christian texts in which they serve as a starting point for religious contemplation.[13] It is therefore likely that the *Arma* existed as an independent pictorial motif significantly earlier than generally assumed. In their meaning as a sign of triumph, the *Arma* refer to the victory of Christ-like trophies, which is sometimes visualized with recourse to the ancient *tropaion*, a rack displaying the captured weapons of a defeated enemy.[14] The *tropaion* motif is echoed in the Prayer Book of Bonne with the crown of thorns hung on the cross. It is more obvious, however, in the drawing of the Utrecht Psalter, which is regarded as one of the earliest known independent depictions of the *Arma Christi* (Fig. 12.2).[15] On fol. 12r, the objects attached to the cross or positioned close to it (scourge, the crown of thorns, lance, the sponge rod, and two other items that cannot be identified clearly) refer to the 21st Psalm.[16] The objects form a cluster or accumulation which emphasizes the close connection between the individual elements. In their agglomeration in the Utrecht Psalter, the items are recognizable as a unit and function as such. They allude to the sufferings of Christ culminating in the crucifixion, but through the reference to the *tropaion* they also are reminders of the victorious triumph over his suffering.[17] In her studies on the mentions of the *Arma Christi* in early Christian texts, Mary Agnes Edsall has pointed out the rhetorical figure of *accumulatio* often used there (see 2014a). It can be assumed that this list-like quality of the *Arma* in texts, among others by highly regarded authors such as Augustine, also influenced the *enumeratio* of the *Arma* in visual art. Like the *tropaion*

Fig.   12.2 Utrecht   Psalter,   area   of   Reims,   probably   820–830, Universiteitsbibliotheek   Utrecht,   Ms.   32,   fol.   12r,   image   credits: Universiteitsbibliotheek Utrecht

motif, some of the text passages quoted by Edsall are also characterized by the notion of victory: in the Acts of Thomas, for example, the objects and actions that cause suffering (such as being spit on) function as a support for the Christian in his struggle against the devil or for receiving divine grace (Edsall 2014a, 31–32).

The shift in Christ's perception from glorious ruler to the incarnate Savior, the emergence of Passion piety, and a turn toward the suffering of Jesus in worship, prayer, and devotion were accompanied with a change in the very notion of the *Arma Christi* in the twelfth century: they were integrated into the meditation on the Passion. In this context, the *Arma* are no longer imagined as signs of victory but as those objects and actions that inflicted mental and physical suffering on Christ. In the context of the private practice of piety, images of the instruments of the Passion became useful for religious contemplation and compassion. This new functionality of the motif in the late Middle Ages becomes visible in the vital artifacts of private devotion, texts, and images. Henceforth, the *Arma* have frequently appeared in prayer texts and books, small-format panel paintings, and, from the fifteenth century onward, in single-sheet prints and devotional booklets. However, the meaning of the *Arma* as symbols of victory did not disappear entirely; their visual accentuation as signs of triumph or instruments of the Passion still depended on the individual representation. One meaning did not always exclude the other; composition and context provide indications of the intended reading. Furthermore, the apotropaic power attributed to the *Arma Christi*[18] and the indulgence that could be obtained through them suggest a connection to the imagination of victory and the overcoming of suffering.

Narration and Enumeration

Despite their shared origins, a different functionality was ascribed to the events of the Passion in narrative images and the enumeration of the *Arma Christi*, which can be illustrated using the example of an ivory picture booklet made in the second quarter of the fourteenth century (Figs. 12.3a and b).[19] Between the ivory book covers, which are decorated with carved scenes, there are six thin plates, also made of ivory, whose depictions are not carved but painted. The first pages each show a scene from the Passion, followed by the sequence of the instruments of the Passion starting on the recto page of the fifth panel with a full-page depiction of the *Vera Icon*. The list continues on the verso side with the hand that struck Christ at the

Fig. 12.3 (a, b) Ivory booklet with scenes of the Passion and the *Arma Christi*, ca. 1330–1340, Victoria and Albert Museum, London, Museum number 11–1872, 5v–7r, © Victoria and Albert Museum, London

top and Christ with one of his tormentors below.[20] Opposite, on the recto side of the sixth inner panel, the bucket, the side wound, the sponge rod, and the crown of thorns are presented. On the next double page, three nails, the hammer, pincers, the blindfold, the thirty pieces of silver, and blood-stained footprints of Christ are shown on the left, while the staff of reed, the robe and three dice, the scourge, the ladder, the lance, and the sarcophagus (seen from above) are positioned on the right on the inside of the booklet's back cover.

Concerning the arrangement, it is striking how sequence and accumulation coincide in this booklet and form a discernible contrast: the scenes of the Passion are aligned one after another, and as the turning of the pages is required to advance within the narrative, a linear reading is stipulated. While it is also necessary to turn the pages to see the *Arma Christi* in their entirety, the mode of organization changes after the introductory full-page picture of the *Vera Icon*. From this point on, each page shows several individual elements, which are no longer arranged in a row like the narrative images. Although the page with the hand and the Christ-group still suggests a direction from top to bottom, on the opposite page we find a disordered accumulation with no obvious reading direction. Unlike in the Prayer Book of Bonne, there is no central element directing the gaze here; a hierarchical or compositional center does not exist. The same applies to the following double page. Here, long and narrow objects are positioned adjacently, and nails, the hammer, and pincers (the tools used in the nailing to and in the deposition from the cross) as well as the dice[21] and Christ's robe form units, but it is impossible to spot distinct chronological, hierarchical, or narrative structures. Further, the semblance of order is alluded to even as it is denied: nails, the hammer, and pincers might be read from left to right, but since the hammer in the middle projects above the items to its sides and takes a higher position, the horizontal reading direction is interrupted and challenged by the vertical. Since the booklet begins with a chronologically linear narrative, the deliberate disorder in the second part is even more striking.

It becomes clear that the two modes of organization offer the viewer different approaches for contemplating Christ's suffering. In the ivory booklet, the artist acknowledged the functionality of narration and enumeration and made use of it to offer the beholder multiple ways for contemplation.[22] While the former allows the events to continuously move toward the climax of salvation history, the latter obstructs an integration into the linear narrative scheme. Through their detachment from the

Passion narrative and their establishment as an independent motif, the *Arma* provide access to the Passion by means of the materiality and agency of things.[23] In narrative sequences of the Passion, the steadily increasing agony of Christ is paralleled with the intensifying acts of violence against his soul and body. With the *Arma Christi*, however, the observer does not see the harmed body of Christ in repetition but beholds the various objects (and sometimes people) related to Christ which cause him suffering. *Contemplatio* and *compassio* thus are activated by the instruments of violence rather than by their victim.[24]

This aspect of refocusing on the objects is already linked to the structural character of the *Arma* as an enumeration. Through their enumeration, the individual instruments are removed from the context of the narrative, and a list is created. And yet another effect arises: the enumerated elements separated from the narration are fanned out and achieve heightened visibility. In other words, the readers' or viewers' perception is reconfigured and directed toward supposedly trivial or secondary matters. Wolfgang Schmidgen has described this process of moving-into-sight using the example of lists in Daniel Defoe's *Robinson Crusoe*.[25] He describes how things rather ordinary on the ship—"two or three bags of nails and spikes, a great skrew-jack, a dozen or two of hatchets, and above all, that most useful thing called a grindstone" (Defoe 1985, 72–72, qtd. in Schmidgen 2001, 21)—are granted special attention after being salvaged from the wreck and enumerated. Unlike this case, however, the *Arma Christi* are not a list already drawn up in the Passion narrative; each individual *Arma*-enumeration only originates in the treatment of the theme. Despite the detachment, the Passion is maintained as a context and as the source of the *Arma*. In other words, while outside of the novel Robinson's list would not reveal that the objects were recovered from a shipwreck, the *Arma Christi* ran no risk of being misunderstood as anything else by contemporary Christian observers.[26]

LISTS AND THE PRACTICE OF PIETY

It seems that precisely the combination of separation and increased visibility of the elements generated by a list was considered most useful for the integration of images of the *Arma Christi* into late medieval piety practice. In various depictions, access to the *Arma* and their function was created by the contrast of merging and separating. The applied strategies, however, varied, as can be seen in the following three examples. The Ulm woodcut showing the Man of Sorrows and the *Arma Christi*, the *Arma Christi* grid of the *Omne Bonum* manuscript in the British Library, and the illustrated Middle English poem "O Vernicle," are related to texts that integrated the images in the functional context. As such, the combinations of text and image shed light on the potential regarding the engagement of the recipient obviously ascribed to the enumerating form. Whereas the first two works, the woodcut from Ulm and the *Arma Christi* grid, are combined with an indulgence text,[27] the "O Vernicle" is a poem enumerating the *Arma Christi*.

The single-leaf woodcut made in Ulm in approx. 1470–1485,[28] (Fig. 12.4) shows structural similarity to the image in the Prayer Book of Bonne of Luxembourg. In both pictures, the body of Christ forms the nucleus and is surrounded by the other items, which are represented on a much smaller scale. But while the *Arma* in the manuscript are neatly arranged next to the side wound and give an impression of clarity and a certain order, the small individual pictures in the woodcut remain scattered over the page, their positions arbitrary and interchangeable. Arrangement in purposeful disorder, as found in the Ulm print, is a frequently encountered characteristic of *Arma Christi* representations. Robert Suckale has acknowledged this interplay between overview and disorder as a peculiar benefit for meditation. For him, the simultaneous conception, with everything synchronously juxtaposed and a clearly emphasized center, offers an outset to the observation but no end and no defined "lines of sight" ("Blickbahnen") either. This arrangement aligned with the abundance of the *Arma* would create a high degree of repeatability without being exhaustive (Suckale 2003, 36). Lisa Cooper and Andrea Denny-Brown follow Suckale's ideas when they describe the *Arma Christi* as a "devotional image cluster" that generates meaning through the sheer number of collected objects and their cultural significance (2014b, 1). Marius Rimmele also has taken the disorder of the *Arma* as a vantage point to reflect on the meaningful processes of pictorial and cognitive combination. Rimmele stressed the activation of the viewer, describing how he or she becomes a co-author when looking at the *Arma* and drawing individual and associative connections between the objects themselves and between them and the body of Christ (Rimmele 2010, 227–228).

Indeed, the additional value of the *Arma Christi* depictions arises from the individual elements, which offer a range of possibilities to create meaning (Rimmele 2010, 228) and thus succeed the functional level of

Fig. 12.4 Man of Sorrows with the *Arma Christi*, single-sheet woodcut, ca. 1470–1485, Germanisches Nationalmuseum, Nuremberg, Inv. No. H 9, image credits: Germanisches Nationalmuseum, Nuremberg

mnemonic aids recalling the Passion. The basic idea, however, is not about generating a collective sum of meaning from all the parts and their respective concrete arrangement, but rather about recognizing the productivity of each distinct unit. In the Ulm woodcut, the unit is used purposefully to stimulate the viewer's attention in devotion. This strategy becomes clear when reading the text below the picture. Here, the prayer granting indulgence is introduced by a set of instructions: "Wer dis gebet spricht mit andacht der het als mengen tag aplas als menig wonden vnser herr / ihesus christus het enphangen durch vnsern willen" ("Whosoever speaks this prayer devoutly will receive as many days of indulgence as our Lord Jesus Christ suffered wounds for our sakes").[29] But the viewers of the print are called upon to not only say the prayer for indulgence but also, if they wish to know the outcome of their actions, to look closely at the picture, ponder the wounds of Christ, and deduce their number.

"Wounds" not only mean the body's physical injuries here, but also those actions that caused inner pain such as the mockery of spitting or Pilate washing his hands of guilt. The Man of Sorrows motif, which is often combined with the *Arma*, serves as a point of reference for the smaller pictures arranged around it, but the actual relationship between instrument and wound must first be established by the viewer during his or her devotional contemplation and meditation. Through an enumeration of the *Arma*, Christ's suffering is broken down into its parts and laid out with all its aspects visible to the viewer.

The depiction of the *Arma* on fol. 15r of the *Omne Bonum* manuscript[30] (approx. 1360–1375; Fig. 12.5) is also based on the effect of separation. The image on the 45.5 × 31 cm page is a regular grid of 5 fields × 8 fields. Like in a typesetting box, each instrument of the Passion is placed inside its own field of the same size, only the crucifixion and, below, the resurrection being exceptions and occupying compartments twice as large. Apart from the last line, there is a small text space underneath each box, in which an inscription names the presented object.[31] The placement of the objects in the individual fields does not reveal any systematic order, but as in the Man of Sorrows woodcut and the Prayer Book of Bonne, the central vertical axis is accentuated. Here, the body of Christ appears in various forms in the grid's central column, evoked either directly or indirectly through a reference. Read from top to bottom, this time a chronological order is indicated: the series begins with the Host in the chalice (the Last Supper), followed by the spitting (first mockery of Christ), the face of

Fig. 12.5 *Omne Bonum* manuscript, England (London?), around 1360–1375, British Library, London, Royal MS 6 E VI/1, fol. 15r, © The British Library Board

Christ as it appeared on the Veil of Veronica (bearing of the cross), the crucifixion, and finally the resurrection. Rather irritatingly, the sequence is interrupted by the cock of Peter's denial, which is positioned between Christ's face and the crucifixion and thus not only interferes with the chronological order but also severely disrupts the series of Christ's manifestations. The rooster seems to have been inserted as a deliberate break, as the side wound can also be found in the grid. Its placement in the central column would have been a logical consequence, but instead it is found in the penultimate field of the fifth column.

As in the single-sheet print, there is also an indulgence text written below the *Arma Christi* grid.[32] The prayer "Ave facies praeclara" written in red ink is preceded by a note in brown ink indicating that, according to Pope Innocentius, the prayer would bring three years of indulgences. The prayer text is followed, again in brown ink, by a reference to the *Arma* grid above: "Quicumque arma superius descripta sive insignia domini nostri iesu christi devote inspexerit, a summis pontificibus subscriptam indulgenciam consequetur" ("Whoever devotedly contemplates the *Arma*, that is the insignia of Our Lord Jesus Christ, depicted above, will obtain the indulgence from the supreme pontiffs spelled out below").[33]

Finally, the next and last paragraph on the page mentions the indulgences granted by various popes. Unlike the previous section, this text does not run across the full width of the text space but forms four columns, written alternately in red and brown ink and separated by red-blue filling. Thus, the enumerating verses become discernible in a tabular list-like appearance, although the entries are not made line by line. Instead, the verse pattern is blended with the list in form and content with the verses of the rhyming text going from top to bottom in each column. The lower sections' layout thus repeats what has already been observed in the grid: a visual ordering structure is created, but the content stored in it undermines this same structure by following its own formal rules and principles. Through this aesthetic inversion, an intriguing moment of irritation arises, which keeps the reader-viewer focused and probably motivates him or her to engage even more with the contents of the page. Yet, the text is also revealing as to the dynamics evolving between text and image, for the expression *devote inspexerit* together with the reference to the *Arma Christi* shown above (*superius descripta*) refers to the visual aspect of contemplation. As each item is given its own space in the list-grid, devotional contemplation could be dedicated either individually to one compartment at a time or could be continued successively from field to field and thus be extended in time.[34]

ORGANIZING VISUAL PERCEPTION

From this type of visual organization, in which the grid provides a formal order, albeit one that is undermined by the disorderly placement of objects within the grid, a tension unfolds between the cohesion of the whole and the separation of the parts. The grid provides for both and thus acquires an ambivalent functionality also to be found in other representations of the *Arma Christi* as well as other enumerating motifs. This ambivalence is substantial for the list, which must always be accessible as a whole and in its parts at the same time. As mentioned above, a list is defined by its structure. The functionality of a list cannot be guaranteed if its elements are not recognizable, specific, and distinct. This very aspect of distinction, however, also requires a visible merging that marks each object as belonging to the list.[35] The challenge of establishing visual or content-related coherence is less obvious in images such as the Man of Sorrows woodcut from Ulm or the *Omne Bonum* grid, as the space of the picture and its boundaries are clearly defined. However, if the *Arma Christi* are part of a visual program in which they are combined with other motifs, perhaps even other enumerations, the set must be recognizable as such. In the *tropaion* motif discussed above, for example, the elements appear as a group because of their proximity: they are clustered and overlap each other in an agglomeration. And in the Prayer Book of Bonne, a visual reflection on enumeration already unfolded through the aspects of demarcation and belonging. There, as in the *Omne Bonum* manuscript (but elsewhere as well), a frame was employed to visually consolidate the list. Both examples show how differently the artists made use of framing devices. While in the Bonne-manuscript only one item is singled out by the frame, each of the *Arma* is separated in the *Omne Bonum* grid. And just like in the prayer book, the frame in the *Omne Bonum* is deeply intertwined with the aesthetics of enumeration, too. Firstly, the division between the *Arma* and the narrative representations also integrated into the grid is made in a very subtle way. The crucifixion and resurrection are not represented by the cross and the sarcophagus, but by the Man of Sorrows in the open coffin and the crucifixion scene, in which Christ is joined by the two thieves, whose addition to the *Arma* would be more than unusual in visual art. Unlike the pictures of the instruments of the Passion, both representations occupy double spaces in the grid and thus stand out from the enumeration of the *Arma*.[36] In addition, this skillful ordering principle of the grid engages the beholder in its own way as the attention is directed to the structure itself. Just as in the Bonne-manuscript, the meticulous design not only points to a thoughtful examination on the side of the artist, but is also used to make things more appealing, to hold the recipients' gaze on the page, and thus stimulate and focus contemplation.[37] The innovative use of framing exhibited in the examples cited thus far is evidence of a thoughtful awareness of *enumeratio* as a pictorial device and shows how reflection on the characteristics and functionalities of a list played a crucial role in the design.

A summary-like overview, possible in the grid despite the separation of its elements, is denied to recipients of the "O Vernicle" rolls (Fig. 12.6).[38] In these long, narrow strips of parchment, the individual *Arma* are arranged one below another; a linear viewing is the only option. The pictorial representations of the *Arma* are interwoven directly with the poem "O Vernicle," in which various *Arma Christi* are addressed one after another. It begins with the invocation of the *vernicle*, the Veil of Veronica, preceded by a pictorial representation of the *Vera Icon*. Pictures also introduce the respective verses in the following. They are placed either between the sections of text or to the left of them, resulting in a two-column view. Considering the handling of such a roll, sometimes over two meters long but only ten or fifteen centimeters wide, which was either unrolled completely or wound on sticks like the larger scrolls, a complete view of the *Arma* which captures Christ's sufferings simultaneously could not have been intended.[39] Only the section being read would be viewable; the reader-viewers needed to move step-by-step through the successive units of the list. In contrast to the works considered so far, however, disorder does not seem to have been the decisive principle here.

Soon after the beginning, the arrangement of the individual verses is aligned with the chronology of events. In the edition by Nichols (2014) the veil is followed by the circumcision knife and the pelican, but then a chronologically consistent sequence starts with the thirty pieces of silver. The objects of betrayal and imprisonment are succeeded by the instruments of mockery. After this, the way to Calvary is evoked with footprints before the objects of crucifixion are mentioned: nails, the hammer, gall vessel, sponge, and lance. The sequence continues with the ladder of the deposition but then the order is interrupted by the spitting and carrying of the cross before ending with the tomb of Christ.

Fig. 12.6 "O Vernicle" roll, England, early fifteenth century, Scottish Catholic Archives, Edinburgh, MS GB 0240, opening sequence, image credits: Scottish Catholic Archives, Edinburgh

Although the vertical sequence is determined by the medium, the long and narrow parchment, it is evident that separation as a rhetorical form achieved by the principle of enumeration was known and purposefully used by the author to focus the reader-viewer's attention on the most crucial aspects. This already becomes clear in the first verse about the veil, which contains various enumerations itself. The theme is the face of Christ preserved in the Veil of Veronica. In the text, the face is initially divided into its parts: "His mouth, his nose, his eghen two, / His berde, his here dede al so." It is interesting to see how the functionality takes upon these individual parts binding them back together: "Schilde me fro all þat in my life" (ll. 5–7). The speaker has sinned with all his five senses: "I haf synned with wittes fyve, / Namelich with mouth of sclaunderynge, / Fals othes and bakbytyng / And made bost with tong also / of synnes þat I haf i do / Lord of heuen, forgif it me / For þe figure þat I here se" (ll. 8–14; Nichols 2014, 354). As mentioned above, the poem is preceded by a picture of the face of Christ on the Veil of Veronica, and it is this very image that should now be contemplated while speaking the text. The listing of the details in the text changes the viewer's perception; after reading the verse, he or she sees not only the face as a whole but discerns its components. Of particular importance is the mouth, since the speaker enumerates his sins committed with speech, and the reader-viewer can use the image to relate to his own sinful behavior and its sensual aspects. The intermedial enumeration in "O Vernicle," therefore, proves itself a highly complex system that influences perception and guides contemplation.

Despite the diversity of visual possibilities inherent to the *Arma*—of which only a few could be explored here—it becomes clear how the pictorial motif of the *Arma Christi* is characterized by its enumerative nature per se. As in literature, the list emerges as a *dispositif* deployed strategically.[40] Through the use of the *enumeratio*, the viewer's attention is redirected several times: not only do the objects contained in a list come into focus, the list itself and thus the enumeration also become subject of observation. "Lists can be self conscious, asking readers to think as much (or more) about the list as they do about the individual objects on it," as Katherine C. Little has pointed out (2019, 118) and, as shown, the visual design can force the perception and reflection of the list itself. An attention-shifting aestheticization of enumeration occurs, for example, in the *tropaion* motif when a cluster is created or when the impression is given that in the carefully laid out grid structure more attention is paid to the presentation of the contents than to their actual depiction, as in the *Omne Bonum* manuscript.

In the *Arma Christi*, as the examples have shown, the aesthetics of enumeration have always been combined productively with the function of representation. In the interaction of content and form, the motif of the *Arma* gained a particular effectiveness for the practice of piety. Representations of the instruments of the Passion demonstrate how, in the visual arts, enumeration is both a figure of artistic conception and a visual-rhetorical device of operational usefulness.

NOTES

1. The Prayer Book of Bonne of Luxembourg, Duchess of Normandy, before 1349, Paris. New York, Metropolitan Museum, The Cloisters Collection, accession number 69.86.
2. The wound caused the main interest in fol. 331r so far, see for example Tammen 2006; Olsen 2015.
3. How access to salvation is granted through the wounds of the tormented body of Christ is described by Lentes 1995.
4. "Nous monstre tres dous diex votre tres grant largesce. Quant vousistes pour nous souffrir tant de destresce" (Transcription and German translation from Tammen 2006, 96). The text is part of a known prayer about the wounds of Christ, see also the excerpt from the Book of Hours Paris, Bibliothèque de l'Arsenal, MS 570 (see Meyer 1901, 52, no. 9).
5. On the depiction of the birds see Vaurie 1971.
6. Here, the potential of the frame becomes evident. It creates a polarity of inside and outside, inclusion and exclusion, but can also be crossed. The artistic play with the frame and its possibilities on fol. 331r can also be found in other images of the manuscript.
7. For a basic study of the *Arma Christi* in visual art, see Berliner 1955; Schiller 1968; Suckale 2003 [1977]; Rimmele 2010 examines questions of composition and the interrelations of the single elements. The materiality of the *Arma* is explored in the volume by Cooper and Denny-Brown 2014a.
8. Suckale 2003 [1977], 29, sees the reason for this diversity in the variety of relations facilitated by freely distributed elements and encouraging the imagination, but also in a desire to see the objects closely.
9. Suckale 2003 [1977], 27–29, also refers to the new combination of the elements for every new work.
10. Regarding visual rhetoric, an important impulse is provided in the volume by Knape 2007.
11. Although art history has thoroughly examined the combination of motives and images in recent years, visual enumeration has rarely been considered

to date. It can be assumed that the reason for this lies in the supposedly "simple form" of the list (see also von Contzen 2017a). Seminal works on the plurality of images are Ganz and Thürlemann 2010; Blum, Bogen, Ganz and Rimmele 2012; Thürlemann 2013.

12. Basic works with important impulses for the visual arts are Belknap 2000; Mainberger 2003; Jullien 2004a; Stäheli 2011; von Contzen 2017a, b.

13. For example, they are listed in the Acts of Thomas and the work of John Chrysostomos and other sources. See Edsall 2014a.

14. On the *tropaion* and *tropaeum crucis* as precursors to the *Arma Christi*, see Edsall 2014a, 42–43.

15. Utrecht Psalter, ninth century. Utrecht, Universiteitsbibliotheek, Ms. 32. The complete digitalization and an annotated edition can be found at https://bc.library.uu.nl/utrecht-psalter.html. Accessed 29 April 2020.

16. According to present-day numbering, Psalm 22.

17. The well-known words from Psalm 21, "O God, my God, look upon me: why hast thou forsaken me?" that Christ speaks on the cross, see Mt. 27,46 and Mk 15,34.

18. Berliner 1955, 51–52, already presumes an apotropaic effect; see also Vizkelety 1995; Edsall 2014b explores the *Arma Christi* rolls regarding their possible use as amulets.

19. Booklet with scenes of the Passion and the *Arma Christi*, elephant ivory with painted and gilded leaves, ca. 1330–1340, Germany, 10.6 × 6 cm. London, Victoria & Albert Museum, Museum number 11–1872. http://collections.vam.ac.uk/item/O92726/devotional-booklet-devotional-booklet-unknown/. Accessed 13 April 2020.

20. This is probably a reference to the first mocking of Christ, during which he is spat upon. The spitting is already cited as part of the *Arma* in early Christian sources (see examples in Edsall 2014a).

21. The soldiers played dice for Christ's robe beneath the cross.

22. Berliner 1955, 51–52, already drew attention to this aspect. He recognized a meaning in the *Arma* pictures that exceeds the purpose of remembering the stations of the Passion and presumes an apotropaic function in beholding the *Arma*.

23. The aspect of materiality was already addressed by Berliner 1955; Cooper and Denny-Brown 2014a, focused on this aspect as well.

24. Images grouping the *Arma* around the Man of Sorrows or focusing on the side wound open a bifocal perspective, whereby the viewer's gaze connects the objects with the Body of Christ through proximity.

25. "Crusoe's list removes things from concrete contextualized relationships and encloses them in a zone of heightened visibility" (Schmidgen 2001, 21).

26. For the problems of interpreting a list and deviating its function from its elements see Mainberger 2003, 18–20.

27. On the *Arma Christi* in the context of indulgences, see Lewis 1992; Vizkelety 1995.

28. Signed "Michil," 41.4 × 27.6 cm. Nuremberg, Germanisches Nationalmuseum, Inv. No. H 9. See Parshall and Schoch 2005.

29. The subsequent prayer reads: "Herre ihesu Christe Jch ermanen dich dines gõtlichen volkomnen rates. Vnd dines guden willen. Vnd diner gũtten ler. Vnd diner unuerdrossen dinstes / Vnd diner demutigen gehorsami. Vnd diner ewigen wisheit: Vnd diner ymer werenden warheit. Vnd / bit dich l[ie]ber herre durch din gros erbarmhertzigkeit. Das du alles das an mir volbringest dz. / es dir loblich sige in der ewikeit Vnd mir trostlich sige in dire zit Amen". Transcription from Parshall and Schoch 2005, 248.

30. James le Palmer: Omne Bonum, around 1360–1375, folio 45.5 × 31 cm, text space: 34.5 × 19 cm. London, British Library, Royal MS 6 E VI/1. On the manuscript, which consists of a total of four parts bound in two volumes, see Sandler 1996. For fol. 15r, see vol. 1: 94 and vol. 2: 12.

31. A transcription of the inscriptions can be found in Sandler 1996, vol. 2, 12.

32. A complete transcription with a German translation is provided by Zimmermann 1997.

33. Transcription and translation from Sandler 1986, 230, no. 30, and Sandler 1996, vol.1, 163, no. 60.

34. "Like the five wounds, the instruments of the Passion could be separated so that each received its own space on a page or roll and its own time within the devotion, extending visually and verbally the reader/viewer's contemplation of them" (Kamerick 2002, 173).

35. See also Belknap 2000, 36–37: "Lists must be examined from two opposing viewpoints: we look at the individual units that comprise a list (what does it hold?), and we look at the function or purpose of the list as a whole (how does it hold together?)".

36. Further divisions by grid-like structures are found in two prayer books associated with the Bohun family, the Oxford Book of Hours (Bodleian Library, MS Auct. D.4.4) and the Passional of Kunigunde (Prague, National Library of the Czech Republic, Sign. XIV A 17).

37. The significance of framing for enumerations and their visual disposition has been rarely examined; on the significance of framing in depictions of the Fifteen Signs before the Last Judgement, see Wagner 2016.

38. Ten roll manuscripts are known, all of them illustrated. In three of them, the poem "O Vernicle" is followed by a promise of indulgence. On the "O Vernicle" rolls, see Robbins 1939; Nichols 2009, 2014; Newhauser and Russel 2014; Edsall 2014b.

39. On the context of use, see Edsall 2014b.

40. Jullien sees the practical effective power of the list as a specific *dispositif* made effective by strategic use of the relationships of antagonism and correlation to ensure the renewal of dynamics and their continuity (2004b, 12).

References

Belknap, Robert E. 2000. The Literary List: A Survey of Its Uses and Deployments. *Literary Imagination* 2: 35–54.

Berliner, Rudolf. 1955. Arma Christi. *Münchner Jahrbuch der bildenden Kunst* 6: 35–152.

Blum, Gerd, Steffen Bogen, David Ganz, and Marius Rimmele, eds. 2012. *Pendant Plus: Praktiken der Bildkombinatorik*. Berlin: Reimer.

Cooper, Lisa H., and Andrea Denny-Brown, eds. 2014a. *The Arma Christi in Medieval and Early Modern Material Culture: With a Critical Edition of 'O Vernicle'*. Abingdon: Taylor & Francis Ltd.

———. 2014b. Introduction: Arma Christi – The Material Culture of the Passion. In *The Arma Christi in Medieval and Early Modern Material Culture: With a Critical Edition of 'O Vernicle'*, ed. Lisa H. Cooper and Andrea Denny-Brown, 1–20. Abingdon: Taylor & Francis Ltd.

Defoe, Daniel. 1985 [1719]. *Robinson Crusoe*. London: Penguin.

Edsall, Mary Agnes. 2014a. The Arma Christi Before the Arma Christi: Rhetorics of the Passion in Late Antiquity and the Early Middle Ages. In *The Arma Christi in Medieval and Early Modern Material Culture: With a Critical Edition of 'O Vernicle'*, ed. Lisa H. Cooper and Andrea Denny-Brown, 21–51. Abingdon: Taylor & Francis Ltd.

———. 2014b. Arma Christi Rolls or Textual Amulets? The Narrow Roll Format Manuscripts of "O Vernicle". *Magic, Ritual, and Witchcraft* 9 (2): 178–209.

Ganz, David, and Felix Thürlemann, eds. 2010. *Das Bild im Plural: Mehrteilige Bildformen zwischen Mittelalter und Gegenwart*. Berlin: Reimer.

Jullien, François, ed. 2004a. *Die Kunst, Listen zu erstellen*. Berlin: Merve Verlag.

———. 2004b. Einleitung. In *Die Kunst, Listen zu erstellen*, ed. François Jullien, 7–14. Berlin: Merve Verlag.

Kamerick, Kathleen. 2002. *Popular Piety and Art in the Late Middle Ages: Image Worship and Idolatry in England 1350–1500*. New York/Basingstoke: Palgrave MacMillan.

Knape, Joachim, ed. 2007. *Bildrhetorik*. Baden-Baden: Verlag Valentin Koerner.

Lentes, Thomas. 1995. Nur der geöffnete Körper schafft Heil: Das Bild als Verdoppelung des Körpers. In *Glaube Liebe Hoffnung Tod* (Exhibition Catalogue), ed. Christoph Geissmar-Brandi and Eleonora Louis, 152–155. Vienna: Kunsthalle Wien.

Lermack, Anette. 2008. Spiritual Pilgrimage in the Psalter of Bonne of Luxembourg. In *The Art, Science, and Technology of Medieval Travel*, ed. Robert Bork and Andrea Kann, 97–111. Abingdon: Routledge.

Lewis, Flora. 1992. Rewarding Devotion: Indulgences and the Promotion of Images. In *The Church and the Arts*, ed. Diana Wood, 179–194. Oxford: Blackwell.

Little, Katherine C. 2019. The Politics of Lists. *Exemplaria* 31 (2): 117–128.

Mainberger, Sabine. 2003. *Die Kunst des Aufzählens: Elemente zu einer Poetik des Enumerativen*. Berlin/New York: De Gruyter.

Meyer, Paul. 1901. Prières et poésies religieuses: Tirées d'un manuscrit lorrain (Arsenal 570). *Bulletin de la Société des anciens textes français* 27: 43–81.

Newhauser, Richard G., and Arthur J. Russel. 2014. Mapping Virtual Pilgrimage in an Early Fifteenth-Century Arma Christi Roll. In *The Arma Christi in Medieval and Early Modern Material Culture: With a Critical Edition of 'O Vernicle'*, ed. Lisa H. Cooper and Andrea Denny-Brown, 83–112. Abingdon: Taylor & Francis Ltd.

Nichols, Ann Eljenholm. 2009. O Vernicle: Illustrations of an Arma Christi Poem. In *Tributes to Kathleen L. Scott: English Medieval Manuscripts: Readers, Makers and Illuminators*, ed. Marlene Villalobos Hennessy, 139–169. Turnhout: Harvey Miller Publishers.

———. 2014. O Vernicle: A Critical Edition. In *The Arma Christi in Medieval and Early Modern Material Culture: With a Critical Edition of 'O Vernicle'*, ed. Lisa H. Cooper and Andrea Denny-Brown, 308–392. Abingdon: Taylor and Francis Ltd.

Olsen, Vibeke. 2015. Penetrating the Void: Picturing the Wound in Christ's Side as a Performative Space. In *Wounds and Wound Repair in Medieval Culture*, ed. Kelly DeVries and Larissa Tracy, 313–339. Leiden/Boston: Brill.

Parshall, Peter W., and Rainer Schoch. 2005. *Die Anfänge der europäischen Druckgraphik: Holzschnitte des 15. Jahrhunderts und ihr Gebrauch* (Exhibition Catalogue). Nürnberg: Germanisches Nationalmuseum.

Rimmele, Marius. 2010. Geordnete Unordnung: Zur Bedeutungsstiftung in Zusammenstellungen der Arma Christi. In *Das Bild im Plural: Mehrteilige Bildformen zwischen Mittelalter und Gegenwart*, ed. David Ganz and Felix Thürlemann, 219–242. Berlin: Reimer.

Robbins, Rossell Hope. 1939. The "Arma Christi" Rolls. *The Modern Language Review* 34 (3): 415–421.

Sandler, Lucy Freeman. 1986. Face to Face with God: A Pictorial Image of the Beatific Vision. In *England in the Fourteenth Century: Proceedings of the 1985 Harlaxton Symposium*, ed. W. Mark Ormrod, 224–235. Woodbridge: Boydell and Brewer.

———. 1996. *Omne Bonum: A Fourteenth-Century Encyclopedia of Universal Knowledge: British Library MSS Royal 6 E VI – 6 E VII*, 2 vols. London: Harvey Miller.

Schiller, Gertrud. 1968. *Ikonographie der christlichen Kunst, vol. 2: Die Passion Jesu Christi*. Gütersloh: Gütersloher Verlagshaus Mohn.

Schmidgen, Wolfgang. 2001. Robinson Crusoe, Enumeration, and the Mercantile Fetish. *Eighteenth-Century Studies* 35 (1): 19–39.

Stäheli, Urs. 2011. Das Soziale als Liste: Zur Epistemologie der ANT. In *Die Wiederkehr der Dinge*, ed. Friedrich Balke, Maria Muhle, and Antonia von Schöning, 83–101. Berlin: Kulturverlag Kadmos.

Suckale, Robert. 2003 [1977]. Arma Christi: Überlegungen zur Zeichenhaftigkeit mittelalterlicher Andachtsbilder. In *Stil und Funktion: Ausgewählte Schriften zur Kunst des Mittelalters*, ed. Peter Schmidt, Robert Suckale and Gregor Wedekind, 15–58. Munich: Deutscher Kunstverlag.

Tammen, Silke. 2006. Blick und Wunde – Blick und Form: Zur Deutungsproblematik der Seitenwunde Christi in der spätmittelalterlichen Buchmalerei. In *Bild und Körper im Mittelalter*, ed. Katrin Kärcher, Kristin Marek, Raphaèle Preisinger, and Marius Rimmele, 44–85. Munich: Wilhelm Fink Verlag.

Thürlemann, Felix. 2013. *Mehr als ein Bild: Für eine Kunstgeschichte des "hyperimage"*. Munich: Wilhelm Fink Verlag.

Vaurie, Charles. February 1971. Birds in the Prayer Book of Bonne of Luxembourg. *The Metropolitan Museum of Art Bulletin* 29 (6): 279–283.

Vizkelety, András. 1995. Ein Beispiel zur Funktion und Praxis der Arma-Christi-Andacht im Spätmittelalter. In *Sô wold ich in fröiden singen: Festgabe für Anthonius H. Touber zum 65. Geburtstag*, ed. Helmut Birkhan and Carla Dauven-van Knippenberg, 521–530. Amsterdam: Brill.

von Contzen, Eva. 2017a. Grenzfälle des Erzählens: Die Liste als einfache Form. In *Komplexität und Einfachheit*, ed. Albrecht Koschorke, 221–239. Stuttgart: Springer.

———. 2017b. Die Affordanzen der Liste. *Literaturwissenschaft und Linguistik* 47: 317–326.

Wagner, Daniela. 2016. *Die Fünfzehn Zeichen vor dem Jüngsten Gericht: Spätmittelalterliche Bildkonzepte für das Seelenheil*. Berlin: Reimer.

Zimmermann, Andrea. 1997. *Jesus Christus als "Schmerzensmann" in hoch- und spätmittelalterlichen Darstellungen der bildenden Kunst: Eine Analyse ihres Sinngehalts*. PhD dissertation, University of Halle. Retrievable at: https://sundoc.bibliothek.uni-halle.de/diss-online/97/98H110/prom.pdf.   Accessed 2 May 2020.

CHAPTER 13

Et Cetera Photobooks? Reflections on Conceptual Documentary Photography as Visual Enumeration

Anja Schürmann

Photography has thus far been conceptualized not as a list but as a series. This contribution aims to question the photographic series in terms of enumerative functions and modes of representation. I will ask whether visual enumeration is a viable possibility and, if so, how. I will ask whether photography, and in this particular case the Conceptual Documentary photobook,[1] is particularly suited to assign an enumerative, a "serial" function to the image and how that enumerative function is communicated to the viewer. One thesis is that the role of the viewer in the CDp is strengthened. The viewer is not "only" the recipient but active constructor of the work. We can define an enumeration as a kind of inventory or catalogue, if they represent a characteristic (like names), we can speak of a register. An archive or inventory of categories presents the user with a series of instances without a narrative thread; the book form, however,

A. Schürmann (✉)
Institute for Advanced Study in the Humanities Essen (KWI), Essen, Germany
e-mail: anja.schuermann@kwi-nrw.de

R. A. Barton et al. (eds.), *Forms of List-Making: Epistemic, Literary, and Visual Enumeration,*
https://doi.org/10.1007/978-3-030-76970-3_13

275

suggests and inevitably creates a sense of progress from beginning to end.[2] Yet, how are these opposing dynamics reconciled and transformed when the archive or list is reproduced in the form of a photobook? Both the book and the list satisfy a need for order, for a distinct selection. However, if the list is generated from the anthropological need to name and order unknown things, there should be no visual lists, as the act of naming is (necessarily) precluded. Images are not distinct signs. I argue that in order to become enumerative, the image must have a marked grasp on the word. To speak of visual lists is possible through the adaptation of verbal sign systems on several transmedial levels. However, the image has to undergo various operations to achieve this alignment. The image must be reduced and semantically limited in order to become a distinct and isolated item with a countable element. In order to achieve this, unifications are necessary that align the individual images with each other. To put it in a nutshell: at least to some degree, the photographic series must become a serial work.

In the following I introduce the term "et cetera photobook" in order to attribute another, more serial component to the Conceptual Documentary photobooks discussed in this chapter. As I will later explain in more detail, this term highlights the process of continuously adding new items and the aesthetics associated with this additive mode of presentation. To a certain extent, I owe this phrase to Peter Bexte. In his book *Konjunktur & Krise* he examines the conjunction "and" in images and texts, not only as a linguistic phenomenon but also as a structure of thought (see Bexte 2019). With this term I want to make clear that seriality in the photobook cannot be defined only by a certain set of themes, as is the case in the documentary discourse on concepts such as power, memory, and testimony. The visual plural also functions as a formal criterion and forms its own aesthetics.

From Series to Photobook, from Photobook to Conceptual Documentary Photobook (CDP)

In scholarly research little has been said about the visual list. The following considerations will take up the concept of plural images as *hyperimages* as described by Thürlemann (2013).[3] He mainly emphasizes two principles that are at work when we deal with images in the plural: first, the principle of reciprocal sharpening and, second, the principle of distancing.[4] Both principles negotiate the connection between parts and the whole and are therefore important for any consideration of visual series (see Thürlemann 2013, 16). A series refers to an artistic work which consists of parts that are independent but which together form a whole. A series is an umbrella term that has many manifestations. A painted medieval winged tartar can be considered a series, as can a comic strip or Upper Italian Renaissance frescoes that embellish representative villas. Another form is serial works. As a demarcation to series, serial works are characterized by a "numerical or otherwise systematically predetermined process (permutation, progression, rotation, reversal)" (Bochner 1967, 23). The sequence in turn designates the way in which those parts are arranged.

Visual series have recently been the subject of two studies that discuss the minimum number of images that can be considered a "series." The question also seems relevant for the discussion of lists. Martina Dobbe allows serial orders to begin with six or more objects, since each element then "resists separation through perception" (see Dobbe 2013, 38). Bettina Dunker later also lets her "picture plural" begin with six; she explicitly excludes diptychs and triptychs—also because of their "religious horizon(s) of meaning" (Dunker 2018, 11).

However, there is such thing as an "excess" of pictures, as Dobbe and Dunker make clear. Where "the equivalence of the individual elements is lost" (Dobbe 2013, 39), where "repetition and variation of a certain pictorial pattern" (Dunker 2018, 12) are lost in the mass, the plural overtaxes the series. Dunker concludes her considerations with the thesis that image-sets in which "the individual image [...], as well as the arrangement and the exact number" (Dunker 2018, 12), are interchangeable, do not represent serial concepts.[5] These considerations suggest that lists and enumerations can also express and represent some kind of "information overload" rather than providing order or structure. Can lists express order and abundance at the same time? The question nicely leads us to the photobook as both a plural and a comprehensive picture compilation. In a conventionally bound book three principles of order can be distinguished: the double page, possibly chapters, and the material body of the book as a whole. Before I consider whether (and how) photography becomes enumerative in the context of the photobook, I will first present a few basic considerations about the photobook and its encounter with Documentary Conceptual Art.

THE CONCEPTUAL DOCUMENTARY PHOTOBOOK (CDP)

In this paragraph I would like to introduce the concept of the CDp, which was essentially coined by Melissa Miles (see Miles 2010) and transfers the approach of Conceptual Documentary Art to photography and the photobook. Since the three photobooks I will analyze all belong to this "genre" to varying degrees, I find it helpful to highlight those characteristics influenced by Miles, starting with a brief definition of the photobook. One of the most informative definitions of the photobook comes from Andrea Nelson:

> Photobooks are publications characterized by the careful sequencing and editing of photographic images in order to convey visual arguments. They imply authorship by a photographer or photo-editor and are not intended to describe a book simply containing photographs nor a compendium of photographs illustrating a text. (Nelson 2007, 10)

The formulation "careful sequencing" used by Nelson does not distinguish between artists' books and books that are not produced in an artistic context. Her definition strengthens the thematic openness of the photobook. The photobooks discussed in this paper are also "photobookworks" in the sense that they interrelate "between two factors: the power of the single photograph and the effect of serial arrangements in book form" (Sweetman 1985, 187). Clive Scott states that the photobook is able "to capitalize on our natural need to read series as sequence, and sequence as consequence" (Scott 1999, 215). The photobook of Conceptual Documentary photography deliberately frustrates the expectation of "consequence." Conceptual Documentary photobooks do not create a narrative with a beginning, climax, and end. Melissa Miles explains that

> Conceptual Documentary photography is characterized by a desire to explore a single, often banal idea from many different angles [...]. Rather than submerging themselves in dramatic events, Conceptual Documentary photographers seek out and frame their subjects according to a predetermined idea or scheme. Processes of repetition and categorization are central to Conceptual Documentary. (Miles 2010, 50)

As we see, the concept has set out to respond to the criticism against humanist photography[6] by combining the tradition of humanist photography with ideas of seriality and Conceptual Art. The humanist—or "concerned"—photographer is someone who not only thinks and sees through his camera but also decidedly "feels" and thereby hopes to transport that feeling into the photographs. He thus abandons the objectivity usually typical for documentary art as he concentrates on his subjective feelings, often assuming that objectivity is hardly attainable in complex situations.[7] Although they are often conceived with a decidedly political stance, the CDps—unlike in humanistic photography—do not show close-ups of suffering victims, no photography of dismay.

Aesthetically, the CDp certainly has precursors within photobook production. In the following paragraph I introduce some of the works that are important for contextualizing the enumerative function of photography, as these can provide an idea of the historical development of the visual characteristics of the CDp. The first work I want to discuss is one of the first photobooks ever: William Henry Fox Talbots' *The Pencil of Nature* from 1844.

Order and orientation were two of the most important functions with which Talbot promoted his invention of the photographic negative. According to him, a photo was a lot more efficient, faster, and precise when it came to documenting a collection of Chinese porcelain, for example, than a written inventory: "The more strange and fantastic the forms of his old teapots, the more advantage in having their pictures given instead of their descriptions".[8] Carol Armstrong calls the resulting genre "inventorial photograph" (Armstrong 1998, 127). The inventorial photograph already reveals some basic visual assumptions that later become relevant for the CDp (Fig. 13.1).

The Chinese porcelain is shown in such a way that the objects maintain a constant distance not only from each other but also from the viewer. The picture ground is parallel to the picture planes and identical to the shelf wall; the oculus is in the middle of the picture; the horizontal lines run parallel with the edges. The spatial depth is minimal, the illumination uniform. For Friedrich Weltzien, these photographs are not only archival aids but at the same time function as an "Enlightenment movement of tidying up and sorting" with regard to "an ideal of clarity" and politeness, since correct distancing and appropriate spacing were becoming synonymous with civility in the Enlightenment (see Weltzien 2006, 29). The distance described (polite and respectful) is also important with regard to the CDps. In the context of CDps, the photographer is not a "concerned photographer," but someone who tries to keep and maintain distance, both toward his objects and toward the viewers and their perception.

Fig. 13.1 William Henry Fox Talbot, *Articles of China*, 1844, Detroit Institute of Art, Creative Commons CC0 1.0 Universal Public Domain Dedication

While the origin of the visual list as we find it in the collection inventories—which are often arranged according to specific criteria—is limited to a single page, our next example, Karl Blossfeldt's photobook *Urformen der Kunst* (1928)[9] (Fig. 13.2) shows how the elements of the single page can be distributed throughout the length of a book.

Blossfeldt's plant photographs were not only botanically innovative: the isolation and sculptural arrangement of the natural objects went beyond Talbot's even spacing. For Ed Ruscha, Blossfeldt's sacrosanct "uniformly operative principle of form" (see Molderings 1977, 73)—both in nature and in technique—turns profane.[10] His books have had a significant impact on the CDp: he implements the serial element of repetition in his works,

Fig. 13.2 Karl Blossfeldt, *Urformen der Kunst* (Berlin 1928), 3, Rijksmuseum Amsterdam, Creative Commons CC0 1.0 Universal Public Domain Dedication

be it with small fires, with petrol stations, or parking lots. Indeed, such repetition tends to reinforce the image. Its formal and aesthetic aspects are amplified, while the relevance of the depicted is diminished.[11] Ute Eskildsen recently suggested that conceptual artists like Ruscha, who conceived photography as the epitome of mass media, gave new impulses to the CDp and the photobook as a high-circulation artist's book in general (see Eskildsen 2004, 27). The three photobooks presented in the following acknowledge this serial and conceptual legacy but combine it with another, namely, the political and socially critical heritage of humanist photography.

RICARDO CASES, EL PORQUÉ DE LAS NARANJAS, MACK 2014

On opening Ricardo Cases' photobook *El porqué de las naranjas* we see (next to the title) a photograph in which an orange is trapped between a curb and a car tire. This remains one of the few oranges that Cases depicts, even though the title translates as *The Reason for Orange(s)*. Cases explains in an interview that the fruit is "one of the symbols of the Levante region," as well as of "tourism and construction" (Pantall 2014). When we turn the page, the orange fruit transforms into the color that collects as oil in the middle of a paella pan (Fig. 13.3). Later in the book the leitmotif, the color of orange, reappears in leaves that turn orange or wooden slats, plastic tarpaulins, and small or large fires (Fig. 13.4).[12] Even if the color detaches itself from the object in the course of the book, as a surface color it often remains associated with the background in the picture. Cases' colors are bright and saturated because the sun plays a significant role in his portrait of the Levante region. His use of light gives the work a penetrating and relentless presence: no shadow remains unexplored, nobody

Fig. 13.3   Ricardo Cases, *El porqué de las naranjas* (London 2014), n.p., © Ricardo Cases

Fig. 13.4 Ricardo Cases, *El porqué de las naranjas* (London 2014), n.p., © Ricardo Cases

can hide. The sharp-edged overexposure is often aided by flashes; these give the objects a surprised, even trapped look as if they had been caught. That flashlight aesthetic resonates with the local past: the Levante has been a tourist destination, once very popular, today a victim of real estate speculators and financial crisis. The transitions of the image are often formally motivated: a round object is correlated with a likewise round object in the next picture; the exposure time has changed from one picture to the next. Although Cases, in line with the cinematic principle, only sets one image per double page, the book is primarily arranged in pairs of images, not in larger sequences. Despite the luminosity of the colors, it must be viewed from a short distance, especially since the photos are printed relatively small, which increases individual attention. In terms of reception aesthetics, the reader repeatedly tries to discover the color orange in this series of images. And the reader usually (yet not always) succeeds. This dissolves the form into abstraction while simultaneously endangering it with such clear instructions such that the search for the color is abandoned as soon as it is found.

Due to the differentiated use of the color orange, sometimes lighter, sometimes darker, sometimes used extensively or as a small accent, the search is never easy or unconditional. In this search, the contexts of this withered and emaciated region cannot be ignored. Just as the color orange repeatedly reappears and cannot be overlooked, so, too, the economic crisis that shapes the region is omnipresent—even if only in minor and easily overseen details.[13] The enumerative quality of the book is obvious. The title of the book works as a connecting hypernym, while the formally designed sequence has linearity in its compositional geometry, although it is still far from being diagrammatic.

The enumeration refers—regardless of the object—to signifiers (see Eco 2009, 118), while Allison Stewart and Stephen Gill, the authors of the photobooks introduced in the following, count the signified. This means that Cases' use of the color orange emphasizes the expressive side of the sign, whereas—as we will see in the following—Gill and Stewart tend to highlight the thematic aspects of their enumeration. Cases has pointed out several times that he wanted to start his project "openly", that he viewed the photographs as "autonomous" (Pantall 2014), an autonomy that, since the degree of staging is relatively low in Cases, remains visible—in contrast to Stewart and Gill.

Allison Stewart, *Bug Out Bag: The Commodification of American Fear*, Self-Published 2018

If the fairly discrete elements in Cases were arranged one behind the other on different pages, in *Bug out Bag* they lie next to each other on the same page. "Bug out bags" are bags that are intended as basic equipment for disaster preparedness and serve either as a 72-hour survival kit or as a means to rebuild civilization. The spiral-bound book, which also focuses on the commercialization of prepping by showing trade fairs and other places of supply for utilities, is visually reminiscent of a manual, a printed aid, or guide that provides instructions in case of emergency. As functional as this travel occasion may be, the photos by Allison Stewart show that each bag allows individual conclusions to be drawn about the character of the packer, about his idea of society and solidarity, and about order and control in situations that are hard to imagine. If one understands the list as a phenomenon of crisis (see Bexte 2014, 27), as a possibility to create order and thus assert control in a disordered world, Stewart's work is doubly relevant for the theme of this essay: on the representational as well as on the iconic level.

The objects in the photographs are singularized, intentionally exempted. They do not attempt to tell a story but rather stage specific isolated (and more or less deliberately constructed) scenes. Stewart uses her mobile photo studio to show the unwrapped emergency backpacks on an even white background. They are central to the content, which is arranged more or less in a row around them. In this microcosm, the objects certainly function as stimuli or references to a narrative (see Wolf 2002, 43): while Mike from Texas encounters the apocalypse with tequila and phenobarbital (Fig. 13.5), Sam's backpack reflects his need for communication by packing "walkie talkies" and a radio (Fig. 13.6).

The sparse titles assigned to the panels activate the viewer as a (co-) constructor of the narrative.[14] The intended viewers would complement and connect the given image with Mike's or Sam's idea of what would be important in and after the expected catastrophe. It seems that the more

Fig. 13.5 Allison Stewart, *Bug Out Bag: The Commodification of American Fear* (2018), self-published, 23, © Allison Stewart

Fig. 13.6 Allison Stewart, *Bug Out Bag: The Commodification of American Fear* (2018), self-published, 25, © Allison Stewart

sparingly explanatory elements or narrative stimuli are used, the more active the viewer has to be. Although Stewart, like Talbot in his inventory (Fig. 13.1), combines the objects in one image, the oversight and inequality of the objects create a different effect: due to the singularizing type of recording and the neutral perspective afforded by the overhead perspective, the objects become findings or clues in a crime scene that not only function prospectively but also retrospectively. The objects depicted could be instructions but also the legacies of their owners, posthumous testimonies after the catastrophe. A similar representation where the photos qualify as found objects can also be observed in the photobook by Stephen Gill, in which people are identified by what they leave behind.

Stephen Gill, a Series of Disappointments, Nobody 2008

The pages in Stephen Gill's *A Series of Disappointments* are heavy and slightly larger than a usual piece of paper. Also photographed from above, they display differentially illuminated objects on a black background (Fig. 13.7).

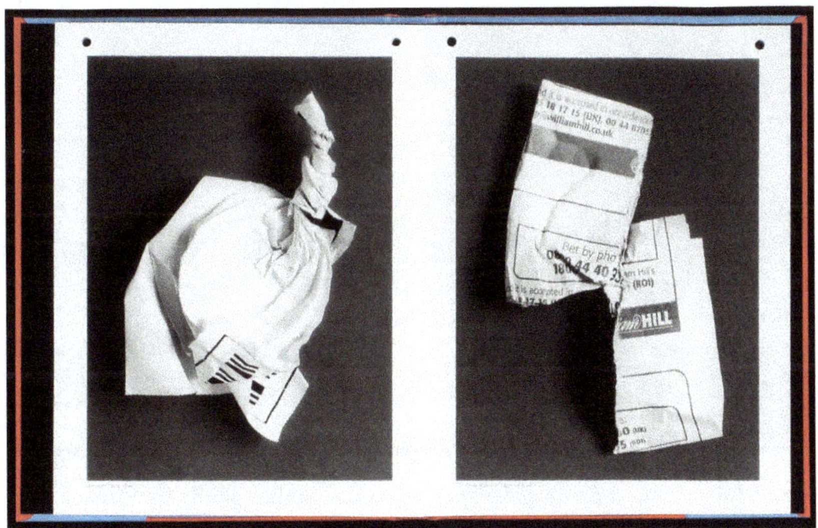

Fig. 13.7 From *A Series of Disappointments* (London 2008) by Stephen Gill, n.p. Copyright © 2008, Stephen Gill

Watches, too, were advertised in this way, in black and white, as were jewels and other valuable products. Gill, however, has photographed discarded betting slips—that is, objects of no or of negative financial value, to be precise. The 36 slips were found in Hackney, a district of London that has three times as many betting shops as the rest of the city (see Miles 2010, 64). Although the lack of color and the two-sided positioning of the photographs have the effect that the objects are aligned more closely than in Stewart's photobook, they simultaneously possess a distinct individuality.

In the truest sense of the word: the two-dimensional slip becomes three-dimensional through the body of the bettor: "(N)ervous tension and grief" (Gill 2008) is what Gill called the emotions he sees as responsible for the fact that we do not see rectangular notes but rather types of death, crumpled up piles, torn, artfully turned or otherwise transformed pieces of paper that "began as hope, were shaped by loss or defeat, then cast aside" (Gill 2008). The failed bets are placed sparingly as text attached to the images (Fig. 13.8).

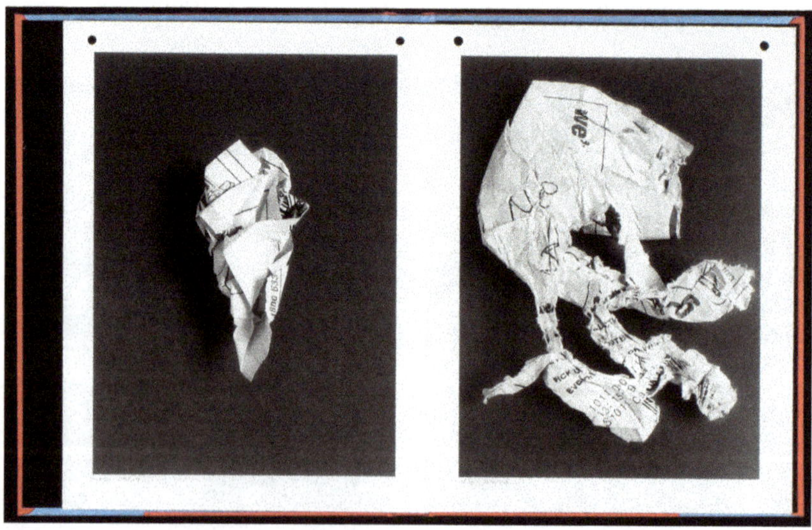

Fig. 13.8 From *A Series of Disappointments* (London 2008) by Stephen Gill, n.p. Copyright © 2008, Stephen Gill

In addition to the act of leafing through, and printed as a fanfold, the book allows for a different mode of reception, which further differentiates the issue of value: owners of *A Series of Disappointments* are encouraged to hang their own exhibition of the book. The book contains within it instructions for the removal of the text block from its cover and on how to properly hang the pages on small nails using the holes punched in the cover. The resulting long, continuous line, the "Series of Disappointments," underlines the extent of the loss and the repetition of frustration.

Melissa Miles stresses that this form of repetition is also typical for the CDp: "The repetition of photographs of a single, often banal subject has the effect of protracting and merging the photographed moments" (Miles 2010, 64–65). The disappointed hopes become one big disappointed hope, which is individualized by the formal difference of the betting slips. And yet the sheer amount of betting slips combined with the greatest standardization of the recording situation is a reductionist gesture that could be called a visual form of the list: the book is just an option for the display; the pages give the appearance of a showcase, an exhibition of living dead. There is no narrative, no dynamic owed to it. This visual list is neither complete nor discreet but produces surplus in the psychological charging of the form and received kinetic energy.

Formally, the betting slips have been transformed into signs—signs that refer to the structural change in Hackney and the poverty of the population as well as to the next page, which could possibly be showing the identical betting slip in a different form. This sculptural kind of aesthetic with its differentiated shades of gray borrowed from product photography, which in Walker Evans' and Karl Blossfeldt's work (Fig. 13.2) referred to the beauty of everyday life and pure form, is here called into question by a cultural product that—unlike Evans' pliers—has a negative rather than a low value. The simple listing emphasizes the loss of value, since the identical photographic treatment of the slips turns them into a singular mass, further stressing the huge loss of collective value. This practice is counteracted. The various deformations of the betting slips refer to the individuality of their owners. The kinetic energy, which is evident in the betting slips, highlights the extent of economic loss as well. It appears paradoxical how much money seems to be associated with a simple sheet of paper. Eventually, the book also draws our attention to the bizarre nature of banknotes, where value is again just a matter of agreement. As in Gill's series *Billboards* (2002–04), the fantasy worlds of advertising are visually provided with an ironic, yet highly political commentary.

ET CETERA PHOTOBOOK

In the following sections I would like to broaden my methodological focus and talk about cultural and literary approaches. This will allow me to work out the intermedial functions of the visual list more strongly and also to distinguish the enumerative qualities of the photobooks presented. So again: why do I use the term "et cetera photobook" in the title? I do not intend to define a new genre but rather to highlight a shared function of these books that the term Conceptual Documentary does not sufficiently emphasize. It is about the "and" and the "and so on," that is the connectors and the endings of enumerative systems. Peter Bexte has written several texts about the "and" and explored it not only as a verbal but also as a philosophical and visual phenomenon (see Bexte 2019).

Unlike analysis, the list is a form of synthesis. Like the word "and," it stands for connection as such, without its modality having yet been clarified. If one follows Bexte's argument, the list becomes a constructive phenomenon, a remedy against the crisis; the dissolution and the disintegration can at least be countered by a mere list.[15] Lists turn against a causal logic. This can be linked to the CDp's claim that visual series are directed against humanist photography, which often works with dichotomies. As already emphasized by Melissa Miles, the CDp is also to be understood as a partial response to the crisis of representation in humanist photography. As a swan song to the pity-generating single image, it creates a series of images that, following no causal or chronological narrative, seems most likely to be associated with an "and." According to Bexte, the "and" (like the "or") is a disjoint conjunction, for it divides as it connects (see Bexte 2019, 21). He also emphasizes that conjunctions and prepositions have no meaning of their own in contrast to conceptual categories but that "their meaning always arises from the context" (Bexte 2019, 51). This contextuality of the "and" is constitutive for the verbal and visual enumeration. Only in and with the context does the mode of enumeration open up; only then does it become clear whether one counts in an archival, typological, or hierarchical manner.

Due to the specificity of its medium, photography is particularly suitable for creating visual lists. The uniqueness of photographic textuality lies in the referential or indexical sign-like nature of the photographic image (see Hughes and Noble 2003, 4). The indexicality of a photograph—its reference to a reality located in front of the image—creates a closer connection to the depicted than other media. Moreover, as Victor Burgin wrote in 1977, photographs—like language—are seen as part of the environment, "whereas paintings and films readily present themselves to critical attention as objects" (Burgin 1982, 143). The depicted can thus be more strongly present as a countable and delimitable sign, as evidenced by the numerous archival impulses in photo history (see Fig. 13.2), which can promote its list-likeness. It is also through this indexicality and through other characteristics such as the reproducibility, distributability, and cropping of a photograph that it is most context-sensitive, as photo theory argues.[16] Abigail Solomon-Godeau points out that an evidential history of photography could therefore not be written without a "history of photographic uses" (Solomon-Godeau 1991, xxiv). And like the photo, the "and" is an "unsecured, because context-related meaning of connectors, brackets, couplings, etc." (see Bexte 2014, 32). Still, the "and" emphasizes a lack of hierarchy between the parts as a conjunction, which is most likely to remain invisible (see Bexte 2019, 15). This lack of hierarchy between the individual photos is also present in the CDp.

The contextualizing word produces repetitive loops, and yet it is important to emphasize that the "bidirectional directionality" (Selmani 2012, 171) of the "and" means that the law of exchange does not apply. As Bexte has shown, the words "father and son" have a different quality than "son and father" (see Bexte 2014, 31). Unlike in mathematics, neither literary, visual, nor semantic elements in general can be exchanged without consequences, a phenomenon already pointed out by Meyer Schapiro (see Meyer Schapiro 1969). In the examples shown here, for instance, the formal sequencing of Cases was needed to give coherence to the series, which otherwise had hardly any underlying ordering parameters. This coherence offers the basis for further considerations such as how the color orange is reflected in the work.

The "et cetera" can refer not only to the "and" but also to the "etc." and thus to the end of lists. The "et cetera" is then to be understood as a gathering, as an end that could go on. As already emphasized above, a bound book necessarily has an end, even if it appears as a fanfold. This seclusion is counteracted by the incomplete nature of the discrete individual elements: the "et cetera" is about the basic possibility of a subsequent rereading, a reassessment of what the agreement actually consisted of in the first place (see Garfinkel 1967, 74).

The gaps and interstices are what I initially called the discursive power of the list. Therefore, Sabine Mainberger is to be agreed with when she states that enumeration—she deliberately avoids the word list—is "often marked as incomplete" but does not have to be "in principle infinite" (Mainberger 2018, 95–96). Thus, the photobooks dealt with here correspond to Mainberger's third category of infinity: "A finite number of items cannot be written down in full" (Mainberger 2018, 95–96). The "et cetera" is therefore not a sign of infinity but of detail.[17]

The CDp relies on the affordance of photography to freeze time, to isolate subjects from their surroundings, and to put them in a new context in which new associations and meanings can be forged. As the viewer has to recontextualize its isolated and thus abstracted objects, here the CDp shows itself in its openness and revisionality as well-behaved postdocumentary (see Gevers 2005). This postdocumentary quality is also evident in the sensitivity toward figural representation. Humanist photography has been criticized for, among other things, cementing injustices rather than helping to overcome them by representing unfortunate and needy people. People are not depicted in Stephen Gill's book, and hardly in Allison Stewart's and Ricardo Cases' books.

Of the examples shown here, the betting slips by Gill are most list-like in nature. The "and" between them can be understood as hung and leafed through; they are literally connected and, as such, are exhibited as a unit. This unity is further reinforced by the reduction of contexts already emphasized above: due to the many constant parameters, color, perspective, display, and background, the comparison is directed at the form of the betting slip and thus indirectly at the psychological condition of the owner—an owner who is not shown. This connects Gill's series to Stewart's backpacks: they both do not show the owners of the photographed objects. The color orange is an object-overlapping phenomenon for Cases as well. This representational void, together with the non-hierarchical order of the individual images, gives the viewer the opportunity to expand them imaginatively—both on the personal and on the political level.

This openness and revisionality are shared between visual and verbal enumerations. Literature is fascinated by lists because they seem to unite incompatible things very simply. Eva von Contzen emphasizes that lists in literary texts underline the constructiveness of the discourse, since they deflect classical reception expectations such as immersion: "Lists resist the immersive impetus and challenge readers on a cognitive level, requiring, to varying degrees, strategies of familiarization and narrativization in order to make sense of their meaning" (von Contzen 2016, 246). This refusal of immersion—or of narrative—is also inherent in the examples that I have presented in this article.

Horizons of Reception

Christiane Frey and David Martyn begin their essay on knowledge in and through lists with a remark on reception aesthetics: we would read "over the individual elements of a list" (see Frey and Martyn 2016, 91) if we knew the heading, the category under which the elements would be subsumed. The authors speak of horizons of expectation with which the reader is equipped. If we ask ourselves when and who is equipped with which horizons of expectation, then we have a clear winner: *Bug out Bag* is too well known as a term and too ubiquitously understood than to have to guess for a long time what kind of unpacked backpacks might be depicted. But neither Cases nor Gill allows such simple conclusions to be drawn from the title of the work on display: the fact that the color orange could become the smallest common denominator within Cases' enumerative structure is something the viewer, despite the title, only realizes after turning the pages several times; no text is assigned to the pictures that could guide the viewer in Gill's work to associate the disappointment mentioned in the title with the betting-slip sculptures. Even if "3.20 Hereford Earcome Sannie £ 5 to win" provides only very fragmentary information about the betting context, it is the combination of visible fonts in the image and the captions that slowly makes the viewer aware of the fact that they are seeing betting slips. It is also the suggestive materiality of the book (the way in which it reminds us of the black-and-white photography as is typical for jewelry catalogues) that meaningfully leads the viewer astray. If the category or/and a certain hierarchy is given in advance, the following would no longer be a "mere" list but a catalogue, that is, a "hierarchical subsumption of particulars under general terms" (Frey and Martyn 2016, 96). This differentiation can also be applied to visual forms of cataloguing. What works as a list when, how, under which conditions, and in which media also depends on the viewer's stance. The list is an associative principle that exists primarily in a cognitive capacity as "object and process" (Bronfen et al. 2016, 8). However, if a list is a cognitive tool, as Eva von Contzen emphasizes (see Frey and Martyn 2016, 96), we have to ask how the concept of a visual list comes about. In the beginning, I put forward the thesis that it is a reductionist and abstracting act that aligns the polysemic image to the disjointed sign. Abstraction occurs through countable repetition and formal reduction, a principle that the CDp has adopted from serial art. The reduction is achieved amongst others by equalizing the shooting parameters that the photographer imposes on his series, which is often accompanied by a high degree of staging.

Conclusion

A cluster is not a list because the elements are not discrete but overlap. Visual lists therefore rely on conjunctions, the "and" must be exposed to show the enumerative quality of the image. This can be realized in various ways. In my examples it is the page and the associated page turning as a visual blink that creates that structure. Even though lists can do both, separate and connect, they are more visible when they separate. But to what extent does the list then strive for its own erasure and to what extent does it expose itself?

Sabine Mainberger suggested that enumerative texts either "accentuate the diversity of the individual elements" and as a result appear 'objective' and 'factual'" or emphasize "the equalizing" and "repetitive," which makes them appear "'ritualistic' and 'obsessive'" (Mainberger 2003, 95). It is not quite that simple with visual enumerations: Ricardo Cases' photographs attach less importance to repetition than to difference, yet on the pictorial level it is primarily the exaggerated colorfulness and the access to objects, which oscillates between surreal and expressive, that contradicts attributions such as "objective" or "factual." However, the thesis seems to apply to Stewart's photobook. Her prepper-hauls emphasize diversity and create order at the same time. The individual objects gain meaning through their connection to the other objects and through their relationship to the whole of the bag. Stephen Gill's enumerations seem most repetitive, but not obsessive. Yet, one of his aims is certainly to represent the mass of betting tickets in Hackney. Creating a list is always an act of abstraction. When a list is created, the individual items become both reduced and more complex: reduced because they are cut off from previous (semantic) contexts, and more complex because they are entangled in new semantic structures within the list.

Martin Parr has described humanist photography as much too preachy (see Miles 2010, 57). Lists cannot preach. The CDp abstracts/reduces its theme to a list in order to allow further (crisis) description. As a serial work, the visual list can be both politically and conceptually coherent. Gill and Stewart use the camera's dyadic power to isolate its object and remove it from its social context in order to generate a much more open conceptual economy for Contemporary Documentary photography.

Following my initial thesis, various ways in which signs emerge can be distinguished in the photobooks: the enumerative character is less obvious in Cases, as he does not singularize his objects like Gill or Stewart. Nevertheless, one looks for the color orange. By the time you find it, you have seen a lot of the once rich but now disused region around Valencia and have experienced the way in which light is able to illuminate the worn, peeled, and dried up plains. Through the back door of a narrative that deflects to be subsumed, Cases is thus able to draw attention to the forgotten contexts of the region. Stewart's glass cabinet backpacks, on the other hand, are most closely based on the photographic tradition of the inventory—an isolated, future inventory that receives its sign-like aspects from the absence of the owners. Every canned tuna, every battery thus refers to someone who is only present as a first name in the book. Stephen Gill's photobook *A Series of Disappointments* is best described as a visual list, while with regard to Stewart and Cases it seems more appropriate to speak of enumerations or enumerative systems, for in addition to the necessary reduction involved to create a discrete sign, Gill's work also adjusts another parameter: that of space.

If you turn the pages of Cases' book, the place where the photo was taken changes on every page. Sure, we are always in the same Spanish region, but in very different places, where the viewer is confronted with very different things. This changes with Stewart: here, the place seems to be the same, and yet the viewer is aware that Stewart had different backpacks unpacked at different places, in which she found different things. This distinction also disappears in Gill's series: you always see the same thing in the same place. Because the recording situation is unchanged, the viewer can respond more quickly to the depicted objects and their similarities and differences. The betting slips are arranged differently, but they always remain betting slips that he has picked out and photographed in black and white on a neutral surface. The fanfold, which makes it possible to display the pages as a row or as a line, also refers to a spatial continuity—and thus to a further alignment with the writing. Similarly, Gill's camera is the only one that is static, while Stewart changes the distance of the camera to her objects to visually match stuffed and not so stuffed pockets.

I began this text by arguing that lists create surplus. Visual enumerations in the documentary photobook also create this surplus: disappointed hopes with Stephen Gill, dystopian fears with Allison Stewart, and tourists' desires with Ricardo Cases. Strictly speaking, this surplus is not visually represented in their books, but it is still present. A semantic and an affective surplus, an emotional level of perception that is generated for and ultimately also by the recipients themselves. The CDp makes use of the apparently non-hierarchical and unfinished structure of enumeration in order to counter the hierarchical problem of humanist photography. Additionally, it emphasizes the interpretive gaps between individual images and thus creates a receptive autonomy, which is also an important representational goal in other approaches to Postdocumentary Art. It uses the decontextualization of space, time, and presence to emphasize the photo as a sign and to counter the crisis through a series of signs, the first step of which can be an "et cetera," a list.

Notes

1. I will use the acronym CDp for the term in the following.
2. Andrew Piper describes this process: "They convey a sense of the development of readerly thought" (2012, 52–53).
3. For research on diagrammatics see also Schmidt-Burkhardt (2012).
4. Distance refers to an act of reception: as soon as the viewer compares a work with other works, it no longer stands on its own but at the same time also exemplifies the aesthetic set of rules that justifies its inclusion in the overarching system of presentation. See Thürlemann (2013, 16).
5. The list as a means of expressing excess can also be found in literature. Monika Fludernik quotes a passage from Oliver Twist, in which the protagonist's sensory overload in a market is communicated via an excessive description. See Fludernik (2016).
6. I am referring here to criticism of Western Documentary or humanist photography, which, by portraying the "non-Western" as deplorable and in need of help, consolidated rather than helped to overcome this asynchronicity. See Solomon-Godeau (2003).
7. Cornell Capa, the brother of Robert Capa and director of the International Center of Photography in New York, defines the approach of the concerned photographer as follows: "The concerned photographer finds much in the present unacceptable which he tries to alter" (Cookman 2009, 130). Capa was also the one who established the expression "concerned photographer" for his photographs, because the images should have a humanitarian impulse. There are two anthologies titled *The Concerned Photographer*, published by him in 1968 and 1972, which define the genre. See Capa (1968) and (1972).

8. Fox Talbot (1844).
9. Blossfeldt (1928). Blossfeldt was not a photographer by profession but a sculptor. His photographs were taken in the 1890s as illustrations for the art educational writings of his first employer, Moritz Meurer, and later as models for his own lessons in "modelling from living plants" at the Unterrichtsanstalt des Kunstgewerbemuseums Berlin, where Blossfeldt taught from 1899 to 1930.
10. See Ruscha (1964). Additionally, Walker Evans should not go unmentioned here. His work *Beauties of the Common Tool* was published in July 1955 in the magazine *Fortune*, which he also edited as picture editor. Even here, in the contextless formal aesthetics of pliers, scissors, and spatulas, a profanation of Blossfeldt's approach can be observed. See Campany (2014).
11. For Ruscha, photography is not "arty" and is already dead as an art form. In an interview about his books he said in 1964: "Thus, it is not a book to house a collection of art photographs—they are technical data like industrial photography. To me, they are nothing more than snapshots" (quoted after van der Weijde 2017, 125).
12. Herein as well as in terms of the diversity of the thematic framework, the book recalls Ed Ruscha's *Various small Fires and Milk* (1964).
13. Although he works with color, this aspect is most closely related to the tradition of Ed Ruscha, who also depicts fires in his photobook *Various Small Fires and Milk* (1964).
14. See Scheuermann (2010, 203). David Herman considers the question how the viewer is guided to narrative conclusions as an important element of postclassical narratology: see Herman (1997, 1057).
15. When considering the list as a form of montage, a remark by Bernd Stiegler might prove enlightening here, who observes montages particularly in situations of upheaval. Such situations give rise to new cultural forms; these forms, however, need not be homogeneous and can retain their heterogeneity. See Stiegler (2009, 310).
16. See Solomon-Godeau (1991, xxiv).
17. Umberto Eco had already pointed this out when he said that the painting *The Ten Thousand Martyrs* by Jacopo da Pontormo did not have to depict 10,000 people to do justice to this title. See Eco (2009, 39).

References

Armstrong, Carol M. 1998. *Scenes in a Library: Reading the Photograph in the Book, 1843–1875*. Cambridge, MA: MIT Press.

Bexte, Peter. 2014. ‚und': Bruchstellen im Synthetischen. In *Synthesis – Zur Konjunktur eines philosophischen Begriffs in Wissenschaft und Technik*, ed. Gabriele Gramelsberger, Werner Kogge, and Peter Bexte, 25–40. Bielefeld:

transcript. https://www.degruyter.com/document/doi/10.14361/transcript.9783839422397.25/html

———. 2019. *Konjunktur & Krise: Vom ‚und' in Bildern und Texten.* Berlin: Kadmos.

Blossfeldt, Karl. 1928. *Urformen der Kunst.* Berlin: Verlag Ernst Wasmuth. Rijksmuseum Amsterdam. http://creativecommons.org/publicdomain/zero/1.0.

Bochner, Mel. 1967. The Serial Attitude. *Artforum* 6 (4): 28–33.

Bronfen, Elisabeth, Christiane Frey, and David Martyn. 2016. Vorwort. In *Noch einmal anders: Zu einer Poetik des Seriellen*, ed. Elisabeth Bronfen, Christiane Frey, and David Martyn, 7–16. Zürich/Berlin: diaphanes.

Burgin, Victor. 1982. Looking at Photographs. In *Thinking Photography*, ed. Victor Burgin, 142–153. London: Macmillan.

Campany, David. 2014. *Walker Evans: The Magazine Work.* Göttingen: Steidl.

Capa, Cornell. 1968. *The Concerned Photographer.* New York: Grossman.

———. 1972. *The Concerned Photographer 2.* New York: Grossman.

Cookman, Claude Hubert. 2009. *American Photojournalism: Motivations and Meanings.* Evanstone: Northwestern University Press.

Dobbe, Martina. 2013. Einsheit und Vielheit: Zur Bildökonomie des Seriellen. In *BildÖkonomie: Haushalten mit Sichtbarkeiten*, ed. Emmanuel Alloa and Francesca Falk, 29–53. Munich: Wilhelm Fink Verlag.

Dunker, Bettina. 2018. *Bilder-Plural: Multiple Bildformen in der Fotografie der Gegenwart.* Paderborn: Wilhelm Fink Verlag.

Eco, Umberto. 2009. *Die unendliche Liste.* Trans. Barbara Kleiner. Munich: Hanser.

Eskildsen, Ute. 2004. Photographs in Books. In *The Open Book: A History of the Photographic Book from 1878 to the Present*, ed. Andrew Roth, 11–29. Göteborg: Hasselblad Center.

Fludernik, Monika. 2016. Descriptive Lists and List Descriptions. *Style* 50 (3): 309–326. https://doi.org/10.5325/style.50.3.0309.

Frey, Christiane, and David Martyn. 2016. Listenwissen. Zu einer Poetik des Seriellen. In *Noch einmal anders: Zu einer Poetik des Seriellen*, ed. Elisabeth Bronfen, Christiane Frey, and David Martyn, 89–103. Zürich/Berlin: diaphanes.

Garfinkel, Harold. 1967. *Studies in Ethnomethodology.* Englewood Cliffs: Wiley.

Gevers, Ine. 2005. Images that Demand Consummation: Postdocumentary Photography, Art and Ethics. In *Documentary Now!* ed. Frits Gierstberg et al., 82–99. Rotterdam: NAi Publishers.

Gill, Stephen. 2008. Description in the Webshop. https://www.nobodybooks.com/product/a-series-of-disappointments-blue-red. Accessed 15 May 2020.

Herman, David. 1997. Scripts, Sequences, and Stories: Elements of a Postclassical Narratology. *PMLA* 112: 1046–1059.

Hughes, Alex, and Andrea Noble. 2003. Introduction. In *Phototextualities. Intersections of Photography and Narrative*, ed. Alex Hughes and Andrea Noble, 1–16. Albuquerque: University of New Mexico Press.

Mainberger, Sabine. 2003. *Die Kunst des Aufzählens: Elemente zu einer Poetik des Enumerativen*. Berlin/New York: de Gruyter.

———. 2018. 2.9 Ordnen – Aufzählen. In *Handbuch Literatur & Materielle Kultur*, ed. Susanne Scholz and Ulrike Vedder, 91–98. Berlin/Boston: de Gruyter.

Miles, Melissa. 2010. The Drive to Archive: Conceptual Documentary Photobook Design. *Photographies* 3 (1): 49–68. https://doi.org/10.1080/17540760903561108/.

Molderings, Herbert. 1977. Überlegungen zur Fotografie der Neuen Sachlichkeit und des Bauhauses. *kritische berichte* 5 (2/3): 67–88.

Nelson, Andrea Jeannette. 2007. *Reading Photobooks: Narrative Montage and the Construction of Modern Visual Literacy*. PhD dissertation, University of Minnesota.

Pantall, Colin. 2014. The Reason of Oranges. *British Journal of Photography Online*, September 23. https://www.bjp-online.com/2014/09/the-reason-of-oranges. Accessed 26 June 2020.

Piper, Andrew. 2012. *Book Was There. Reading in Electronic Times*. Chicago: University of Chicago Press.

Ruscha, ed. 1964. *Various Small Fires and Milk*. Anderson, Richie & Simon: Los Angeles.

Schapiro, Meyer. 1969. On Some Problems in the Semiotics of Visual Art: Field and Vehicle in Image-Signs. *Semiotica* I: 223–243.

Scheuermann, Barbara J. 2010. Narreme, Unbestimmtheitsstellen, Stimuli – Erzählen im fotografischen Einzelbild. In *Die fotografische Wirklichkeit: Inszenierung – Fiktion – Narration*, ed. Lars Blunck, 191–205. Bielefeld: transcript.

Schmidt-Burkhardt, Astrit. 2012. *Die Kunst der Diagrammatik: Perspektiven eines neuen bildwissenschaftlichen Paradigmas*. Bielefeld: transcript.

Scott, Clive. 1999. *The Spoken Image: Photography & Language*. London: Reaktion Books.

Selmani, Lirim. 2012. Durch 'und' hervorgerufene mentale Prozesse. *Deutsche Sprache: Zeitschrift für Theorie, Praxis, Dokumentation* 2: 166–185.

Solomon-Godeau, Abigail. 1991. *Photography at the Dock: Essays on Photographic History, Institution, and Practices*. Minneapolis: University of Minnesota Press.

———. 2003. Wer spricht so? Einige Fragen zur Dokumentarfotografie. In *Diskurse der Fotografie: Fotokritik am Ende des fotografischen Zeitalters*, ed. Herta Wolf, 53–74. Frankfurt/Main: Suhrkamp.

Stiegler, Bernd. 2009. *Montagen des Realen: Photographie als Reflexionsmedium und Kulturtechnik*. Munich: Wilhelm Fink Verlag.

Sweetman, Alex. 1985. Photobookworks: The Critical Realist Tradition. In *Artists' Books: A Critical Anthology and Sourcebook*, ed. Joan Lyons, 187–207. Rochester: The Visual Studies Workshop Press.

Talbot, William Henry Fox. 1844. *The Pencil of Nature*. Plate III: Articles of China. http://www.fotomanifeste.de/user/pages/manifeste/1844-Talbot-PencilOfNature/faksimile-talbot.pdf?g-bd986df0. Accessed 23 June 2020.

Thürlemann, Felix. 2013. *Mehr als ein Bild. Für eine Kunstgeschichte des 'hyperimage'*. Munich: Wilhelm Fink Verlag.

van der Weijde, Erik. 2017. *This Is Not My Book*. Leipzig: Spector.

von Contzen, Eva. 2016. The Limits of Narration: Lists and Literary History. *Style* 50 (3): 241–260. https://doi.org/10.5325/style.50.3.0241.

Weltzien, Friedrich. 2006. Die Bildtechnik der Höflichkeit. William Henry Fox Talbots kontrollierte Affekte. In *Fotografische Leidenschaften*, ed. Katharina Sykora et al., 19–32. Marburg: Jonas Verlag.

Wolf, Werner. 2002. Das Problem der Narrativität in Literatur, bildender Kunst und Musik: Ein Beitrag zu einer intermedialen Erzähltheorie. In *Erzähltheorie transgenerisch, intermedial, interdisziplinär*, ed. Ansgar Nünning and Vera Nünning, 23–103. Trier: WVT.

Index[1]

---

[1] Note: Page numbers followed by 'n' refer to notes.

© The Author(s) 2022

R. A. Barton et al. (eds.), *Forms of List-Making: Epistemic, Literary, and Visual Enumeration*,

https://doi.org/10.1007/978-3-030-76970-3